Desert Passions

« HSU-MING TEO »

Desert Passions

ORIENTALISM AND ROMANCE NOVELS

University of Texas Press ⟁ AUSTIN

First edition, 2012
First paperback edition, 2013

Requests for permission to reproduce material from this work should
be sent to:
    Permissions
    University of Texas Press
    P.O. Box 7819
    Austin, TX 78713-7819
    http://utpress.utexas.edu/index.php/rp-form

LIBRARY OF CONGRESS CATALOGING-IN-PUBLICATION DATA

Teo, Hsu-Ming, 1970–
Desert passions : Orientalism and romance novels / by Hsu-Ming Teo.
    p.   cm.
Includes bibliographical references and index.

ISBN 978-0-292-75690-8 (paperback)
1. Orientalism in literature.   2. Love stories—History and criticism.
3. Women in literature.   4. East and West in literature.   5. Orient—In
literature.   I. Title.
PN56.3.O74T46   2012
809′.933585—dc23   2012003761

Contents

Acknowledgments

In 2006, Ned Curthoys asked me to revisit my earlier work on sheik novels and Orientalism for a conference at the Australian National University that he and Debjani Ganguli were organizing on the legacy of Edward Said. The idea for this book came out of that conference. I amassed so much material that Angela Woollacott suggested I write a book on the subject, and this is the result. So thank you both very much, Ned and Angela! Angela, in particular, has been a good friend and a generous mentor throughout my academic career.

This book could not have been written without financial support from Macquarie University via the Macquarie University Research Fellowship and Macquarie University New Staff Grant. I am very grateful to my various research assistants who have helped with different parts of the book: Kathleen Evesson, Annemarie Lopez, Bridget Deane, and Sofia Eriksson.

I am particularly indebted to Eric Murphy Selinger for his specialist knowledge about romance fiction, invaluable critiques, and welcome suggestions for how to improve the whole book, to John Docker for encouraging me to think more flexibly about certain topics by sharing his various insights on Bakhtin and the romance novel, and to Margaret Sampson who, in the space of a fortnight, proofread and critiqued the final draft of this book despite being overwhelmed by Orientalism and suffering from a surfeit of sultans. I have also benefitted greatly from the insights of the following people, who have read and critiqued various chapters of this work: Amy Burge, Sande Cohen, Lisa Featherstone, and Gennaro Gervasio. All remaining shortcomings in the work are, of course, my responsibility.

My special thanks to Stuart Ward and Richard White for their friendship, intellectual and moral support, and encouragement in all my various endeavors over the years. I also appreciate very much the support and friendship of Toni Johnson-Wood, and Juliet Flesch, who has been most generous with sharing her knowledge of Australian romance novels.

I am most fortunate to work with warm and wonderful colleagues, so thanks to my colleagues in the Department of Modern History, Politics, and International Relations, particularly Mary Spongberg, for creating a congenial and enjoyable work environment that facilitates research and writing. I am also grateful to my colleagues in the Department of English who listened to an early draft of Chapter 1 and provided valuable feedback. I appreciate very much the intellectual support and encouragement of the International Association for the Study of Popular Romance, who acted as a sounding board for various bits and pieces from this book over the last few years and who, again, put up with Orientalism and sheik romances for a long time.

Thanks to Jim Burr, Jullianne H. Ballou, and other editorial staff at the University of Texas Press for their encouragement and help in editing and publishing this book.

Finally, thanks to David Teo and Siew Ching Lai for their unstinting love and support, and to my friends who keep me grounded and constantly remind me of the things that matter in life.

Desert Passions

Introduction

I'm the Sheik of Araby
Your love belongs to me
At night when you're asleep
Into your tent I'll creep
And the stars that shine above
Will light our way to love
You'll rule this land with me
The Sheik of Araby.

HARRY B. SMITH AND FRANCIS WHEELER, 1921

When E. M. Hull's *The Sheik* was published in 1919 and made into a film starring Rudolph Valentino, "sheik fever" was unleashed in the Western world. In the United States, the book went through fifty printings in 1921 alone, and it was one of the first novels to appear on the best-seller list for two consecutive years (Raub 120). It was continually reissued in paperback from the 1920s to the 1960s, and it had sold 1,194,000 copies in hardback by 1965 (Blake 2003: 67). Upon the film's release in 1921, the *New York Telegraph* estimated that over 125,000 people had seen *The Sheik* within weeks of its opening. It screened for six months in Sydney, Australia, and ran for a record forty-two weeks in France (Leider 167–168). The word "sheik," which originally referred to a Muslim religious leader or an elder of a community or family, suddenly took on in the West new connotations of irresistible, ruthless, masterful, and over-sexualized masculinity, before ending up as a brand of condoms in America by 1931. *The Sheik* made a dramatic impact on the literary genre of Eastern love stories in Britain, reviving the popularity of the early twentieth-century "desert romance" novel pioneered by authors such as Robert Hichens and Kathlyn Rhodes and spawning a series of forgettable imitations in other novels and short stories in women's magazines. In the United States, the Tin Pan Alley hit "The Sheik of Araby" was composed in response to the film and rapidly became a jazz standard, especially in New Orleans, before being reworked by the Beatles in 1962. Hull's sequel, *The Sons of the Sheik* (1925), and Valentino's performance in the film version of the novel in 1926, brought the craze for all things romantically "Oriental" to its zenith in fashion and film.[1] Arabic fabrics, clothing, jewelry, cigarettes, cosmetics, interior decorations, and design motifs proliferated, as did dozens of copycat films such as *Burning Sands* (1922), *Arabian Love* (1922), *The Tents of Allah* (1923), *The Arab* (1924), *Sahara Love* (1926), and *Love in the Desert* (1929). The film even affected the world of musical theatre when an operetta, *The Desert Song*, opened in New York in November 1926 before being made into a movie in 1929.

Sheik fever died down by the 1930s, but its impact on Western popular culture was already indelible, particularly as fodder for spoofs and satires. It did not take long for the first mockery to appear. The 1923 film *The Shriek of Araby* lampooned the abduction scene in *The Sheik*, where Valentino rides across the desert sands and snatches Agnes Ayres from her horse, throwing her over his saddle and snarling: "Lie still, you little fool!" The horseback abduction scene was a rich source of mockery, especially for American cartoonists and illustrators such as Dick Dorgan, who wrote a satirical review of *The Sheik*, accompanied by the illustration below, for the film magazine *Photoplay*.

Spoofs and sly references to *The Sheik* continued in American culture long after the desert romance as a literary subgenre had petered out. This was partly because the tropes of abduction, captivity, sexual slavery, opulent harems, and dancing girls in *The Sheik* were derived from a rich Western tradition of Orientalism, and particularly from a spectacular, "Arabian Nights" Orientalism that developed in the United States through world's fairs, circuses, carnivals, and Wild West shows during the nineteenth and early twentieth centuries. This was an Orientalism that fed dreams of consumption and playful experimentations with identity, as well as sexual titillation and romantic desires. These traditions of Orientalism provided potent and plentiful sources for Hollywood fantasies about harems. In the midst of the Second World War, Bob Hope, Bing Crosby, Dorothy Lamour, and Anthony Quinn were featured in *The Road to Morocco* (1942), a film that satirizes the fantasy of Westerners being kidnapped and incarcerated in harems by featuring American men as

He tackled her at the five yard line, picked her out of the saddle
and yelled, "Home, James!"

FIGURE 0.1. *Dick Dorgan,* Photoplay Magazine, *April 1922*

the abductees imprisoned in the Moroccan princess's harem. Throughout the mid-twentieth century, a number of Bugs Bunny cartoons made ridiculous references to abductions and harems and even had the "wascally wabbit" dressed as a belly dancer in one episode. References to *The Sheik* repeatedly cropped up in numerous comics and television shows, as well (Michalak 7, 13–14). In 1984, John Derek's film *Bolero* featured his wife, Bo Derek, playing a young, 1920s American flapper enamored with Valentino as Sheik Ahmed Ben Hassan. The film begins with Bo Derek gazing up longingly at a poster of *The Sheik*. She travels to the Middle East determined to lose her virginity to a sheik, but her plan goes awry when the sheik who has agreed to deflower her falls asleep instead.

Satires and spoofs were not the only legacy of *The Sheik* throughout the twentieth century. Although the British-authored "sheik novel" had run out of steam by the 1930s, the 1970s saw a revival of the subgenre, particularly in the form of the newly emerging, female-authored, erotic historical romance novel (also known more disparagingly as "bodice ripper") produced primarily in the United States. These historical romance novels found their counterpart in American film and television shows of the 1980s such as the Brooke Shields film *Sahara* (1983) and William Hale's television miniseries *Harem* (1986). Historical romance readers' and writers' renewed interest in the Orient may have been sparked by the growing awareness of the importance of Middle Eastern politics and oil to Western political and cultural life—especially after the Six-Day War of 1967, the oil shocks of the 1970s, the rise of Palestinian-related terrorism, improved relations with Egypt under Anwar Sadat, and the Iranian Revolution and subsequent hostage crisis of 1979. However, for reasons explained in Chapters 5 and 6, it was more than likely the result of an attempt by female writers to use one of the most well-known pornographic motifs in nineteenth- and twentieth-century Western culture—the Oriental despot and his harem—to explore female sexuality and create a new language of heterosexual, female-centered erotica in the wake of sexual liberation and the second-wave feminist movement. Orientalism as a discourse was never simply about legitimating the extension of Western power over the Middle East; it served many varied and changing purposes over time.

In the last quarter of the twentieth century, increasing media coverage of Middle Eastern affairs created a public awareness of the region that manifested itself in rather peculiar ways in global Western popular culture. Where Western women's romance fiction was concerned, the transnational and corporate nature of romance publishing in the late twentieth century consolidated the creation of a modern-day "sheik romance" subgenre produced by authors from various parts of the British Commonwealth and the United States. Australian and Canadian female novelists had joined the British in writing Orientalist romance novels by the mid-1980s, but the genre became thoroughly Americanized after the First Persian Gulf War, in 1991, and grew steadily in terms of the output of American-authored publications and sales.

The al-Qaeda attacks on September 11, 2001, saw no diminution in the popularity of these novels about love relationships between white women and Arab or Muslim men. On the contrary, 2002 saw the peak of publications, with at least twenty-two different contemporary sheik romance novels and four historical harem romance novels published that year. In 2005, sixteen sheik romance novels were published for the estimated fifty-one million romance readers in the United States, prompting ironic commentary in American and British newspapers and *Time* magazine (Whitaker 2006, Reardon 2006).

In his landmark 1978 work, *Orientalism*, Edward Said makes a passing reference to the puzzling connection between the Orient and sexu-

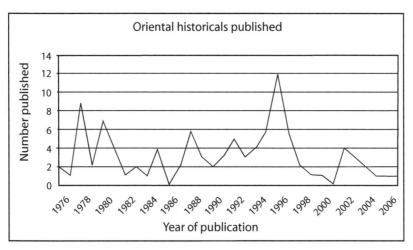

GRAPH 1. *Oriental Historicals Published*

ality: "Why the Orient seems still to suggest not only fecundity but sexual promise (and threat), untiring sensuality, unlimited desire, deep generative energies, is something on which one could speculate" (1995: 188). He, however, declines to probe the issue. A huge body of scholarship on Orientalism has been produced since Said's original work, yet despite many critiques of the association of Orientalism with sexuality, few attempts have been made to understand the long historical process by which the Orient became associated with sexual promise and romantic love in Western culture. Derek Hopwood's *Sexual Encounters in the Middle East: The British, the French and the Arabs* (1999), Ruth Bernard Yeazell's fascinating cultural history, *Harems of the Mind: Passages of Western Art and Literature* (2000), and Mohja Kahf's *Western Representations of the Muslim Woman: From Termagant to Odalisque* (1999)—a masterly historical survey of changing (male) representations of Muslim women in European literature from the twelfth to the nineteenth century—are perhaps the only works that consider aspects of Orientalism, sexual desire, and romantic love in Western culture. Still less has there been any analysis of how Western *women* understood and represented Oriental love affairs and interracial relationships, particularly during the growth of women's novel writing in the late nineteenth and twentieth centuries—a period of efflorescence in fiction that coincided with the age of empire.

As is well known, in colonial discourse other colonized "natives" were attributed the same inferior character traits as Orientals: savagery, ignorance, irrationality, childishness, cunning, deceit, laziness, despotism,

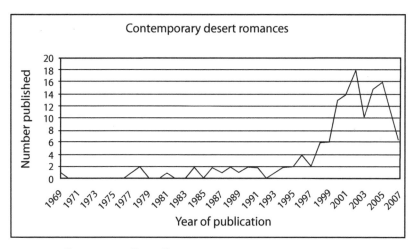

GRAPH 2. *Contemporary Desert Romances*

cruelty, and moral and sexual depravity. Yet it was particularly the Islamic Middle East and North Africa—from Morocco to present-day Iran—that came to be understood as a *locus sensualis* long before E. M. Hull wrote *The Sheik* in 1919. Just how did the Orient become Orientalized in the Western imagination in this particular way? That is, how did it become constructed as a place of barbarism and savagery but also, paradoxically, as a space of sensuousness and opulence, sexuality and romantic love? What purposes did it serve for different audiences at different times? More problematically, how did the Orient come to be associated with abduction and rape, particularly of English virgins, and why did this seem so thrillingly romantic to a particular generation and culture obsessed with *The Sheik* in the early twentieth century? Did these Oriental rape romance stories, when written by *women*, have the same meaning as when they were written by men? And what impact did the civil rights movement, sexual liberation, second-wave feminism, antirape politics, and American involvement in the Middle East have on the perpetuation and meaning of such fantasies in the present day, through historical novels such as Connie Mason's *Sheik* (1997) and Bertrice Small's *Love Slave* (1995)? Or in contemporary Harlequin romance novels such as Jacqueline Diamond's *Captured by a Sheikh* (2000), Penny Jordan's *The Sheikh's Virgin Bride* (2003), Emma Darcy's *Traded to the Sheikh* (2005), Susan Stephens's *The Sheikh's Captive Bride* (2005), Miranda Lee's *Love-Slave to the Sheikh* (2006), Sarah Morgan's *The Sheik's Virgin Princess* (2007), and the myriad other novels emphasizing "sheik(h)s" in their titles, which alludes to the topos of Western virgins abducted and sold into sexual slavery to sheiks?[2]

This book is a cultural history of the Orientalist representation of interracial, cross-cultural, sexual, and romantic liaisons between Western women and Arab men in the popular culture of romance throughout the twentieth and twenty-first centuries. I argue that whether or not romance writers are aware of their Orientalist literary heritage, the motifs they rework in their historical harem novels or modern-day sheik novels are drawn from a centuries-long literary engagement between Europe and the Muslim world. Certain literary texts have been significant in developing or popularizing these romantic motifs, which have become part of the Western world's cultural warehouse of images, ideas, stock characters, and standard plotlines of Orientalist romance. In this book, therefore, I begin with a survey of the historical evolution of the romantic East in Europe's literary engagement with its Islamic other, beginning with twelfth-century verse romances written in response to the expansion of Islamic Spain and to the crusades in the Holy Land from the eleventh to the end of the thirteenth century. I trace the development of the classic themes of Orientalist romance in seventeenth- and eighteenth-century writings and drama, including abduction by "Barbary" pirates; white slavery; the fear of renegades; the despot and his harem; the figure of the powerful concubine exemplified in the French Roxane/Roxelane tales of the eighteenth century, whereby the irrepressible concubine Roxelane tames and makes monogamous the sultan Soliman and, finally, fantasies of escape from the harem typified in Mozart's opera *Die Entführung aus dem Serail* (*The Abduction from the Seraglio*, 1782).

Although alternative readings of the Oriental harem were provided by women travelers in the eighteenth and nineteenth centuries, beginning with Lady Mary Wortley Montagu's authoritative *Turkish Embassy Letters* (1763), female-authored accounts that desexualized the seraglio and showed it as a domestic space comparable to the bourgeois home (Melman 1995, Lewis 1996) had little impact on the general European romantic imagination. Instead, Western ideas of the harem and the romantic East continued to be shaped by male authors, especially Byron, whose Eastern tales created a palimpsest of Orientalist characters and topoi recognizable in twentieth-century romance novels. The Byronic Orient gave way to the overtly erotic East in the anonymously authored novel *The Lustful Turk* (1828) and other nineteenth-century pornographic novels, pictures, and periodicals. The slow but steady accretion of such motifs as the abduction and rape of the English virgin and the problematic issue of the heroine's sexual desire for the Arab male found their way into late Victorian romance novels set in the Orient at a time of increasing French and British encroachment in that region, laying the groundwork for E. M. Hull's *The Sheik*—one of the first "blockbuster" novels and films of the twentieth century.

The Sheik dramatically transformed the character of these Orientalist interracial fantasies because it feminized the genre and made white women central to Orientalist discourse as producers, consumers, and imagined participants in Eastern love stories. This trend became especially marked in the last quarter of the twentieth century. The eroticization of romance fiction, which gave rise to the historical bodice ripper, also brought the rise of the erotic Orientalist historical romance novel as well as the revival of modern-day sheik romance novels published by Harlequin Mills & Boon. However, dramatic differences in the purpose and function of Orientalist motifs between novels of the early and late twentieth century are evident, shaped inevitably by the civil and women's rights movements that had developed in the intervening decades. Where early twentieth-century sheik romances are obsessed with the specter of miscegenation, and emphasize white women's responsibility to respect and uphold the boundaries of whiteness, their modern-day counterparts are more concerned with the incorporation of the ethnic (male) other into modern Western society. In both cases, far from the imperial West being portrayed as the male "self" penetrating the Oriental female "other," the West is in fact represented by the white female whose attitude toward, and acceptance or incorporation of, racial or cultural male others is moderated by prevailing Western social mores.

Furthermore, these modern-day romances are often engaged in a project that Joyce Zonana terms "feminist Orientalism": "figuring objectionable aspects of life in the West as 'Eastern'" in order to redefine the feminist project as "the removal of Eastern elements from Western life," thus making the goals of feminism more palatable to a Western readership (594). In Zonana's work, the discourse of feminist Orientalism is not directed externally toward European relations with the Muslim world, nor is it motivated by a feminist desire to reform the harem system. Rather, the social and political function of feminist Orientalism is aimed at the "transformation of Western society—even while preserving basic institutions and ideologies of the West" (595). Examining the writings of late eighteenth- and nineteenth-century female writers such as Mary Wollstonecraft, Elizabeth Barrett Browning, Margaret Fuller, Charlotte Brontë, and Florence Nightingale, Zonana argues that "images of despotic sultans and desperate slave girls became a central part of an emerging liberal feminist discourse about the condition of women not in the East but in the West" (594). British female writers used "images of oriental life—and specifically the 'Mahometan' or 'Arabian' harem" to "articulate their critiques of the life of women in the West" (594). By setting up gender inequality as "Eastern," these feminist writers encouraged their own society to become more "Western" by improving the status, rights, and opportunities afforded to women. Similarly, female romance novelists in the late twentieth and twenty-first centuries argued for their heroine's right to a fulfilling career and life outside the domestic sphere, while also "de-Orientalizing" the sheik hero in order to assimilate him into Western society. Feminist Orientalism is thus a "rhetorical strategy (and a form of thought) by which a speaker or writer neutralizes the threat inherent in feminist demands and makes them palatable to an audience that wishes to affirm its occidental superiority" (595).

The intervention of Western female writers in the discourse of romantic Orientalism is significant particularly where late twentieth- and twenty-first-century representations of Arabs and Muslims are concerned. Said argues that since the advent of the Arab-Israeli wars and the oil crises of the 1970s, the figure of the demonized Arab has become pervasive in American popular culture:

> In the films and television the Arab is associated either with lechery or bloodthirsty dishonesty. He appears as an oversexed degenerate, capable, it is true, of cleverly devious intrigues, but essentially sadistic, treacherous, low. Slave trader, camel driver, moneychanger, colorful scoundrel: these are some traditional Arab roles in the cinema. (1995: 286)

Copious works have been produced enumerating the negative stereotypes of Arabs in American songs, jokes, fiction, television programs, political cartoons, comics, and movies (e.g., Morsy 1983, Christison 1987, Orfalea 1988, Simon 1989 and 2010, Michalak 1988, Shaheen 1994 and 2001, Suleiman 1999). Of course, as Melani McAlister (2001) points out, such representations were never static, nor did they serve the same political, economic, or cultural functions in America over the course of the twentieth century. Extant discussions of negative stereotypes almost always omit the valorization of Middle Eastern Muslim cultures by black American men who identified with Islam as an alternative way of carving out a cultural identity and political position for themselves, particularly within mid-twentieth-century American society (McAlister Chapter 2). Nevertheless, as many scholars have shown, the sheer weight of negative representations of Arabs in American popular culture is undeniable and serves as a cultural warehouse from which stock images and narratives can be wheeled out to explain international events or to justify foreign and domestic policies.

In this respect, the modern, female-authored, sheik romance subgenre provides an interesting contrast. These novels certainly rehash classic Orientalist discourses, but not necessarily with the aim of differentiating, distancing, and denigrating the Arab or Muslim other in modern Western society. Because of the formal plot demands of the genre of romance fiction (see Regis 30), cultural commonality and shared human interests and emotions are often emphasized instead of ineluctable difference. In many cases, the strength and stability of the Oriental family is celebrated and contrasted favorably against the high divorce rates in the West, or the dysfunctional families that conservative authors fear have come to both characterize and destabilize the nation. Quite often, interracial, interreligious, cross-cultural unions between white women and Arab men represent a healing of the family and society, as well as a wistful, nostalgic return to a more idyllic, ordered national utopia that accommodates both women and ethnic others. This is not to say that these novels are free of Orientalist stereotypes, of course. Certainly, the sheik is often initially portrayed as harsh and unenlightened in his view of gender relations, and with a tendency toward authoritarian behavior. Yet the Middle Eastern potentate is not completely demonized or beyond redemption by a good, liberated, liberal Western woman. British imperialism's Christianizing and civilizing mission of the nineteenth century lives on in these novels, hybridized with strands of the American national mission to bring liberty, democracy, and modernity—especially in the form of liberal feminism—to the developing postcolonial world. Within their plots, contemporary sheik romances seek to rescue the Middle East from the effects of social and technological backwardness and ignorance, particularly where the treatment of women is concerned. But they also seek to normalize depictions of Middle Eastern people to a certain extent, to celebrate the strength and vitality of Oriental family life and cultural traditions, and to renew social bonds between the East and West by incorporating ethnic difference and ethnic culture into contemporary Western societies. Especially during the era of the American war on terror, this is by no means insignificant.

My methodological approach in *Desert Passions* is that of a feminist cultural historian engaging primarily with three ongoing scholarly conversations: the first involves Orientalism and Western culture; the second, Western women and imperialism; and the third, the new wave of scholarship in romance fiction. The lineaments of Said's thesis laid out in *Orientalism* are well known by now.[3] Said argues that since the eighteenth century, Western aesthetic, scholarly, and (a)historical representations of the Middle East have homogenized a geographically and culturally diverse region and peoples, portraying them as Europe's inferior other in order to extend, consolidate, and justify Western imperial rule over the region. Said writes, "Orientalism, which is the system of European or Western knowledge about the Orient, thus becomes synonymous with European domination of the Orient" (1995: 157). In the process of producing the Orient, Europeans simultaneously created an identity for themselves as a superior "race" that was "rational, virtuous, mature, 'normal'"—and therefore fit to be imperial masters (1995: 40). In the three decades since the publication of *Orientalism*, numerous works have appeared exploring the production of Orientalist discourse in art, literature, and travel (e.g., de Groot 1989, Lewis 1996, Alloula 1986, Said 1993, Behdad 1994). Many of these critique flaws in Said's work, arguing that Orientalism was never a unified or homogeneous discourse; that the binaries produced by Orientalism were never stable and did not always favor the characteristics associated with the West; that the meaning and function of this discourse varied according to when it was produced, and by which gender; and that the simplistic application of a discourse created during the European age of empire was not without problems when applied to the United States after the Second World War because of the complicating factors of the Cold War. In the second half of the twentieth century, America had different political alliances with various decolonizing and postcolonial countries in the Middle East, while the racial and cultural diversity of the United States itself produced heterogeneous others within its national borders, complicating the straightforward "othering" of Orientals against a unified American self (Lowe 1991, Spivak 1985, Melman 1995, Lewis 1996, McAlister 2001). Still, as Suzanne Conklin Akbari comments about Said's work today, "There is clearly no point in belaboring the limitations of a theory introduced in the late 1970s in the context of a very different political and academic climate" (5).

More recent studies, while recognizing the limitations of Said's original thesis, have nevertheless continued to utilize the concept of Orientalism to explore the particular moments of its production, paying attention

to how its function and meaning changed according to different historical, political, and cultural contexts. This book is located within such historically specific revisions of Orientalism and Western culture. One of
the ways in which I extend the study of Orientalism is by considering
how *women* produced such discourses in *popular culture*. Following Said's
lead, scholars of Orientalism and Western culture have primarily focused
on high culture (fine arts, music, literature) and travel writing, giving
some attention to popular culture in the form of Hollywood films (Said
1993, Edwards 2000, Benjamin 2003, Tromans 2008). Many of these analyses conclude with the end of the nineteenth or the early twentieth century, often using the First World War as the end point of their studies. In
the twentieth and twenty-first centuries, however, Orientalist ideas have
been conveyed most pervasively and effectively through popular culture.
Yet apart from some studies on Orientalism and film (Marchetti 1994,
Bernstein and Studlar 1997, Shohat 1997, Semmerling 2006, Shaheen
2008), and a few articles on *The Sheik* and contemporary sheik romances
from feminist and/or postcolonial perspectives (Melman 1988, Raub 1996,
Bach 1997, Chow 1999, Caton 2000, Blake 2003, Gargano 2006, Teo 2007
and 2010), no extensive work has focused careful and sustained historical attention on Orientalism in popular culture or analyzed the changing meaning of Orientalist tropes resulting from shifting imperial and
geopolitical realities. In this book, I not only situate popular Orientalist
romance novels within their historical contexts and draw out the connections to relevant imperial and geopolitical circumstances; I also provide
a cultural history of the development of Orientalist motifs in Western literature from the twelfth century to the present day, examining what these
motifs meant to different societies at different times, and how they function in contemporary popular culture. The fundamental question I ask,
in other words, is: What purpose did different components of Orientalist
discourse serve for different audiences? For example, narratives of abduction and sexual slavery in the harem had very different meanings in the
sixteenth to the early eighteenth century, when Ottoman power was for-
midable and such occurrences were a reality, than in the late eighteenth
to the early twentieth century, when British and French global power as-
cended to their imperial zenith, and the late twentieth and twenty-first
centuries, when such narratives can be read as postmodern pastiches of
colonial fantasies in an age of American global power and intervention in
the Middle East.

In the United States, a growing body of work—much of it affiliated
with the American-Arab Anti-Discrimination Committee—has exam-

ined the perpetuation of Orientalist discourse in popular culture through analyses of negative images of Arabs and Muslims particularly after the Second World War. In this corpus, however, as with the scholarship on high culture, the focus is on Western *men's* representations of Muslims, Arabs, and the Orient. Despite the feminist interventions of Billie Melman, Reina Lewis, Lisa Lowe, Ruth Bernard Yeazell, Joyce Zonana, and Emily Haddad, among others, male representations of the Orient continue to be taken as the norm, and stand for "the West" as a whole. With the exception of Lady Mary Wortley Montagu's *Turkish Embassy Letters* and E. M. Hull's *The Sheik*, discussions of women and Orientalism tend to focus on Western men's sexual fantasies about and representations of Oriental women. Even Mohja Kahf's nuanced and sophisticated analysis of the changing image of "the Muslim woman" in Western literature—from the outspoken and powerful medieval princess to the subdued figure of the sexualized and oppressed harem concubine of the eighteenth and nineteenth centuries—limits Orientalist discourse to Western men (with the usual inclusion of Montagu as the sole female representative), because her study ends in the early nineteenth century. What is missing, therefore, is any serious, sustained examination of Western women's production and consumption of Orientalist discourse in popular culture, particularly in the twentieth and twenty-first centuries. This is what I seek to redress in *Desert Passions* through a study of the female-authored Orientalist romance novel.

In focusing upon Western women's Orientalist fantasies, I inevitably engage with and build on the existing feminist scholarship on Western women's involvement with imperialism. Since the mid-1980s, a growing body of feminist scholarship has explored European women's historical participation in colonization and the production of imperial culture and identity. Some authors have argued that women were less racist and Orientalist than men in their encounters with colonized peoples because they were constrained by nineteenth-century domestic ideology and the "discourses of femininity" that shaped both writing and behavior (Stevenson 1982, Melman 1995, Foster 1990, Mills 1991, Blake 1992). Others, by contrast, have asserted that living in the empire actually offered women alternative, more "masculine" roles, or that the constraints of traditional femininity vanished after the First World War, and there was then little gendered difference to be discerned in the production of colonial discourse (Procida 2001, Teo 2002). Ann Laura Stoler's work shows how relations in the private sphere were imbricated with colonial and racial ideas. European women in the colonies helped produce bourgeois racial, imperial, and European identities through the careful policing of sexual desire to ensure the legitimacy of offspring. They enforced a rigid code of middle-class maternal behavior as well as the racialized ordering of the domestic sphere (Stoler 1995). Such findings affirm Joanne Nagel's (2003) argument that racial or ethnic boundaries are always sexual, or "ethnosexual," boundaries that can signify danger, distance, and pollution or, alternatively, the opportunity for assimilation and incorporation into the body politic.

I argue that white women's engagement with Orientalist discourse was always characterized by ethnosexual tension, but that in the European age of empire, the "white woman's burden" to ensure racial purity and enforce the boundaries between colonizer and colonized meant that flirtations with interracial romance and miscegenation were ultimately rejected by British writers. However, because of America's different historical circumstances of immigration, and the heterogeneity of "whiteness" as a racial category in the United States, Hollywood films offered the possibility of incorporating ethnic others—including Arabs, on occasion—into the body politic long before Britain did. By the late twentieth century, civil rights and the politics of multiculturalism dominated Western women's Orientalist discourse and the crossing of interethnic boundaries was something to be celebrated. Yet such contemporary stories still bear the vestiges of earlier Western colonial discourse. Western women continue to represent civilization and modernity, while their individuation and exaltation to the status of romantic heroines take place at the expense of those who Chandra Talpade Mohanty calls "third world women," who are either absent from the text or who are represented as backward, unenlightened, oppressed, and in need of salvation (333–358). In this book, I thus extend feminist postcolonial analyses of imperial culture to the area of women's popular culture. I build on and engage with Susan L. Blake's (2003) and Elizabeth Gargano's (2006) works on race and imperialism in *The Sheik* while providing a literary lineage for Hull's novel and examining its continuing influence in women's popular romance fiction throughout the twentieth and twenty-first centuries.

Thus, *Desert Passions* contributes to a third, burgeoning scholarly conversation about women's popular culture. The turn of the twenty-first century has seen the rise of a new wave of critical scholarship on romance fiction, driven largely by Eric Murphy Selinger and Sarah S. G. Frantz's efforts showcasing new academic responses to romance novels, and formally institutionalized by the establishment of the International Association for the Study of Popular Romance in 2009. This new body of interdisciplinary work signals a significant departure from the earlier "first-wave" critique of romance novels that focused on "images of women" debates and expressed feminist concern for female romance readers as the dupes of the patriarchy. The first wave of romance scholarship began with feminist and socialist criticism in the 1970s and early 1980s and was initiated by denunciatory critiques of the genre by feminists such as Germaine Greer (1970), Ann Douglas (1980), and Kay Mussell (1984). Greer's work on romance in *The Female Eunuch* excoriates romance novels and accuses them of indoctrinating young girls with impossible dreams of romance and marriage; of maintaining sexist ideas that women's inequality in work and gender relations is natural and even desirable (192–212). Ann Bar Snitow (1979) is more judicious, arguing that Harlequin romance novels are "neither an effective top down propaganda effort against women's liberation, nor a covert flowering of female sexuality" (143) but, rather, they provided limited pleasures and fulfilled women's needs in a society where American culture's rich myths about individuality and transcendence over socioeconomic situations largely excluded women (150). While Snitow argues that romance novels were *not* the female equivalent of pornography because of their insistence that sexual activity be "treated not primarily as a physical event at all but as a social drama, as a carefully modulated set of psychological possibilities between people" (160), Ann Douglas (1980) disagrees, and deplores the exhibition of powerful, punitive male behavior that takes place at the expense of the heroine's economic, physical, and sexual well-being. Additionally, Kay Mussell (1984) contends that romantic fiction portrays the heroine as passive and infantile, thus undermining women's sexual and financial independence and autonomy.

This early scholarship thus expressed feminist anxieties about the ideological indoctrination of female readers through the supposedly backward images of women presented, and about the perpetuation of patriarchy and capitalism. The debates revolved around whether romance novels were essentially liberating or oppressive for women. Carol Thurston (1987) comes down on the side of liberation, while Tania Modleski (1982), Jan Cohn (1988) and Bridget Fowler (1991) support arguments that romance novels perpetuate the patriarchal, capitalist oppression of women. Meanwhile, one of the most noted scholars in this debate, Janice Radway (1991), equivocates, but inclines toward the latter position. As Selinger and Frantz (2012) note, this body of work is important because it takes "popular romance fiction seriously." Critics "read the novels themselves in search of subtexts, self-contradictions, and other complexities, just as one reads any other text. Their attention to subtexts of *power*, in particular, has proved useful both for scholars and for romance authors" (4). This conversation more or less stuttered to a halt when American romance writers defended their craft in *Dangerous Men and Adventurous Women*, a volume edited by Jayne Ann Krentz which, Selinger and Frantz argue, ushered in the "second wave" of romance scholarship because it showed that "romance authors could serve, like literary authors, as critics and theorists of their chosen genre" (5). An attempt was then made to bring writers, readers, and academic critics together in a special issue of the journal *Paradoxa* (1997) focusing on popular romance fiction, but as Selinger and Frantz note, "In retrospect, the *Paradoxa* gathering was more a harbinger than a transformative event. The issue did not circulate widely enough to displace those early, foundational studies" (7).

While echoes of this earlier debate about whether romance reading is "good" or "bad" for women still resound in volumes such as *Empowerment versus Oppression* (Goade 2007), the recent wave of romance fiction scholarship generally revisits the genre by utilizing a more traditional literary tool kit loosely drawn from New Criticism or New Historicism (Selinger 2007, Selinger and Frantz 2012). The most authoritative account in this third wave thus far is Pamela Regis's taxonomic evaluation of the genre, *A Natural History of the Romance Novel* (2003), a formalist undertaking that establishes archetypes of romance fiction and identifies canons of the genre in a project rather similar to Northrop Frye's magisterial work, *The Secular Scripture: A Study of the Structure of Romance* (1978). Other studies analyze subgenres and intergeneric trends in romance fiction, translations of romance novels, and the representations of different types of sexualities, among many other thematic and interdisciplinary approaches. They explore historical change and pay attention to individual authors rather than assume the ahistorical and interchangeable nature of romance novels. An especially insightful overview of the current scholarship in this field can be found in Selinger and Frantz's introduction to their edited volume, *New Approaches to Popular Romance Fiction* (2012).

In *Desert Passions*, I build on this body of work, but I do not approach romance fiction from a framework of literary theory; rather, mine is a historical contextualization and reading of Orientalist interracial love stories that crosses genres and media and examines how the romance novel exists in dialogical relationship with other historical and contemporary texts. Treating *Desert Passions* as a historical work inevitably limits my engagement with the first wave of feminist scholarship on romance fiction. While some feminists argue that romance novels represented oppressed working-class women's daydreams of gaining access to wealth, status, and power via marriage with the hero in a patriarchal, capitalist society, the two most influential works from the first wave of romance fiction scholarship focus on psychoanalytic interpretations of women's romance reading behavior. Tania Modleski's *Loving with a Vengeance* (1982) and Janice Radway's *Reading the Romance* (1984) contend that romance reading fulfills women's emotional need to experience love and nurturance that, as wives and mothers, they give out to men and children but do not receive in return. In Radway's words:

> The romance readers of Smithton use their books to erect a barrier between themselves and their families in order to declare themselves temporarily off-limits to those who would mine them for emotional support and material care. . . . I try to make a case for seeing romance reading as a form of individual resistance to a situation predicated on the assumption that it is women alone who are responsible for the care and emotional nurturance of others. . . . Romance reading creates a feeling of hope, provides emotional sustenance, and produces a fully visceral sense of well-being. (12)

Although Radway professes a respect for romance readers, such an argument reiterates a position that has been well-rehearsed since Q. D. Leavis's *Fiction and the Reading Public* (1932) and the Frankfurt School's modernist analysis of mass culture: that mass-market popular culture, particularly when manifested in the form of romance fiction, is the "opiate of the missus," serving to reconcile working-class consumers with the fact of their oppressed status quo in a capitalist, patriarchal society. The feminist agenda, then, should be to encourage romance readers to deliver their protests "in the arena of actual social relations" and to "imagine a world whose subsequent creation would lead to the need for a new fantasy altogether" (Radway 220).

Desert Passions does not engage with psychological or psychoanalytic readings of disparate women, nor does it prescribe what these female writers and readers should or should not do to usher in a utopia for women. I am neither interested in condemning nor defending romance novels and romance readers. I simply approach my subject as a fascinating historical and cultural phenomenon, and with a feminist respect for the women who write and read these works. I do not believe, moreover, that generalizations can be made about "the female romance reader," because such a term takes an essentialist view, ignoring differences among class, race, ethnicity, education, religion, age and generation, national and regional identity, habits of cultural consumption, and professional and social experiences, among other complex markers and shapers of identity. These contingencies change the perception as well as the practice of romance reading for different women, as is evident in blog postings, reader reviews of the novels from the Amazon.com website, and reader responses to various contemporary sheik romance novels, which I discuss in Chapters 5 and 9.

Radway's book has arguably been the most influential work on romance fiction to date, especially outside the field of romance fiction scholarship, because of the seemingly solid empirical base of her interviews with romance readers. Because of its status and visibility, *Reading the Romance* has attracted significant critiques in the years since its publication (e.g., Purdie 1992, Jackson 1993, Harris 1994, Hermes 2000). The most problematic flaw in Radway's study, as far as I am concerned, is the fact that her entire hypothesis was drawn from interviews conducted between 1980 and 1981 with sixteen white, middle-class, American homemakers in the small town of "Smithton" who were recommended to her by one bookseller. These interviews were supplemented by forty-two questionnaires completed by customers of the same bookseller. The findings from this small and narrow group with limited interests in the genre were then extrapolated to represent "the romance reader." If we take another sample group, however, the meaning of romance reading is transformed. Radhika Parameswaran's work on readers of contemporary Mills & Boon romance fiction in India, for instance, demonstrates that the women she interviewed have a high status because they can read English, so here romance reading is a mark of privilege, education, and Westernization associated with the urban upper and middle classes (Parameswaran 1999 and 2002). In any case, as most avid readers know, reading is a highly promiscuous affair: readers are rarely faithful to purely one genre of literature. Radway's own findings bear this out, for as she notes, "62 percent of Dot's customers claimed to read somewhere between one and four books *other* than romances every week" (60). Moreover, it is obvious from the epigraphs found at the start of many romance novels that there is not only a familiarity with—or even veneration for—the traditional Western canon on the part of romance novelists, but the boundary between romance literature and the canon is frequently breached through the borrowing of plots, motifs, conventions, and characters. This is what I argue with respect to the discourse of Orientalism, which was associated with high literary forms prior to the twentieth century and then became more widely dispersed in the modern Orientalist mass-market romance novel written overwhelmingly by women.

Although male authors such as Jefferey Farnol and Stanley Weyman were still writing romance fiction in the early twentieth century, the genre became "feminized" over the course of the late nineteenth and early twentieth centuries, perhaps because, as Rita Felski argues, the aesthetics of modernism increasingly denigrated romance as idealized, "cloying feminine sentimentality" (79–80, 117). By the interwar years, women were the major producers and readers of romance fiction (Beauman 6). All the writers of contemporary Orientalist romance fiction discussed in this book are female, and among the writers of Orientalist historical romance fiction, only one discussed here is male: West Indian-born British novelist Christopher Nicole, who wrote the bodice ripper *The Savage Sands* (1978) under the pseudonym "Christina Nicholson."[4]

The novels studied in this book were selected in various ways. I first came across the early twentieth century "desert romance" novel through my previous research into British women's travel writing about the Middle East in the late nineteenth and early twentieth centuries. Female travel writers such as Rosita Forbes and Lady Dorothy Mills also produced romance novels set in the countries that they visited. It was in this context that I came across E. M. Hull's travel book *Camping in the Sahara* (1926), which I read before moving on to *The Sheik* (1919) and *The Sons of the Sheik* (1925), the original sheik romances that prompted my interest in Orientalist romance fiction. Although hundreds of romance novels were written by British women in this period, little work has been done on this genre apart from Rachel Anderson's *The Purple Heart Throbs: The Subliterature of Love* (1974), Nicola Beauman's *A Very Great Profession* (1983), and Billie Melman's *Women and the Popular Imagination in the Twenties: Flappers and Nymphs* (1988). These works were very useful for helping me to locate desert and sheik romance stories from the early twentieth century.

Novels from the late twentieth and twenty-first centuries were far easier to find, thanks to the Internet databases put together by fans of the subgenre. I compiled a database of known Orientalist romances from the following websites:

http://romancing-the-desert---sheikh-books.blogspot.com/
http://shabbysheikh.blogspot.com/

http://sheikhs-and-desert-love.com/
http://romancereaderatheart.com/sheik/Authors.html
http://splumonium.com/DIR_romance/research.htm

Additionally, I did keyword searches of combinations of "sheik/sheikh," "romance," "love story," and "Orientalism" through library catalogues and I then read as many of these novels as I could find. Prior to 2000, the number of Orientalist romances published made this task a relatively easy one. The graphs on pages 5 and 6, compiled from the "Sheikhs and Desert Love" site, show that until 2000, the maximum number of sheik romance novels published annually was six. This increased dramatically until it spiked at twenty-two novels, in 2002. The number of novels published up to the date of my studies meant that it was fairly easy to compile and read the majority of these books, which is why I have been able to isolate some of the more interesting and unusual ones for extended analysis and discussion in the following chapters.

I should note, however, that although the Orientalist historical novels studied are all "single-title" novels of varying length (often between three hundred and four hundred pages), that include subplots not directly related to the unfolding romance between hero and heroine, the contemporary romance novels discussed are almost all "category" romance novels: that is, novels of a certain page length that are released regularly (e.g., monthly), focus almost exclusively on the unfolding romance between the hero and heroine, and are sold under particular publisher imprints or series lines, such as Harlequin Presents, Harlequin Intrigue, Silhouette, and so forth. This difference in selection follows from my methodology described above. If the search terms are not in the titles, and if single-title romance novels featuring Arab Americans or sheiks do not feature in the online bibliographies and databases, then they are virtually impossible to find because of the sheer scale of romance publishing and the innumerable romance novels published over the course of the twentieth and twenty-first centuries.

This book is divided into nine roughly chronological chapters. In Chapter 1, "Loving the Orient: The Romantic East and European Literature," I trace the historical evolution of the romantic East in Europe's literary engagement with its Islamic other; an engagement that produced the foundational topoi seen in Orientalist romance novels today. I begin by focusing on the literary lineage of cross-cultural, interracial, and inter-religious sexual desire and romantic love in Europe's mythical Orient. I explore the transmission of ideas about unrequited, unfulfilled romantic love ("Udhrah" love) from Islamic Spain to Europe, and I examine the imaginary engagement, via Crusade epics, of Europeans with the Muslim threat. In these poems, cross-cultural, interreligious romantic unions were used as a plot device to effect conversions and extend the realm of Christendom. I then trace the development of classic themes of Orientalist romance in writing and drama from the seventeenth and eighteenth centuries, when the Muslim threat moved eastward from Islamic Spain to the Ottoman Empire, and I argue that the topos of Muslim abduction formed the focus of European anxieties in the seventeenth century, whereas eighteenth-century European fantasies placed more emphasis on the Western woman in the harem. In addition to the widespread popularity of Galland's *The Thousand and One Nights* (1704–1717), comic opera such as Favart's *Les trois sultanes, ou, Soliman Second* (1761) and Mozart's *Die Entführung aus dem Serail* (1782) ushered in a vogue for *turquerie* or "turcomania" and brought attention to the reformist role of Western women in the harem. The Orient enjoyed another fashionable phase during the early nineteenth century, when Byron published his Eastern tales, beginning with *The Giaour*, in 1813. Byron was influential in creating a memorable cast of noble "outlaw heroes" who made the Orient their playground. He also redirected attention to the fleshy delights of the harem in *Don Juan* (1821). The rise of pornography in Britain during the eighteenth and early nineteenth centuries made use of existing Orientalist motifs, especially in the anonymously authored Victorian porn classic, *The Lustful Turk* (1828). *The Sheik* shares a number of common motifs with *The Lustful Turk*, particularly the abduction of the virginal heroine, the character of the sadistic rapist hero, and the idea that an Englishwoman can be raped into feelings of love. Through a brief examination of the highly contradictory cultural ideologies of virginity in European literature, I consider why the virgin was such a figure of ambivalence that her rape was titillating to readers. The invention of the pornographic East needs to be read against the slow decline of Ottoman power and the rising encroachment of European nation and empire building at its expense. It was against this backdrop that, starting in the early nineteenth century, British authors began to turn their attention away from the Ottoman harem, with its corruption and consequent loss of power, to the romanticized desert of the stalwart, liberty-loving "noble Bedouin"—thus paving the way for the setting and story of *The Sheik*.

In Chapter 2, I look at the evolution of the desert romance novel as a subgenre of the female-centered romance novel of the nineteenth century. Spirituality and a fascination with the occult characterized late Victorian romance novels, thus the desert romance began as a space for spiritual transcendence in addition to romantic love. This chapter examines key texts in the subgenre in the early twentieth century: Robert Hichens's *The Garden of Allah* (1904) and the novels of Kathlyn Rhodes, whose exotic romances, often set in Egypt and North Africa, combine the concerns of new woman novels about passion, independence, and companionate marriage with more conservative misgivings about sexual feelings and a strong injunction against interracial unions. The popularity of this subgenre preceded *The Sheik*, but it was Hull's novel that undoubtedly transformed the "desert romance" into the "sheik romance" in its twentieth century incarnation. I conclude this chapter with a discussion of the desert romance subgenre in British culture after the publication of *The Sheik*, focusing particularly on how romance novelists treated the taboo issue of miscegenation.

In Chapter 3, I focus on *The Sheik*. I review the extant feminist scholarship on this novel before arguing that the production and reception of the book in Britain need to be contextualized with reference to the First World War and Britain's racial problems domestically and in its colonies after the war. Melman's, Blake's, and Gargano's works have emphasized the imperialist aspects of *The Sheik* but little has been said about British imperial rivalry with France in the novel and its sequel, *The Sons of the Sheik*. This neglected aspect of the novel is discussed in this chapter, along with an analysis of what racial "whiteness" means in the context of imperialism in the Middle East, and how it functions in *The Sheik*. The complex meaning of whiteness is evident in both of Hull's novels as well as in the Hollywood film versions of these novels.

In Chapter 4, "The Spectacular East: Romantic Orientalism in America," I contextualize the production and contemporary reception of the Hollywood film of *The Sheik* within discourses of American Orientalism; discourses that, by the early twentieth century, produced the Orient as a site of consumable goods as well as "Arabian Nights" fantasies. I chart the rise of Orientalist discourses of abduction, seduction, and romance in the United States from the Revolutionary period to the early twentieth century. I trace overlaps with European Orientalist motifs, analyze concerns that arose especially from America's own encounters with Barbary states, and outline the development of middle-class consumer culture in the postbellum period. By the late nineteenth century, Orientalism in the United States was propagated through visually spectacular theatrics, whether in exhibitions, carnival sideshows, staged productions of desert romances such as Robert Hichens's *The Garden of Allah* (1909), early films, and, of course, the Famous Players-Lasky (later Paramount) versions of *The Sheik* (1921) and *The Son of the Sheik* (1926). In my discussion of the translation of Hull's two novels into film, I argue that although the film of *The Sheik* maintains the novel's imperialist agenda, when read against the United States' specific history of immigration, whiteness, and race relations in the early twentieth century, *The Sheik* becomes a story about the incorporation of white "ethnics" into mainstream "Anglo-Saxon" society via the body of the middle-class white woman. I conclude this chapter with a consideration of how the Valentino film influenced romantic Orientalism in American film and television throughout the twentieth century.

In Chapter 5, I explore the rise of the Orientalist harem historical romance novel in the last quarter of the twentieth century and its incorporation of motifs developed in Victorian Orientalist pornography. I focus particularly on the eroticization of the historical romance in the 1970s—an extraordinary development that Carol Thurston (1987) terms the "romance revolution," which followed the sexual revolution and formed alongside women's liberation. The harem historical romance novel draws from several longstanding Orientalist motifs in European literature: the Crusades; Byronic "giaours" (infidels), who were also associated with nationalist, anticolonial freedom fighters; abduction by renegade Barbary corsairs; slave markets; harem life; escape from the seraglio; and the reworking of the Roxelane theme discussed in Chapter 1, whereby the spirited European heroine tames the despotic Muslim male. One of the most common sexual fantasies that found expression in these harem romances was the fantasy of seduction through rape. Therefore, I examine the problem of rape in erotic historical novels to consider how these fantasies might be interpreted, before proceeding to look at how, through the example of Bertrice Small's *The Kadin* (1978), the harem novel could present a challenge to existing Turkish, feminist, and national historiographies of the 1970s. Drawing from reader reviews from the Amazon.com site, I end with a brief discussion of contemporary readers' responses to some of the most popular or controversial novels in this subgenre.

In Chapters 6 to 9, I deal with the contemporary sheik romance novel, which developed in the 1970s and has continued to grow in popularity, beginning with the publication of *Blue Jasmine* (1969), Violet Winspear's reworking of *The Sheik*. In Chapter 6, I outline the historical background to this subgenre, tracing the rise of the "category" romance novel in the twentieth century and examining the influential role of Mills & Boon and Harlequin publishers in creating a mass-market brand synonymous with "romance novel" in the last quarter of the twentieth century. I describe significant historical changes in the nature of these novels resulting from second-wave feminism and the civil rights movement. The desert or sheik romance novel experienced a renaissance in the midst of the growing prominence of the Middle East in international affairs after the 1967 Arab-Israeli war and the oil shocks of the early 1970s. The revival began as a British affair and, in line with its early twentieth-century counterpart, produced somewhat realistic depictions of Western women finding professional opportunities in Middle Eastern countries such as Kuwait and the former Trucial states—countries that had historical and political ties to Britain. Australian authors began writing sheik or desert romances in the mid-1980s, and their involvement marked a turn away from actual geopolitical entities toward a fantasyland of make-believe Oriental countries with little grounding in contemporary Middle Eastern reality.

In Chapter 7, "Harems, Houris, Heroines, and Heroes," I evaluate continuities and changes between the contemporary sheik romance novel and its earlier, 1920s counterpart, as well as in the European discourse of romantic Orientalism that developed over the centuries. I analyze the influence of feminism on heroines, especially in American-authored novels from the 1980s to the twenty-first century, and I examine how changing ideas of masculinity are portrayed through the figure of the de-Orientalized sheik hero. Much of this had to do with the gradual Americanization of this subgenre throughout the 1990s to the present day. American authors began to produce contemporary sheik romances after the Gulf War, and while they adopted the strategy of setting their Oriental stories in fictional Arabic states, they also drew from a century-long tradition of Orientalist Hollywood films to frame their "Arabian Nights" fantasies. Today, this subgenre is largely dominated by American authors who have transformed the sheik romance. American heroines have broken loose from the patriarchal authority of the sheik hero to assert their equality and partnership with these men, who are paradoxically portrayed as priapic but also boyish, companionate, and good father figures—the domesticated "sheik daddy" of Barbara McMahon's eponymous novel of 1996.

In Chapter 8, "From Tourism to Terrorism," I analyze recurring discourses in the contemporary sheik romance. Travel and tourism are prominent discourses in the British sheik novels of the 1970s and 1980s, and are drawn from the early twentieth-century tradition of combining the sheik romance with a travel narrative. Much late nineteenth-

and early twentieth-century British Orientalist discourse was produced through travel books about the Middle East. In this chapter, I explore how the discourse of travel not only idealized and exoticized the Middle East and North Africa, but also imagined a dreary, poverty-stricken, class-bound Britain that heroines were desperate to escape. I argue that this portrayal of the home country is markedly different in Australian and American sheik romance novels. I look at how representations of the ancient and exotic Orient are juxtaposed against discourses of development and modernization, and how these discourses allow authors to touch lightly on political conflicts while limiting what they can actually say about real problems in the Middle East. I analyze two remarkable romances—British novelist Sara Wood's *Perfumes of Arabia* (1986) and American novelist Elizabeth Mayne's *The Sheik and the Vixen* (1996)—which are notable for their authors' attempts to critique Middle Eastern relations with the West—relations that have been filtered through a history of British imperialism and American neo-imperialism. The fragmentation of the American romance market into niche subgenres, such as the romantic thriller and suspense novel, has even enabled some authors to consider American engagement in the Gulf War, terrorism, and contemporary war in the Middle East.

Chapter 9 is a brief account of reader reviews of modern sheik romance novels from the Amazon.com site and other blogs. I argue that these reviews and accompanying blogs indicate ways of interpreting and interacting with the novels that are sometimes very sophisticated and also driven by readers' own agendas. This is particularly true for American readers' heated discussion about race in response to the first black American sheik romance: Brenda Jackson's *Delaney's Desert Sheikh* (2002).

In many ways, these Orientalist romance novels represent white women's desires to promote liberal and multicultural agendas, and to foster interest in, and respect for, Middle Eastern cultures and peoples. These are no doubt often flawed and problematic attempts that not only reinstate Orientalism, but that also resurrect and attempt to reapply American modernization theory to the Middle East. I do not dwell overly much on the post-9/11 era since most of my focus is on the twentieth century; only in the last few years have romance novelists started engaging with issues of terrorism and American wars in the Middle East. However, in the wake of the Gulf War and the al-Qaeda attacks on September 11, 2001, it is important to recognize that there is a significant strand of popular culture that does not demonize Arabs and/or Muslims but, on the contrary, seeks to humanize and include them, and attempts to negotiate an understanding (however imperfect) of American relations with the Middle East. This is greatly significant in light of the discrimination against Muslims and Arabs that has occurred since the 9/11 attacks in the United States and the July 7, 2005, Islamist terrorist attacks in Britain. Contemporary romance writers are often middle-class, university-educated women, but women who have limited knowledge and understanding of the Middle East. In this respect, their novels are also a valuable historical archive, because they show how ordinary, educated women understand and interpret Arabs, Muslims, citizenship and belonging, and Western relations with the Middle East. Their interpretations are inevitably fraught with the long cultural history of Western fascination with, and desire for, the imaginary Orient.

ONE

Loving the Orient: The Romantic East and European Literature

My heart is open to all the winds:
It is a pasture for gazelles
And a home for Christian monks,
A temple for idols,
The Black Stone of the Mecca pilgrim,
The Table of the Torah,
And the book of the Koran.
Mine is the religion of love.
Wherever God's caravans turn,
The religion of love
Shall be my religion
And my faith.

IBN AL-ARABI, "THE INTERPRETATION OF LONGINGS"

In 1146, the French king Louis VII embarked on the Second Crusade to Jerusalem accompanied by his wife, Eleanor of Aquitaine. Eleanor had not been in the Holy Land for very long before rumors began spreading of her love affairs with various Muslim men. Included in the list of her supposed lovers was the great Salah ad-Din Yusuf ibn Ayyub, known to the English as Saladin, the Kurdish sultan of Egypt and Syria who later became famous for his chivalrous treatment of his foe Richard the Lionheart during the Third Crusade.[1] The rumored affair between Eleanor and Saladin was impossible; he was still a very young child and it is unlikely the two even met. Nevertheless, Eleanor's presence in the Orient produced the first of many European tales about white women's sexual or romantic desire for Muslim men. As Maria Menocal notes, in all the scandalous tales that circulated about the queen, Eleanor was always assumed to be complicit in her own seduction (1987: 51).

Eleanor came from a family with a history of involvement with both the Crusades and the aristocratic poetry of romantic love developing in southern France around the twelfth century—a genre recognized to be one of the earliest and most important literary traditions in western Europe (Rougemont 5). She was the granddaughter of the ninth Duke of Aquitaine, William "the Troubadour," who was one of the leaders of the Crusade of 1101, and who popularized the poetry of "courtly love"[2] throughout France. Eleanor's daughter Marie of France was the patroness of one of the most well-known troubadours of the twelfth century, Chrétien de Troyes. Marie's own husband, Henri I, Count of Champagne, also took part in the Second Crusade with his father-in-law, Louis VII. Eleanor and those who traveled with her would thus have been steeped in the French culture of romantic love; so just what was it about the Muslim world of "the Orient" that appealed to these Europeans' fantasies about romance and seduction? Why did a connection develop between crusading and courtly love during the High Middle Ages (Heng 1998), especially since the Orient of the Crusades was supposedly populated by Muslim enemies who were sometimes portrayed as monstrous black idolaters? What made the Orient romantic to that generation as well as to the Western women who, eight centuries later, would thrill to the thought of being seduced by an Arab sheik?

In this chapter, I examine how the Muslim world became associated with love even while European writers portrayed it as a place to be feared and derided. I trace the ways in which many of the tropes that are found in contemporary Orientalist romance novels developed in Europe from the twelfth to the twentieth century. Whether or not modern romance writers are aware of it, the Orientalist motifs that abound in contemporary sheik romance novels derive from a long European literary tradition of imagining and interpreting the Orient. Accordingly, I look at how ideas of romantic love spread from Islamic Spain throughout Europe, before considering how Europeans wrote about cross-cultural, interreligious romantic unions during the late medieval and early modern period. I follow the development of classic themes in Orientalist romance novels during the seventeenth and eighteenth centuries, when the Muslim threat to Europe moved eastward from Islamic Spain to the Ottoman Empire. I explore topoi such as abduction by Barbary pirates, slavery, the renegade hero, the Oriental despot and his harem, the figure of the liberty-loving European concubine who has the power to convert the Oriental monarch, and fantasies of rescue and escape from the harem—all of which can be found in romance novels today, as can the figure of the Byronic hero as the noble outlaw or outcast from a society that has wronged him.

Beginning in the nineteenth century, ideas about the Orient were influenced by Romanticism, especially the poetry of Byron, who probably did more to romanticize the East than anyone before him. But as Steven Marcus suggests, Byron's successors not only eroticized the Orient; they made it a site of European pornography, especially in the anonymous classic of nineteenth-century erotica, *The Lustful Turk* (206). Women's historical romance novels, or bodice rippers, would revive the pornographic Orient in the mid-twentieth century, as discussed in Chapter 5. The pornographic Orient developed in response to the decline of Ottoman power. In the British imagination, the sexual excesses of the Ottoman system—represented by the harem—had produced a weak and effete empire over time. During the nineteenth century, British writers began to turn their attention away from the Ottoman harem, instead romanticizing the fierce, liberty-loving Bedouin of the North African desert.

THE ARABIC CULTURE OF ROMANTIC LOVE

That Eleanor's companions on the Second Crusade recognized the seductive sexual and romantic appeal of their Muslim enemies should not surprise us. The Muslim world had a well-developed culture of romantic love long before Europeans "invented" it in the twelfth century (Rougemont 5, 50). The Arabic poetry of romantic love preceded the Muslim era, beginning as early as the sixth century and developing alongside the rise of Islam throughout the seventh and eighth centuries (Zeldin 76). Wealthy and influential women in cities such as Mecca and Medina were particularly important in fostering the writing and performance of love poetry, acting as the patrons of Arabic and Persian bards. By the time Arabic love poetry entered its golden age in Basra and Baghdad during the eighth and ninth centuries, romantic love had been glorified to a transcendent ideal, at its most noble and pure when it was unrequited or impossible to fulfill (Zeldin 77–80). The idea that desiring an impossible love represented a kind of martyr's death—what the Arabs called "Udhrah love"—would be elaborated in the troubadour tradition in twelfth- and thirteenth-century France and Britain. It spread to Western Europe via al-Andalus, or Moorish Spain (Giffin 8–9, 59).

By the early eighth century, the Islamic Empire had expanded westward from the Arabian peninsula to include the region known in Arabic as al-Maghrib—"the West"—stretching along the North African coastline from present-day Libya to Morocco. In 711, Muslim forces crossed the narrow straits at the mouth of the Mediterranean and invaded Spain from Morocco. Under the Arabic Umayyad rulers, al-Andalus became an epicenter for music and the arts. Even after the original Umayyad dynasty was toppled by subsequent dynasties, the arts continued to flourish because the Mediterranean had become a conduit for cross-cultural interaction among Greeks, Persians, Arabs, and northern Europeans. The Moorish culture of al-Andalus was important to northern European culture in many ways. As Norman Daniel (8–9), Dorothee Metlitzki (37), Thomas Glick (287), Zachary Lockman (26), and many others argue, medieval Europeans recognized that Moorish Spain was culturally and technologically superior to the rest of Europe. Metlitzki points out that Spain and Sicily were vital channels for the transmission of Arabic goods and knowledge to Western Europe, so much so that Arabs "became the teachers and inspirers of the West at the very heart of its cultural life: its attitude to reason and faith" (249).

The influence of Arabic literary and romantic culture on Spanish life was evident by the mid-ninth century, when Paul Alvarus of Córdoba complained about the popularity of Arabic literature among Spanish Christians: "The Christians love to read the poems and romances of the Arabs; they study the Arab theologians and philosophers, not to refute them but to form a correct and elegant Arabic" (Lockman 26). In Moorish Spain, the literary trope of "Udhrah love" was reworked by Ibn Hazm (994–1064) of Córdoba, who became famous for *The Ring of the Dove*, a meditation on the nature of love. After Ibn Hazm, Ibn al-Arabi (1165–1240), another Andalusian poet from Murcia, further exalted love's importance, proclaiming: "The religion of love shall be my religion and my faith" (Zeldin 81–82). Ibn al-Arabi was but one of many poets from Moorish Spain who expanded the Arabic-Islamic literature of love from the eleventh to the thirteenth century (Menocal 1987: 29).

Scholars have argued that via the trade, pilgrimage, and crusading routes over the Pyrenees, the Arabic culture of romantic love spread from the Iberian Peninsula to twelfth-century southern France, influencing the Provençal tradition of courtly love that came to dominate Europe over the next few centuries (Menocal 1987: 30–32, Abu-Haidar 2001, Boase 1977). Whatever the extent of Arabic influence on the troubadour tradition, by the twelfth century, educated Europeans would have been aware that Islamic societies possessed a sophisticated system of beliefs about love, seduction, sexuality, and the pleasures of the senses. This awareness of Islamic romantic and sensual pleasures, coupled with Crusade-enforced ideas of "monstrous" and sexually deviant Saracens, formed the contradictory crux of European imaginative engagement with the East during the High Middle Ages (Strickland 49).

THE CRUSADES AND CROSS-CULTURAL LOVE

Maxime Rodinson argues that western Europeans became more aware of the Islamic world during the eleventh century (6). There were several reasons for this. In the Iberian Peninsula, Alfonso I of Portugal (ca. 1109–1185) was spectacularly successful in wresting large parts of Moorish Spain for the County of Portugal. During the years that Alfonso and other Christian monarchs in Spain were engaged in the *Reconquista*— the Christian reconquest of Spain from Moorish powers—crusaders flocked to the peninsula to roll back the borders of Islam. This Iberian crusade was part of the larger crusading project launched in 1095, when Pope Urban II called upon European Christians to come to the aid of the besieged Byzantine emperor in Constantinople and free the Holy Land from the control of Seljuk Turks so that Christian pilgrimage to Jerusalem could resume. The First Crusade, launched in 1096, concluded satisfactorily for the Europeans when Jerusalem was captured in 1099 and a series of Christian principalities were established along the Palestinian and Syrian coastline. Over the next two centuries, Seljuk Turks gradually reconquered these areas, prompting calls for new crusades from 1145 until 1291, when the Mamluks—a military caste of emancipated Muslim slaves—captured Jerusalem. The city would remain under Muslim rule until it was yielded to British forces in 1917. Although the *Reconquista* continued in Spain until 1492, major crusades to the Holy Land had ceased by the end of the thirteenth century.

The Crusades were particularly fertile for European cross-cultural love stories between Christians and Muslims, giving rise to the earliest examples of Orientalist romance in verse romances such as Orderic Vital's *Historia Ecclesiastica* (1130–1135), the anonymously authored *Floire et Blancheflor* (ca. 1160), *The King of Tars* (ca. 1330s), *Bevis of Hampton* (ca. 1324), and *The Sowdone [Sultan] of Babylone* (ca. 1400).[3] In these crusade romances, the ultimate triumph was not the death of the Saracen, but his or her conversion to Christianity through love and marriage. The French verse romance *Floire et Blancheflor* was one of the first crusade verse romances to gain widespread popularity, especially when it was translated into various English versions as *Floris and Blancheflour*[4] in the thirteenth and fourteenth centuries. In the French version of this tale (the English Auchinleck version begins when Floris and Blancheflour are twelve), Fenix, king of al-Andalus, attacks a group of Christian pilgrims on their way to the popular medieval shrine of Santiago de Compostela, killing a knight and capturing his recently widowed daughter, whom Fenix presents to his wife as her new lady-in-waiting. Fenix's wife and the Christian widow give birth respectively to a boy and a girl—Floris and Blancheflour. The Muslim prince Floris loves Christian Blancheflour but Fenix separates them by selling the "pagan" Blancheflour to a merchant. Blancheflour is locked away in the Tower of Maidens by the emir of Babylon, a serial monogamist who selects a new bride from the tower each year.

Floris and Blancheflour thus presents an early example of three European motifs that would come to dominate subsequent Orientalist romances: the slave trade (focusing particularly on white slavery), the incarceration of females in a prototypical harem, and the sexually insatiable and despotic Muslim monarch who cannot be content with one woman but must have his pick of many. Significantly, however, the romance presented Europeans with two types of Muslims distinguished not only by sexual behavior, but also by geography: the lecherous emir from "Oriental" Babylon and the virtuous Floris from Muslim Spain, which was nevertheless part of Europe.[5] Floris eventually rescues Blancheflour but, in a turn in the plot that would later appear in Mozart's opera *Die Entführung aus dem Serail* (*The Abduction from the Seraglio*, 1782), the lovers are discovered by the emir. The Muslim monarch ultimately permits them to leave freely because he recognizes the higher value of romantic love. However demonized or "othered" Muslims might have been in European culture during the Middle Ages, it was assumed that they, too, recognized the higher priority of love. Floris and Blancheflour return to al-Andalus when Fenix is dead, and since Floris has converted to Christianity, he proceeds to convert his subjects as well. *Floris and Blancheflour* was thus a potent tale that reinforced the message of triumphant Christian reconquest and forced conversion that was ubiquitous in Spain between the twelfth and fifteenth centuries. In the French and English imagination, at least, the romance held out the possibility of cross-cultural, interreligious unions— providing the Muslim protagonist converted.

Conversion to Christianity was also central to the plot of *The King of Tars* (ca. 1330s), in which the Muslim sultan of Damascus is persuaded to convert after his child, a monstrous abomination born of the inter-religious union between the sultan and his Christian wife, is baptized and transforms into a perfectly formed baby boy. A second miracle occurs when the sultan is christened: his black skin turns completely white. Whiteness in these verse romances was associated with sexual innocence, purity, morality, Christianity, and Europeanness. It was the color of salvation (Lampert 401). This was especially the case for women, but it also applied to all Christians generally. Debra Higgs Strickland notes that during the fourteenth century, "Christian artists portrayed non-Christian enemies with distorted physiognomy and dark skin as a sign of their rejected status" (49). Thus white skin—the sign of normality and humanity—was eminently desirable, as we shall see in many of the love stories that followed from these epics, including Orientalist romance novels of the twentieth century.

If Christian heroines had the power to transform their Muslim husbands, Christian heroes, too, had the power to convert Muslim princesses in verse romances such as *Bevis of Hampton* or *The Sowdone of Babylone*, both of which feature Saracen princesses who betray faith and father for love of a Christian knight. What is unusual about these Muslim heroines is that they possess a great deal of agency.[6] In *Bevis of Hampton*, the Muslim princess, Josian, pursues and woos Bevis and promises to convert to Christianity if he will marry her.[7] She is resourceful and clever, working to earn money when necessary and skilled in the use of herbs for medicinal purposes. The initiative and daring of Muslim heroines is particularly evident in the *Sowdone of Babylone*, in which the sultan's daughter Floripas falls in love with Charlemagne's noble knight Guy of Burgundy. When Guy and the other peers are captured by the sultan, Floripas persuades her father to let them live and later plots their escape. Rana Kabbani criticizes such depictions of Muslim women, arguing that the women are shown to be inherently lustful, deceitful, and unscrupulous in their pursuit of love (15–16). However, as Mohja Kahf points out, these Muslim princesses are also portrayed as unveiled, wealthy, powerful, and assertive. As such, they form a distinct contrast to European women of the time, who were represented as generally passive. The princesses are also a far cry from the veiled, silenced, and submissive *odalisque* sequestrated in the harem, who would come to epitomize European ideas of Muslim women by the eighteenth century (4–6). To a late twentieth and twenty-first century romance readership familiar with resourceful, independent, and assertive heroines, there is something far more appealing in these entrepreneurial Muslim princesses who frankly admit to sexual desire and risk everything for love, transgressing gender roles and embarking on epic adventures to achieve a happy ending with their beloved.

In these stories of cross-cultural, interreligious love, racial identity is notably less significant than it would be in nineteenth- and twentieth-century literature. "Race" in the Middle Ages has been given much attention in the last decade, with a *Journal of Medieval and Early Modern Studies Special Issue* devoted to the subject in 2001. Many of the issue's articles are responses to Frank M. Snowden's claim in *Before Color Prejudice* (1983) that in ancient cultures, physiological differences—especially in skin pigmentation—conveyed ideas of ethnicity without connotations of inferiority or superiority (Snowden 63–87). Contributors argue that "race" in ancient and medieval cultures was far more complex than had been hitherto acknowledged. Robert Bartlett's etymological study of the terms used to describe race shows that they could imply biological descent groups, tribes, and nations, as well as groups determined by geography, climate, language, and cultural practice. In fact, he contends, "The medieval situation was one where 'race' almost always means the same thing as 'ethnic group'" (53). While acknowledging the complexity of medieval understandings of race, Jeffery Jerome Cohen also points out that physical differentiation remained an important consideration, because other races—whether Saracens, Jews, or the "monstrous races" that populated Greek and medieval texts, such as the cynocephali (a dog-headed people), the large-eared panotii, or the one-footed sciapods[8]—were defined according to the degree by which they differed from the ideal Christian body. Cohen argues:

> Strictly speaking, the Christian body did not have a race (just as, ideally, it did not have a gender or a sexuality), because the body of the other always carried that burden on its behalf. In writing embodied race out of the Middle Ages, a medieval logic is being reenacted. Anatomical appearance, the medical composition of the body, and skin color were in fact essential to the construction of difference throughout much of this period, especially in Christian representation of the Jews who lived in their midst (gens Judaica) and of Iberian and eastern Muslims (Saraceni). (116)

Suzanne Conklin Akbari agrees, suggesting that in the Middle Ages, "difference of faith and diversity of skin color appear as two sides of a single coin, each aspect reinforcing the other" (1). Religious heresies were manifested through flesh that deviated from Christian norms. She notes, however, that in contrast to Jewish bodies in literature, the bodies of Muslims "were thought to be open to assimilation: through conversion, the female Saracen was especially available to the Christian community, her pollution erased both through a change in faith and through the physical bond of marriage within the Christian community" (4). This was true of Saracen men as well.

Religion apart, the physical and cultural boundaries between Christians and Muslims were remarkably porous in medieval literature. While Saracens were frequently depicted as stock monstrous types (e.g., black skinned and/or giants), many were also presumed to possess the same noble characters as their Christian counterparts. Infidels though they might be, they were nevertheless classified as civilized people endowed with a history, rather than as so-called barbaric tribes "devoid of history, development, and individual distinction" (Augstein x–xi). As Kahf notes, in crusade tales Muslim Saracens and Christian Franks bear marked similarities to each other: "They not only have the same equipment, but also the same values, the same concepts of shame and honor, the same type of feudal hierarchy" (24). Muslim women might be depicted as powerful, overbearing, loquacious queens, but such traits were condemned as unfeminine by Muslims and Christians alike. When a Muslim woman converted to Christianity because she fell in love with the Christian hero, she was incorporated into the universal gender order espoused by Europeans: she was silenced and became submissive to men (Kahf 36–38). Similarly, when a Christian woman married a Muslim monarch who fell in love with her—as in *The King of Tars* and *Floris and Blancheflour*—she became the active agent in his conversion to Christianity, which resulted in the conversion of his subjects as well. The realm of Christendom was thereby extended through romantic love, marriage, and the conversion of the king. Muslims, then, were different and inferior because of their heretical beliefs, but they were not entirely other in terms of their biology, culture, or gender hierarchies, especially if they were of royal or noble blood. "Race" was not yet an insurmountable barrier to unions in literary romances, even if, in reality, various canon and civil sumptuary laws in western European societies required that a person's race and religion be marked on his/her clothing to discourage different groups from associating (see Brundage 1987: 95, 207, 1995: 57–65).

Enthusiasm for crusading in the Holy Land had been exhausted by the end of the thirteenth century. In 1492, the last remaining Muslim stronghold of Granada was surrendered to the joint monarchy of Aragon and Castile. Al-Andalus was no more.[9] Consequently, the Crusades ceased to be a source for interreligious, cross-cultural romances by the early sixteenth century. The great Italian epics about Charlemagne's knight Roland—Boiardo's *Orlando Innamorato* (1495) and Ariosto's *Orlando Furioso* (1516–1532)—provided a fillip to the gradually vanishing crusade romance, as they were replete with stories of love between Christians and non-Christians: Orlando and Rinaldo's rivalrous infatuation with Angelica, the princess of Cathay, for example; or the Amazonian, Italian female knight Bradamante's love for the Moorish prince Ruggiero who, in accordance with the conventions of the genre, had converted to Christianity. In the Italian epics, however, the focus was less on crusade and the imminent Muslim threat to Europe than on the interplay of fabulous stories about battles, chivalry, romantic love, and knightly valor in a bygone era. The framing tale of Ariosto's *Orlando Furioso*—the most celebrated literary work of its age—is the love story between Bradamante and Ruggiero, told ostensibly to provide the Italian House of Este with legendary and heroic ancestry (Waldman xiv). In the epic poem, the biological fact of Ruggiero's Moorish ancestry is incidental, subordinated to his heroic status as a converted Christian knight. To be of the same religion (Christianity) and class (royalty or aristocracy) was still more important to Ariosto than to be of the same race. Yet race was soon to become a problem in cross-cultural literary romantic unions.

Giraldi Cinthio's short story "Un Capitano Moro" in *Hecatommithi* (1565), which provided the rough lineaments for Shakespeare's *Othello* (1603), places a strong emphasis on the Moorish lineage of the Christian-converted captain when transforming him from the valiant hero of Venice to the vengeful villain who slays his wife. No good could come from an interracial union, even if the Muslim lover had converted. The stains of race and culture were indelible. In "Un Capitano Moro," Cinthio makes his heroine articulate a warning that Shakespeare more delicately left out of *Othello*. Cinthio's Desdemona begs "Italian ladies" to "learn from me not to wed a man who nature and habitude of life estrange from us" (4). It seems that a shift was taking place during the sixteenth century, whereby conversion to Christianity was no longer sufficient to overcome differences in "nature" (biology) and "habitude of life" (culture) in literary romances. While great Italian Renaissance epics such as Boiardo's *Orlando Innamorato*, Ariosto's *Orlando Furioso*, and even Torquato Tasso's *La Gerusalemme liberata* (1581; about the taking of Jerusalem during the First Crusade) could entertain plots about interreligious, interracial love vaguely set centuries before in the crusade era, the prospect of these unions occurring in near-contemporary Venice was evidently more disturbing. By the time *Othello* was performed in 1604, the Muslim threat to Europe had moved from the south to the east. Othello, a converted Moor, is recruited to lead the Venetian armies against the onslaught of the Turks on the island of Cyprus. The westward march of the Ottoman Empire forms the backdrop to *Othello* and many other tales of cross-cultural romantic unions from the late sixteenth to the eighteenth century.

RENAISSANCE RENEGADES AND MUSLIM WOMEN

As Turkish tribes spread throughout the Anatolian Peninsula after the eleventh century, capturing Constantinople by 1453, the threat of Islamic encroachment upon Christendom was palpably real to Europeans. Under the leadership of Suleiman I ("the Magnificent," r. 1520–1566), the Ottoman Empire reached its zenith as an imperial power, extending from present-day Iran to the gates of Vienna. Zachary Lockman (2004) and Margaret Meserve (2008) point out that educated Europeans in the sixteenth century were awed and dazzled by the opulent wealth and seemingly unstoppable military might of the empire, which compared favorably to their own in many ways. Niccolo Machiavelli approved of the Ottoman sultan's enormous personal power and commended the Ottomans for possessing "many of the virtues associated with the great empires of antiquity, including Rome" (Lockman 44). Ogier Ghiselin de Busbecq, the Habsburg ambassador to the Sublime Porte, admired the Ottoman civil administration and the military for their meritocracies (Lockman 43). Unlike in European governments of the same period, slaves and people from different faiths and cultures could be incorporated into Ottoman institutions and rise to high ranks. Nevertheless, to uneducated Europeans, Turkish military prowess reinforced the idea that the Turks were a fearsome, cruel, barbaric people, while medieval myths about the "dog-Turk"—a "man-eating being, half animal and half human, with a dog's head and tail"—emphasized the bestial nature of the Muslim Turk to a Europe just beginning to explore a world that still seemed to be populated by "monstrous races" (Karlsson 62–64).

Despite these misgivings, the preeminence of Ottoman power meant that by the sixteenth century, European monarchs were anxious to enter into diplomatic negotiations with the Sublime Porte regarding trade, political alliances, and piracy along the Barbary Coast (i.e., the Mediterranean coastline of North Africa from present-day Morocco to Libya inhabited by Berbers—Muslim peoples indigenous to the region). The

French were among the first of the Western European courts to do so, for they regarded the Ottomans as natural allies against the growing might of the Habsburgs on their eastern and southern borders. The English soon followed, anxious to gain access to Ottoman-controlled Mediterranean trade. By the turn of the seventeenth century, English trade entrepôts had been established throughout the Islamic Mediterranean, in Istanbul, Aleppo, Alexandretta, Tunis, Tripoli, and Algiers. Words like "pasha," "dey," and "bey" (a local ruler who was nominally a subject of the Otto-man sultan, but who often retained considerable independence and au-tonomy) were introduced into the English vocabulary along with "Bar-bary corsairs" (also misleadingly referred to as "Turkish pirates") Arab, Berber, Morisco, and Ottoman sailors who began to raid the Irish and southern English coasts from their strongholds in North Africa during the early seventeenth century (Colley 43–63, Davis 2004).

Official contact with Eastern culture was supplemented by recre-ational travel, which added to Europe's storehouse of Orientalist lore. European travelers to the Ottoman Empire created a new Orientalist lit-erature encompassing histories, travelogues, translations of Turkish tales, and Orientalist plays. Between 1558 and 1642, at least forty-seven plays dealing with Oriental material were generated by the major British play-wrights of the day (Wann 427). The public was obviously fascinated by the East, no doubt because fears of Ottoman power and expansionist aims as well as Muslim pirate predation along the Mediterranean and Atlan-tic coastlines were very real. Unlike the later Orientalist literature of the eighteenth to the twentieth century examined by Edward Said in *Orien-talism*, early modern European literature about the Orient was produced in a context where the Ottoman Empire was still the dominant Mediterra-nean and eastern European power of the day. Europeans were supplicants to the Ottoman sultan for trade and travel purposes, but they were also potential victims of Muslim abduction and conversion to Islam (Vitkus 146–147, Colley 44–45). The Orientalist motifs that developed during this period included captivity by corsairs, fear of renegades, the association of Islam with violence and sensuality, the mystery of the harem, and the despotism of the Islamic ruler. These literary motifs resonated differently with maritime audiences aware of their position as potential colonies or abductees than with Europeans of the late eighteenth and nineteenth cen-turies, when the British and French were building their own empires and chiseling away at the slow-crumbling edifice of the Ottoman Empire.

Miguel Cervantes's *Don Quixote* (1604) contains one of the earliest stories of Islamic abduction, escape from Muslim lands, and cross-cultural romance. In "The Captive's Tale," a Spaniard and a veiled woman—the first in Western literature to be depicted as veiled and different from European women (Kahf 83)—arrive at an inn where Don Quixote is resting. The Spaniard recounts how, while fighting the Turks at the Battle of Lepanto (1571), he was captured and imprisoned in Algeria. Zoraida, a beautiful and wealthy Moorish princess, fell in love with him and, like Floripas in *The Sowdone of Babylone*, or the more contemporary Jessica in Shakespeare's *The Merchant of Venice* (ca. 1596–1598), betrayed her father, rescued her lover, converted to Christianity, and fled with her lover to Christian lands. The continuities with medieval crusade epics are clear: the Christian warrior hero who is captured, the Muslim woman he seduces, her conversion to Christianity, and the triumph of the Christian West over its Islamic foe on levels personal, sexual, military, and political (the Turks were defeated at the naval Battle of Lepanto). Yet Cervantes's short story marked a turning point in the genre, for few other captivity narratives had a triumphant ending; rather, they were characterized by the presentation of European men as victims of abduction by Barbary pirates and physical and even sexual slavery by Muslim potentates.

The seventeenth century saw an efflorescence of pirate abduction tales in Britain, undoubtedly because throughout the 1600s, Barbary corsairs were regularly sighted in the English Channel and thousands of English and Irish men, women, and children were captured and shipped to the slave markets of Algiers and Istanbul (Colley 44–63). Linda Colley estimates that "over the course of the seventeenth and eighteenth centuries, there were probably 20,000 or more British captives of Barbary" (44). (All this, of course, occurred at a time when the English were developing and consolidating their own transatlantic African slave trade as well as engaging in Mediterranean piracy. The Malta-based Knights of St. John were particularly infamous for capturing Muslim vessels and selling their passengers into slavery on a regular basis [45].) In stories of British enslavement, the captives appeared as helpless, passive victims on the verge of converting to Islam. Where "The Captive's Tale" still proclaimed the power of the Christian warrior hero to convert Muslim princesses through romantic seduction, seventeenth-century English travel writers and dramatists feared that the reverse was actually the case: captured Englishmen would be tempted to convert to Islam for social and economic opportunities and because they were sexually tempted by Muslim women, who had emerged as a potent symbol of the sensual and seductive Orient. Constrained by the rigidly hierarchical, class-controlled economic system of Western Europe, lower-class Christian European slaves found that their Muslim masters sometimes provided them with opportunities for advancement as well as manumission (Matar 1993: 489). It was thus unsurprising that many Englishmen chose to convert or stay in Ottoman lands rather than be ransomed and rescued. For English soldiers abroad, the temptation to desert or convert was strong. Colley notes that in the British port of Tangier (acquired during the reign of Charles II as part of the dowry of his Portuguese wife, Catherine of Braganza), rates of desertion increased throughout the late seventeenth century as "pay fell into arrears, and excitement and professionalism faded into boredom and loss of hope" (40). Deserters caught by the British were executed or enslaved by their own kind, especially if they were suspected of "turning Turk"— that is, converting to Islam.

Decisions to abandon Protestantism and embrace Islam created great consternation in Britain. Daniel Vitkus notes that "post-Reformation anxiety about conversion produced a discourse about 'renegades' and 'convertites' which applied to those who converted to Catholicism as well as those who turned Turk" (152). These anxieties were reinforced by real-life cases, as when Captain Hamilton was sent by Charles II to rescue Englishmen enslaved along the Barbary Coast, only to discover that they had no wish to return to England. Hamilton concluded in his report: "They are tempted to forsake their God for the love of Turkish women who are generally very beautiful" (Matar 491). Conversion thus portrayed was not only a betrayal of one's faith, but of one's nation. Furthermore, it was motivated by desire for Muslim women. The fascinating allure of Muslim women was celebrated in one of the most popular English ballads about Barbary captivity, the so-called Lord Bateman ballad, which appeared in 112 different versions from the seventeenth to the nineteenth century. The ballad is about a north countryman who is captured at sea by "Turkish pirates," imprisoned, and liberated by the Muslim governor's beautiful daughter. Colley notes that "in certain versions of the story," the Muslim heroine "follows him to England, where he abandons his local, Christian fiancée for this 'Turkish' bride, who brings with her a jeweled belt worth more than all the wealth of Northumberland" (83).

Plays about Protestant English male renegades who "turned Turk" were regularly produced throughout the seventeenth century, and in almost all of these, the irresistible attraction of the Muslim woman is emphasized (Matar 497). Her charms were all the more potent for being entirely imagined, because no Englishman, including those who traveled to Muslim lands, had ever encountered any Muslim women from the wealthier classes. Nevertheless, European writers associated Islam with, and criticized it for, excessive and depraved sexual practices. The sexual excesses of Muslims were believed to derive from their religion, which permitted polygamy, but Muslim sexuality also became linked to the sexual practices of the Moors and black Africans, who were imbued with deviant or animal-like sexuality in Western European culture (Gilman 1985, Vitkus 159, Morgan 167–192). The description of the renegade as one who "turns Turk" therefore had additional racialized, sexual connotations. The site of such male anxieties and envious desires was, of course, "the harem"—that imaginary locus of lust where any number of beautiful, enslaved women existed solely for the pleasure of their Islamic masters, and gratified a variety of deviant sexual desires.

THE HAREM IN THE EUROPEAN IMAGINATION

Ruth Bernard Yeazell argues that any "study of the West's relations with the harem must be in large part a study of the [Western] imagination," for there is no such place as *the* harem; "there are only harems, as various as the individual households, of many different countries and times, in which separate quarters have been set aside for the seclusion of the women" (1). The word *haram* in Arabic means forbidden or sacred and refers to Islamic women who wear the veil in public spaces, as well as forming the root of the Turkish word *haremlik*—the place (*lik*) of the sanctuary (*harem*) that was filled with "the spirit of majesty" (Wheatcroft 2). Its counterpart was the *selamlik*: men's space within the household, where business with the outside world was conducted. There was nothing in the original etymology of *haram*, or in Turkish culture, to suggest that women were locked away or imprisoned or sexually enslaved in the harem. Unless they were from the wealthier classes (in which case they were sequestered), women were generally free to come and go as they pleased. However, the Turco-Persian word that Western travelers heard, *sarayi*, meaning palace, as in the Topkapi Saray, came to be confused with the Italian verb *serrare*, meaning to lock up or enclose (Yeazell 2). By the end of the sixteenth century, the French word *sérail* and the English word "seraglio" referred not merely to the Turkish women's palace, but to the women's quarters or even to the women themselves, who were imagined as exotic prostitutes. In fact, by the time Samuel Johnson produced his English dictionary in 1755, "seraglio" was tantamount to "brothel" (Yeazell 60, 100). To Europeans, the seraglio was synonymous with the harem, and both terms connoted sexual slavery as well as the decadent wealth of the Ottoman Empire. The harem was a source of obsessive fascination and envy for European men, who imagined a variety of women incarcerated solely for the pleasure of the Oriental despot. Thus was born a recurrent colonial fantasy of chivalric rescue: the heroic European male breaching the walls of the harem to rescue the imprisoned beauties.

This was a change indeed from the sixteenth- and seventeenth-century abduction narratives in which the European captives in need of rescue had been *men*—from the Spanish captain in *Don Quixote* to the numerous Englishmen enslaved by Barbary corsairs and forced to "turn Turk" in English plays and so-called memoirs. One of the earliest pirate abduction and captivity tales to focus on the plight of European women was Jean-François Regnard's *Le légataire universel* (*The Sole Heir*, 1708), which purportedly told the true story of how Regnard and a Frenchwoman, Madame de Prade, were abducted from their ship by corsairs and sold into Sultan Achmet-Talem's harem. Regnard was eventually ransomed by his relatives, but Madame de Prade was never heard from again. This French tale was compounded by numerous English stories by Penelope Aubin, Eliza Haywood, and Elizabeth Marsh over the course of the eighteenth century (Hoeveler 46–71). As Colley notes, until the publication of Elizabeth Marsh's *The Female Captive* (1769), Barbary abduction and captivity had not been presented as a sexual threat for British women; rather, the focus had been on the menace of sodomy to British men (128). Colley argues:

> Sodomy in the context of writings on Barbary and the Ottoman world before 1750 was rather a metaphor, a particularly acute expression of the fear and insecurity that Britons and other Western Europeans continued to feel in the face of Islamic power and, as they saw it, aggression. . . . Those who accused Muslims of sodomy in the context of discussions of corsairing and captivities were rarely primarily concerned with whether North African and Ottoman males allowed themselves to be sodomized. Rather, the burden of these expressed anxieties was that captive British and other European males were the potential victims. It was *they* who might be penetrated and invaded. *They* who might be forced into the passive role. Accusing the Barbary powers, and the Ottoman empire in general, of practising sodomy on Christian captives was yet another way in which Britons gave vent to their insecurities and to ancient fears that Islam might in the end use its strength to reduce them to submission. (129–130)

Only after Britain had consolidated its position as a global European power in the mid-eighteenth century—after the Seven Years' War and the conquest of Bengal—did captivity writers lose interest in the possible sodomizing of British male slaves. Only after Ottoman power began to recede in the Mediterranean and in eastern Europe during the eighteenth century did "British and European fears of penetration from without" decline, so that captivity narratives began to include fantasies of "titillation rather than terror," focusing on European women enslaved in the Sultan's harem for his pleasure (130–131).

Although no men other than family relations were permitted within the women's quarters, European male travelers to the Ottoman Empire nevertheless expended much time and ink imagining a location they had never seen. From the sixteenth to the early eighteenth century, writers and travelers such as William Painter, Thomas Dallam, Sir George Courthope, Ottaviano Bon, Paul Rycault, and Antoine Galland, among many others, described the harem in painstaking detail, reiterating myths about the insatiable sexual appetites of Muslim women and the sexual violence of the Oriental despot ruling tyrannically over his enslaved harem. Galland's best-selling multivolume, *Les mille et une nuits* (*The Thousand and One Nights*, 1704–1704), ushered in a new vogue for Orientalism in the eighteenth century, as ever-increasing numbers of Europeans traveled to Istanbul and beyond. Those who stayed at home eagerly consumed a growing body of European Orientalist literature, the dominant motif of which was the harem or the seraglio. It is ironic that in an age of increasing engagement with, and knowledge about, Eastern lands, the one site that was forbidden to European male travelers—the one site about which they were profoundly ignorant and had little hope of gaining accurate knowledge—came to represent all that was Oriental about the East.

French tales about the Oriental harem were part of a broader Enlightenment project critiquing the centralization of the French state and the increasing power of the French crown from the time of Louis XIV (r. 1643–1715) until the French Revolution (Grosrichard 3–25, 123–188). Perhaps the most famous in this genre was Montesquieu's *Lettres persanes* (*Persian Letters*, 1721), an epistolary novel comprising 161 letters exchanged between two Persian travelers visiting Paris, and including the story of their wives and the eunuchs who oversee their harems in Persia. The increasing tyranny of the harem owner Usbek over his harem slaves results in rebellion and chaos in the harem until even his favorite, the European woman Roxane, whom he trusts implicitly, cuckolds him and commits suicide, scornfully declaring that while she may have outwardly submitted to Usbek, her will to love and her mind were always her own:

> How could you think that I was such a weakling as to imagine there was nothing for me in the world but to worship your caprices; that while you indulged all your desires, you should have the right to thwart me in all mine? No: I have lived in slavery, and yet always retained my freedom: I have remodeled your laws upon those of nature; and my mind has always maintained its independence. (350)

As in so many eighteenth-century harem tales, race is not ostensibly the issue here. Slavery and tyranny versus freedom and independence in relationships of all kinds is what really matters. Yet it is telling that the outwardly enslaved European woman should be the one to rebel and raise the banner of liberty in the harem of the Muslim despot. This must surely be one of the first of such depictions that would become so popular in late twentieth-century Orientalist romance novels.

That Usbek's most prized possession, the spirited rebel, should be called Roxane was no coincidence, for by the eighteenth century, Europe had a tradition of associating strong European harem women with variations of the name Roxane or Roxelane. The original Roxelane was the favorite concubine of Sultan Suleiman I. She was kidnapped from Russia or the Ukraine between 1517 and 1520 and sold into the Ottoman imperial harem. European visitors and historians subsequently referred to her as "Roxelane," "Roxolana," "Rosselane," "Roxa," or "Rossa" because she was believed to originate from Russia (Yermolenko 234). When she became Suleiman's favorite concubine, she was renamed "Hurrem," meaning "joyful" or "laughing one" (234). Suleiman broke many Ottoman traditions in order to marry Hurrem Sultan, keep her at court, and permit her to bear several of his children (235–236). In the sixteenth and seventeenth centuries—the age of strong royal women in Western Europe, such as Queen Mary, Elizabeth I, and Catherine de Medici—Europeans had portrayed Roxelane as a scheming, power-hungry woman who held an unprecedented degree of political authority in the Ottoman court. By the eighteenth century, however, the figure of Roxane/Roxelane would be transformed into one that was heroic, sympathetic, a rebel in the harem, a champion of liberty, and fundamentally French.

The key to this transformation was Jean-François Marmontel's short stories, collectively published in 1761 as the *Contes moraux* (*Moral Tales*). Of these anecdotes, "Soliman II" became one of the most popular.[10] "Soliman II" reinterpreted the Suleiman I-Hurrem Sultan story, transforming the Russian slave into the French woman Roxelane who, although not particularly beautiful, nevertheless captivates the sultan because of her charm, wit, impudence, unyielding independence of spirit, and love of liberty. It is her mission to teach him how to love as only Europeans, with their inborn experience of liberty, can truly love. Roxelane laughs at the sultan, scorns his attempts to impress or command her, and rejects his attempts to court her without liberating or empowering her. If Soliman loves her, she says, he will not only manumit and marry her, but he will also share his power with her. She will have none of him otherwise. "Is this all you know about love?" she asks him incredulously:

> Glory and grandeur, the only good things worthy to touch the soul, are reserved for you alone; shame and evil . . . are my portion. And you would have me love you! If my lover had but a cabin, I would share his hut with him and be content. He has a throne; I will share his throne or he is no lover of mine. If you think me unworthy to reign over the Turks, send me back to my own country where all pretty women are sovereigns and have more power than I have here, because they reign over hearts. (Marmontel 52–53, my translation)

Significantly, what wins the sultan's heart is Roxelane's mental and governmental capabilities, not just her sexual allure or availability. Perplexed, exasperated, and irresistibly seduced by her zest for life, love of liberty, and striking originality, Soliman undergoes a transformation of character to the point that Roxelane is able to love him for his "good heart" and "many virtues." She is then rewarded with power, a throne, and a companionate marriage celebrating the bourgeois domestic ideal. At the end of the play, Roxelane frees the women of the *sérail*, thus promoting their liberty as well as ensuring Soliman's subsequent monogamy.

Historically, the more influential version of this tale was Charles-Simon Favart's *opéra comique*, *Les trois sultanes, ou Soliman Second* (1761, music by P. C. Gibert), based on Marmontel's story. Favart's version is a romantic comedy that sets up rivalry in the harem not merely between European and Oriental concubines, but among the Europeans themselves. Marmontel's French concubines are now given different nationalities. Elmire is Spanish in Favart's version, while Délia becomes a Circassian. Only Roxelane—cheerfully helping her rivals to capture (unsuccessfully) the sultan's lust and love, and blithely unconcerned about the petty politics of the seraglio—remains French. There is a hierarchy of modern European femininity at play here, with the French coming out on top. Roxelane continues to laugh at the sultan, to disdain his attempts to impress or command her, and to reject his attempts to court her. She "attracts the sultan's interest with her native understanding of sovereignty, her brash critiques of life at the court and, more significantly, her apparent indifference to the Sultan," which "affords her a moral soapbox of sorts, from which she preaches opposition to the Sultan's harem politics in favor of a by now familiar message of liberty, equality and fraternity" (Elmarsafy 13). "Love craves liberty," she tells Soliman, "It must have equality" (Favart 69, my translation). Only when he gives in, frees his harem, and announces to his people that he intends to marry her does she relent and tell him that he has "pierced her soul" with his love and many virtues. In a significant departure from Marmontel's original version, Favart's Roxelane then willingly submits to Soliman's lordship, gives him her liberty, and acknowledges him as her "sultan, hero and master" (Favart 53–72).

In this French heroine we see the prototype for the heroine of many twentieth-century sheik romance novels, whose stubborn independence and love of liberty thwart the lust of the Arabic sheik hero, and whose utter difference from other women—Western and non-Western alike—causes the sheik to fall in love with her and relinquish his rakish ways for monogamous, middle-class marriage. That the rough lineaments of Favart's plot are recognizable in many modern-day Orientalist romance novels is unsurprising; Favart's *opéra comique* gripped the European imagination in a most potent and influential way. It was translated, plagiarized, and performed in many parts of Europe, and it found its way into other musical forms: Haydn's Symphony No. 63 was subtitled "La Roxelane," while Mozart's pupil Franz Xaver Süssmayr adapted it as another opera after the decade-long success of Mozart's *Die Entführung aus dem Serail* in Vienna (Elmarsafy 22).

However, eighteenth-century Orientalist romances were not always cross-cultural and did not always feature a European heroine striving to reform the Oriental potentate. The rescue of an abducted and enslaved European woman from the Oriental despot's harem was an equally popular Orientalist fantasy, especially in vaudevilles of the *théâtre de la foire* (theatres at carnivals or fairs) and at the opera (Meyer 480). *Die Entführung aus dem Serail* was among the most popular of these operas, resulting in no less than forty-four productions from 1782 to 1792 (Stone 115). Like other Orientalist fare of the eighteenth century, *Die Entführung* features a European heroine kidnapped by Barbary pirates and sold into the harem of a wealthy Muslim ruler. She virtuously resists Pasha Selim's attempts at both seduction and coercion and is eventually reunited with her Spanish lover when he tries to rescue her from the seraglio. Selim is particularly interesting because he confounds European stereotypes of the lustful, vengeful, violent Turk (although his vizier, Osmin, conforms to that role). Selim initially appears as the typical Muslim tyrant, but he ultimately reveals himself to be more capable of understanding the sacrifices of love than the European protagonists—Konstanze, the captive he desires, and Belmonte, Konstanze's Spanish lover of noble rank, who jealously accuses her of having surrendered her virtue to the pasha. Selim also proves more generous, forgiving, and magnanimous than the Christians. Although Belmonte deceitfully gained entrance into the palace, although he broke into the seraglio and helped Konstanze escape and, most importantly, although his father stole Selim's land and wealth before sending him into exile, Selim overcomes his understandable urge for revenge. He forgives the lovers and sets them free, declaring that "it gives me far greater pleasure to reward an injustice with justice than to keep on repaying evil with evil." He will not stoop to the level of Belmonte's father. The Muslim monarch, in fact, proves more "Christian" than the Christians, and the opera concludes with a paean of praise for the pasha.

Die Entführung is thus an example of the reformist ends to which Enlightenment Orientalist discourse could serve. As Alain Grosrichard (1998) notes in his nuanced discussion of despotism during the Enlightenment, the concept of Oriental despotism served two groups well during the socioeconomic turmoil and political change in the eighteenth century: "The rising bourgeoisie could denounce the proponents of the old order as riddled with the despotic disease, bearers of an irrational privilege and perpetuators of slavery. The aristocracy could present democratic demands as an extension of despotic levelling, soulless deindividualization, loss of rank and distinction" (Dolar xiv). Written and performed for the Austrian emperor Joseph II, *Die Entführung* used the Orientalist topos of the tyrannical Muslim monarch to make the implicit argument that a despot could be transformed by romantic love, and that if even a Muslim could behave with such magnanimity, then how much more so should a Christian European monarch.

In all these stories we see the beginnings of a tradition of romantic stories about Western women—rather than Muslim women—incarcerated in and dominating the harem. It is this tradition that modern-day historical harem romances and sheik novels are heir to. Beginning in the late eighteenth century, Muslim women became sidelined and marginalized in their own sphere, reduced to an undifferentiated mass of "other women," or occasionally singled out for negative treatment as the jealous concubine or possessive, power-hungry mother of the Muslim despot. Two other developments during this era are worth noting. First, it is clear that cross-cultural, interracial sex and romance were still not yet a serious issue for Europeans as long as the Muslim protagonist involved was the sultan or a suitably upper-class ruler. Second, when these Orientalist harem tales found their way into English literature, the heroine's virginity became much more important.

The emphasis placed by the English on the virginity of their heroines in Orientalist romances had been notable since *Floris and Blancheflour* and *Bevis of Hampton*. Blancheflour has to undergo a virginity test to prove her virtue and chastity before the emir will release her to Floris in the English version (Kelly 2000: 9), whereas in the French version, *Floire et Blancheflor*, the emir discovers the lovers in bed (Segol 234). In *Bevis*, the patriarch of Jerusalem tells Bevis that he must only marry a virgin. When the plot of Favart's *Les trois sultanes* was poached by Isaac Bickerstaffe for his play *The Sultan, or, A Peep into the Seraglio* (1775), the English heroine Roxalana is transformed into a virgin (1782: 310–326), whereas French Roxelane flippantly boasts of her lovers to Soliman in *Les trois sultanes*. The virginity of the English heroine was certainly essential for a happy ending by the time the rise of the novel saw sustained assaults on English heroines' virtues in epistolary works such as Samuel Richardson's *Pamela, or Virtue Rewarded* (1740) and *Clarissa* (1748). In English literature of the eighteenth to early twentieth century, heroines were generally rewarded with marriage if they managed to preserve their virginity, whereas defloration—even through rape—resulted in death. Richardson's eponymous heroine in *Pamela* famously induces the lecherous nobleman Mr. B. to fall in love with and marry her because she refuses to surrender her virginity at any price, whereas Clarissa, who loses her virginity when she is drugged and raped in a brothel by the villainous Robert Lovelace, has to die in order to redeem her virtue. This was why *The Sheik* was so shocking to early twentieth-century readers: the raped heroine falls in love with her rapist and lives happily ever after.

The plot of the enslaved English virgin who conquers and softens the despot of the seraglio through love, thereby achieving her own liberty and asserting her equality with him in a companionate marriage, was popular because it was a variation of *Pamela*. It would be echoed in twentieth-century American historical harem romances such as Johanna Lindsey's *Captive Bride* (1977) and *Silver Angel* (1988), Connie Mason's *Desert Ecstasy* (1988) and *Sheik* (1997), and many contemporary desert romance novels. The harem or seraglio in all these stories is often a place where the Western virgin triumphs over the septic jealousies and vicious intrigues of competing concubines and overcomes the ruthless plots of the *kadins* (the highest ranking females who had born children to the sultan). She either escapes the debauched sexual appetites and tyranny of the Muslim despot or brings him to his knees by virtue of her beauty, intelligence, uncompromising love of freedom, and vision of an egalitarian Western companionate marriage.

To be sure, an alternative vision of the harem was introduced by female travelers, beginning with the posthumous publication of Lady Mary Wortley Montagu's *Turkish Embassy Letters* in 1763. The harems that Lady Mary visited challenged male imaginings of the space. While she emphasized the novelty of naked women bathing together in the *bagnio* and admired the exoticism of harem fashions and furnishings, she also compared the sexual politics of the harem and the typical eighteenth century European court, provocatively declaring that because Muslim women could own property and were afforded public anonymity by the veil, they were more "free" than European women (letter XXIX). Following Montagu's lead, subsequent female travelers to the East represented the harem as a domestic space similar to the bourgeois home. In contrast to male harem fantasies, the travel accounts by these nineteenth-century women presented the harem as a living area where fully dressed women cared for their children, kept themselves busy with domestic work, such as embroidering, and engaged in communal activities, such as eating together, which the open space of the harem facilitated (Melman 1995, Lewis 2004). Here was the opportunity for friendship, companionship, and sisterhood, rather than resentful rivalries and murderous jealousies. Here, too, women could lead fulfilled, autonomous lives in one another's company. They did not simply wait to be summoned to the master's bed, nor did their sexual subjugation and frustration lead to adulterous and/or lesbian acts, as in Montesquieu's *Persian Letters*.

Nevertheless, the female-centered narrative of the harem failed to displace the conventional European male fantasy of the harem, not only in male-authored literature but in female-authored romantic novels of the twentieth century as well. For Westerners, the harem remained ineluctably connected with the leitmotifs of abduction, sexual slavery, sexual plenitude and variety for the despotic master, jealousy and rivalry among women, and the ever-present threat of violence. Its women needed a particular type of hero to rescue them, and they found him in Byron's Eastern tales of the early nineteenth century.

THE BYRONIC HERO AND THE ROMANTIC ORIENT

By the late eighteenth century, power relations were shifting between Western Europe and the Islamic East in favor of the former as Britain and France consolidated and expanded their colonies around the world. This, of course, is the period Said focuses on in *Orientalism*. Nigel Leask points to the connection between the expansion of British colonial rule—particularly in India—and the principal exponents of Romanticism (18-19). Leask argues that many of the Romantic writers treated the trope of the Orient as the literary equivalent of an imported luxury commodity, a product of the mercantilist economics of eighteenth-century Europe's involvement with the East Indies (19). William Beckford's *The History of the Caliph Vathek* (1786) is generally considered the turning point in European Orientalist literature, as it marked the moment when the eighteenth-century Oriental tale transitioned to nineteenth-century Romantic verse. *Vathek*'s narrative alone is not particularly influential as far as later Oriental romance novels are concerned. What is significant is the novel's scope and supposed accuracy of detail: the cornucopia of Oriental customs, manners, folklore, objects, food, and clothing that Byron would later call "costume" (20). Other writers of the Romantic era—Goethe, Coleridge, Hugo, Flaubert, Lamartine, and Byron (Hopwood Chapter 2)—would follow suit, gleaning inspiration from the ornate, Oriental "decoration" of Beckford's work. As Mohammed Sharafuddin suggests, it was not merely the brilliant East, the sensuousness, the mockery, and the dark horror of *Vathek* that influenced Byron, but the very fact that Beckford's Orient "became an opportunity for *experience*—certainly for intense personal fantasy and gratification." For Sharafuddin, "*Vathek* is part of [Byron's] inner world. It is a projection of an amoral, secret life into the public domain; it gives rein for the first time to what could well be called the outlawed self" (xxxii). This "outlawed self" was what Byron celebrated, especially in his Eastern tales, produced between 1813 and 1816, and it would prove immensely influential in the configuring of romantic heroes thereafter. In this section, therefore, I look at the rise of the Romantic outlaw hero: an über-masculine figure like Sheik Ahmed Ben Hassan, who bears bitterness against a world that has wronged him, but who is admired and worshipped as a godlike figure by other men.

Like Beckford before him, Byron was one of the Romantic poets who actually went to the Orient, embarking on his own Grand Tour from 1809 to 1811. Out of his travels came the semi-autobiographical *Childe Harold's Pilgrimage: A Romaunt* (1812–1818), in which the world-weary, youthful hero travels through Spain, Greece, and Turkey, commenting at large on his experiences as well as on cultural scenes and contemporary political events. The huge success of *Childe Harold* prompted Byron's publisher, John Murray, to urge Byron to produce more tales with an "Oriental" flavor. The first of Byron's Oriental verse romances, *The Giaour* (1813), also received great popular as well as critical acclaim. Byron's Advertisement to the first edition, published in the *Morning Chronicle*, declares that his tale is "founded upon circumstances now less common in the East than formerly"; namely, the story of "a female slave, who was thrown, in the Mussulman manner, into the sea for infidelity, and avenged by a young Venetian, her lover, at the time the Seven Islands were possessed by the Republic of Venice." Rumors spread that Byron had saved the life of just such a young woman who had been condemned to drown in a sack for her infidelity. Byron seemed to confirm this story when he wrote to E. D. Clarke that "the Athenian account of our adventure (a personal one) which certainly first suggested to me the story of the Giaour . . . is not very far from the truth" (Sharafuddin 222–223). The motif of the English aristocrat saving an adulterous harem concubine from death-by-drowning would be reworked in Julie Fitzgerald's historical romance novel *Royal Slave* (1978), albeit with a considerably different role for the Englishman.

The Giaour (*giaour* being a Turkish slur for an infidel) consists of a series of disjointed fragments recounting the Giaour's love affair with Turkish Hassan's favorite Circassian concubine, Leila, who disguises herself as a "Georgian page" in order to steal out to meet her lover. When "black Hassan" discovers Leila's treachery, he has her seized and thrown into the Aegean, where she inhabits a watery grave. Enraged, grief-stricken, and bent on revenge, the Giaour and his "robber clan" of Arnauts (Albanians) ambush Hassan and his Tartar guards. After an epic battle, Hassan and his men are slaughtered, and the Giaour takes himself off to a remote monastery to brood over his savage crimes and torture himself over Leila's loss until his unrepentant death. To the very end, he proves to be a *giaour* with respect to both the Muslim and Christian faiths, true only to an internal moral code of his own. Where the renegade in Jacobean dramas was a villain unless he could be reconverted, in Byron's hands the renegade was a Cain or (Miltonic) Satan figure—one exiled from society, who exemplified the fierce pride, individualism, and private code of honor so prized by Romanticism. *The Giaour* was an immediate hit upon its release, with several editions published in the first year and fourteen editions in print by 1815.

The Giaour is important for the motifs it introduced or reinforced in the Oriental romance. It fuses the Romantic penchant for medieval chivalric quest romances with Oriental passions and despotism. From medieval *chansons de geste* and verse romances, *The Giaour* inherits and reintroduces into Western Romantic literature the European hero who is skilled with swords and steeds. Indeed, our first glimpse of the Giaour is as he rides furiously "like a Demon of the night" on horseback—as is Diana Mayo's first glimpse of Sheik Ahmed Ben Hassan in *The Sheik* (1919), and the Berber Princess Zara's initial sighting of Sheik Jamal in Connie Mason's *Sheik* (1997). As for swordplay, the clash of steel between the Giaour and Hassan (while both are on horseback) inspired Delacroix to recreate this scene in *Combat of the Giaour and Hassan* (1826). The interchangeable qualities of horse and warrior—cheval and chevalier—and the association of this Romantic image with medieval chivalry and crusades are also demonstrated in Delacroix's paintings *Entry of the Crusaders into Constantinople on 12 April 1204* (1840) and *Arabian Horses Fighting in a Stable* (1860). Significantly, in this age of slow-declining Ottoman power, the focus of the Oriental romance moved from the harem of the Topkapi palace to the harsh desert environment inhabited by noble Arab warriors. In Delacroix's paintings, as in Byron's poems, the division is less prominent between men of different faiths than between leaders and followers: the solitary heroes on horseback, and those who bow their knees to the warriors who master both horses and other men.

Along with Childe Harold and Conrad in Byron's *The Corsair*, the Giaour embodied the "Byronic hero," whose influence can be seen in Charlotte Brontë's Rochester, Emily Brontë's Heathcliff, and countless other fictional romantic heroes. The Giaour is an aggressive and domineering man of action ruled by dark passions, with a "mind that broods o'er guilty woes." He views the world with a deep-seated cynicism that "mocks at Misery" and is physically manifested in that famous "bitter smile"—the "curl and quiver" of his pale lip (ll.848, 853). He is inherently aristocratic, instantly recognizable to others as a "noble soul" with "lineage high," even though he is a troubled, misanthropic (though never misogynistic) exile, misunderstood by the wider world and rejected because of his crimes of passion; crimes spurred by the fervid heat and physical sensuality of the East. Byron claimed that love in northern Europe differed from love in the Orient, where passion was felt to a far greater degree. The Giaour declares:

> The cold in clime are cold in blood,
> Their love can scarce deserve the name;

But mine was like the lava flood
That boils in Aetna's breast of flame. (ll.1099–1102)

And yet this "Oriental love" turned out to be strangely similar to the European courtly *ideal* of monogamous (even if paradoxically adulterous) romantic love portrayed through Lancelot's love for Guinevere, for example, or Tristan's for Iseult, Dante's for Beatrice, Petrarch's for Laura, or Shakespeare's for his Dark Lady (Lewis 1936). Toward the end of the poem, the dying Giaour defiantly confesses his crimes to the monk and claims that only the understanding and experience of true love redeems him:

With havock I have marked my way:
But this was taught me by the dove,
To die—and know not second love.
This lesson yet hath man to learn,
Taught by the thing he dares to spurn:
The bird that sings within the brake,[11]
The swan that swims upon the lake,
One mate, and one alone, will take. (ll.1164–1171)

These lines suggest that the ideal of courtly love celebrated by European poets is more honored in the breach than in the observance. The "lesson yet hath man to learn" certainly applies to Oriental Hassan with his harem of women, but the universal use of "man" implies that Europeans, too, have yet to understand and practice not merely monogamy, but single-minded and single-hearted devotion to only one lover throughout an entire lifetime. Apparently, only the Giaour understands true love. Byron thus individuated the Giaour by attributing a unique devotion to him, and grouping all other Europeans and Orientals together in matters of love. The Byronic hero's understanding of passionate love and his unwavering fidelity to one woman are repeated in *The Corsair* (1814), with its famous closing couplet: "He left a Corsair's name to other times, / Linked with one virtue, and a thousand crimes" (Canto III, ll.1863–1864).

The Giaour is a poem in which seeming binaries blend or overlap. The fiery love of the Orient merges with European monogamy. The pattern of difference and convergence of West and East occurs between the hero and villain, as well. The villain, "stern Hassan" (the adjective is repeated several times), is a recognizable type, whose villainy is chiefly demonstrated through his cruel treatment of women. The poem repeats the European canard that Muslim men treat their women callously because they do not believe women have souls. It is, presumably, the Giaour's noble treatment of Leila that wins her "tender" heart and prompts her to betray Hassan. The motif of the Muslim woman who chooses the Christian European hero over her Muslim master was, by then, a longstanding convention: Josian falls in love with Bevis, Floripas with Guy of Burgundy, and Zoraida with Cervantes's Spanish captive. The qualities of the European gentleman that make him an unassailable romantic hero—chiefly, his chivalry and tenderness toward women—are also evident in Pasha Selim's and Osmin's frustrating inability to seduce Konstanze's and Blonde's hearts away from their European lovers in *Die Entführung aus dem Serail*. In order to successfully woo a European woman, according to Marmontel's and Favart's Roxelane, the Muslim despot needs to be transformed into a type of de-Orientalized European gentleman. The Giaour, however, fits uneasily into the mold of the traditional European hero, because apart from his unwavering fidelity to Leila even after her death, he proves to be a mirror image of the villain in many ways. He admits that had Leila betrayed him like she betrayed Hassan, he would have acted no differently from Hassan; he, too, would have killed her (ll.1061–1069). In acknowledging that Leila's death was "deserved" from Hassan's perspective, the Giaour shows his own values and demands of women to be in some ways as tyrannical as his enemy's. Vengeance and murder are the solutions to personal betrayal in *The Giaour*.

There is no doubt that much of the hero's force and appeal as a romantic lover derive from his extravagant outpouring of feeling for Leila. Yet in a curious twist, Hassan elicits as much emotion from, and certainly far more actual engagement with, the Giaour than does Leila. Hate and revenge are but the counterpart of love and passion, as the Giaour is the counterpart of Hassan. Indeed, the mortal combat between the two arch-enemies is described like lovemaking:

> Ah! fondly youthful hearts can press,
> To seize and share the dear caress;
> But Love itself could never pant
> For all that Beauty sighs to grant
> With half the fervour Hate bestows
> Upon the last embrace of foes,
> When grappling in the fight they fold
> Those arms that ne'er shall lose their hold:
> Friends meet to part; Love laughs at faith;
> True foes, once met, are joined till death! (ll.647–654)

That the object of hate should be inextricably bound to the object of love—that it should be the flip side of affection—is an idea that is later found in *The Sheik*. The paramount difference there, however, is that the protagonists in Hull's "embrace of foes" are the hero and heroine. Sheik Ahmed Ben Hassan's rape of Diana Mayo springs from a desire that is birthed from his hatred of the English. He uses her body to punish his foe. Since we later learn the secret that he is half English, his hatred for his foe is also a form of self-hatred, and in this way, he also echoes the Giaour. For Diana Mayo, what begins as "the fervour Hate bestows" is eventually transformed into an equally desperate love that promises redemption for the villain-hero sheik, whose proud mutiny against society, natural leadership of his loyal tribe, inflexible will, murderous aggression toward all foes, and private code of honor mark him again as another descendant of the Giaour—with one critical exception, of course: the Giaour would never rape or brutalize women the way the sheik and Byron's Hassan do.

In *The Byronic Hero*, Peter Thorslev classifies the Giaour as a type of "sensitive Gothic Villain" (150). He is a synthesis of the eighteenth-century hero of sensibility (exemplified in Goethe's Werther, and Ann Radcliffe's Valancourt in *The Mysteries of Udolpho* and Vicentio Vivaldi in *The Italian*), who is distinguished by his "capacities for feeling, mostly for the tender emotions—gentle and tearful love, nostalgia, and a pervasive melancholy"—and the Gothic villain: striking, handsome, aristocratic, and possessing an air of mystery and an "indomitable will," though not necessarily the classic villain's "unmitigated evil" (Thorslev 35, 52). Crucially, whatever wrongs the Byronic hero may have perpetrated—and they are innumerable even though unnamed—he is "invariably courteous toward women, often loves music or poetry," and he has a "strong sense of honor." He has been "ensouled and humanized" (Thorslev 8). In fact, it is the Giaour's tenderness toward Leila (like Conrad's toward all women in *The Corsair*) that makes him a hero to her, even though he is a villain in the eyes of society. This character type is surely recognizable to readers of romance fiction especially from the 1970s, even though in his treatment of women, he differs dramatically from E. M. Hull's cruel, brutal sheik and all the rapist heroes of 1970s Orientalist bodice rippers discussed in Chapter 5.

The Giaour was followed by several more Eastern tales: *The Bride of Abydos* (1813), *The Corsair* (February 1814), *Lara* (August 1814; Byron indicated this was a sequel to *The Corsair*), *The Siege of Corinth* (1816), and *Parisina* (1816). *The Bride of Abydos* plays little part in the evolution of the twentieth-century Oriental romance novel. It largely falls into the "escape from the seraglio" subgenre. Thorslev points out, however, that the hero in this poem, Selim, is "the first of Byron's fully developed Noble Outlaws"—a type of hero characterized by exile and solitude, driven to outlawry by a personal wrong inflicted by society or a loved one. The noble outlaw, a "transformed eighteenth-century villain," is "invariably fiery, passionate, and heroic; he is in the true sense bigger than the life around him." His inherent leadership abilities, recognized by his robber band of brothers, stem from his aristocratic lineage, for he personifies "the Romantic nostalgia for the days of personal heroism, for the age when it was still possible for a leader to dominate his group of followers by sheer physical courage, strength of will, and personal magnetism" (66–69). Byron's noble outlaw is important, for in none of the other recognized antecedents to the modern romance novel—neither Samuel Richardson's *Pamela* (1970) nor Jane Austen's *Pride and Prejudice* (1813)—do we see such a character developed as romantic hero. Yet this is recognizably the figure of Ahmed Ben Hassan in *The Sheik*.

Byron's archetypal noble outlaw, however, is indubitably Conrad in *The Corsair*, the verse romance that tells the tale of the pirate Conrad, whose "name on every shore / Is famed and feared." Conrad leads a band of pirates who follow him loyally because of his proven success in their ventures and his "power of Thought—the magic of the Mind" that "moulds another's weakness to its will" (ll.182, 184). He is a dangerous, ascetic, and solitary figure; a "man of loneliness and mystery, / Scarce seen to smile" (ll.173–174). His crimes do not dismay him, for he sees them as appropriate vengeance on a cruel society that has made him the way he is:

> His soul was changed, before his deeds had driven
> Him forth to war with Man and forfeit Heaven.
> Warped by the world in Disappointment's school. (ll.251–253)

His one love in life, his one redeeming virtue, is his lover, Medora, who, Penelope-like, marks the boundaries of home and hearth as she stays in the tower overlooking the pirates' bay, watching for Conrad's return, only to die of grief when she believes him captured and executed.

Since the days of Robin Hood, outlawry has been glamorized and associated with personal liberty. This connection is reinforced in the opening lines of *The Corsair*, where the pirate band sings: "O'er the glad waters of the dark blue sea, / Our thoughts as boundless, and our souls as free." Of course, European liberal discourse on the Orient had involved considerations of liberty and despotism, especially in the eighteenth century. The underlying anxiety in much of the discourse, however, was that Europe was not as free, nor as different from the Orient, as Europeans might wish. This was especially voiced in French criticisms of monarchical power and the growing centralization of the state. Nevertheless, until Lady Mary Wortley Montagu provocatively proclaimed that Turkish women enjoyed more freedom than European women, it was a truism that however many liberties might be curtailed in Europe, the continent was still more free than the Orient, where endemic slavery was symbolized by the harem system. In *The Corsair* and *Lara*, Byron blurs this dichotomy between West and East. His Europe, like the Orient, is also quite literally a site of slavery and despotism, with the feudal structure of thanes and serfs in *Lara* forming the background to the hero's return home, where he finds himself an outcast. As Leask argues, Byron's depiction of a degraded and hypocritical Europe as the moral equivalent of the Orient does little to undermine the discourse of Orientalism identified by Said, for it leaves intact the qualities assigned by the West to the East. It is simply that, in its nascent age of empire, Europe was equally characterized by the "fatalism, violence, eroticism, [and] intoxication" that it had previously ascribed to the Islamic Empire (61). Caught between the corruption of the East and the West, and bitterly rejecting both in a universal misanthropy born from unnamed wrongs, the Byronic hero turns instead to exile and outlawry. The trope of the rootless hero is sometimes repeated in historical harem romances of the late twentieth century, in which the protagonist and heroine have to leave both Europe and the Orient to begin a new life in the New World.

Byron seems to have exhausted his store of tortured noble outlaw heroes by the time he created Don Juan, the sixteen-year-old scholar who is seduced by twenty-three-year-old Julia, wife of Don Alfonso, and who is sent away from Seville as a result. The unfinished, seventeen-canto mock epic tells of Don Juan's Oriental adventures as he is shipwrecked, seduced, kidnapped by pirates, sold as a slave in the markets of Istanbul, and bought by the sultana Gulbayez—the sultan's fourth and favorite wife. Gulbayez smuggles Don Juan into the palace harem, where he is disguised as a woman, giving rise to the famous scene in the seraglio "where the ladies lay / Their delicate limbs; a thousand bosoms there / Beating for love, as the caged bird's for air." *Don Juan* (1821) sealed Byron's reputation as a poet of the romantic, sensual Orient, confirming the status of the Byronic hero for the next two centuries and ensuring that his mere reference would conjure a frisson of sexual tension and excitement. The Byronic Orient, as scholars have argued, proved highly adaptable for the development of pornography in the nineteenth century (Marcus 209, Colligan 7).

SEX AND SULTANS: THE PORNOGRAPHIC EAST

When the women's historical romance novel took an erotic turn beginning in the 1970s, the Oriental harem, with its centuries-long association with romance, sensuousness, seduction, and pornographic sex became a popular setting for female erotica. That the East should have turned into a favored locus of European pornography was foreseeable. European pornography originally developed as a form of political and social critique (Hunt 1993), and by the eighteenth century, the Orient had acquired all the characteristics of society that came to be mocked and satirized in porn: corruption, tyrannical power, oppressive state and religious institutions, and hypocritical social mores. Importantly, the Orient offered an alternative—possibly utopian—social and sexual order to that of Europe. What was surprising was how long it took Europeans to portray the Orient in explicitly pornographic terms.

It was inevitable that an attack on despotism and tyranny through pornography would invoke the Turk even as it offered the titillating pleasures of polygamy. The British tradition of Orientalist pornography began in the 1820s, when the caricaturist Thomas Rowlandson depicted the harem as a sexual paradise in his engravings. In *The Harem*, the dark-skinned, turbaned Muslim master, with the long stem of his pipe pointing rather redundantly to his large erection, gazes at a multiplicity of naked, white-skinned female bodies lined up in two tiers and fading off into the distance.

The fantasy was a clichéd one by then, but Rowlandson further reinforced its appeal in his engraving *The Pasha*, where the master of the harem—naked except for his turban—entertains five women: each of his arms is around a naked woman, with two women kneeling before him—one grasping his erect penis and the other lying prostrate in the background caressing herself—and the fifth lying back on the divan, watching.

The Oriental harem, always sensual and erotic in the European imagination, had become overtly pornographic by the 1820s (Sigel 42). This hypersexualized Orient is emphasized in the anonymously authored novels *The Lustful Turk* (1828, 1829, 1848, 1860–1864, 1893), *The Seducing Cardinal's Amours* (1830), *Scenes in the Seraglio* (ca. 1820–1830, 1855–1860), and *A Night in a Moorish Harem* (ca. 1900). *The Seducing Cardinal's Amours* has

FIGURE 1.1. *Thomas Rowlandson, "The Harem," n.d.*

an explicitly polemical message that is not dissimilar to earlier eighteenth-century arguments made by Montesquieu in *Persian Letters* and Montagu in her *Turkish Embassy Letters*: namely, that there is a sexual equivalence between women in Europe and women in the Oriental harem, and that women in the harem might well be better off. As Lisa Sigel points out:

> According to the novel, the Catholic Church forced women into decadence, while the Turkish harem allowed them to enjoy their own natural sexuality. Likewise, although women were purchased and abandoned nightly in the brothels of France, they were purchased and then cosseted in the harem. The contrast of women's treatment in the harem . . . with their treatment in the West showed the harem to be superior for women as well as men. (42)

The "cosseting" of harem women, however, depended entirely on their willing sexual submission to the harem master, as *The Lustful Turk* makes abundantly clear.

The Lustful Turk is an epistolary novel that draws heavily from long-established Oriental literary conventions, such as renegade pirates, abduction, and the sexual enslavement of white women in the harem. As

FIGURE 1.2. *Thomas Rowlandson, "The Pasha," n.d.*

mentioned above, one of the most popular farces in the late eighteenth century was Bickerstaffe's *The Sultan, or, A Peep into the Seraglio* (1775), which celebrates the triumph of English womanhood and liberty over the mental, physical, emotional, and sexual slavery of the harem. Bickerstaffe's short play challenged traditional gender relations by having the English slave Roxalana declare:

> Men were not born to advise; the thing is expressly the contrary—We women have certainly ten thousand times more sense. Men, indeed! Men were born for no other purpose under heaven, but to amuse us; and he who succeeds best, perfectly answers the end of his creation. (315)

By the end of the play, virginal Roxalana rules over the sultan, telling him to liberate the seraglio, marry her, and raise her to the position of his consort. She assures him that "should she interpose on behalf of the unfortunate, relieve the distressed by her munificence, and diffuse happiness through the palace, she would be admir'd, she would be ador'd; she'd be like the queen of the country from where I came" (326). It is precisely these female pretensions to physical and sexual integrity, personal liberty, and a role in the public sphere, along with their habit of laughing at men, that are attacked and subverted in *The Lustful Turk*.

The novel opens with a letter from the heroine, Emily Barlow, written to Sylvia Carey, the sister of Henry, the man Emily loves. In the tradition of sentimental fiction, Emily's parents have cruelly separated the lovers because of Henry's impecunious circumstances. They are sending Emily, along with her maid, Eliza, to India to stay with an uncle who is obviously a wealthy nabob who has made his fortune there.

Various scholars have remarked on the link between empire and pornography (Hyam 1990, Colligan 2003): the expansion of British power in India was accompanied by investigations into Indian sexuality; pornographic depictions of the Turk "buggering" European women at a time when the Ottoman Empire was still a force to be reckoned with later gave way to an obscene ditty about the British Prime Minister Gladstone "buggering" the Turk in a jingoistic display of British imperial might at the end of the nineteenth century; and the European penetration of North African and Middle Eastern deserts was accompanied by studies of Arab pederasty and homosexuality (Sigel 3, 9, Colligan 2003, Kennedy 2000). *The Lustful Turk* was written at a time when Europeans were beginning to encroach on Ottoman territory in North Africa, though the Muslim Empire still encompassed significant swathes of eastern European territory (territory that was nonetheless under threat by central and eastern European imperial ambitions and internal nationalistic aspirations). Nevertheless, the throwaway reference in *The Lustful Turk* to Britain's Indian concerns is significant as a fleeting reminder of the economic underpinnings of growing British imperial might.

Emily sails from Portsmouth, lamenting her separation from Henry who, in true sentimental hero mode, is distraught by their separation but is fairly useless at actually doing anything about it. When the ship is attacked by "Moorish pirates," Emily and her maid are captured by an "Algerine Corsair"—in fact a renegade Englishman—who brings them to Algiers as a present for Ali, dey of Algiers. Inside the dey's palace, Ali rapes Emily until he reduces her "chastity to a bleeding ruin," but she quickly learns to enjoy sex with the dey. His penis—of which there are many repetitive descriptions, leading Steven Marcus to complain of its "immense overestimation" (212)—is transformed from a "terror of virgins" to the "delight of women" (19). Emily then meets the dey's other European concubines and discovers how they ended up in his harem. The three European women—Emily, Honoria, and Adianti—share similar stories: their initial love for a hero of sensibility who proves no match for the powerful, aggressive, and sexually ruthless dey. Henry Carey, Emily's English love, is voiceless and unseen in the novel. We learn that following his separation from Emily, he is wretched and dejected and keeps to his room. Adianti's lover, Demetrios, was "eloquent, poetic, romantic, enterprising, and a lover of the arts" (43), but this didn't prevent him from being slain at the altar, or Adianti from being abducted by the local Turkish ruler of their Greek town. Like Henry, Ludovico, the nobleman in love with Honoria, is equally emasculated by the European culture of gallantry for which Honoria's Italian city is famed. She tells Emily: "It is common there for a gentleman to profess himself the humble servant of a handsome woman, wait upon her to every public place for twenty years together, without ever seeing her in private, or being entitled to any greater favour than a kind look, or a touch of her fair hand" (24). This is the treatment Honoria metes out to Ludovico, whose mind she loves but not his body.

These honorable but effete European men later reappear in *The Sheik* as well as in late twentieth-century Harlequin Mills & Boon British sheik romance novels. They throw into stark relief the sexual potency and appeal of the Muslim hero, whose sexuality defines his aggressive and domineering masculinity. When the frigid Honoria resists the dey's advances, the dey has her flogged and Honoria articulates the difference between the Muslim tyrant and her European lover: "There was a change, Madame, from the respect of poor Ludovico. The smallest favour was not granted to him until after the most urgent persuasions, whilst the Dey took every liberty he thought fit, and I believe thought he was conferring an honour upon me" (28). That the dey is granting her a favor is a perspective that Honoria, like Emily, eventually comes to share, due to the wonderful power of his magical penis. Honoria's submission to the dey brings out the "passionate and tender," "most devoted and even submissive lover" in him—as long as she continues to obey him and offer her sexual services willingly, of course. All potential resistance from Honoria, however, has been put to flight; she has been properly reeducated in her role as a woman and sexual receptacle. She even learns to luxuriate in the dey's perverse passion for anal sex; a passion that is characterized as typically Muslim in this and subsequent Orientalist pornography and romance novels. The fact of the dey's Muslim identity is continually emphasized by his apostrophes of agonized pleasure to Allah and "Holy Mahomet" during his rapes of the European virgins.

Like *The Sheik*, *The Lustful Turk* makes the point that European civilization, with its artificial culture of chivalry and gallantry and its high valuation of virginity and chastity, has emasculated its men and desexualized its women. Only the dey's aggressive hypermasculinity—the masculinity of the Gothic villain—can revive sexual passion within European women and unleash their natural appetites, transforming them into "real women." It is because of this that the women grow to love him and yearn for his sexual attention. This pattern of abduction, rape, seduction, and love forms, in essence, the plot of *The Sheik*. Like Honoria, Diana easily and impatiently deflects the attention of her European and American admirers; it is only the Sheik's ruthless rape that ignites her sexuality and causes her to eventually fall in love with him. Rape and the experience of phallic penetration are thus presented as ultimately liberating, because they awaken women's "natural" or "animal" passions. In masculinist libertine philosophy, virginity and chastity are artificial, repressive constructs of society that need to be subverted in order to unleash women's— particularly virgins'—natural sexual urges.

The raped virgin fantasy had, in fact, been in circulation for centuries since Greek chastity romances, or martyrological narratives (Kelly 49, 56). Maud Burnett McInerney notes that martyrological narratives often catered to a female audience and are

> characterized by a special emphasis on dramatic confrontations between protagonist and antagonist, between virgin martyr and pagan tyrant, cast in the form of interrogations that alternate dialogue with torture. All express a double pair of features that distinguish the stories of virgin martyrs from those of their male counterparts: physical passivity is linked to an aggressive eloquence and an eroticized martyrdom to imperishable sexual integrity. (50)

It is precisely this tradition of virginal chastity and resistance unto death that was under assault in European pornography, particularly in narratives such as *The Lustful Turk*, that showed women's resistance to be due to their ignorance of the pleasures of sex.

Moreover, virgins were historically troubling because they encoded a paradox of cultural desires and fears. The virgin signified chastity, religiosity, innocence, purity, authenticity, and future reward. As an object of male desire and a commodity of exchange, the virgin's value lay in novelty. The virgin object could be traded for wealth or social status by her father, while for her husband, as Margaret Ferguson remarks, "the virgin item's cultural value lies partly in the fact that it has *not yet* been used" (7). However, these meanings pertained only as long as the virgin was under male control: her father's, brother's, or husband's. The "active virgin," on the other hand—the woman who independently chose a perpetual state of virginity—was potentially threatening to society and the state. As Richard Halpern points out, the "'active virgin' is often depicted as *wandering* rather than remaining quietly in the enclosure of the patriarchal *domus*"—an activity that allied her to the other public woman, the prostitute (Ferguson 9). Thus the active virgin and the prostitute both signified the woman who had escaped patriarchal control. The active virgin also caused uneasiness because she was a potential figure of power and authority, as demonstrated by two of the most famous European virgins: Joan of Arc and Elizabeth I. She was, in addition to a potential whore, also an androgynous Amazon—a virago. Little wonder, then, that in *The Sheik*, Diana Mayo's virginity is commented upon disapprovingly by society matrons as well as potential husbands, and that although she delights in wearing feminine dresses, she thinks of herself as androgynous. As an active virgin, she will not consent to remaining in the domestic sphere; she insists on her right to wander in the desert where, of course, she is abducted and raped by the sheik, who thus puts an end to her virgin status and—as happens to European women in *The Lustful Turk*— initiates her into the true purpose of womanhood.

The eighteenth and early nineteenth centuries formed the transitional period of confused and contradictory ideas about virginity and women's sexuality: when old ideas about women's voracious sexual appetites jostled for primacy with new ideas about women's lack of passion; when virginity was simultaneously innocent and yet already tainted with the shadow of sexual knowledge. Virginity was a sign of truth and authenticity, but perhaps also a charade of dissemblance; a guarantee of virtue, but perhaps also a cynical commodification of the virginal body for trade in the sexual marketplace (LeGates 22–23). In such a climate, as Jon Stratton observes, deflowering a virgin became a male obsession—the height of sexual stimulation and fantasy in European culture: "In London a book published in 1760 stated that a virgin cost fifty pounds. In the nineteenth century we find the author of *My Secret Life* spending much time and money procuring young virgins" (19). Samuel Richardson's novels were ultimately focused on the virgin who either preserved her virginity or lost it through rape. Sade was similarly obsessed, not only with the defloration but with the utter degradation and abasement of the mystical, beatified virgin.

This was the immediate historical context in which the dey of Algiers in *The Lustful Turk* hungered after virginal bodies to rape and initiate into sexual pleasure. At a time when the ideology of the asexual "angel in the house" was gaining ascendancy, the anonymous author of *The Lustful Turk* defiantly asserted an older, erotic libertine fantasy of the insatiable female sexual appetite unleashed in a violated virgin who is imprisoned in the harem of a brutal and sexually depraved Eastern potentate. It was a fantasy that proved enduring, recurring in women's historical harem romance novels of the late twentieth century, and alluded to in modern Harlequin romance titles like *The Sheik and the Virgin Secretary* and *The Sheik and the Virgin Princess*, though these novels do not feature the violent rapes of *The Lustful Turk*.

FROM BEYS TO BEDOUINS: ROMANCE AND
THE DECLINE OF THE OTTOMAN EMPIRE

The gleeful mockery of Muslim potentates in British pornography such as *The Lustful Turk*; William Dugdale's weekly periodical, *The Exquisite: A Collection of Tales, Histories, and Essays, Funny, Fanciful and Facetious* (1842–1844); and the jingoistic 1878 ditty "Who'll bugger the Turk?" in *The Pearl* magazine were all symptoms of growing European imperial might and expansion that took place at the expense of the ailing Ottoman Empire. European assaults on Muslim territories in North Africa had begun with Napoleon's invasion of Egypt in 1798. Although French occupation was short lived, driven out by the British and their Ottoman allies in 1801, it brought the Rosetta Stone to Europe, produced the multivolume Orientalist study of the country, *Description de l'Egypte* (1809), and "inaugurated a new era in which the lands of the Middle East and North Africa would be increasingly subject to a European economic and political encroachment, and finally European colonial rule" (Lockman 71). In 1830, the French invaded Algeria, and by 1883, Tunisia had been made into a French protectorate. By 1912, after the resolution of the gunboat standoff between France and Germany that came to be known as the Agadir Crisis, most of Morocco had fallen under French governance, as well. The French thus gained control of the gateways to the Sahara—the setting of *The Sheik*.

British colonial interests lay further east: in India, Persia, the arid Gulf region, and Egypt. In the mid-nineteenth century, the Egyptian government became increasingly indebted to French and British financiers. Nationalist attempts to throw off the yoke of European financial control of Egyptian affairs led to the British invasion and occupation in 1882, the establishment of the "Veiled Protectorate," and the conquest of Sudan in 1898. Although Egypt nominally gained independence in 1922, the last British troops would not leave the country until 1954. The British also seized the Gulf port of Aden in 1839, which they turned into a coaling station en route to India, and the British government then entered into alliance with sheikdoms along the Persian Gulf coast via the Perpetual Maritime Truce of 1853, under which provision of law these sheikdoms were administered by the British government in India.

As the nineteenth century progressed and the Ottoman Empire shrank under the onslaught of internal nationalist aspirations and European imperial expansion, it was increasingly the North African desert, rather than the traditional Ottoman harem, that formed the new locus of English romantic fantasies and sexual longing. The North African and Middle Eastern deserts were unknown entities to Europeans for most of the period covered in this chapter because Mediterranean and overland trade routes touched only the coastal areas of these regions. European travelers such as William Lithgow and Laurent d'Arvieux made journeys into North Africa in the seventeenth century, but it was only in the nineteenth century that the Arabian desert was explored by increasing numbers of European travelers, including Jean Louis Burckhardt, Gifford Palgrave, François-René de Chateaubriand, Charles Doughty, Richard Burton, and Wilfred Scawen Blunt, among others. These men were highly individualistic, observant travelers as well as gifted writers. There is no single stereotype of "the Bedouin" common to all their works. However, certain ideas came to be accepted as truisms: namely, that town Arabs had become corrupted by foreign contact and that the "true" Bedouin was the Bedouin of the desert, descended from a pure racial lineage, who spoke the purest Arabic (Tidrick 28–29). It was this Bedouin who was exalted among Orientals, far above the lazy, corrupted, depraved Turk, whose decline was associated with the pornographic pleasures of the harem.

If Bedouins were romanticized, so was the forbidding desert in which they lived and warred. Carsten Niebuhr's *Travels through Arabia* (1774–1778) waxes lyrical about the spiritual, sublime desert with its hash climate and melancholy landscape, the mirages that worked so powerfully on the Romantic imagination, and the effect of the desert's danger, harshness, and solitude on Arab character. And Byron was, of course, influential in establishing the desert as a space of the Romantic sublime—an empty stage for the Romantic ego writ large—as in the following lines from *Childe Harold*:

Oh! that the Desert were my dwelling-place,
With one fair Spirit for my minister,
That I might all forget the human race,
And, hating no one, love but only her!
Ye elements!—in whose ennobling stir
I feel myself exalted—Can ye not
Accord me such a being? (Canto IV, st. 177)

Romantic interest in the expansive space for the dramas of the self was followed by further travel and literary as well as scholarly interest in the desert and its inhabitants over the next century. Once considered a wasteland populated by wild and savage tribes to be avoided at all costs, by the end of the nineteenth century the desert had become an essential part of the European traveler's journey through the Orient. The very emptiness of the desert (in European understanding, at least) made the land a fitting stage for the projection of the European self. It was a space of mysticism and spirituality where, in the tradition of the three great monotheistic religions, spiritual revelation was received. For Europeans struggling to come to terms with perpetual change, industrialization, urbanization, and the increasing pace of modern life, the desert seemed timeless, unchanging, and fixed in history. It was the clichéd "pastness" of the desert that made it so pleasurably melancholic as well as romantic for some travelers, as Ali Behdad notes in *Belated Travelers* (1994). It was a space that was ripe for the enactment of Orientalized romantic love, and middlebrow British novelists obligingly led the way.

TWO

The Rise of the Desert Romance Novel

Could, in truth, East mate with West? Would not the separate
viewpoints of the two clash, make discord instead of harmony?
Customs, religion, standards of various kinds would be at variance
between the two; and would it be the part of the woman to forget
her heritage, to yield up her private convictions, to sink in many
ways her individuality?

KATHLYN RHODES, *THE DESERT LOVERS*

At the age of thirty-two, Domini Enfilden is released from the
burden of caring for her father—a harsh, embittered man
whose half-Hungarian wife eloped with a musician while
Domini was still a child. Orphaned, unmarried, alone in the world, but
endowed with fortune and freedom for the first time in her life, Domini
flees "England and the people mewed up in it for the winter." She has had
enough of doing dreary "things without savour, without meaning, without salvation for brain or soul" (5). Looking for purpose and passion, she
boards a ship for North Africa.

> She wanted freedom, a wide horizon, the great winds, the great sun, the
> terrible spaces, the glowing, shimmering radiance, the hot, entrancing
> moons and bloomy, purple nights of Africa. She wanted the nomad's
> fires and the acid voices of the Kabyle dogs. She wanted the roar of the
> tom-toms, the dash of the cymbals, the rattle of the negroes' castanets,
> the fluttering, painted figures of the dancers. She wanted—more than
> she could express, more than she knew. (5)

What Domini wanted, British and American readers apparently wanted as well—more than they knew, but certainly not more than Robert Smythe Hichens could express. Hichens's *The Garden of Allah* was published in 1904 and ran through five editions in that year alone, with seven more editions published in 1905. The novel took America by storm: department stores and restaurants were draped in "Garden of Allah" themes, while "Garden of Allah" lamps, *objets d'arts*, and perfumes were developed for the burgeoning Orientalist consumer market in the States (Edwards 45). *The Garden* was adapted into a spectacular and successful play in New York in 1909, featuring whirling sandstorms and camels on stage. The first Hollywood film version of the book premiered in 1916 and was remade in 1927, and in 1936, when Marlene Dietrich's and Charles Boyer's respective portrayals of the tragic, star-crossed lovers Domini and the renegade Trappist monk Boris Androvsky were immortalized in the tagline "They loved each other with the fierceness of those who have been denied love!"

The Garden of Allah launched the early twentieth-century craze for the "desert romance," a romantic subgenre that *The Sheik* capitalized on and transformed in the 1920s. In this chapter, I examine the rise of the desert romance novel as a subgenre. I begin by considering the tropes that characterized the Orientalist romance novel in the late nineteenth and early twentieth centuries; motifs such as spirituality and the occult, the sexualization of the Sahara Desert in Hichens's novel, and the exploration of new woman issues such as women's sexuality, marriage, and miscegenation. These topics, which concerned romance novelists from the late nineteenth century through to the 1920s, when the desert romance reached the height of its popularity, are also evident in the Hollywood films that tried to cash in on the success of Famous Players-Lasky's *The Sheik* (1921). Because *The Sheik* merits its own chapter, so that it can be discussed at length, I leave Hull's novel to the next chapter and focus here on changes in the desert romance.

THE RISE OF THE DESERT ROMANCE NOVEL

By the time *The Garden of Allah* was published in 1904, the romance novel had been going strong for more than one-and-a-half centuries. Scholars of romance novels usually trace the foundational plots and characters of the genre back to Samuel Richardson's *Pamela* (1740), Jane Austen's *Pride and Prejudice* (1813), and Charlotte Brontë's *Jane Eyre*

(1847) (Ramsdell 6, Dubino 103, Regis 16, 63). These are novels whose heroes and heroines, cast of supporting characters, and archetypal romantic plots are still easily recognizable in countless romance novels today. However, they were by no means typical of the average romance novel in the nineteenth century. In Britain and the United States, nineteenth-century romance novels were distinguished by their sentimentality, intense religiosity, and moral and inspirational lessons. This was as true of the American domestic sentimentalist novelists who dominated the Civil War era as of the British novelists who wrote for Mudie's Select Library or W. H. Smith's railway bookstalls from the 1840s to the 1880s. Romance novels were looked at askance from their very inception. Detractors of the genre cast doubt upon its moral utility and objected to its potentially pernicious influence over weak female minds. The novels could only be justified by being packaged as "light literature" promising to "carry pleasantly to the minds of the young, germs of precious truth, which time and the blessing of heaven may cause to take root and spring up to the present and future well-being of the soul" (quoted in Anderson 20). As Margaret Dalziel notes:

> The characters who are meant to attract the reader's sympathy are usually represented as pious, at any rate in the sense of showing deference to the deity. Heroines in particular have recourse to prayer, and there is a good deal of rolling of eyes to heaven in a more or less prayerful way. Sorrows and joys are commonly regarded as sent from on high, moral laws are given a religious foundation, and moral decisions are based on religious considerations. (Anderson 20)

The religiosity of mid-nineteenth-century romance novels showed the influence of Evangelicalism in British and American societies. By the late nineteenth century, however, the foundations of mainstream religion were shaken by the proliferation of Darwinist ideas. In response, romance writers turned increasingly to the occult to create in their novels a heightened sense of transcendence, wonder, and the uncanny. In this regard, romantic fiction was heir to Romanticism, which prized the sublime, the mystical, and the irrational, along with the sensation of acute emotions over reason, practicality, and the unexciting, prosaic qualities of daily life. Since mainstream romance novels would not return to alternative spiritualities until the final years of the twentieth century, late Victorian and Edwardian romantic fiction was therefore significantly different from the secular realist form that came to dominate the twentieth century. The late

Victorians' preoccupation with spirituality and mysticism found an exotic outlet in the non-Western world, as increasing trade, travel, and colonialism brought knowledge and consumable goods back to Western cities.

The Orientalist literature associated with European colonial ventures in the Middle East and North Africa in the nineteenth century is well known. In addition to scholarly translations of Arabic and Persian texts, it includes the travel writing—often purporting to be ethnographies—generated by Edward Lane, Richard Burton, Wilfrid Scawen Blunt and Lady Anne Blunt, Harriet Martineau, François-René de Chateaubriand, Alphonse de Lamartine, and Gérard de Nerval, as well as the historical novels of Benjamin Disraeli and Gustave Flaubert, among others. From a less exalted literary plane came middlebrow colonial adventure romances such as Ouida's (Mary Louise Ramé) *Under Two Flags* (1867), which features the French tomboy Cigarette as the café singer in French Algeria who sacrifices her life for the aristocratic English exile Bertie Cecil while fighting with the French Army of Africa. Because of France's extended presence in North Africa, many nineteenth-century British-authored Oriental novels tend to be set in Algeria. These were followed at the turn of the century by celebrations and various renditions of the story of General Gordon at Khartoum: for example, William Le Queux's *The Eye of Istar* (1897), A.E.W. Mason's *The Four Feathers* (1902), Gilbert Parker's "While the lamp holds out to burn," in *Donovan Pasha* (1902), and Hall Caine's *The White Prophet* (1909) (Diamond Chapter 3).

Other late Victorian romance novelists were more interested in exploiting the occult Orient through sensational thrillers than in documenting and jingoistically supporting European colonial rule. Published in the same year as Bram Stoker's *Dracula*, and equally part of the apocalyptic genre of fin de siècle invasion literature, Richard Marsh's *The Beetle* (1897) signaled imperial fears of reverse colonization. In this novel, a sinister, hermaphroditic, shape-shifting Oriental pursues a British politician back to London, where the Oriental hypnotizes the politician and threatens to wreak havoc on his political ambitions and his romantic relationship with the English heroine. Marie Corelli, the most popular romance novelist of the late nineteenth century, combined ecstatic spirituality, Oriental mysticism, and the sinister occult in two of her best-selling novels, *The Soul of Lilith* (1892) and *Ziska* (1897). *The Soul of Lilith* tells the story of the Egyptian magician El-Rami, who experiments with bringing a twelve-year-old Egyptian girl back to life by trying to trap her soul in her body because he is in love with her beauty. Corelli virtuously punishes El-Rami for dabbling in matters best left to the Creator: Lilith's body blisters, chars,

and disintegrates into dust when the magician kisses her. El-Rami consequently becomes insane and ends his days confined in the Monastery of
the Cross in Cyprus. *Ziska* takes a turn for the torrid occult as it breath-
lessly charts the French painter Armand Gervase's overwhelming passion for the exotic Russian princess Ziska. Corelli describes the couple
as strangely Oriental looking, resembling Arabs of the "purest caste and
highest breeding" (55). Gervase is, in fact, later revealed to be the reincar-
nation of a cruel ancient Egyptian warrior who murdered a dancer he
loved, and Ziska is the reincarnated dancer, who has returned to take her
revenge. The story ends predictably enough in death.

What is notable about these late Victorian romances is that, in contrast to the pre-nineteenth century Orientalist plays and opera discussed
in the previous chapter, racial boundaries are never crossed. The Egyptian El-Rami falls in love with an Egyptian girl, and Gervase and Ziska are
both European, while their ancient incarnates are both Egyptian. Moreover, romantic love in the Orient was not only associated with the purple
prose of sublime, irrational passion, but often with the tragic death or
separation of the lovers. There was nothing new about this as a topos in
passionate, romantic love, of course, as Rougemont has pointed out in his
analysis of the Tristan and Iseult myth (15–155). Even today, millions of
viewers of *Gone With The Wind*, *The Bridges of Madison County*, or *Titanic*
continue to identify these films featuring lovers who are tragically parted
as archetypal romantic films. But it bears emphasizing that these endings
were particularly characteristic of Orientalist love stories at the turn of the
twentieth century, such as Robert Hichens's best-selling desert romance.

THE GARDEN OF ALLAH

The Garden of Allah would be barely recognizable as a romance novel
by modern readers. In some ways more of a travelogue than a novel, it
tells the long-winded, emotionally fraught story of Domini Enfilden, who
seeks solace from her troubled life in the Sahara desert after the lingering death of her English father, an embittered atheist who abandoned his
Catholic faith after he was betrayed by his Catholic wife. Domini inherits
from her mother her "dark beauty" and Bohemian "quick vehemence and
passion," but fortunately she also possesses the sterling English qualities of
common sense, strength, and athleticism, in addition to a reassuring lack
of Continental vanity. Like many adventurous women of the nineteenth
century who had to wait until the deaths of parents or husbands endowed

them with the wealth and liberty to travel (Blake 1992: 21), Domini had spent much of her adolescence and early adulthood suppressing her emotional, physical, and psychological needs in order to care for her father. Such self-sacrifice is rewarded by the opportunity to travel after his death. The desert—the "garden of Allah," which is also the "garden of oblivion" (20)—brings Domini peace, nourishes her soul, and provides her with the opportunity for romantic adventure when she meets the dark, brooding, half Russian, half British Boris Androvsky. Cast in the mold of Byron's tortured Eastern heroes, Boris is prone to social awkwardness and possesses the uncanny ability to make crucifixes shudder or fall off walls when he passes by. Nevertheless, Domini and Boris fall in love, marry, and sustain a few brief moments of euphemistic passion. Their relationship ends unhappily when Boris reveals himself to be a runaway apostate Trappist monk who has stolen the secret recipe for the monastery's famous "Louarine liqueur." The two reluctantly agree to part so that Boris can save his soul by returning the liqueur recipe to the monks and renewing his vow of silence. Domini goes back to her house with its little "Moorish garden" at the edge of the desert, where she is comforted by her and Boris's son and the caressing winds of the desert.

Hichens showed himself in many ways to be more enthralled with the desert than he was with his hero and heroine, or their tragic love story. He reserved his most earnest passages of exalted prose to describe the desert, "with its pale sands and desolate cities, its sunburnt tribes of workers, its robbers, warriors and priests, its ethereal mysteries of mirage, its tragic splendours of colour, of tempest and of heat," (15) and the "legions of freeborn, sun-suckled" Bedouin tribesmen who lived there (144). Indeed, one could argue that it is the anthropomorphized desert that constitutes Domini's true love and passion. Inhaling the "pure, clean" desert air is like a kiss from the East:

> When two lovers kiss their breath mingles, and, if they really love, each is conscious that in the breath of the loved one is the loved one's soul, coming forth from the temple of the body through the temple door. As Domini leaned out . . . she was conscious that in this breath she drank there was a soul, and it seemed to her that it was the soul which flames in the centre of things, and beyond. (17)

In the tradition of nineteenth-century British travelers' attitudes toward the Middle East, the desert in this book is associated with "boundless freedom." It is a great, rolling emptiness upon which the Romantic

European ego can project itself, but where the self is also realized through an experience akin to sexual intercourse. Traveling on a train through the desert induces an experience of ecstatic sensation in Domini that positions her hermaphroditically as both the penetrated female swooning from love and sex, and the male penetrator invoking a classic trope of European colonial conquest of virgin territory:

> The entrance into this land of flame and colour, through its narrow and terrific portal, stirred her almost beyond her present strength. The glory of this world mounted to her heart, oppressing it. The embrace of Nature was so violent that it crushed her. . . . When all the voices of the village fainted away she was glad. . . . Suddenly she knew that she was very tired, so tired that emotions acted upon her as physical exertion acts upon an exhausted man. (25)

Boris's tortured affections can scarcely compete with this orgasmic consummation of desire for the desert. Hichens later assures us that "entry into the desert had been full of such extraordinary significance" because Domini instinctively understood that Boris and the desert were "as one in her mind"—but it is the desert that "summons" her and evokes the most sexualized sensations described in the novel (265). After their marriage, for instance, as she and Boris journey into the desert in a palanquin on a camel's back, Domini shuts her eyes because she "did not want to see her husband or to touch his hand. She did not want to speak. She only wanted to feel in the uttermost depths of her spirit this movement . . . towards the goal of her earthly desires" (284). The desert invades and overwhelms all her senses.

The Garden of Allah is ostensibly about Boris's redemption from apostasy through his love—romantic and sexual—for Domini, which balances the cosmic scales whereby her father's love for his unfaithful wife led to his own apostasy from his faith. But Hichens's personal romance is really with the desert, as is further shown in his subsequent book, *The Spell of Egypt*, (1910) in which he did away with the pretense of a plot and focused solely on a romanticized and rhapsodized Eastern landscape. He lost no readers in doing so; *The Spell of Egypt* enjoyed much literary success.

It seems that Edwardian readers could not get enough of Egypt or the desert as a landscape of the exotic—a primitive, romantic geography contrasting with jaded, decadent, over-industrialized and over-urbanized modern Europe (Anderson 183). The popularity of the late Victorian imperial adventure romance novel—Henry Rider Haggard's *King Solomon's*

Mines (1885) or *She: A History of Adventure* (1886–1887), for example—attests to this yearning to escape civilization but to also, paradoxically, open up the "uncivilized" world for European exploration and exploitation. In addition to this adventure genre, Rita Felski notes the parallel existence of

> another influential cultural tradition of imagining non-Western cultures as exotic zones of spiritual plenitude and erotic transfiguration. Instead of affirming the hegemony of modern civilization over less developed territories, this latter motif privileges those very territories as a redemptive refuge from an overbearing modernity. (137)

Women as well as men indulged in such fantasies, but this access of Eastern enthusiasm, this idealization of the Orient, nevertheless arose alongside, and overlapped with, increasing European encroachment in the region. Indeed, the rhetoric of the occult Orient bears striking similarity to the rhetoric of imperialism. As Felski argues, the "desire to escape the constraints of Western culture expressed itself in fantasies of exploring new, uncharted realms, whether actual or metaphysical; the spirit world was yet another territory to conquer, another enticing frontier" (136). Therefore, despite the wealth of information about Egyptian life, and despite the overblown and soulful descriptions of the desert, the plots of British novels before the First World War were focused primarily on European relationships staged against an exotic background figured as primitive, mystical, and unchanging. They did not attempt to engage with modern Egyptians or Arabs, or to include them in their plots.

THE NEW WOMAN AND THE DESERT ROMANCE

Where late Victorian and Edwardian anxieties about the status of religion and the lure of the occult were explored through Egyptian tales, other fin de siècle preoccupations raised by the new woman literature of the 1890s and early 1900s, such as the relationships between men and women, the independence of women, and the role of sexuality inside and outside of marriage, also found expression in Eastern settings. This is evident in the novels of Kathlyn Rhodes, whose concerns about the impact of the new woman movement on gender and romantic relations remained constant throughout her novels of the first three decades of the twentieth century, even as she became increasingly obsessed with the strict demarcation of racial boundaries after the First World War. None of the women in Rhodes's romance novels are new women; she tended to favor the traditionally feminine heroine. However, the gender issues raised in her romances—the desires of women to experience greater liberty and a wider life, to pursue professions, to give expression to sexual drives, and to enjoy sex outside of marriage—had all been put on the table by new woman novels.

In *The Desert Dreamers* (1909), the influence of new woman themes can be seen in Rhodes's treatment of premarital sex. Like E. M. Forster's Leonard Bast in *Howard's End*, Rhodes's hero, Richard Allison, is an impoverished bank clerk toiling out his days in a bleak London office, his dreams and poetic ambitions stifled by soulless modernity. When he receives a bequest from an estranged uncle, he forsakes his respectable occupation and journeys to Egypt, where he meets an old school friend who lends him his house in the middle of the "lonely, palm-guarded desert" (10). There, Richard's artistic genius and passion for life begin to revive. He meets and falls in love with an intense young Irish woman, Emer Linsvane. There is, however, nothing simple about falling in love during the fin de siècle; like all romance novelists at this time, Rhodes uses lofty language to describe love:

> Love at first sight may be termed, truly enough, a physical love rather than a love of the soul; yet its claims are after all as just, and frequently more insistent. For the voice of passion is not always a base and clamorous voice; sometimes it speaks in accents as pure and as holy as any voice of prayer or benediction.
>
> To the true lover the body of the woman he loves is a treasure worthy of a reverence as great and deep as the Holy Grail to the knights of old. That he longs to make it his own in no wise detracts from the purity of his worship; his longing is the incense he burns before her shrine, the homage which is the most fitting and natural tribute to the beloved. (19)

In other words, the true male lover will refrain from sex before marriage. These frequent explications of love by Edwardian writers are quite possibly due to the fact that cultural understandings of romantic love in the Western world were undergoing a transformation at this time. Scholars of romantic love argue that although sexual attraction was an important, albeit unstated, aspect of romantic love in the nineteenth century, what distinguishes nineteenth-century love from its modern twentieth-

century counterpart is the excessive emphasis placed on the intensely private, exalted, spiritual nature of love (Rothman 1987, Lystra 1989, Seidman 1991). We have already encountered this in the many references by
Corelli, Hichens, and others to the capacity of love to facilitate spiritual
redemption. By the early twentieth century, however, spiritual love was
giving way to a secularized notion of love that was associated with sexual
attraction and the commodification and consumption of romance (Illouz
1997). Like Rhodes's elucidation in *The Desert Dreamers*, turn-of-the-
century meditations on love were thus an attempt to mediate this changing understanding. They sought to find a place for passion while upholding traditional social and sexual mores.

As Lucy Bland (1995) shows, although there was a proliferation of
clubs and organizations highlighting and debating the role of sexuality in
gender relations in the late nineteenth and early twentieth centuries, there
did not exist a public forum where British women could voice their views
from a platform of personal experience rather than having to recourse to
"scientific evidence." In the face of self-confident, university-educated
men claiming the authority of science and objectivity — in Karl Pearson's
Men's and Women's Club, for instance — women who attempted to invoke the importance of the emotions, and to argue for the emancipation
of women, were quickly daunted and silenced. The Men's and Women's
Club eventually disbanded because of "the unbridgeable chasm between
the desires and aspirations of women and men" (Bland 1995: 41). Where,
then, were ordinary, middle-class women to turn in order to explore or
voice their opinions about sexuality? The romance novel naturally served
as such a forum. Not only was it concerned with romantic love, but it was
also focused on gender relationships and the emotions. Within the pages
of the romance novel, female characters could reflect upon the significance of sexuality for their lives and relationships. This is certainly demonstrated in *The Desert Dreamers*.

Richard and Emer want to get married but are trapped in their desert
village by the onset of the *khamsin*, the notoriously fierce desert wind. In
the midst of the storm, they give in to their passions and make love, then
continue living together in a state of "halcyon happiness" (59) for weeks.
The desert made them do it; or perhaps they were "unconsciously influenced by the fatalism of the Arabs among whom they lived" (60). The
Orient disarms even the best of Britons. When the desert storms subside,
Richard and Emer leave for Cairo to be married, but on the way Emer is
thrown from her horse and dies in the desert — deflowered and unwed.
Two years later, Richard meets Emer's sister Diana in Paris and the two

fall in love. After they are married, Diana is horrified to discover that her husband "had allowed, nay, encouraged, her sister to imperil her immortal soul by committing a sin for which no words could be black enough" (154). Much marital discord ensues until Richard returns to Egypt and has the revelation in the desert that "he and Emer had proved unworthy of their own high ideals of love and morality. Their love . . . might have been a finer, greater thing if they had been strong enough to deny themselves the gratification of their passion until they were lawfully wedded in the sight of God" (219). Humbled and made penitent by this realization, he is then permitted a second chance at happiness with Diana, who has meanwhile learned not to hold a man's former transgressions against him.

Marital discord and the meaning of a woman's sexual desire also form the basis of Rhodes's *Flower of Grass* (1911), which was republished as *The Relentless Desert* in 1920. This novel is significant because for the first time in her career as a romance writer, Rhodes raises the possibility of a white woman's sexual desire for a nonwhite man, and the problems that such illicit desire might provoke. The heroine, Phillida Gordon, marries the English Egyptologist Owen Cassilis and the two travel to Egypt together. Owen returns to his work, leaving his highly romantic and passionate wife with a lot of spare time on her hands. This is bound to lead to trouble, for we are told at the start that Phillida is half French, which accounts for her alien, un-English sense of chic and her ardent longing for a "thrilling" life "crammed full of adventurous things, exciting affairs of one sort or another!" (23). She encounters the handsome and sexually attractive, but ultimately evil and predatory, Egyptian Hassan Bey. A "native of the high classes" who has received a "modern education," and who is in "constant intercourse with Western minds," Hassan Bey nevertheless "remained at heart purely Eastern" (154). Despite his two wives stashed away in his desert villa and his countless affairs with other European women, he makes it his goal to seduce Phillida. He very nearly succeeds as well because, in contrast to later twentieth-century romance novels in which the heroine's sexual attraction to a man is a foolproof sign that he is the hero and that she will fall in love with him, a woman's strongly felt "sex-life" in a Rhodes novel is instead troublingly suspicious. Strong sexual attraction signifies a weakness of the will and moral character, an inability to rule the passions of the body. It has little to do with true love, because Rhodes believes that men and women can be sexually mesmerized and blinded by corrupt but charismatic characters. Those who act on their sexual impulses and flout conventional social and sexual mores inevitably live to regret it. Phillida's "sex-life was awakening rapidly in this warm, passionate climate" (159), and sure enough, her sexual senses are "enslaved" by "the glamour of the Oriental's personality" (105). She foolishly agrees to several clandestine meetings with him and is drugged by his kisses. Only when he abducts and imprisons her in his desert villa, and only when she meets his two wives, does she finally realize "what Hassan Bey would have made her," and what he truly is:

> greedy, rapacious, lustful, a creature veneered with a surface charm, a wonderful and deadly magnetism, but beneath the outer fascination of the Oriental a savage, pitiless hunter, marking down his prey with a callousness as revolting as it was inhuman. (251)

She also learns the bitter lesson "which all women learn soon or late": that "a woman's honour is the most valuable and the most easily flawed possession she may ever hope to hold" (251). Suitably chastened and humbled, she is ready to be rescued by her husband, who tells Hassan Bey that Phillida "belongs to me . . . a man of her own race—of her own colour!" (261).

Here, then, are the classic motifs of the Orientalist desert romance on the eve of the First World War: the passionate, independent English heroine who longs for a larger life; the lure and mystery of the desert with its promise to effect a profound transformation in the modern European self; the sexually potent but predatory high-caste Oriental who lusts after the Englishwoman; and his power to entrap her sexually. The world was ready for *The Sheik*, which shocked and thrilled female readers with its tale of the aristocratic English heroine abducted and raped in the desert by an Arab sheik.

MISCEGENATION IN DESERT ROMANCE NOVELS AND FILMS AFTER *THE SHEIK*

The most radical aspect of E. M. Hull's desert love story was not the fact that the heroine is raped and falls in love with her rapist. It was the fact that for most of the novel, readers are led to believe that an Arab man has sex with a white woman. This illusion is exposed at the end of the novel when the Sheik is revealed to be the son of an English earl and his Spanish wife. In the sequel, *The Sons of the Sheik*, Hull draws the line firmly against miscegenation, even though, throughout her career as a novelist, she did more than any other romance writer to place the figure of the Arab sheik at the center of white women's sexual fantasies. I will discuss these two novels, and Hull's subsequent desert romances, in the next chapter, which I devote specifically to *The Sheik*, and I will analyze Hull's novels in their specific historical and cultural contexts. Suffice it to say here that the success of *The Sheik* sparked a revival in the fortunes of the desert romance and brought to the fore questions about nonwhite men's sexual desirability and the problems miscegenation posed to both British and American societies.

To understand the full impact of the depiction of interracial desire and miscegenation in *The Sheik*, we need to remember that the nineteenth-century British Orientalist writings of men such as James Cowles Prichard and Richard Burton describe Arabs, Africans, and animals alike as savage "creature[s] of instinct, controlled by sexual passions, incapable of the refinement to which the white races had evolved" (Kabbani 63). As Michael Diamond shows, novel after novel from the 1890s to the First World War raised the scenario of an Arab man attempting to compromise the virtue of a white woman, only to be strongly rebuffed. In William Le Queux's *The Hand of Allah* (1914), the English who "knew Africa, who knew the Arab" hated "the taint of black blood," and the "sight of their own women introducing their daughters to that oily Egyptian sickened them" (Diamond 77). The heroine in Robert Hichens's *Barbary Sheep* (1909) nearly succumbs to an Arab *spahi* while her husband is engrossed in game hunting, but she realizes just in time that the Arab cavalryman's motive for seducing her is purely mercenary, and "the peculiar disgust which so many white-skinned people feel towards the dark races of the earth suddenly rose up in her" (Diamond 78). A. J. Dawson's *Hidden Manna* (1902) ends with the heartfelt exclamation: "God save us all from mixed marriages, I say!" (Diamond 78). In some cases, British men, rather than God, save their women from mixed marriages; in many other cases, women save themselves by drawing back from crossing racial boundaries. In none of these prewar novels did an Arab man actually have sex with a white woman, which is why *The Sheik* was such a bold and subversive novel for its time, despite its conservative conclusion.

During the 1920s, British fiction—in its popular and middlebrow varieties—flirted with the deliciously tantalizing spectacle of white women abducted and enslaved in Oriental harems. Popular interwar British women's magazines geared toward a more working-class readership, such as *Betty's Paper*, *Peg's Paper*, *The Violet Magazine*, and more serious middle-class periodicals such as *Health and Physical Culture*, published fictional and supposedly real-life stories of white women who fell in love with or, more often, fell into the evil clutches of, Oriental men—

whether Arab sheiks or Indian rajahs (Cadogan 131). In almost all these stories, the color bar was ultimately upheld and the tales served as a stern warning to young women enamored with the "fabulous and romantic" East, or who yearned for the "fierce love-making" of handsome and cultured Arabs (Raoulemont 137).

Sensationalist tales of white slavery were snapped up by these women's periodicals, as were improbable stories of white female derring-do, such as Therese Raoulemont's "Captive in a Sheik's Harem" (1931). Raoulemont's article, published in the interwar women's journal *Health and Physical Culture*, recounts the purportedly true story of the French author's courageous rescue of her compatriot Yolande, who had fallen in love with and married a Moroccan sheik. "The French recognize no colour bar," Raoulemont warns her readers ominously, "and it was not considered unusual that this beautiful girl should fall in love and marry a native official of the French regime" (26–27). Eventually tiring of the hapless Yolande, the perfidious Sheik Rafin "sold her as a slave to a relative of his, who had kept her a prisoner in his harem, waiting upon his native women." There she languishes until Raoulemont draws a pistol on the sheik's guards, effects her own escape (Sheik Rafin attempted to lock her in his own harem), and forces the French commandant in El Akra to arrest the sheik and his white-slave-owning relatives. And just in case any cliché of Orientalist pornography has been neglected from the plot of this "true story," the photographic illustration for this piece depicts a bare-breasted, veiled woman, and is accompanied by the caption "The inmates of the harems are virtually no more than petted and pampered prisoners—until their charms fade; then they become little better than slaves to wait upon their more fortunate sisters" (Raoulemont 26–27). Such lives presented an obvious contrast with that of the resourceful author, photographed in stern profile in the magazine, standing upright and dressed in her colonial travel garb of shirt, riding trousers, and boots.

The proliferation of sheik stories was enough to make the British writer Rosita Forbes complain that on her tour through the United States to promote her travel book *The Secret of the Sahara: Kufara* (1921), her audiences wished only to hear about "sheeks" and romance in the desert rather than her political views about Pan-Arab federalism (1944: 102). Forbes commented that American women "imagined the desert full of lawless and good-looking horsemen just waiting to make love to the first white woman who happened over their horizons!" (1921: 45). Despite her disdain for sheik novels, and despite the success of her own travelogues about the Middle East, Central Asia, and South America, Forbes could not resist the temptation to cash in on the popular desert romance genre in novels such as *Quest: The Story of Anne, Three Men and Some Arabs* (1922), *If the Gods Laugh* (1925), and *Sirocco* (1927). Her preface to *Quest* expresses the pious hope that "the actual conditions of Arab life may be differentiated from the highly-coloured romances which are so often woven round the World of Islam." In this semi-autobiographical novel, many descriptive passages and conversations with various politicians were copied straight out of her earlier travel books, which expound her political views on the Middle East during the First World War; Britain's obligations to the sherif of Mecca, who had promoted the Arab Revolt; her objections to France's ill-executed mandate over Syria; and contrasts between efficient British rule in India and French misrule in Syria. As Derek Hopwood observes: "The British quite sincerely believed that the French were unfit to rule an empire" (60). Forbes was unusual in using romantic fiction as a vehicle for expressing overt political views, and for emphasizing the importance of white women's role in empire building, especially in *If the Gods Laugh*, in which Italy's bumbling attempts at colonization are flayed. Nevertheless, she bowed to the prevailing trend of the time and included several attempted sexual assaults on her heroines in *Quest* and *Sirocco*. The would-be rapists, however, were European men.

Desert romances swiftly proliferated among other middlebrow female novelists in the firm grip of sheik fever. The prewar queen of the subgenre, Kathlyn Rhodes, repackaged some of her earlier stories for the new market: *The Lure of the Desert* (1916) was serialized in *Girls' Own Stories* in 1921, and *Flower of Grass* (1911) was republished as *The Relentless Desert* in 1920. The interwar years were the heyday of Rhodes's romances, with the publication of *The City of Palms* (1919), *Under Desert Stars* (1921), *Desert Lovers* (1922), *A Desert Cain, and Other Stories* (1922), *Desert Justice* (1923), *Allah's Gift* (1933), *Desert Nocturne* (1939), *A Daughter in the Desert* (1940), and *It Happened in Cairo* (1944). There was little apparent difference between the postwar and prewar novels; Rhodes had always taken a firm stance against miscegenation and warned her readers about the perils of succumbing to attractive Orientals. Others jumped on the desert romance bandwagon. Like Rosita Forbes, the aristocratic travel writer Lady Dorothy Mills also attempted a desert romance novel (*The Tent of Blue*, 1922), in addition to her books about Africa. Louise Gerard, who would specialize in romance plots set in various African colonies for the recently established publishing house Mills & Boon, produced *A Sultan's Slave* (1921), in which the English heroine meets a Frenchman, is abducted by him, and discovers that he is the sultan's son. When she falls in love with him, she swears that she "would have given all she possessed—her cherished freedom, her vast riches, her life—to have had him as she once thought him, a man of her own colour, not with this dreadful black barrier between them" (120). He is, of course, revealed to be a white man at the end.

Given the consensus among authors and their readers regarding miscegenation, as well as the conflation of Arabs with negritude in British popular culture (see the next chapter), Joan Conquest's *Desert Love* (1920) is all the more remarkable. *Desert Love* tells the story of Jill Carden, an upper-middle-class Englishwoman thrown into genteel poverty upon the death of her parents. She makes a living as a servant-cum-companion to an exigent older German woman, preferring to preserve her independence rather than marry a portly, nouveau-riche millionaire for his money. On a travel stop in Cairo, she notices a tall, noble Arab staring gravely at her. He is Hahmed, Sheikh el-Umbar, the unbelievably wealthy "Camel King," who provides the British government with stock for their Camel Corps. Hahmed is obviously a "good native" since his commercial interests align with the political interests of the British protectorate. Thinking the desert no great distance away, Jill impulsively approaches Hahmed to hire him as a guide to the desert. He tells her that if she goes with him, he will keep her alone in the desert with him and she will not return to her friends. After resourcefully fighting off an attempted drugging and rape by an evil town Arab, Jill follows Hahmed into the desert because she is in search of adventure and freedom from the constraints of her old life. He is tender, respectful, and loving toward her and does not attempt to touch her until she comes to him of her own free will. They are married, and after a few tempestuous tantrums on Jill's part because she is pregnant and afraid, they settle down to a happy life together in the desert.

Arabs are generally idealized in Conquest's novel as noble, passionate, true, and loyal men of honor, even though they might be rigid and unbending when it comes to gender roles and the protection of their womenfolk. This is particularly the case for Hahmed, who is a Bedouin from southern Arabia and is therefore "purer" than town-bred Arabs, who live closer to the corruption of Europeanized cities. Conquest attempts to assess Bedouin culture on its own merits, explaining Bedouin practices, such as raiding, within their particular cultural context. Arab women, however, are either absent or depicted in a very poor light. The reason Hahmed is still unmarried when Jill meets him is because the bride his family chose was a lesbian, and his wedding night turned into a nightmare when he discovered her in a passionate embrace with her maid.

Arab women are vilified even further in *The Hawk of Egypt* (1922), Conquest's sequel to *Desert Love*. In *The Hawk of Egypt*, the villainy of Arab women is epitomized by Zulannah, the courtesan who falls in love with the English hero, Ben Kelham, and plots against the English heroine with whom Ben is in love. When she is not entertaining men, Zulannah entertains herself by torturing animals and her servants. She eventually dies a horrible and ignominious death when, like Jezebel, she is chased down and consumed by the rabid stray dogs of Cairo. Again, the individuation of the white heroine as well as her endowment with sterling virtues are at the expense of nonwhite women.

What is most surprising about *Desert Love*, however, is the fact that there is simply no discussion of miscegenation; no suggestion that miscegenation is to be regarded as regrettable, if not utterly offensive, to society. Jill's decision to travel with Hahmed into the desert, to entrust her life and reputation into his keeping, along with their mutual love for each other, are presented matter-of-factly as decisions and events that do not require further authorial comment. This is quite unprecedented for this subgenre, especially since there is no authorial legerdemain revealing Hahmed as European-born at the novel's end. Conquest, it seems, was the only author at this time to accept the possibility of interracial, cross-cultural romantic and sexual unions. But did she, really?

Desert Love's sequel, *The Hawk of Egypt*, tells the tragic story of Hugh Carden Ali, the eldest and best-loved son of Jill and Hahmed, who is sent by his parents to study in England—first at Harrow, then Oxford—where he assimilates well enough until he is taunted by a woman for being a half-caste. He never recovers from this racial slur for the rest of his life. He vows that Arab women are not good enough for him, but when he falls in love with the English heroine, he realizes that he cannot with honor marry her because of his "tainted" blood. In the end, he nobly sacrifices his life to save the heroine, preserving her for the English hero. The moral of the story is provided by Jill's English godmother, who tells the grieving Jill that she is suffering the consequences of loving an Egyptian without giving thought to the offspring of their union. Had it really been necessary for her to marry Hahmed, she should have ensured that they never have children. While Hahmed might be socially acceptable because he is a "pure-bred Arab," their half-caste son could never be acceptable to either "great race." As Robert Young argues, colonialism

> was always locked into the machine of desire . . . Folded within the scientific accounts of race, a central assumption and paranoid fantasy was

endlessly repeated: the uncontrollable sexual drive of the non-white races and their limitless fertility . . . At its core, such racial theory projected a phantasmagoria of the desiring machine as a people factory: a Malthusian fantasy of uncontrollable, frenetic fornication producing the countless motley varieties of interbreeding, with the miscegenated offspring themselves then generating an ever-increasing *mélange*, 'mongrelity', of self-propagating, endlessly diversifying hybrid progeny. (181)

The only thing for honorable and heroic "half-castes" to do in the romance novel was to breed themselves out of existence.

From the late nineteenth to the early twentieth century, then, the Orientalist desert romance changed from a focus on the menacing and mysterious Orient—the Orient of Corelli, Hichens, and Rhodes that served as an exotic backdrop to European melodramas—to the Orient as a locus of rape and romance, where the figure of the dangerous Arab was foregrounded alongside the European heroine. As Reeva Simon shows in *Spies and Holy Wars: The Middle East in 20th Century Crime Fiction* (2010: 14–31), beginning with the publication of John Buchan's *Greenmantle* in 1916—"one of the earliest spy novels with a Middle Eastern theme" (1989: 19)—the Middle East became an increasingly popular site for British intrigues and thrillers. The pages of postwar popular fiction became a battleground where a tug-of-war between the desert as a space of male adventure and the desert as a space of female romance was enacted. By the end of the 1920s, the male adventure story—the foreign intrigue or foreign legion tale—won out, probably because of the seemingly insoluble problems (within and without literature) of miscegenation for white heroines, and because the unpleasant realities of growing anticolonial protests in the new mandatory states in the Middle East stripped the region of its romantic aura for contemporary British love stories.

Significantly, women had inserted themselves into the center of Orientalist discourse, both as producers and consumers. The Orient became a place for strong-willed imperialist women to experience romantic as well as imperial adventures. It was also a zone in which women could fantasize about, and test the boundaries of, race and interracial desire. In all the stories where the Arab hero is ultimately revealed to be a European man, it is still significant that the white women, who are desired by other white men, find themselves irresistibly attracted to the Arab persona. Even though these interracial relationships are undermined or debunked in the end, questions about the desirability of postwar Western men and Western masculinity in comparison to Arab men were nonetheless brought to the fore. This was no insignificant matter in interwar Britain where, as Alison Light argues, "masculinity and ideas of the nation were being 'feminized'" (10). However, a pattern emerged whereby authors who flirted with representations of interracial romantic or sexual relationships in one novel disavowed this position in the sequel: Hull with *The Sheik* and *The Sons of the Sheik*; Conquest with *Desert Love* and *The Hawk of the Desert*; and even Maud Diver with her raj romances *Lilamani* (1910) and *Far to Seek* (1921). That the turning point should be around 1920–1921 was no coincidence for reasons that I will elaborate in the next chapter. They include the onset of anticolonial protests after the Paris peace settlements, the race riots in Britain in 1919, and the resulting Aliens Order in 1920.

THREE

E. M. Hull's The Sheik

And he was an Arab! A man of different race and colour, a native;
Aubrey would indiscriminately class him as a "damned nigger."...
She did not care what he was, he was the man she loved.

E. M. HULL, *THE SHEIK*

In 1919, a romance novel by a little-known Derbyshire woman was
published featuring the story of the aristocratic but tomboyish
Lady Diana Mayo, an English virgin who, in her travels through
French colonial Algeria, is kidnapped by an Arab sheik and raped many
times.[1] She eventually falls in love with this "brute" of an Oriental "native"
but then discovers—much to her surprise—that her beloved Arab rapist
sheik is in fact the half English, half Spanish son of a peer of the British
realm. As for the sheik himself, the violent and priapic Ahmed Ben Hassan is reduced to repentance and redeemed by his love for Diana. He re-
verts to "civilized" standards of patriarchal European gender norms and
presumably forsakes rape and promiscuity (though not necessarily his
penchant for strangling evil Arab opponents when he deems this justified). The two live happily ever after in the desert, leaving the reader with
the final spectacle of an aristocratic English couple "gone native," it is
true, but who reign imperialistically over the unruly Bedouin tribes of the
Sahara in an area that was nominally under French colonial control. Edith
Maude Hull's *The Sheik* thus concludes with a reassertion of reactionary
patriarchal gender relations as well as the fantasy of proxy British rule
over French-colonized natives. It was a subtle display of one-upmanship
in British imperial rivalry with the French.

Since the 1970s, feminist, postcolonial, literary, and film scholars have paid intermittent attention to Hull's novel, analyzing its feminist and sexual politics as well as its racial and imperial implications. In this chapter, I discuss existing scholarly work on *The Sheik* before arguing that when we read Hull's novel, considerations of Britain's experience of sexuality and violence during the First World War are crucial, as are understandings of the influence of whiteness and imperialism in British history.

FEMINIST RESPONSES TO *THE SHEIK*

The Sheik elicited a polarized and visceral reaction upon publication in 1919. Billie Melman claims that its sales in Britain surpassed all other best sellers at the time. Yet while it achieved instant cult status among its mainly female readers, literary critics and self-appointed guardians of social morality were appalled, dismissing it as "a typist's daydream" and condemning it for its overt portrayal of sadomasochistic sexuality—a response that has been repeated by feminists throughout most of the twentieth century (Melman 1988: 90). However, since the 1990s, a growing body of scholarship on *The Sheik* has revised earlier hostile opinions and now offers increasingly sophisticated analysis of issues of gender, power, race, and imperialism in the novel.

The earliest responses by feminist scholars to *The Sheik* echoed contemporary reviews that condemned it as a "poisonously salacious" novel, in the words of the 1921 *Literary Review* (Blake 2003: 69). Objections did not focus on its portrayal of Arabs and the Orient so much as on its portrayal of sex and the treatment of women. In *The Purple Heart Throbs: The Subliterature of Love* (1974), one of the first book-length surveys of romance fiction, Rachel Anderson declares:

> *The Sheik* is the most immoral of any of the romances, not because of lewd descriptions of sexual intercourse . . . but because of the distorting view Miss Hull presents of the kind of relationship which leads to perfect love, and the totally unprincipled precept that the reward of rapists is a lovely English heiress with a look of misty yearning in her eyes. (188–189)

Melman describes *The Sheik* as "a prudishly told tale of masculine dominance and complementary feminine masochism and passivity" (1988: 102), while Mary Cadogan argues that the novel is not only an "antifeminist tract in which rapist behaviour is rewarded," but also a "justification of racism" (131).

Since the late 1980s, scholars considering the novel within its historical context have reexamined issues of gender and sexuality. Melman's comprehensive chapter on the appeal of the "desert romance" in *Women and the Popular Imagination in the Twenties* (1988) was among the first publications to pay sustained scholarly attention to *The Sheik*. Along with Michael Diamond's detailed discussion in *"Lesser Breeds": Racial Attitudes in Popular British Culture, 1890–1940* (2006), Melman's work is still one of the most useful delineations of this subgenre. Melman points out that beyond the "rape-*cum*-redemption" story, what caused the greatest outrage in the 1920s was not just the "prurience" or "obscenity" of *The Sheik* and similar "sex novels," but the fact that they were written for *women*. These novels were regarded as "pornographic literature, manufactured by female writers for the consumption of a sex-starved mass female audience" whose work opportunities during the First World War and its aftermath afforded them increased spending power, especially for leisure activities (Melman 1988: 92–93, 104). Underlying the outrage was a deep anxiety that traditional gender, sexual, and social mores were being subverted. The happy ending of the novel—such as it is—ultimately promotes the idea that the "modern sexually emancipated woman can pursue pleasure without being punished for her presumption"; for unlike the heroines of traditional novels, Diana does not die and is not emotionally or socially destroyed by her rape or her subsequent enjoyment of sex (Melman 1988: 93, 102–103). Whatever other literary crimes *The Sheik* might have been guilty of, it gave credence to women's sexual desires and sexual autonomy, contributing to a modern understanding and conversation about sex in the 1920s.

The exact era when women's sexual desires were legitimated has been a subject of some debate. For Ann Ardis, *The Sheik* did not so much herald the radical legitimization of female sexual desire in the 1920s as perpetuate an "advanced" view of sexuality that dated back to the new woman novels of the 1890s (287–296). Ardis focuses particularly on the androgynous figure of Diana Mayo. Where Melman interprets Diana as an interwar flapper, Ardis argues that Diana is actually a new woman and, like so many other new women in novels of the 1890s, she initially rejects heterosexuality, marriage, and domesticity. Attempts to assign a period to the novel have received little attention apart from Ardis's work. Careful reading of the novel, however, makes plausible both Melman's and Ardis's views. Ardis has reason to date the work as an early twentieth-century novel, but she does so by tying its themes to Hull's sequel, *The Sons of the Sheik*, which alludes to German espionage in French North Africa and the implications for the coming Great War. In the film of *The Sheik*, however, the setting, clothing, and hairstyles date it as a contemporary 1920s story. Both authors nevertheless agree on the importance of *The Sheik* in sanctioning female desire in the 1920s. Ardis also credits it with

> legitimizing the female adventure plot . . . for the operant fantasy here is not just about having an erotically satisfying relationship with an early twentieth-century version of a New Age sensitive and virile man; it is about galloping with him across the desert or hunting wild apes with him in the Sub-Saharan jungles. In the context of post-war efforts to redomesticate women, Hull's romances insist upon women's continued access to the public sphere, albeit in an extremely privileged way. (294)

Feminist critics in the 1990s thus began to move away from reading *The Sheik* as a reactionary narrative of sadistic patriarchal lust visited upon a masochistic, victimized woman suffering Stockholm Syndrome. Instead, they looked at the radical and potentially liberating aspects of sexual representations and attempted to descry Diana's empowerment. Although Patricia Raub acknowledges that "in some respects, *The Sheik* can be read as an object lesson to young women who attempt to be too independent and self-reliant," she agrees that "Hull was the first to celebrate sex from the perspective of the female partner," and she goes on to argue that the novel demonstrates Diana's access to power (120, 122). Drawing on Jan Cohn's Marxist-feminist thesis in *Romance and the Erotics of Property* (1988), Raub argues that Diana achieves wealth, status, and power over the sheik's tribesmen via her relationship with Ahmed, while the sheik's exercise of power over Diana is overturned by the novel's end: "Almost against his will, the hero is himself captured by the heroine; he acknowledges his love for her. The heroine has been able to 'remake male sexuality, to subordinate it . . . to love'" (126).

Such an argument is not without its problems. As Karen Chow comments, although the sheik repents of his earlier autocratic treatment of Diana, he is equally dictatorial and disregarding of her wishes when he decides to return her to England in order to make amends. Her attempts to seduce him fail, and it is only when she takes the drastic step of trying to shoot herself that he relents and gives way to her wish to stay with him. Diana may be empowered by forcing Ahmed to love her tenderly, against his will and prejudices, but his seeming transformation is limited. As he himself admits, and as his actions and Diana's occasional fear of him in *The Sons of the Sheik* demonstrate, he cannot change what he is; indeed, he warns her that "you will have a devil for a husband" (296). For Chow, however, the novel fulfills its function of empowering female consumers if not Diana herself. Chow argues that "ultimately, it is not Diana the character but the woman reader, writer, and filmgoer in the material world who is liberated by reading these steamy passages and creating a sex symbol in the figure of Rudolph Valentino" (73).

Although these scholars recognize the imperialistic background to *The Sheik* and mention Hull's seemingly radical breaching of racial boundaries in the sheik's rape of Diana and her love for an Arab, little is made of these aspects of the novel beyond passing comments. As Melman reads it, the revelation of Ahmed's "real" identity as a European, followed by Diana's insistence that she cannot think of him as other than an Arab, are "gratuitous" since they occur so late in the novel (1988: 102). The works of Susan Blake (2003) and Elizabeth Gargano (2006), however, focus more attention on the racial and imperial themes of the novel through postcolonial readings of the plot. Gargano argues that "*The Sheik* enacts an apparently transgressive erotic daydream, which first questions and then ultimately reaffirms the Englishman's capacity for domination" (175). For her, the novel explores the crisis of masculinity that beset British culture in the wake of the First World War. Significantly, none of the European or American men are able to woo Diana successfully because they "embody a demoralized post-war passivity" in the face of the masculinized modern woman (176). The hypermasculine, violent, primitive, sexually potent sheik succeeds where "civilized" but emasculated modern Western men have failed. But the sheik is, of course, a European, and Gargano compares his disguise with that of the famous "white sheik" of the war years and after: Colonel T. E. Lawrence, or "Lawrence of Arabia." Both Englishmen are presented as "'better' Arabs than the Arabs," and this serves to underline the fact that "an Englishman, raised under the same conditions of unimpeded freedom, absolute power over his subordinates, and constant physical activity, is still superior," thus reaffirming Britain's imperial mission and providing a suggested cure to enervated postwar British masculinity (Gargano 182).

Where Gargano argues that *The Sheik* is indeed an example of Orientalist colonial discourse perpetuating racial stereotypes, Susan Blake allows for more heteroglossic and contrapuntal interpretations. Blake's reading of *The Sheik* against contemporary issues of race and divorce led her to conclude that the novel presents two competing stories about imperialism, gender, race, and miscegenation—told respectively by Raoul de Saint Hubert (the French novelist who is the sheik's best friend) and Diana. How readers interpret these issues at the novel's end ultimately depends on whose voice they choose to listen to (Blake 2003: 75). For Blake, the central puzzle to be solved is how,

> in a culture that divided humanity into biologically fixed and hierarchically ranged races, *The Sheik* creates a character who "is" both Arab and English. In a culture terrified of miscegenation, it permits an English lady not only to fall in love with a man she believes to be Arab, but to continue to think of him as Arab after his "real" identity is revealed and to settle into implied marriage with him in an Arab environment. As a popular novel, *The Sheik* necessarily supports the prevailing ideology of its time, but the nonconforming facts raise the question of what else it is doing. (70)

Blake contends that in Saint Hubert's story—a story by no means without its own internal contradictions—race is understood as biological. Saint Hubert tells the tale of the sheik's European parentage, which permits Diana to remain with and love him without the taint of miscegenation. This story thus supports conventional ideas about class, gender, imperialism, and race, because at its close an aristocratic British couple, both performing traditional gender roles, rules over a tribe of Arab "natives." In Diana's story, however, the sheik remains an Arab and she loves him for being an Arab. Blake suggests that Diana's understanding of race is cultural rather than biological, which is why she is able to continue regarding Ahmed as Arab (75–78). In fact, Diana *needs* Ahmed to be Arab rather than English because the English are associated with violence twice in *The Sheik*: first with the sheik's father, the Earl of Glencaryll, whose abusiveness led his wife to flee their marriage; and then with the sheik himself, who wreaks vengeance on the English because of his father's domestic violence. Diana's story thus subverts two interconnected and strongly held imperial and patriarchal tenets about race, gender, and sexuality at that time: namely, that "sexual threat comes from the Other," and that "protection [comes] from the English," particularly within the shelter of the family and the domestic sphere (79). The novel, Blake argues, is "double-voiced" in every way, hinging on the "race" and subsequent identity of the sheik.

Raoul's identification of the Sheik yields to the pressure of imperialist discourse to identify any Other as inferior . . . [but] Diana's insistence that the man she loves is "Arab"—Other and equal, if not superior—resists that pressure and thus functions as a counter discourse. (78)

However, I would argue that Orientalist discourse and the very text of *The Sheik* pose limits to the effectiveness of this counter discourse. Ahmed's being Arab will not save Diana from domestic violence, for the novel confirms in one incident after another that Arabs are a brutal, cruel people who show a "callous indifference to suffering" (Hull 1921: 137). For instance, when Ahmed breaks in a horse with extreme brutality, "his fellow-savages acclaimed him for his cruelty" (103), and after Diana is captured by the villain Ibraheim Omair, she sees him strangle and stab one of his Arab concubines who has a "sullen face and vindictive eyes" (212), and who is jealous of Diana. Throughout the novel, Hull makes repeated references to "ruthless Arab cruelty" and the "primitive ways and savagery" of "wild tribesmen." Arab methods of punishment are ruthless, and "the position of a woman in the desert was a very precarious one" (112). Arabs had an "Oriental disregard of the woman subjugated," and to them "the feelings of a woman were non-existent." (92)

Nevertheless, this body of insightful scholarship illuminates *The Sheik* in many ways and explains its popularity as well as its widespread appeal. It is particularly important to recognize that readers—both then and now—do not simply respond to a straightforward, univocal, monolithic story whose meaning is predetermined and closed off to alternative interpretations. Different or changing ideas about acceptable gender behavior, sexual desire, fantasies and fears about race and miscegenation, and varying attitudes toward imperialism, can all be accommodated within this text—albeit some more easily than others. Thus far, however, scholarship has focused principally on the reception and cultural impact of *The Sheik* in the 1920s. Little consideration has been given to the direct circumstances out of which the novel arose. Moreover, studies of the novel and film have conflated British and American attitudes toward *The Sheik* and toward imperialism, race, and miscegenation.

In this chapter and the next, I will explore more carefully the specific imperial, national, and racial histories of Britain and the United States in the first quarter of the twentieth century, and then compare the British novels with the American films in order to tease out variations in plots and characters that create different meanings for the audience.

E. M. HULL'S *THE SHEIK* AND THE FIRST WORLD WAR

Edith Maude Henderson was born in 1880, the daughter of a New York ship owner and his Canadian wife. As a child she traveled widely with her parents, even visiting Algeria—the setting of her sheik novels. In 1899, she married Percy Winstanley Hull in London and the couple moved to Derbyshire in the early 1900s, where Percy became an agricultural-ist. After the publication of *The Sheik*, the press would run descriptions of Hull as "the shy wife of a Derbyshire pig farmer," because the image seemed so incongruous with the shocking sex and exotic setting of the novel. Percy did indeed breed prize-winning pigs, in addition to pursuing various agricultural projects, but he had begun his professional life as a civil engineer. During the First World War, he served in the armed forces. In a rare interview with *Table Talk* magazine (March 2, 1922), Hull com-mented that it was her husband's absence during the war that prompted her to begin her literary career. She began writing *The Sheik* "not with any idea of it being published, but rather as a means of distraction at a time when I felt very much alone" (Hull papers). The particular circumstances of the novel's composition, which likely occurred in the later years of the war, since it was published in London in 1919, are significant in shedding light on certain of its features: namely, its focus on sex, violence, and the Middle East.

The Sheik carries on a literary tradition of abduction and rape motifs that can be traced from Samuel Richardson's *Clarissa* to Gothic novels and Victorian melodramas. The Indian Rebellion of 1857 had also given rise to a spate of rape novels within the British colonial context, as Jenny Sharpe and Nancy Paxton have shown. Sharpe argues, however, that "rape is not a consistent and stable signifier" in either British colonial or metropolitan discourse, "but one that surfaces at strategic moments" of cultural or political tensions (3). In the case of Anglo-Indian writing, Paxton notes, the rise and circulation of "rape scripts" after 1857 served to consolidate British justifications for increasing imperial control in the colonies—especially India—as well as to attempt a remasculinization of British domestic politics at a time of increasing female independence (112). Novels featuring violence against women—especially middle- or upper-class women—were few and far between in the late nineteenth and early twentieth century. The new woman novels and other sensationalist prewar "sex novels," such as Elinor Glyn's *Three Weeks* (1907), were more con-cerned with establishing women's sexual desires and sexual identities, or debating the merits of extramarital sex ennobled by love—love being "the one motive which makes a union moral in ethics" (3), as Glyn explains in the introduction to the American version of her novel. Glyn's Slavic Lady in *Three Weeks* certainly articulates the idea of the sadomasochistic sexual love found in *The Sheik*, telling her young lover Paul Verdayne:

> A man can always keep a woman loving him if he kiss her enough, and make her feel that there is no use struggling because he is too strong to resist. A woman will stand almost anything from a passionate lover. He may beat her and pain her soft flesh; he may shut her up and deprive her of all other friends—while the motive is raging love and interest in herself on his part, it only makes her love him the more . . . . (64)

However, the hero in *Three Weeks* does not actually brutalize the Lady, for she willingly surrenders herself to him. In fact, what the Lady loves about Paul is his "straight and true" manhood, which makes him chivalrous toward her. Rather than debase himself and the Lady with sadomasochistic passion, Paul is inspired by their love toward "vast aims and noble desires for future greatness" (3).

If, as Sharpe contends, rape stories materialize during times of social tension, then what trauma was *The Sheik* written in response to? It was during the First World War that sex, violence, and rape came to the forefront of British culture and consciousness in a most dramatic way. A number of wartime developments were responsible for this: the onset of "khaki fever" among young women at the start of the war; tales of German atrocities in occupied Belgium and France that were used by the British government for propaganda purposes; and the return of war-traumatized veterans, which briefly resulted in an increase in public and domestic violence.

As Angela Woollacott shows, the outbreak of war in Britain was accompanied by an "epidemic of khaki fever" whereby, according to the press, adolescent girls and young working women flocked to military camps, sexually propositioning and harassing soldiers in towns and cities (325). Khaki fever problematized overt displays of sexuality by women in public. In the nineteenth century, the open display of sexual desire or sexual behavior was associated with prostitutes. When the "amateurs" or "free-lance girls" succumbed to khaki fever in 1914, they were perceived in their pursuit of soldiers to display a prostitute's sexual aggression and shamelessness. Even more ignominious than prostitutes, however, the "amateurs" were not motivated by a need to make a living. They also displayed an independence of mind and spirit that was much deplored. As such, they "threatened a subversion of the gender as well as the moral order" (326). In response to this, the Women Patrols Committee and the Women Police Service were established to control gendered and sexual behavior in public spaces. Middle-class women patrolling the streets took it upon themselves to censure and separate "couples thought to be embracing too closely," by "following those they suspected might be about to embark on unsavory courses of behavior, and warning youngsters of the dangers of overly casual behavior" (Levine 45). Khaki fever died down by mid-1915, when women were co-opted into war work and other forms of patriotic contribution to the war effort, but concern over women's sexual behavior and the spread of venereal diseases meant that middle-class women continued to police working women's expressions of sexuality in public places during the war (Woollacott 331).

If khaki fever brought to public consciousness an uneasy awareness of women's dangerous sexual desires and autonomy, then tales of German atrocities trickling back from the continent introduced rape and sexual violence into public discourse. The German invasion of neutral Belgium on August 4, 1918, had been Britain's ostensible *casus belli* to declare war on the Central Powers. To make the case for war to the British public, the government invoked complex legal arguments about obligations incurred by Britain under the 1839 Treaty of London. Such arguments were soon replaced by simpler, sensationalist accounts of German atrocities — particularly the rape, abuse, and torture of women and children — in newspapers, war pamphlets, and posters. The "innocent, virtuous" raped Belgian woman came to symbolize the violated borders of Belgium in many propaganda posters; "Belgium became a frail and ravished *jeune fille*, weeping and broken on the floor as the *uhlan*, the helmeted German cavalryman, leaves the bedroom" (Harris 180).

Other artists depicted a female Belgium stripped, bound, and raped. These images, which were widely circulated and believed, acquired more force as stories of rape and violence were amassed in Lord Bryce's official *Report of the Committee on Alleged German Outrages* (Gullace 714, Ward 29). By 1916, the British were compiling documents about the abduction of women and children for forced labor — including sexual labor — in *The Deportation of Women and Girls from Lille*. The bishop of Lille appealed emotively to a British and American audience, telling them that "promiscuity . . . inevitably accompanies removals *en masse*, involving mixture of the sexes, or, at all events, of persons of very unequal standing. Young girls of irreproachable life . . . have been carried off" (Gullace 742).

The "rape of Belgium" was also used as propaganda to persuade the

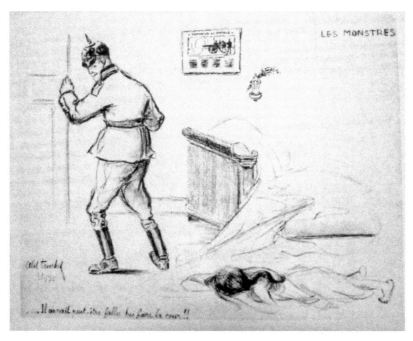

FIGURE 3.1. A. Truchel, Les Monstres, *"He might at least have courted her. . ." poster*

United States to enter the war. When the United States joined in 1917, at least two U.S. war posters (figures 3.2 and 3.3) referred to the raped Belgian woman, demonstrating just how widely this image had spread in popular culture. In all these accounts, violence toward women and children was depicted as typifying the behavior of the German other. The behavior of English soldiers, by contrast, was supposedly characterized by "honour, decency, rightness, and fair play" (Harris 29). This notion of honorable English or British masculinity and the chivalric treatment of women and children became more problematic in the later years of the war and its aftermath because of increases in domestic violence in all belligerent nations (Thébaud 68).

The Great War had a traumatic effect on a whole generation of young men. Literature on the war and demobilized soldiers has usually portrayed these men as either shattered, shell-shocked neurasthenics, or angry young men nursing bitter grudges against those who sent them to war (Adams 1990, Fussell 1975). Demobilization was always going to be a difficult experience for men: if soldiers were discharged during the war, it was probably because of physical or psychological injuries; and after returning home from the war, all men had to face the problems of "find-

FIGURE 3.2. *American First World War Liberty Bonds poster*

FIGURE 3.3. *American First World War recruitment poster*

ing a job, resuming family life," and "curbing aggression" that they had been encouraged to develop and display during the war (Nye 430). The effects of the war on men's lives were visible not only through the large number of amputees in public spaces, but also in the behavior of former soldiers. Men suffering from shell shock walked with a "shivering, shuddering, fainting, halting, 'mincing gait'" that distressed those who witnessed it (Leed 99). Such behavior undermined the "manliness" of shell-shocked victims because of the prevailing belief in late nineteenth- and early twentieth-century Europe that a "true man" was in control of his passions and his body (Mosse 101). If the "shivering" neurasthenic veteran symbolized the trauma of war, so, too, did the embittered and violent veteran—often said to be of working-class origins—who could not control his passions.

As soon as the guns fell silent in November 1918, members of the ruling class and the British press began to express alarm about "brutalized" working-class soldiers turning to violence and theft. According to *The Times* in May 1919, the commissioner of the Metropolitan Police feared that a battle-hardened husband might now murder his wife rather than, as before the war, administer "just a clip under the ear"' (Emsley 175). British war correspondent Philip Gibbs

> believed that a significant minority of front-line soldiers had returned seriously altered by their experiences: They were subject to queer moods, queer tempers, fits of profound depression with a restless desire for pleasure. Many of them were easily moved to passion when they lost control of themselves. Many were bitter in their speech, violent in opinion, frightening. They had gone through "an intensive culture of brutality." Equally, and this he implied had prompted sexual assaults, "sexually they were starved. For months they had lived out of the sight and presence of women." (Emsley 175)

Emsley argues that by and large, moral panics about the return of a whole generation of psychologically scarred, brutalized men were unfounded, and that the statistics for indictable assaults show no significant increase in the postwar years. It is probably true that the majority of soldiers returned to the private life of "Little Englanders" and eschewed imperial masculinity and politics for the quiet pleasures of tending the garden, smoking their pipes, and doing crossword puzzles (Light 1991). There is currently insufficient research into the First World War and domestic violence in Britain to warrant any detailed or conclusive statements about a surge in wife and child abuse, and it is certainly worth noting that nations on the losing side experienced the greatest political, social, and domestic violence (Nye 431). However, Susan Kingsley Kent's (1993) work on violence against British women during the war and Elizabeth Nelson's (2007) work on the war and domestic violence in Australia both suggest a correlation between war trauma and increased rates of wife abuse. Additionally, Simona Sharoni's (1995) study of gender and the Israeli-Palestinian conflict likewise documents an increase in male violence against women and children during military conflicts that legitimize the brutalization of society. The fact that divorce rates in Britain rose after the war suggests increases in adultery as well as "cruelty," or wife abuse, because while men could petition for divorce solely on the grounds of adultery, until 1923, women had to prove abuse in addition to adultery (Blake 2003: 81). An initial rise in male domestic violence would not be unexpected because returned soldiers felt "resentment toward those who had stayed behind, including their wives, and the traditional patriarchal obligation to control one's wife was a particularly exigent aspect of militarized masculinity" (Nye 430).

The social and sexual context of wartime and postwar Britain is important to *The Sheik* in obvious ways. It explains why female sexuality in this novel is so fraught with confusion and contradiction, and why passion is intermeshed with violence. In the new woman novels of the 1890s and 1900s, the heroines exploring their sexual identities are middle class. In *The Sheik*, to be aware of and express her passionate, sexual nature at the start of the novel would declass the aristocratic Lady Diana Mayo immediately, since wartime anxieties about female sexual behavior mainly concerned working- and lower-middle-class women. Middle- and upper-middle-class women were the ones who patrolled and tried to regulate young women's sexual behavior, just as in the novel, Lady Conway, like the imperial memsahib abroad, tries to uphold the rules that govern acceptable British behavior. Diana's rape allows her to experience sex while absolving her from agency, thus maintaining her status as a virtuous heroine. Not only does Diana endure rape, but she comes to enjoy sex and to participate in it, and thereby transforms intercourse with her rapist into the suggestion of a modern, companionate relationship. As her months of captivity progress, despite the sheik's occasional reversion to cruelty, she comes to treasure the late nights when Ahmed "told her all the incidents of the day's visit to one of the other camps, and from his men and his horses drifted almost insensibly into details connected with his own plans for the future, which were really the intimate confidences of a husband to a wife who is also a comrade" (Hull 1921: 283). The confused attempt to reconcile romantic, companionate love with sexual passion and violence within the home must have resonated with readers whose male family members had returned from the frontlines traumatized and, unable to cope with the transition back to domesticity, sometimes prone to violence.

That Hull should have conceived of abduction and rape as a central plot device in the novel is therefore comprehensible, since during *The Sheik*'s conception, rape stories were in wide circulation in British society. The problem, of course, was that rape was associated with German wartime atrocities and there was no way that rape in a European context could possibly be anything but horrifying. Not until American troops began arriving at the Western Front in huge numbers after April 1918 did the tide of the war begin to shift decisively in favor of the Allies. In fact, it is possible that when Hull was writing the novel, the outcome of the war was still uncertain, with Germany favored to win after the collapse of the Eastern Front following the Bolshevik Revolution of November 1917. Hull sidestepped these problems to a large extent because she formulated her plot within the subgenre of the desert romance novel, which solved many of the dilemmas created by the war.

During the First World War, the Middle East was the only arena where fighting in any way resembled glamorized ideas of noble heroes testing themselves on the field of blood. The static war on the Western Front diminished soldiers and often left men in the "feminized" position of cowering fearfully in the trenches, helpless in the face of heavy bombardment before being mowed down by an enemy they could not see. By contrast, the war in the Middle East—particularly the Sinai and Palestine Campaign and the Great Arab Revolt—was active and mobile, featuring cavalry charges that conjured pre-modern images of chivalric warfare. In particular, the Great Arab Revolt, initiated by Sharif Hussein bin Ali in June 1916, brought Lieutenant Colonel T. E. Lawrence to prominence as a result of the sensationalist reportage of the American journalist Lowell Thomas in 1918. Thomas's dramatic war film *With Allenby in Palestine and Lawrence in Arabia* debuted in London in 1919 and featured Lawrence himself as the "white sheik" who, together with Sharif Hussein's sons Faisal and Abdullah, leads the Arab uprising against the Ottoman Empire (Long 25). Given the timing, it is unlikely that Hull saw this film before she wrote her novel. However, similar claims have been made about the leadership qualities of Ahmed Ben Hassan and T. E. Lawrence: both of them are Englishmen who masquerade as Arab sheiks, and who alone are capable of uniting and leading the unruly tribes of the desert.

GENDER, WHITENESS, AND IMPERIALISM IN THE MIDDLE EAST

It was not just the Middle East that invoked the plethora of ideas about the Orient that had been circulating in Britain since the eighteenth century. In Britain, the North African desert also conjured ideas about noble Bedouins as "true" Arabs (in contrast to their much-derided town counterparts), as well as evocations of European women who had found in the desert a space to be free from European conventions limiting sexual and social behavior (Tidrick 1989). In the scholarship on women's travel writing, much attention has been paid to the constraints of nineteenth-century femininity upon female travelers and their behavior abroad (Foster 3–25, Mills 1991). Despite these well-documented constraints, however, European women traveling abroad were certainly aware of the possibility of sexual liaisons with Oriental men. A few women (Lady Jane Digby, Lady

Hester Stanhope, Isabella Eberhardt, Emily Keene, and Margaret Foun-
taine, for example) even acted upon their sexual desires and entered into
long-term relationships with non-Western men. These relationships were
not technically illegal. At no time did the British government actually pass
legislation forbidding interracial unions within the United Kingdom or its
colonies, unlike the postbellum United States, where miscegenation was
prohibited in various states and only gradually repealed state-by-state,
until the U.S. Supreme Court ruled such laws unconstitutional in *Loving v.
Virginia* in 1967. Perhaps it was because of the porousness of racial boundaries in Britain that British popular literature at the turn of the twentieth
century became obsessed with interracial sex, as we have seen in the last
chapter. Behind the idea that Oriental men possessed a mysterious and
fatal attraction for British women lurked anxieties about the outcome of
such unions: racially mixed offspring who confounded an imperial order
based on the white imperial race ruling nonwhite "natives." Because
there were no legislative barriers against interracial unions between white
women and nonwhite men (unions between white men and nonwhite
concubines were tacitly accepted), the full weight of social opprobrium
was brought down upon the practice in the genres of popular culture. In
The Sheik, if Diana will not or cannot redeem herself and embrace her
traditional literary fate—death—resulting from rape, let alone interracial
rape, then Hull the author must save her through the timely revelation of
the Sheik's English and Spanish parentage (albeit with an uneasy hint of
Moorish blood in his heritage), thus shoring up the boundaries of white
racial identity to appease her readers and potential critics.

From the start of *The Sheik*, readers are reminded that this is both
an Oriental and an imperial tale. Diana represents the white race and
British imperial prestige; her gendered behavior reflects the rival merits
of the British and French *mission civilisatrice* that accompanied and justified colonial expansion in the late nineteenth and twentieth centuries.
Intermittently throughout the novel, then, British and French culture
and colonial successes are subtly compared. French colonial control over
Algeria is shown to be sadly wanting when Diana's desert party is ambushed by Arab raiders. Moments before she realizes the seriousness of
her situation, just before she is swept off her saddle and abducted by the
sheik, "Diana's first feeling was one of contempt for an administration
that made possible such an attempt so near civilization" (48). It is precisely the feebleness of such an administration that permits the fantastical
ending: the British aristocratic couple exerting feudal rule over warrior-
like Bedouin tribes in French colonial Algeria. In this novel, it seems that

the French are mainly lauded for their loyalty to the British protagonists: the sheik's faithful valet, Gaston, is French, as is his best friend, Raoul de Saint Hubert, who helps the couple realize their love for each other (a fitting role for the Frenchman in the British imagination!), and who chivalrously sacrifices his own love for Diana in order to facilitate her relationship with the English Ahmed Ben Hassan.

Because Diana is cast as a victim throughout much of *The Sheik*, there is limited opportunity for her to undertake any of the usual roles of imperial women in the colonies: the memsahib organizing expatriate domestic life and policing the boundaries of sex and race (Stoler 2002); the maternal missionary or social reformer shouldering what Antoinette Burton (1994) calls the "white woman's burden," rescuing helpless, downtrodden native women from their Oriental plight; or the intrepid female traveler traipsing insouciantly into villages where no white woman has ever been, the amused cynosure of all eyes and the compassionate dispenser of medication and cheap trinkets (Teo 1998). Nevertheless, Diana's imperial identity is established through the fact that as a white British woman, she has traveled widely throughout the world and even gone tiger hunting in India. Imperial prestige shadowed by the threat of imperial violence enables her to embark on a journey into the desert by herself, dressed in "manly" riding clothes, without any regard for local custom or sensibilities. Diana's authoritative imperial identity is further emphasized through her intimidating use of her "imperial eye" to subjugate natives—their eyes waver and fall beneath her haughty gaze (36, 212), whether in India or in the North African desert. In fact, Hull is at pains to tell us that the only "native" whose gaze does not fall beneath hers is the Sheik, who is of course English. When Diana first stands before Sheik Ahmed Ben Hassan—a figure formed in the image of the Gothic villain, with "the handsomest and cruellest face that she had ever seen"—his "fierce burning eyes . . . swept her until she felt that the boyish clothes that covered her slender limbs were stripped from her, leaving the beautiful white body bare under his passionate stare" (56–57). Since she (and the reader) believes him to be Arab at this point, a clichéd trope of colonial relations is inverted: the all-seeing, all-commanding gaze of the imperial eye gives way to the predatory, penetrating gaze of the supposed native, whose hungry stare consumes the imperialist's white body, here transformed into a sign of her gendered vulnerability.

There are repeated references to Diana's whiteness throughout the novel: the sheik's lascivious glances at her "beautiful white body" (Hull 57), for instance, or the villain Ibraheim Omair's awareness of the "white woman who was Ahmed Ben Hassan's latest toy" (196). As we have seen in Chapter 1, whiteness in Western literature has long been associated with Europeanness, sexual purity, innocence, salvation, and virginity. Diana certainly represents all of these things when we first meet her, particularly as the Amazonian virgin/virago who flaunts her independence and has little use for men. Although she quickly loses her sexual purity and innocence, she retains the other qualities associated with whiteness: she is always European, with all that this implies in the age of empire, and she is the Sheik's racial and moral salvation. Diana initially takes her white privilege for granted; she cares little about upholding the prestige of her class and race and scornfully flouts the gender restrictions imposed upon other white women in the colonies. However, her experiences in the novel teach her solidarity with other white races. Trapped in an ambush by the bandit sheik Omair later in the novel, with only the French valet Gaston at her side, Diana becomes aware that whiteness takes precedence over stratifications of class. At the moment when she and Gaston face possible death together, "all inequality of rank had been swept away . . . they had been only a white man and a white woman together in their extremity" (211). While Diana's aristocratic British imperial identity is important, therefore, it can also be subsumed within a broader white European identity, within the context of colonization and resistance against nonwhite natives.

If Diana's whiteness establishes her sexual desirability to white and nonwhite men alike, it also confirms the significance of her rape, since the only rape that mattered in Western imperial culture was the rape of a white woman; the far more common historical scenario of a nonwhite woman's rape by a white man received little comment. If rape has degraded her, it is Diana's interaction with social and racial inferiors within the colonial context that restores her sense of identity; it is her "childish" Bedouin maid Zilah who "in some indefinable way gave back to Diana the self-control that had slipped from her" (Hull 62); it is the French valet Gaston who serves her as devotedly as he serves the sheik who returns to her a sense of her due as an aristocratic Englishwoman (277). Yet any such sense of recovered status fluctuates. Over a month of repeated rapes, she comes to realize that "her life was in [the sheik's] hands, that he could break her with his lean brown fingers like a toy is broken . . . She was utterly in his power and at his mercy—the mercy of an Arab who was merciless" (78).

As discussed in the previous chapter, *The Sheik* challenged the prewar gender and racial order by depicting Diana's growing desire for an apparently Arab hero, thus invoking the threat of hybridity—the great taboo of the age of empire. Prewar novels set in the Orient required their white female characters to police their own sexual desires and uphold the integrity of the white race. However, *The Sheik* broke with this convention to depict "proud Diana Mayo who had the history of her race at her fingers' ends" (275) refusing her duty and choosing instead to abase herself before her love and sexual desire for the Arab man she believes the sheik to be. Fortunately for her, then, the sheik is actually European, a British peer of the realm. This racial legerdemain was an important plot maneuver, for it excused Diana's inexplicable attraction to the supposed native, dissipated the horrible specter of miscegenation, and provided the means of Ahmed's repentance and redemption and, consequently, the novel's happy ending. Moreover, it meant that Diana would remain British in nationality, for the 1914 British Nationality and Status of Aliens Act stated that "the wife of an alien shall be deemed to be an alien." Not until 1948 could women from the United Kingdom retain their own nationality regardless of whom they married (Baldwin 522).

Hull returned to the themes of miscegenation, imperialism, love, and rape in the sequel, *The Sons of the Sheik* (1925); but in this novel, the strictures against miscegenation are more pronounced, uttered by the sheik himself when he discovers that his son Ahmed has raped a Moroccan woman (who, of course, turns out to be the daughter of a French aristocratic family). The truly radical moment in *The Sons of the Sheik* occurs at the end of the novel, after the heroine (by that stage pregnant with young Ahmed's child) is abducted and savagely raped by the German villain—a spy collecting information and stirring up the "natives" against the French in anticipation of the forthcoming war. In the final pages, Ahmed decides that the heroine's rape does not matter to him because his love for her is worth more than the fact that she has been violated by another man. This must surely be one of the first of such episodes for a mainstream novel, whereby the rape of the heroine by a man other than the hero is not punished by her death, and which still concludes in the romantic union of the heroine and hero. Significantly, at the end of *The Sons of the Sheik*, Hull finally presents readers with the rapist Hun of British wartime propaganda, whose brutality makes young Ahmed's pale by comparison. Yasmin is, in fact, depicted in the typical posture of the raped Belgian woman: "crouched half naked on the ground, bearing all the marks of a desperate struggle, with her unbound hair streaming over her bare shoulders, she lay moaning and writhing in agony, her face hidden against the crumbling wall" (358).

While Hull flirted with the possibility of interracial sex between a white woman and an Oriental man in *The Sheik*, she denounced miscegenation in *The Sons of the Sheik* and her subsequent novels. What had happened in the interim? If Arabs and other colonized peoples were "noble savage" allies during the war, their cause personified and glamorized by T. E. Lawrence, things changed rapidly after the ceasefire. In 1919, the year Hull's novel was published in Britain, the Amritsar massacre, in which nearly four hundred anticolonial protesters in the Punjab were gunned down by the British Indian Army, exacerbated colonial anxieties about race relations in the Indian subcontinent and revived Mutiny-era narratives of Indian rape of English women (Sharpe 123). After the Paris Peace Conference, the Treaty of Sèvres, in 1920, and the Treaty of Lausanne, which replaced it in 1923, resulted in much of the Ottoman Empire in the Middle East being carved up and placed under British and French control as League of Nations mandatory states. Egypt had been a British protectorate since 1914. To Britain's growing empire in the Middle East was added Palestine, Transjordan, and Iraq. From the start, the assertion of British power in place of Ottoman suzerainty was strongly resisted in its newly acquired Middle Eastern territories. In 1920, fourteen thousand British and Indian troops stationed in Iraq put down an Arab uprising at the cost of four hundred fatalities. In Somaliland in 1920, the British bombed Muslim encampments when a Muslim leader rose up against British rule. In Iraq, where the British had installed Sherif Hussein's son Faisal as a puppet king, revolts broke out sporadically throughout the 1920s and were met by Royal Air Force bombings before the British mandate was ended in 1932. Anticolonial sentiment throughout the 1920s must have reverberated uncomfortably through the Orientalist romantic fantasies of novelists and readers, probably leading to the decline of the sheik romance novel by the 1930s, when it was replaced by the growing popularity of adventure stories about the French Foreign Legion inspired by P. C. Wren's *Beau Geste* trilogy.

Meanwhile, domestic events in Britain exposed fears about "reverse colonization" and interracial unions. A sizable "black" population (including Arabs and South Asians as well as Africans) had lived in London and other British port cities, such as Liverpool and Cardiff, for a few hundred years, but it increased during the First World War, when colonial workers and seamen were recruited to make up shortfalls in British manpower (Tabili 9). Just as women's contributions to the British war effort resulted in women being gradually enfranchised after the war, colonized men who had contributed gained a sense of entitlement as subjects who had sacrificed for the British and began to demand citizenship rights. In such an environment, interracial boundaries began to be breached. The postwar years saw incidents of black men marrying white women. As Lucy Bland argues, for white Britons this meant returned servicemen finding black men in their jobs, houses, and beds, which partially contributed to the outbreak of race riots in Cardiff, Liverpool, and London in the first half of 1919 (2005: 34). Newspapers screamed of "The Black Peril" (indeed, they had been doing so since 1917) and blamed black men for taking white men's jobs and women (2005: 35, 37). In response, the British Parliament passed the Aliens Order in 1920, restricting nonwhite immigration.

Arab men became a specific focus of concern in 1923, during the murder trial of Madame Fahmy, a thirty-two-year-old Frenchwoman who had married and murdered a wealthy Egyptian prince ten years her junior. A connection was made between the trial and the immense popularity of "sheik" romances, as the *Daily Mirror* editorialized:

> Too many of our women novelists, apparently under the spell of the East, have encouraged the belief that there is something especially romantic in such unions. They are not romantic, they are ridiculous and unseemly; and the sensational revelations of the trial . . . will not be without their use if they bring that fact home to the sentimental, unsophisticated girl. (Bland 2005: 47)

Indeed, Fahmy's defense barrister argued in his summation: "Her greatest mistake — possibly the greatest mistake any woman could make — was as a woman of the West in marrying an Oriental" (2005: 46). Although Britain had no legislation against interracial unions, public sentiment regarding miscegenation was made abundantly clear.

These events, both domestic and foreign, undoubtedly had an impact on both the production and reception of Hull's output in the 1920s. Her subsequent novels, such as *The Sons of the Sheik* (1925) and *Captive of the Sahara* (1931), like those of fellow desert romance novelist Kathlyn Rhodes, insisted on the impossibility and outright danger of interracial unions between Europeans and Orientals. Even prolonged intercourse of any sort was detrimental to one or the other — usually to the Oriental. The most dangerous figure in these later stories was the hybrid male: the half white or culturally white Arab or Egyptian. Occupying the status of both hero and eventual villain, the sheik who affected whiteness would inevitably reveal his dark desires and his degenerate Oriental self. According to novelists such as Hull and Rhodes, despite the sheik's desire for racial and

cultural whiteness, he was helpless to control the baser instincts resulting
from his biological race. Relinquishing his desire for the white woman, or
even sacrificing his life for her, ultimately constituted his one heroic act.
In Hull's *Captive of the Sahara*, the Bedouin sheik ends up dying to protect the English heroine, whom he fell in love with and imprisoned in his
desert stronghold, the City of Stones. His self-sacrifice, and the fact that
he—an actual Arab, unlike Sheik Ahmed Ben Hassan—never forces himself upon her, are his only virtues in a tragic tale of unrequited love and
misguided anticolonial ambition. The native's love for the white woman
threatens her reputation and destroys him. Whatever timorous gestures
The Sheik had made toward breaching the boundaries of the white imperial race through the body of the white woman, the vast majority of
English novels in this subgenre during the 1920s and 1930s reverted to the
argument that it is the white woman's responsibility to uphold this boundary and to police ruthlessly her own dark desires for the sake of all "races."
Interestingly enough, none of these storylines was ever as popular as the
suggestion of the taboo interracial union presented in *The Sheik*.

The specific historical circumstances of E. M. Hull's novels thus
shaped the contours of her plots and changed the social taboos she was
willing to test or break. Although in *The Sheik* she was willing to challenge
social attitudes toward women's sexual desire and the significance of rape
for women, miscegenation was not a boundary she was ready to breach.
However, when *The Sheik* was translated into an American film, the per-
meability of white boundaries—gendered, corporeal, social, and political—was once again challenged, as was the meaning of whiteness itself.

FOUR

The Spectacular East: Romantic Orientalism in America

Here is romance. Red-hot. . . . The best-selling story by E. M. Hull, scoffed at by the higher-browed critics, but read and re-read by two-thirds of the women in this country, has been made into a very exciting, very old-fashioned photoplay.

"THE SHEIK," *PHOTOPLAY*, JANUARY 1922

When *The Sheik* was published in the United States in 1921, it went through fifty printings in that year alone (Leider 153). It featured in the American best-seller list for two years, ranking as the sixth best-selling novel in 1921 before achieving second place in 1922 (Raub 119). *The Sheik* was evidently as successful in the United States as in Britain, but did American audiences respond to and understand it in the same way as British audiences? Did they merely draw from European traditions of Orientalism to make sense of the novel and the film, or were there specific American conditions that affected the American experience of sheik fever? In this chapter, I look at how American Orientalism shaped the meaning and reception of *The Sheik* in the 1920s and subsequently influenced Hollywood films rehashing similar themes in the twentieth century. I begin by examining American colonial and early republican relations with the Middle East, and the Barbary captivity literature the United States produced as a result of its interaction with North Africa. This was the start of a native Orientalist tradition in the United States, supplemented by travel narratives in the nineteenth century. Eyewitness accounts of the Middle East, however, were refracted through the prism of the popular *The Thousand and One Nights* or *Arabian Nights' Entertainments* tales, and the Orientalist fantasies from the

Nights were brought to life for domestic audiences in the dizzying spectacles of the 1893 Chicago World's Fair, circuses, traveling exhibits, and Wild West shows staged by Buffalo Bill Cody and others in the late nineteenth century. It was this spectacular Orient that found its way to Hollywood by the early twentieth century, creating a ready and receptive audience for *The Sheik*.

The response of Americans to *The Sheik* was no doubt largely similar to that of the British. However, the translation of Hull's novel into a Hollywood silent film entailed significant differences that are important, especially since the film arguably eclipsed the novel in influence and made the story famous worldwide, not just in English-speaking countries. Beyond plot changes and technological considerations, the differences between the novel and the film arise from the particular historical experiences of gender, race, and ethnicity in the United States. Where these issues in Britain were linked to the colonial context, in the United States they were associated with anxieties about immigration, assimilation, and citizenship. Furthermore, the two countries had different traditions of popular Orientalist discourse: in Britain, Orientalism was anchored in a principally "realist" mode of representing the geopolitical situations of existing colonies; in the United States, Orientalism arose from fairground and merchandising fantasies of "Arabian Nights." I will conclude this chapter with a survey of the influence of *The Sheik* over Hollywood recreations of sheik and harem movies, particularly in the 1980s.

AMERICAN ORIENTALISM FROM BARBARY CORSAIRS TO WORLD'S FAIRS

American engagement with the Middle East began in the seventeenth century, as traders brought timber, tobacco, and sugar to the Mediterranean Basin to exchange for Oriental luxury goods and foodstuffs such as capers, raisins, and figs (Oren 18). Like Europeans engaged in mercantile trade around this region, colonial Americans faced the problem of attacks from North African corsairs—pirates operating privately, but sanctioned by their own governments. These privateers were based in the empire of Morocco, or the Ottoman-dependent regencies of Tripoli, Tunis, and Algiers—an area of the Middle East labeled "al-Maghrib" by Arabs, meaning "the West," but that Europeans called the "Barbary Coast." In 1625, the first colonial American merchant ship was captured by North African corsairs, while in 1678, "Algiers seized another Massachusetts ship and thirteen vessels from Virginia" (Oren 19). British trading ships were more frequently the targets of attack and capture, as discussed in Chapter 1; yet these ships often carried American personnel or passengers who were also subject to imprisonment and slavery while they awaited ransom. Eventually, the British government entered a truce with North African corsairs by paying "tribute" money (i.e., bribes to leave British ships alone) to the Barbary regencies.

After the outbreak of war against Britain in 1775, American ships lost British naval protection and were once again prey to North African piracy. Americans turned to the French for help since they had signed a Treaty of Amity and Commerce with France in 1778, but no assistance was forthcoming because "French leaders were keen to promote their own Mediterranean trade and feared the impact of American competition on the southern ports of Toulon, Nice, and Marseille" (Oren 21). The United States had barely won the War of Independence and gained its status as a new republic, when it was humiliated by the capture of three ships in 1784 — "merely the first of many instances of hijacking and hostage-taking that America later faced in the region" (Oren 23). It was in response to such practices that, in 1794, George Washington signed a bill financing the creation of the U.S. Navy, and the administrations of presidents Jefferson and Madison finally took respective action against North African piracy in the Barbary Wars of 1801–1805 and 1815. The U.S. Navy won these wars decisively and, in 1815, under the leadership of the consul general William Shaler, Commodores William Bainbridge and Stephen Decatur forced the release of all American hostages, bringing an end to the North African powers' demand for tribute. As Michael Oren argues:

> The Barbary Wars altered European perceptions of the United States, but, more decidedly, the victory also transformed Americans' image of themselves. The war infused them with reinvigorated emotions of national pride and a galvanized sense of identity. . . . The audiences that once cringed at Susanna Rowson's jeremiad on American impotence, *Slaves in Algiers*, now thrilled to *The Siege of Tripoli*, James Ellison's paean to American valor. (75)

From the colonial period to the early days of the fledgling republic, American literary engagement with the Orient was shaped by these experiences of captivity and slavery. Much has been written about the Indian captivity narrative as the earliest form of American literature, focusing especially on Mary Rowlandson's *The Sovereignty and Goodness of God: Being a Narrative of the Captivity and Restoration of Mrs. Mary Rowlandson* (1682).[1] Yet as Paul Baepler (1999) and Mark Kamrath (2004) show, the Barbary captivity narrative was equally potent in the literary imagination of colonial Americans because of America's humiliating history of Barbary abduction. One of the earliest examples of the American Barbary captivity narrative is Thomas Atwood Digges's picaresque novel, *The Adventures of Alonso* (1775), which tells the story of how the hero, Alonso, is captured by Moroccan pirates and sold to a rich slave owner. Digges's novel is significant because it introduced the character of the homosexual and/or pedophilic Muslim male who subsequently became a stock figure in Orientalist historical romances of the late twentieth century. (For example, in Julia Fitzgerald's *Royal Slave* [1978; discussed in the next chapter], one of the English characters ends up being sold as a *garzone* for a male harem owner whose predilection is for blond European men. The same novel presents the "Kislar Agha," the Chief Black Eunuch of the Grand Seraglio, as a cruel and callous pedophile.) In *The Adventures of Alonso*, the Muslim master, Aldalid, tries to seduce Alonso and, when he fails, to rape him (Baepler 45). Alonso avoids rape by killing the slave who guards him, and he escapes with another Christian renegade slave. As with British tales of Barbary incarceration, this early American account was more concerned with the rape and penetration of the male body by powerful Muslim men than with the threat Barbary abduction presented to American women (Colley 129–130). Digges's tale set the pattern whereby Oriental practices of slavery and sexual abuse were emphasized and blamed on the influence of Islam in Oriental cultures, while the same practices victimizing African Americans in American society were ignored (Oren 155).

No doubt because of the increased vulnerability of American shipping to piracy during the revolutionary period, the 1780s and 1790s saw a spike of interest in stories about Barbary piracy, abduction, and captivity. Other American Barbary corsair novels include Peter Markoe's *The Algerine Spy in Pennsylvania* (1787) and Royall Tyler's *The Algerine Captive* (1797), and Barbary captivity narratives were occasionally used in stage plays to promote the abolitionist agenda. Among these plays were Susanna Rowson's *Slaves in Algiers* (1794), James Ellison's *The American Captive, or Siege of Tripoli* (1812), David Everett *Slaves in Barbary* (1817), and Maria Pinckney's *The Young Carolinians, or Americans in Algiers* (never produced). The Barbary corsair became such a stock figure in American popular culture by the late nineteenth century that juvenile fiction and dime novels were filled with titles such as *The Algerine, The Corsair Prince, The Boy Bedou-*

ins, *We Three (or, Wrecked on the Desert of the Sahara)*, and *Driven to the Sea; or, The Sailor's Secret, A Story of the Algerine Corsairs* (Baepler 46–50). Women, too, contributed to this genre, with the 1807 publication of the supposedly autobiographical *An affecting history of the captivity and sufferings of Mrs. Mary Velnet, who was seven years a slave in Tripoli, three of which she was confined in a dungeon, loaded with irons, and four times put to the most cruel tortures ever invented by man.* Baepler also notes that

> two other fabricated accounts, by Mary Gerard and Viletta Laranda, as well as several American plays with female captives suggest a public fascination with female captivity, perhaps derived from the Indian captivity tradition and accounts by Mary Rowlandson, Hannah Dunstan, and Mary Jameson among others. (147)

These sensationalist stories were no doubt popular for the spectacle of rape and miscegenation they promised, but they also provided forums for exploring more disturbing social and sexual currents in the new republic.

In his study of eighteenth- and early nineteenth-century American periodicals, Mark Kamrath argues that the contents of Oriental tales feature "related discourses of sentiment, colonialism, and female eroticism," whereby "erotic and, at times, sadistic images are intimately bound with sentimental discourses and a [female] desire for sexual agency and liberation" (4). Over two-thirds of Oriental captivity tales in periodicals such as *The New-York Magazine* (1790–1797), *Massachusetts Magazine* (1789–1796), *The Columbian Magazine, or, Monthly Miscellany* (1786–1792), and *The American Museum* (1787–1792), among others, were authored by Americans (Kamrath 7), thus showing a robust imaginative engagement with an originally European genre. Additionally, magazines such as the *Philadelphia Minerva* (1795–1798) also featured French-authored Oriental tales, which were translated into English and then syndicated in the English-speaking world. One such story, "The Unexpected Discovery: An Oriental Tale," was written by the Frenchman Nicolas Bricaire de la Dixmerie in 1768, then translated and published in the *Philadelphia Minerva* in 1798. The story is a familiar one: Laura, a young "French beauty," is orphaned and escapes to Venice to avoid her guardian's unwanted sexual advances. She is abducted by an "African corsair" en route and taken as a female slave to Alexandria, Egypt, where the "fair captive" is "stripped" of her possessions and auctioned off to the highest bidder, an Oriental despot whose hungry gaze over her "different endowments" enacts a metaphorical rape. The despot's desire to rape a helpless woman is paralleled by his political desire to "ravage the provinces of Greece" and experience the sadistic "pleasures which a commander enjoys after victory" (Kamrath 19). Kamrath suggests that Oriental tales like this one, which were popular with male and female readers alike, enact the "objectification of women's body parts . . . associated with early modern pornography." However, these early republican Oriental tales also express women's sexual yearnings as well as their "desire for female independence, equality, and liberation" since heroines usually overcome their tribulations and gain their freedom (21). These originally European tropes of Oriental imprisonment, sexual seduction, and potential rape thus found their way into American culture especially during times of tension between the new republic and the Barbary states. They had a long-lasting impact on American society, reemerging in the American female-authored erotic historical romance novel (discussed in the next chapter) as well as in the profusion of sheik and harem films that were regularly rehashed in Hollywood throughout the twentieth century.

Fear of Oriental power was soon supplanted by fascination with Oriental pleasures. In the wake of the American victory in the Barbary Wars, Americans began to journey to the Middle East and captivity narratives were supplemented by travel accounts. Many went for trade purposes, while some went as missionaries and educators. The American Board of Commissioners for Foreign Missions was established in 1810, and the first missionaries had ventured forth to the Middle East by the 1820s (Oren 87, 90). Secure in the knowledge that they were protected by U.S. consuls, the number of American visitors to the region climbed steadily throughout the 1830s, as missionaries were joined by scientists, pilgrims visiting Bible lands, professionals curious to see the ancient wonders of Egypt and Petra, adventurers, and tourists (Oren 152–153). From this first batch of travelers came books such as Walter Colton's *A Visit to Constantinople and Athens* (1836) and John Lloyd Stephens's *Incidents of Travel in Egypt, Arabia Petraea, and the Holy Land* (1837). After the hiatus imposed by the Civil War, American tourists resumed their travels to the Middle East, focusing on Egypt, Greater Syria, and Palestine. In Egypt, "the number of American tourists had risen from an antebellum rate of sixty per year to nearly five hundred" after the Civil War (Oren 228).

It was not just the Bible that encouraged Americans to visit the Middle East. As Susan Nance shows, the Orient was also the site of exotic fantasy and "abundant consumption" inspired by American editions of *The Thousand and One Nights* or *Arabian Nights' Entertainments*—easily the most popular and widely sold book after the Bible during the nineteenth century (15, 19). Postbellum American advertisements framed travel to the Middle East as "Oriental tales," claiming that "Authors and editors could explain a voyage down the Nile as 'Ethiopian Nights Entertainments' or a trip to the Tigris River as a visit to 'The Land of the *Arabian Nights*'" (36). The tourist souvenirs travelers sought and bought evoked scenes from the *Nights*, along with the promise of the excessive luxury associated with these tales. The influence of such fantasies was particularly potent in the burgeoning consumer culture of the nineteenth century (45). The *Nights* showed Americans *how* and *what* to consume, from fashion and food-stuffs to folderols.

Many tourists, however, were disappointed with what they found in the Middle East. As Michael Oren remarks:

> Though their backgrounds were diverse, American travelers shared re-markably similar impressions of the Middle East. Accustomed to well-ordered and largely homogeneous American cities, the tourists were disoriented—literally unable to find the East—by the labyrinthine layout of Middle Eastern streets and by their culturally diverse inhabi-tants. (153)

Bible landscapes often failed to impress, as they did not live up to the epic scale of Old Testament tales. Americans arrived in the Middle East already prejudiced against Muslims, and travel merely confirmed their opinion that Islam was a cruel and corrupt religion, and that all the chronic problems of the region could be traced back to this source (154). Contempt for town Arabs was compounded by fear of the Bedouins in the desert, for unlike the British, who increasingly romanticized the Bedouins as freedom-loving, independent, "noble savages" during the nineteenth century (Tidrick 20–31), Americans were convinced the Bedouins were bandits or "swindling scoundrels who commonly exaggerated the dan-gers of passage to negotiate the highest fee possible" (Nance 123). Such negative impressions of Arabs in the Middle East were exacerbated by, and confused with, the phenomenon of "street Arabs"—homeless chil-dren in late nineteenth-century American cities. Arabs and "street Arabs" alike had unsavory reputations for being "tricksters" (Nance 122). These unflattering impressions of the Middle East were consolidated by one of the most popular travel books of the nineteenth century: Mark Twain's *The Innocents Abroad, or The New Pilgrims' Progress* (1869). A satirist by profession, Twain could only be expected to ridicule the region. However, Oren argues that in his travel writing, Twain's "disdain for Muslims was

unrivaled," and his "aversion toward all things Middle Eastern only thick-
ened the more deeply he penetrated the region" (242). *Innocents Abroad*
was the best selling travel book of the nineteenth century, so its influence
was far reaching. Nevertheless, although Americans traveled in increasing
numbers to the Middle East in the nineteenth century and produced volu-
minous writings about their experiences, it would not be from travel narratives that the public gained or reinforced its "Arabian Nights" fantasies
of the Orient, but from the spectacle presented in world's fairs and Wild
West shows that sprang up in the late nineteenth century (Nance 2009).

The first world's fair in the United States—the Centennial International Exhibition—was held in Philadelphia in 1876 and was memorable
for its exotic displays of Oriental life in the form of Egyptian and Moroccan pavilions. But it would be in the 1893 Chicago World's Fair that Oriental exhibits would come to shape American consumer culture in the late
nineteenth and early twentieth centuries. The transmission of Oriental
exotica to America via the Chicago World's Fair owed much to the Jewish-
American entrepreneur Sol Bloom, who was so impressed with an Algerian revue he saw in Paris in 1889 that he acquired the rights to the Algerian village and brought it to Chicago in 1893, after he was appointed the
fair's entertainment director (Oren 299–300). Bloom oversaw the creation
of an entire "Mohammedan world" within the Midway Plaisance of the
fair, complete with Algerian, Egyptian, Moroccan, Tunisian, Sudanese,
and Turkish exhibits and veiled dancing girls. The World Fair: Columbian Exhibition was held to celebrate the four-hundredth anniversary of
Columbus's discovery of the New World. When it opened on May 1, 1893,
President Grover Cleveland was "greeted by dozens of young women in
brazenly diaphanous pantaloons and brightly embroidered vests who
lowered their veils as he passed." "I doubt very much whether anything
resembling it was ever seen in Algeria," he later confessed, "but I was not
at the time concerned with trifles" (Oren 300–301). The Middle Eastern
pavilions swiftly became the most popular sites within the fair, attracting
sixty percent more admissions than the next highest earner, the Ferris
wheel, as Americans flocked to the Turkish pavilion, with its kiosks and
mosques, or "the forty souvenir shops at the Grand Bazar [*sic*]," where
they could also "smoke a water pipe at a *café chantant* while sipping Mecca
coffee or 'Turkish Temperance Drinks,' such as orange juice and lemon-
ade." They crowded the "Moorish Palace, with its hall of mirrors and its
wax museum of horrors, the Persian Tent, and the Kabyle (North African tribal) house," and were enthralled by Cairo Street, with its temples,
mummies, and "ancient" tombs, and its parade of dogs and donkeys,

camels and monkeys, and Egyptians dressed as dervishes (Oren 302). The exotic Orient was inevitably accompanied by its erotic manifestation: the "Palace of Eros," in the Persian Tent, where "women clothed in so-called Oriental dress—translucent skirts, bare midriffs, a profusion of bracelets and beads—performed snake and candle dances" to the music of flutes and tom-toms. More popular than these women were the sensual *danseuses du ventre*—the belly dancers—who Bloom introduced to America, of which the most famous was the Syrian-born Fahred Mahzar, known to her audience as "Little Egypt" (Oren 302–303 Jarmakani ch. 2 and 3). Scenes of belly dancers in gauzy, spangled dress would come to dominate Hollywood films about the Orient in the early twentieth century.

These spectacles of the lavish and sensuous East certainly had their provenance in the centuries-long European tradition of Orientalism discussed in Chapter 1. On the outskirts of the Chicago World's Fair, however, a peculiarly American tradition was developing in the form of Buffalo Bill Cody's "Wild West Show," which advertised, as a side entertainment, "A Group of Syrian and Arabian Horsemen [who] will illustrate their style of Horsemanship, with Native Sports and Pastimes" (Nance 118). As Nance notes, when North Africans and Middle Easterners began immigrating to the United States in the 1870s, a small but significant number of them chose to make their living in "the guise of Arab horsemen and self-starting acrobats in traveling circuses, Wild West shows, and vaudeville," offering "portrayals of Arab athleticism that flattered American patriotism in comprehensibly exotic modes" (16). They fashioned themselves as deliberate counterparts to the American cowboy in circuses and Wild West shows, performing "Wild East" roles of "Bedouin Rough Riders," "Bedouin bandits," and "Nubian" or "Soudanese" horsemen. Audiences were carried away by this novel form of entertainment combining Orientalist notions of the Middle East with American frontier idioms that were already familiar (113–114).

In addition to armed combat, military tournaments, horse races, and acrobatic feats of horsemanship supposedly innate to the Bedouins (even though most performers did not identify as Arab and certainly did not consider themselves Bedouins), immigrants from the Middle East also took part in Oriental tableaux or vaudeville-type shows that presented stereotypical displays of Eastern life. The separate spectacles were connected through the motif of the "Oriental potentate's/sheik's entertainment" which, as Nance explains, was "a way to transition from one part of a production's script to the next in ways that could make the juxtaposition of unrelated performances seem natural" (124). For example, a combined Bill Cody and Pawnee Bill *Wild West and Far East Show* might present the tale of a tourist caravan raided by Arabs. Some of the group are captured and taken to a desert oasis with pyramids and palm trees in the background. When the other tourists arrive with the ransom, the captives are released and all are treated to a sumptuous meal and various types of entertainment—exotic animal parades, acrobats, and so forth— at the behest of the sheik (124). The world's fairs, Oriental exhibitions, circuses, and Wild West shows were immensely popular in the United States during the late nineteenth and early twentieth centuries. They explain why American Orientalism developed as a distinctly carnivalesque visual tradition that was associated with exotic animal parades, displays of horsemanship, acrobats, fire-eaters, and other circus elements in an ensemble that was foreign to European Orientalism. American Orientalism was distinctly spectacular, and it was also decidedly for sale.

THE SPECTACULAR, CONSUMABLE ORIENT

Holly Edwards (2000) and Susan Nance (2009) argue that throughout the course of the nineteenth century, American Orientalism was increasingly associated with the growth of bourgeois consumer culture in an age when urban life was characterized by the commodification of goods, sexuality, physicality, and the exotic Orient (Edwards 17). The Chicago World's Fair of 1893 was especially significant in this transition. The fair aligned and affirmed American visions of the Orient with European imperial hierarchies of ethnographic difference and cultural inferiority through the condescending display of Oriental villages. It also situated the Orient within the modern idiom of salacious sexuality through Sol Bloom's creation of the scandalous but popular "hoochy-coochy" Oriental dance that evolved from the *danse du ventre* (Edwards 39). The dance might have been stimulating for men and scandalous to moral campaigner Anthony Comstock, who tried to shut it down (Oren 303), but it also provided one way for American women to experiment with their sexuality. Self-consciously "modern" women used "the persona of the mischievous Eastern Dancer" as a "vehicle for colloquially feminist, sexually self-aware consumer individuation" (Nance 17). It wasn't just the dance that helped women to experience their bodies in new ways, and to experiment with and create new identities, but it was also the costume of the dance—beads, bangles, scarves, veils, luxury materials, and cosmetics—

and other exotic consumer items—carpets, cushions, and curios—that came to be associated with the dance and Oriental culture.

From the beginning of the nineteenth century, Oriental material culture served as department store and advertising backdrops for selling sensuous luxury items, cigarettes (Mecca, Medina, Omar, and the famous Camel brand), home furnishings, fashion, and film (Jarmakani ch. 3). The paradox of American Orientalism was that while it depicted the Middle East as exotically primitive and racially inferior, it was also a playful cultural discourse through which modern Americans could indulge the pleasures of the senses and experiment with alternative forms of sexuality, gender relations, and mystical rituals. Orientalism was used to explore and transform how Americans related to one another, and this explains the popularity of masquerade balls and the use of Oriental motifs in Freemason and other occult male societies such as the "Shriners."[2] Oriental role-playing offered "the opportunity to try on surrogate identities and taste illicit pleasures while protected by disguise," and "people moved across class and ethnic boundaries to dabble in what were perceived to be risqué behaviors" (Edwards 40). Because the United States had no formal, sustained imperial relationship with the Orient in the early twentieth century,[3] American Orientalism was not so much about the justification and extension of imperial power as about the construction of an imaginary space for American "pleasures, fantasy, and escapism, in the mode of the *Arabian Nights*." For Americans, "the Orient represented the option of luxury and self-indulgence, far from the rigors of a humdrum desk job" (Edwards 23). Therefore, American Orientalism, as William Leach argues, "was symptomatic of changes taking place within Western society—and especially in cities—that had little to do with imperialism or with the desire to appropriate somebody else's property, but that symbolized a feeling of something missing from Western culture itself, a longing for a 'sensual' life more 'satisfying' than traditional Christianity could endorse" (105).

This appropriation of the Orient as an exotic commodity that could satisfy a more sensuous age was further strengthened by the spectacular use of Oriental imagery in the Broadway production of Robert Hichens's *The Garden of Allah*, which premiered in 1907. That the play should have opened in New York, popularly known as "Baghdad on the Hudson" for its commerce and seedy immigrant life, was particularly apt. *The Garden of Allah* featured live camels, technological feats producing whirling sandstorms on stage, and meticulously researched recreations of Algerian scenery (Edwards 44). The visual spectacle of the Orient overshadowed the play's narrative content, which was confusing and quickly forgotten. It ushered in a prewar vogue of hotels and restaurants being decked out in furnishings and all manner of consumables reminiscent of the stage play and associated with the phrase "Garden of Allah"—from women's magazines and perfumes to table lamps. In 1912, the New York department store Wanamaker's even staged a fashion show specifically based on themes from *The Garden of Allah* (McAlister 22). As Edwards notes, "the migration of Garden of Allah imagery from story to product epitomizes the process whereby the Orient was constructed and then disseminated in forms that conformed with American dreams and patterns of consumption" (45).

This is distinctly different from Orientalist discourse in Britain at the same time. Not to say that Britain did not have a tradition of theatrical Orientalism, for clearly it did, from the seventeenth-century stage plays of Barbary abduction, Isaac Bickerstaffe's "The sultan, or, A peep into the seraglio" (1775), and the lavish stage spectaculars of Australian-born actor Oscar Asche, whose "brand of musical orientalism and . . . orientalist musical productions (*Kismet*, 1911–1912; *Mameena*, 1915; *Chu Chin Chow*, 1916–1921; and *Cairo*, 1921–1922) became the most talked about productions of his generation" (Singleton 2). British vaudeville and music halls also translated Orientalism into stereotyped, bawdy, sensuous, and exotic popular entertainment throughout the late nineteenth and early twentieth centuries. Yet British Orientalism during this period was equally notable for its high culture expressions in artistic and literary endeavors, and it was also anchored in travel narratives and scholarly treatises produced by famous travelers and Orientalists. I am not arguing that the British Orientalist discourse of high culture was more "authentic" or "true" to the Orient than the American variant. As Said (1978) has argued persuasively, the discourse of Orientalism was never simply a more or less accurate representation of "the Orient"; it was a discourse that actively "Orientalized" the Orient, investing it with the qualities that made it seem inevitably Oriental to Europeans. In any case, as Timothy Mitchell (1998) shows with regard to Egypt, European colonial authorities sometimes restructured the physical space of the Orient so as to render it comprehensible within the preexisting discourse of Orientalism. In Egypt, villages, army barracks, and towns were all reorganized along the lines of the replicas constructed for world's fairs and exhibitions, exemplary of certain political "truths" about the colonized (Mitchell 1988). The discourse of European Orientalism was thus not necessarily more authentic or true than the discourse of American Orientalism.

Nevertheless, despite this active Orientalizing of North Africa, the British (and French) relationship with the Orient was still constrained by the geopolitical realities of colonialism: different types of political relations with local rulers; the lucrative provisions of financial services; trade, investment, and the building of infrastructure; administration of the civil service; control over the military and containment of anticolonial activities; and the existence of sizable expatriate European populations in key colonial towns and cities, as well as tourists traveling through lands rendered safe by the assertion of imperial dominance and military power. To this extent, then, British Orientalism differed from the extravagant and glamorous Orientalist fantasies peddled by American business and the entertainment industry to whet consumer appetite for new fashions, furnishings, and a more sensuous "national dream life for men and women" (Leach 107).

Even before the publication of *The Sheik* in the United States, American society was already acquainted with a commodified, consumable, "Arabian Nights" Orient that was fashionably modern in its celebration of exotic primitivism. Americans had a longstanding tradition of Barbary captivity narratives extending back to the colonial period and, in fact, the last quarter of the nineteenth century witnessed an increase of such adventure tales in juvenile literature as well as in dime-store fiction (Baepler 49–50). American Orientalism was spectacular and opulent in its "Arabian Nights" manifestation, but it was also hybridized with circus acts and Wild West feats of horsemanship. These elements were reproduced in Hollywood films in the early twentieth century.

THE SHEIK IN HOLLYWOOD

In 1921, Rudolph Valentino became Hollywood's latest matinee idol when he smoldered across the silver screen as Julio Desnoyers in Vincente Blasco Ibáñez's *The Four Horsemen of the Apocalypse.* He was poached from Metro Pictures Corporation by the entrepreneurial Hollywood mogul Jesse Lasky, who then began searching for a vehicle for his new star. Lasky's secretary, who had been reading Hull's novel, urged her boss to cast Valentino in *The Sheik,* for he seemed perfectly suited for the role of the ruthless but romantic Ahmed Ben Hassan (Leider 152). Valentino was also ridiculously cheap for hire at $500 per week, especially when his competition for the role, D. W. Griffith's star, James Kirkwood, was asking for a minimum of $1,250 (Leider 154–155). Despite its initial start featuring famous theatre and opera stars, Famous Players-Lasky (which later became Paramount) was less concerned with film as an art form than as a mass-produced commercial venture that would appeal to large, mainstream audiences and net huge profits (Leider 149–150). This preference would determine how they treated the plot of the controversial, if best-selling, novel. Monte Katterjohn developed and modified the screenplay of *The Sheik*, and in 1921, under George Melford's direction, shooting began in Southern California, with Valentino as the sheik and Agnes Ayres playing the role of Diana Mayo.

Hollywood had shown an early fascination with the East. The Oriental film was one of the most popular genres in the first two decades of the twentieth century, beginning with George Méliès's *The Palace of a Thousand and One Nights* (1905) (Eisele 77). The filtering of the East through the *Arabian Nights* meant that, from the start, Hollywood productions of desert romances differed from their British counterparts (and from the Broadway production of *The Garden of Allah*) in terms of the attempts to recreate the "authentic" Sahara Desert, which British filmmakers often prided themselves in doing well. It may have been that British cultural familiarity with the region—through the writings of its novelists, travelers, Orientalist scholars, and through the realistic paintings of artists such as Ludwig Deutsch and John Frederick Lewis—laid a greater expectation of naturalism and authenticity on British filmmakers. Famous Players-Lasky was bound by no such considerations. Emily Leider argues that a "realistic re-creation of the North African desert wasn't what Melford set out to evoke. Having set his sights on a popular rather than a highbrow audience, he sought a certain staginess and encouraged an exaggerated acting style. . . . This was to be a fantasy film, not an attempt at naturalism" (155–156).

Melford took advantage of the setting and the story to film some dramatic long shots of Arabs riding en masse across the rolling desert dunes, and thus satisfied the American fascination with Bedouin horsemen, while Pathé Company footage of actual Algerian towns were spliced into the film for exterior crowd scenes (Leider 155). However, the interior shots made no attempts at realism. They were often staged within arched doorways or framed by opulent draperies and awnings, creating a proscenium-like effect throughout the film that distanced the audience from the action on-screen and reminded them that they were watching the elaborately orchestrated realm of Hollywood Oriental fantasy (Caton 116). This was the "Arabian Nights" Orient of advertisements and hotel décor, restaurant and department store designs. Melford's habit of using a "keyhole" effect to frame certain sequences within a black circle reinforced this dream-like fantasy and was also reminiscent of Gérôme's *tondo* of his harem fantasy, *Le Bain turc*. Again, no attempts at verisimilitude were made with Valentino's sheik costume or with the interiors of the sheik's tent, which were the fabulous confections of Valentino's partner, Natacha Rambova (Leider 156–158). The film of *The Sheik*, then, was never an attempt to represent a romance in a realistic Orient, but to indulge what were clearly American fancy-dress fantasies of the Orient.

The Sheik opens with the muezzin's call to prayer and the sight of pious Muslims in the desert bowing down in prayer. The film gives far more emphasis to religion—both Christianity and Islam—than does the novel. This is unsurprising given America's history of connecting Protestant narratives of a "chosen people" in the Promised Land to the Biblical landscapes of the Middle East (Edwards 17). The second scene shows a camp in a desert oasis with white-robed men sitting in a circle. This, we are told in the intertitles, is the "marriage market" where, according to ancient custom, "wives are secured for the wealthy sons of Allah." This scene—familiar in Western Orientalist discourse—does not occur in the book, but in the film it performs the crucial role of setting up the sheik as a potential romantic lover. A young Arab woman, Zilah, is about to be sold in marriage to the highest bidder, but "a tribal chieftain protests the sale of his sweetheart." Sheik Ahmed Ben Hassan then intervenes to stop the sale and unite Zilah with the man she loves. The sheik tells the gathering of wealthy Arab men: "When love is more desired than riches, it is the will of Allah. Let another be chosen." The notion that Allah looked after the interests of lovers, and that their destiny—*kismet*—was to be united in spite of adversity, would become popular with the revival of Orientalist romance novels in the 1970s (discussed in the next chapter).

Despite longstanding American suspicions of Islam, particularly in the later nineteenth century, when increasing numbers of Americans began to make pilgrimages to the Holy Land, Islam in popular romance was often portrayed as benign, mystical, and romantic. Certainly, *The Sheik* serves up trite Orientalist motifs of slave markets, harems, and chattels, and Sheik Ahmed Ben Hassan plays the role of the patriarch, disposing of women to his men—but this particular sheik understands and subscribes to the overriding importance of romantic love, even though, as the film proceeds to show, he himself has never experienced it. This American trend toward whimsy and sentimentality represents a crucial point of contrast with Hull's novel, in which the sheik dismisses love altogether. In the novel, when Diana pleads for mercy, asking him: "Are all Arabs hard like you? Has love never even made you merciful?" he derisively replies, "Love? *Connais pas!*" (109).

The film of *The Sheik* differs from the novel in many significant ways, but perhaps the most crucial differences are in the characters of Diana and Ahmed Ben Hassan and in the initial exchange between them. In the novel, Diana's first encounter with the sheik occurs when he abducts and rapes her. But in the film, she first sees the sheik at a hotel casino—the "Monte Carlo of the Sahara"—where again, he is allowed to display a chivalric, gentlemanly side to his nature. He spots Diana as he is entering the casino, which is prohibited to Western guests. She, angry at being kept out of any public place by a "savage desert bandit," is told by a French officer that the sheik is a "rich tribal prince who was educated in Paris," and that in Biskra, "his slightest wish is law." Like the novel, then, the film downgrades the authority of the French in colonial Algeria. The French permit colonial relations to be overturned, such that Arabs are able to keep Europeans out of a space owned and inhabited by Europeans. The casino scene, with its richly patterned hangings, carpets, cushions, robes, and diaphanously clad dancing girls, enabled the display of opulence and exotic entertainment that Americans had come to expect from Orientalist fare.

Diana veils herself, masquerades as a dancer, and gatecrashes the sheik's party, but her white skin gives her away. She is positioned as an arrogant imperialist, telling the sheik that she intruded because "I wanted to see the savage who could bar me from this Casino." Unlike in the novel, where Diana is a passive victim of the sheik's lust, unwittingly drawing his attention because of her beauty, in the film it is Diana's own discourteous action in failing to respect social and racial boundaries at the hotel that brings her to the sheik's attention. She is not without power or agency in their initial encounter, either. When the sheik unmasks her in the casino, exclaiming over the "pale hands and golden hair of a white woman," she draws a revolver on him. Her act mimics in miniature the conquest and colonization of the Middle East: at the barrel of a gun, which she loses in the desert at the moment of her abduction and the loss of her power as an imperial subject. The man who abducts her, however, is not a complete stranger, but one whose attention she has deliberately courted. This is important in ameliorating the shock of the abduction.

The film's abduction scene, which became so famous that it was lampooned two years later in *The Shriek of Araby*, is consistent with the novel, but the rape scene is again different. For one thing, Diana's rape is deferred a number of times. The sheik forces her to change out of her riding clothes and dress for dinner; then after dinner, she tries to escape by running out into a sandstorm. He brings her back, but his kiss, which in the novel leads to the rape, is interrupted when he has to head out into the sandstorm to rescue the men's horses. When he returns, he sees Diana on her knees beside the divan, her hands clasped in desperate prayer, and a jeweled cross displayed prominently on her chest. (There is no such emphasis on Diana's religion in the novel.) He approaches her stealthily, one hand outstretched and ready to debauch her, but he is conscience-stricken at the sight of her weeping prayers. Head bowed in dejection and perhaps in remorse or pity, the sheik leaves the bedroom and sends the Arab maid Zilah to comfort and tend to Diana. What happens next is open to interpretation. Those who were familiar with the novel inferred that the rape had occurred because the caption, "Through the dull slumber of despair—until morning tempts back a desire to live," seemed to suggest the same plot as the novel, as did Diana's subsequent appearance in the costume of a subdued Arab woman. In Kansas City, the widespread understanding that Diana had been deflowered outside of marriage led to the film's ban locally (Leider 166). However, other audiences concluded that Diana was not raped.

This ambiguity was very much due to the fact that Lasky wanted the film to evade the American censors so that it would be as mainstream and popular as possible. As Steven Caton argues, it is entirely possible to interpret the film plot as a shift from intended rape to romantic courtship. The scene where the sheik leaves Diana sobbing in Zilah's arms is in fact full of symbols of phallic detumescence: the sheik's upraised right hand drops in dejection as he leaves, and the lit pipe or cigarette that he habitually holds is nowhere to be seen. Moreover, both the sheik and Diana are fully clothed the following morning: Diana wakes alone in Zilah's presence, and the sheik places a rose on Diana's breakfast tray, thus signaling his intent to court her in the traditional Western manner (115). Leider points out that

> many of the original reviewers of *The Sheik* complained that the movie, in toning down the rape, changed what had originally been the story of a woman overpowered by a man into one about a woman having her way with a compliant male. They argued that Hull's tale had lost its spine in the process of being adapted from book to screen. . . . Woundingly, they used the language of castration, speaking of the movie version as "mealy, emasculated." (167)

A review in a film magazine, for example, castigates the censors for "patting 'The Sheik' into a decorous mood mild enough for the most tender mind. His fierceness—which so delighted the gentle spinster readers—is all gone . . . and his attitude toward the kidnapped heroine is that of a considerate and platonic friend rather than the passionate, ruthless lover." (*Pictureplay* 1922)

It was this latter charge that would make Valentino determined to ensure that there would be no such misunderstanding when he reprised his role in the Hollywood sequel, *The Son of the Sheik* (1926), directed by George Fitzmaurice. In that film, which eliminates one of Diana's sons in the novel and focuses only on the junior Ahmed, we know that the rape occurs—although we do not see it—because of the way Ahmed tosses Yasmin (played by Vilma Banky) onto the divan, removes his belt, and lights a cigarette as he stalks menacingly toward her before the fade-out. The next scene shows Yasmin weeping on the divan while Ahmed skulks around looking guilty. For Valentino, who was notoriously sensitive when he felt that his masculinity and his "honor" had been impugned,[4] the sequel was a chance to correct the aspersions cast on his virility by the turn toward romantic courtship in *The Sheik*—the courtship that eventually prompts Diana to scrawl "I love you Ahmed" in the sand.

The sheik's emasculation is complete at *The Sheik*'s conclusion. Where the novel ends with him wresting a pistol away from Diana's grasp before she shoots herself, Melford's film ends with him wounded and waking from a coma to hear Diana offering her life to God in return for his recovery. The couple is reconciled in a way that emphasizes the sheik's vulnerability. Where Diana is upright, watching over him and playing nurse, the sheik is weak and bedridden. It is a final image not dissimilar to the pietà,[5] or to a well-known First World War Red Cross poster featuring a nurse who is cradling a wounded soldier whose head is bandaged as "the greatest mother in the world." The sheik's turban—symbol of his Oriental otherness—has been replaced by a stark white bandage around his forehead, causing him to resemble the infantilized and emasculated wounded soldier in the Red Cross poster, while his clothes seem no different from a European man's. The transformation from savage Bedouin sheik to wounded white European man, induced by his love for Diana, is encapsulated in his final words: "the darkness has passed and now the sunshine."

The film also follows the novel's imperial agenda, but where the novel emphasizes the role of white men in extending and controlling empire in the Middle East, under Melford's direction, Diana reprises the role of the white woman in the imperial mission, bringing Christianity and European civilization to the Orient and rescuing Ahmed from his racial and cultural apostasy. "Pray God, dear friend, to save his life," she says in the intertitles; "Oh, if He would only accept my life in exchange for his!" Even prior to this, she brings civilizational "light" to the Oriental tents of the sheik: dressing for dinner, reading books, and engaging in "cultured" behavior, especially when the French novelist Raoul de Saint Hubert visits. Diana's attempts to uphold ruling-class European standards of behavior are by no means insignificant. From the mid-nineteenth to the early twentieth century, any white woman who immigrated to the colonies and married a white man was deemed to have fulfilled her duty to the empire. This was because white women—especially if they were middle class—were seen as civilizing influences who would prevent white men from "going native," taking indigenous concubines, and undermining the hierarchical racial structure on which British colonialism was based. As Adele Perry shows with the case of British Columbia in the 1870s, for example, the population was considered to be lacking in white women's influence of culture, gentility, morality, and piety. Without white women, white Canadian men were dangerously exposed to the temptations of "all the evils of heathendom" and "risked becoming a disgrace to the English race itself" (501). English literature set in the colonies around this time similarly emphasizes that the role of an Englishwoman was to marry and be a helpmate to an earnest Englishman whose life was dedicated to the service of the empire, whether his service took the form of involvement in the colonial bureaucracy, in the army, or in public works such as building railways or dams. After marriage, a wife's service to the empire took the form of service to her husband, including creating a pleasant home environment for him (Teo 2004).

The film thus follows the novel's imperial agenda, as did many other Hollywood films of the interwar years. So many Hollywood films were based on British imperial adventure novels that, in 1939, the British *Daily Express* praised Hollywood for "glorifying Britain's empire" and noted that "the British empire need not worry for propaganda while Hollywood does its imperial publicity" (Webster 63). Where the novel of *The Sheik* emphasizes the role of white men in extending and controlling the empire in the Middle East, the film gives equal emphasis to Diana's role as a white woman within the imperial project. Moreover, because of the film's ending, Diana retains her spirit and sense of agency—tempered by love and tenderness—whereas in the novel she is almost driven to suicide. Where the British novel condemns and destroys the new woman, replacing her with a more traditionally feminine woman, the American film applauds a modern, feminist-influenced femininity. Indeed, a few years earlier, Jesse Lasky had requested Cecil B. DeMille and Jeannie Macpherson to "write something typically American that would portray a girl in the sort of role that the feminists in this country are now interested in . . . the kind of girl that dominates . . . who jumps in and does a man's work" (Leider 165).

The imperial civilizing mission, and the role of the white woman as enlightened as well as enlightening in every sense of the word, are visually expressed through the use of film lighting in *The Sheik* to "privilege and construct an idea of the white person" (Dyer 84). Diana's whiteness is first emphasized when she enters the sexualized space of the Oriental casino where the sheik and the other Arabs are engaged in the "marriage gamble where brides are won on the turn of a [roulette] wheel." She stands out from the other veiled women and is unmasked by her whiteness. When the sheik takes her hand, his hands are colored and shown to be much darker than hers. Later, he will stand beneath her hotel room balcony and serenade her anonymously, singing "Pale hands I love beside the Shali-mar"—the popular Edwardian "Kashmiri Song" from *Four Indian Love Lyrics*, composed by Amy Woodfore-Finden.

Film is, of course, a technology of light, and in *The Sheik* and *The Son of the Sheik* light is used to convey stark messages about the civilizational illumination brought by Western women into the benighted lands of the East. As Richard Dyer explains, early film stock tended to show white people as dark skinned, unless lighting was used strategically to highlight skin and to eliminate shadows. During the 1920s, Hollywood developed a convention of using the key light, the fill, and backlight to keep the white figure "separate from the background as well as creating, when wanted, the rim and halo effects of heroic and glamour lighting" (Dyer 87). The latter was particularly associated with virginal, pure, white heroines. In *The Sheik*, the whiteness of the heroine's skin and the effect of light on her, around her, or flowing from her to the hero are carefully created. Although Agnes Ayres, like Diana in the novel, is not blond, her cloth-ing often reflects the light and her hair is backlit in such a way that she is radiant with light. This accorded with the developing traditions of cinema lighting, where "idealized white women are bathed in and permeated by light. It streams through them and falls onto them from above. In short, they glow" (Dyer 122).

In the era of black-and-white silent film, colors and clothing were crudely symbolic. The villain in Westerns wore dark clothes and a dark hat, whereas the Western hero was symbolized by his white hat. The same

FIGURE 4.1. *Rudolph Valentino & Agnes Ayres,* The Sheik

symbolism can be seen in *The Sheik*. When Diana is abducted, she wears light-colored riding clothes—the costume of European imperial authority in the Orient that is also worn by the French novelist Raoul de Saint Hubert. Forced by the sheik to change into a dark evening dress, her white European, Christian identity is then symbolized by the large cross hanging prominently around her neck. However, clothing is more ambiguous for Arab men, particularly the sheik. In the opening scenes, he and the other Arab men are dressed in white robes. By the time he has Diana in his power, his white robes have given way to darker, multilayered, richly textured striped or patterned garments. In the final sickbed scene, when the sheik, through Diana, reclaims his whiteness and literally sees the light, he is simply dressed in a nondescript pale shirt and breeches. Without his characteristic turban, he is indistinguishable from a European man. The same symbolism is at work in the costumes of *The Son of the Sheik*. The junior Ahmed is first seen dressed all in white, but when he believes that Yasmin has betrayed him, and he turns toward revenge and rape, his clothing becomes more variegated and striped with dark and light. Yasmin, meanwhile, is always clothed in light colors and sparkling textures so that she shimmers and glows.

The scenes of conflict between Valentino and Ayres in *The Sheik* em-

FIGURE 4.2. *Valentino & Vilma Banky,* The Son of the Sheik

FIGURE 4.3. *Valentino & Vilma Banky,* The Son of the Sheik

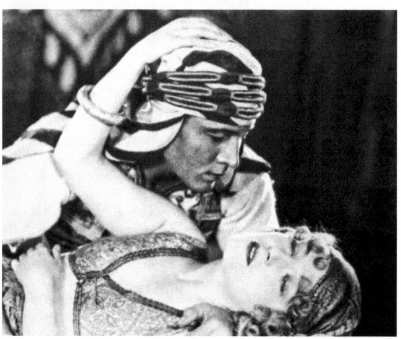

FIGURE 4.4. *Valentino and Ayres,* The Sheik

phasize the contrast between his darkness and her light. His hands were artificially darkened so that they would stand out against her skin and her clothing whenever he held her. Although his face is darker than hers, as befitted all white men when juxtaposed against white women in Hollywood convention, his face nevertheless appears white when he is not in close proximity to her. Leider notes that as a southern Italian, "Valentino's dark complexion might have been highlighted as an asset, since he was playing a hot-blooded, charismatic Arab chieftain." However, given widespread fears of miscegenation and nativist sentiment about white purity, and given the fact that the Ku Klux Klan was on the rise in the 1920s, "the producers played it safe: only in the posters and lobby cards, especially those in color, does Rudy's skin look tan or even black. On-screen, his face appears white, but his hands show darker" (Leider 159). This schizophrenia of lighting and coloring reflected the ambivalence of white Americans toward racial and ethnic others, and toward citizenship and even whiteness itself.

The Sheik was produced in a context of increasing white American concern over immigration from southern and eastern Europe that eventually resulted in the Immigration Act of 1924, also known as the Johnson-Reed Act, which included a "national origins quota" system for Europeans, limiting immigrant numbers to two percent of the existing population group in the 1890 census. As Matthew Frye Jacobson argues, the period of mass European immigration from the 1840s to 1924 "witnessed a fracturing of whiteness into a hierarchy of plural and scientifically determined white races" dominated by Anglo-Saxons. The response of newly arrived European immigrants and their descendants—Irish, Italians, Poles, and Slavs—was to scramble for the consolidation of, and inclusion into, a catch-all white "Caucasian" identity constructed at the expense of black Americans migrating from the agrarian South to the urban and industrial North and West (Jacobson 7–8). For immigrants, the crucial factor for belonging to the American nation was naturalization and citizenship, restricted since 1790 to "free white persons," and extended in 1870 to "aliens of African nativity and to persons of African descent." Rather than challenges to the racial basis of citizenship, the late nineteenth and early twentieth centuries instead saw a raft of legal attempts to have certain marginal groups declared "white."

Significantly, in contrast to Britain, where Arabs were associated with "blacks" until the Second World War, in the United States, Arabs, Syrians, Lebanese, and Turks were declared a "white" race under the landmark 1915 *Dow v. United States* ruling by the Circuit Court of Appeals. The "fact" of Levantine whiteness was established in a series of naturalization cases heard in federal courts between 1909 and 1915. Syrians such as George Dow and his supporters deliberately constructed themselves as white men, appealing to a shared sense of Christian entitlement, their ancient civilization, and the Semitic roots they shared with Jews, who were considered racially white (Gualtieri 42–46). For the new immigrant groups, however, whiteness was unstable and precarious. To southern Americans, Mediterranean, Eastern European, Jewish, and Levantine immigrants were "in-betweens," occupying a status between true whites and true blacks. Inclusion into white identity and white society was provisional, dependent upon a person's occupation, associations, and behavior. European immigrants were only white as long as they upheld the "white man's code." It was possible for these individuals to slip into blackness (and therefore be treated as blacks) if, like Italians in Louisiana, they worked alongside, maintained business relations with, or married blacks (Jacobson 57). In New Orleans, eleven Italians were lynched by the White League in 1891, while in Tallulah, Louisiana, five Sicilian storekeepers were lynched in 1899 (Jacobson 56–58). Levantine immigrants were not exempt either. Syrians were targeted by the Ku Klux Klan in Georgia, while in Florida, the lynching of Nicholas Romey shocked the Syrian community, who were not only outraged, but "bewildered" that he had not been recognized as a white man. In the words of the Syrian-American newspaper *ash-Shaab*:

> The Syrian is not a negro whom Southerners feel they are justified in lynching when he is suspected of an attack on a white woman. The Syrian is a civilized white man who has excellent traditions and a glorious historical background and should be treated as among the best elements of the American nation. (Gualtieri 47)

Valentino's role as the pseudo Arab Ahmed Ben Hassan in *The Sheik* must therefore be contextualized within this history of competing versions of whiteness and citizenship in the United States as well as within discourses of American Orientalism. Rudolph Valentino, née Rodolfo Guglielmi, emigrated from southern Italy to New York in 1913, where he worked at a number of odd jobs and made a living as a "taxi dancer"—a professional dance partner in the popular dance halls of the 1920s—before heading west to Hollywood in 1917. As Leider observes:

> He didn't set his sights on romantic or heroic roles. Physical traits determined casting choices and he knew he looked foreign, which meant he would be typed as a villain. Ethnic and racial stereotypes were still rigidly fixed, and moral qualities attached to skin tone and hair color, as well as nationality. Blonde women tended to be cast as virgins, brunettes as vamps. To American directors and producers, and much of the audience, dark skin implied contamination. The most popular leading men of the moment were all clean-cut, square-jawed, all-Americans . . . like Douglas Fairbanks, Harold Lockwood, and Wallace Reid. (87)

Films featuring Italians—such as *The Criminals* (1913), which focused on the Mafia kidnapping of a child, or D. W. Griffiths' *Italian Blood* (1911)—pathologized them and called their whiteness into question (Leider 50). Griffiths dismissed Valentino as "too foreign looking" for anything but villainous roles, and Valentino, accepting the inevitable, advertised himself in *Motion Picture Studio Directory* as "a New Style of Heavy." In the end, it was white American women—actresses like Dorothy Gish and Carmel Myers, or screenwriter and Metro executive June Mathis—who persuaded male directors to cast Valentino in leading roles. Through these women's assistance, Valentino became Hollywood's first swarthy romantic hero, helping to "redefine and broaden American masculine ideals." Only after Valentino "could a blonde leading lady accept and return the ardent kisses of a screen lover with dark coloring" (4). Even so, he did his best to stay out of the sun, recognizing that he had a propensity to tan and fearing that he would become, in his own words, "like a Negro" and "too black for pictures" (162).

In *The Sheik*, then, the spectacle of Valentino the Italian immigrant representing Ahmed Ben Hassan the supposed Arab raised questions about white identity, civic belonging, and social acceptance determined by the right to marry a white woman. In the context of contemporary debates over whiteness, immigration, and citizenship, Caton argues, the revelation of Ahmed's mixed parentage "has a precise correlate in the contested notions of whiteness and non-whiteness . . . Could Italians in America (Valentino, for example) claim to be white?" (114). And what about the Jewish Americans who flocked to and dominated Hollywood's burgeoning film industry? Caton contends that the "immigrant who is neither white nor black but confusingly in-between could become a 'bourgeois' citizen of the country with the helping hand of the patronizing white woman. . . . Libidinal attraction to a dangerous type is justified and legitimated for the sake of a national melting pot, paid for by the exclusion of the black man" (116).

Originally nonwhite-but-not-black, Valentino/Ahmed can become white through his love of a white woman who tames and redeems him through Christian courtship and marriage. This process of conversion and redemption is in direct contrast to the novel, in which it is Diana's feminist-inflected femininity that is tamed and transformed by Oriental rape. In the film, Diana's second abduction and attempted rape by the evil robber Sheik Omair takes place after Ahmed Ben Hassan, under the Frenchman Saint Hubert's influence, has reluctantly agreed that because he loves Diana, he must send her back to her own people. From this point on, Valentino's/Ahmed's transformation into a white man takes place at the expense of darker others. The sheik's otherness is transferred to the villainous Omair, who is not only much darker in complexion, but who also associates with Africans, in contrast to the Frenchmen with whom Ahmed consorts. Sheik Omair is guarded by a giant Nubian and surrounded by the classic Hollywood iconography of African otherness: nearly nude dancing girls and tom-toms. In the act of rescuing Diana, Valentino/Ahmed survives a near-fatal attempt on his life, whereas black-affiliated Omair and his Nubian guards die. Valentino's/Ahmed's transformation into a white hero thus takes place at the expense of black men. In the final scene, as I have mentioned, Ahmed is stripped of his physical symbols of Oriental otherness—his *thawb* and his turban—and left only with his shirt and breeches, while Diana kneels by his side and lays her head on his wounded breast. As Caton remarks, this is "allegorically significant in the context of American race relations," for "it offers the dream of a partnership between white and ethnic other, implied by the handclasp of Diana and Ahmed before the final fade-out" (116). To American audiences, the film thus offered a message of racial, ethnic, or cultural incorporation that was different from that offered by the British novel.

However, Valentino's—and, hence, other ethnic heroes'—acceptance as a white man was gendered and conditional. While many women idolized him as the "perfect lover," to others, such as a *Photoplay* reader, he looked "wicked . . . maybe because he is not an American" (Studlar 299). In fact, Valentino never became naturalized as an American citizen because he was torn between his homeland, Italy, and the country that had made him famous while consistently questioning his masculinity and his racial heritage. He was reviled by American men who "feared that American women, duped by immigrants—especially those, like tango pirates, who achieved a masquerade of good breeding—would bear offspring who would inherit the ancestry of their dark foreign fathers, an ancestry that was considered to be tainted" (Studlar 299). Just as Arabs could be represented and displaced by a more acceptable "white ethnic" like Valentino, in time swarthy but romantic ethnic heroes in Hollywood would be represented and displaced by "Anglo-Saxon" actors such as Ronald Colman (*The Night of Love*), John Gilbert (*The Cossacks*), Douglas Fairbanks (*The Thief of Baghdad* and *The Gaucho*), and Richard Barthelmes (*The White Black Sheep*). Studlar argues, "Such stars could temporarily satisfy female desire for erotic exoticism without threatening either American men or the nation's Nordic/Anglo-Saxon purity" (301). Therefore, the potential of *The Sheik* to make Americans out of Oriental and ethnic nonwhite-but-not-black men through the body of the white American woman did not survive the early 1920s and was not revived as a possibility until the late twentieth century. By 1926, this was clear. Where Hull's sequel, *The Sons of the Sheik*, again raised the possibility of interracial romance between the English-descended son of the sheik, Ahmed junior, and the Moroccan Yasmin (later revealed to be French), George Fitzmaurice's film *The Son of the Sheik* ignored the miscegenation subplot altogether and made Yasmin indisputably white—the daughter of a Frenchman—from the start of the film.

The sequence of the colonization and displacement of the exotic ethnic/Arab figure by an indisputably "white" man echoes uncannily the transformation of the Arab Ahmed Ben Hassan into the white Earl of Glencaryll (the English title Ahmed inherits) in *The Sheik*, but it also serves to emphasize that these white heroes are at their most erotically charged when masquerading as nonwhite men. This is, of course, the paradox of Orientalism: while being a discourse that creates and propagates images of inferior others, it simultaneously expresses the consciousness of a lack on the part of the Westerner and a yearning for the sexually exciting, darker other.

HOLLYWOOD HAREM FILMS AFTER *THE SHEIK*

As with British desert romance novels of the early twentieth century, Hollywood sheik films of the same era were concerned with ethnosexual relations.[6] However, because it was not always clear whether the relations between Europeans and Arabs were considered white interethnic relations or interracial relations, Hollywood desert romance films did not always draw a firm line against these associations. Indeed, one of the first Hollywood sheik films, Cecil B. DeMille's *The Arab* (1915), features a love story between a white Christian missionary and an Arab sheik. In this film, it is the Arab's decision to relinquish the white woman, rather than the white woman's decision to preserve racial purity and avoid miscegenation, that leads to the parting of the lovers. On the whole, despite the fact that by the First World War, twenty-nine American states were still enforcing antimiscegenation laws prohibiting marriage between "white" Americans and African Americans, Native Americans, Chinese, Japanese, Malays and Filipinos, miscegenation was tolerated between white men and nonwhite-but-not-black women in Hollywood films (Bland 2005: 32). In *The Virgin of Stamboul* (1920), for instance, an American mercenary rescues a Turkish beggar woman from the snares of Sheik Achmet Bey and falls in love with her. George Melford, who had directed *The Sheik*, turned *The Virgin of Stamboul* on its head in *Love in the Desert* (1929), which tells the tale of a spoiled young American libertine whose wealthy parents send him away to Arabia after he refuses to give up consorting with chorus girls. In this film, the young man is abducted before being rescued by an Arab princess with whom he falls in love and marries (much like in the medieval verse romances or Renaissance captivity tales discussed in Chapter 1), to the consternation of his mother. White male relationships with Oriental females were therefore acceptable in Hollywood, not only where the Middle East was concerned, but also in stories about the Far East and the Pacific Islands (see Marchetti 1993).

The romantic success of white women's relationships with Arab men, however, depended on the ultimate revelation of these men's true European identity. Such plots were popular with audiences throughout the 1920s. One such film had, in fact, appeared before *The Sheik* was published in the United States. In Reginald Barker's *The Flame of the Desert* (1919), the English Lady Isabel Channing falls in love with a handsome Egyptian, Sheik Essad, who rescues her when she is seized by a rebellious Bedouin tribe. She discovers that Sheik Essad is really a British army officer in disguise, and all ends well with their romance. Oscar Hammerstein II's musical *The Red Shadow* (1932) features a vaguely anticolonial plot (against the French, as always) whereby a young Frenchman, Pierre Bierbeau, the son of a prominent general sent to Morocco to fight the Arab Riff insurgents, turns on the French and becomes the leader of the Riffs. When Pierre's girlfriend, Margot, visits the French garrison in Morocco, she falls in love with the Red Shadow, not realizing that he is in fact Pierre. In Irving Pichel's *The Sheik Steps Out* (1937), the sheik, who kidnaps and marries the spoiled American heiress to teach her a lesson, is revealed to be the son of a Spanish count. While it may be argued that these women are ultimately attracted to white men, the fact remains that the men first become sexually desirable to the heroines by "browning down" and adopting the masquerade of Middle Eastern masculinity—a masquerade that middle-class American men had been performing in masked balls, *tableaux vivants*, and social clubs since the turn of the century (Edwards 8).

By the mid-1920s, the sheik film and novel had become sufficiently clichéd to the extent that spoofs and comedies began to be produced that mocked, but simultaneously paid homage to, the subgenre. It did not take long for the first spoof, F. Richard Jones's *The Shriek of Araby* (1923), to appear. Long after sheik films and desert romances had petered out in Hollywood, the spoofs and comedies continued, featuring desert sand dunes, palm trees and oases, exotic architecture, luxurious palaces with beautiful slave girls and menacing guards, abduction and wrongful imprisonment, and tyrannical Muslim leaders. In the midst of the Second World War, just before American troops invaded Morocco in November 1942, Bob Hope, Bing Crosby, Dorothy Lamour, and Anthony Quinn starred in David Butler's *The Road to Morocco* (1942), a film about two bumbling American stowaways who are shipwrecked and transported to Morocco, where they find themselves caught up in a comedy of errors and double-dealings replete with warring sheiks, a beautiful princess, slave girls, prophecies of violent death, and a wise man who reads the stars incorrectly because of fireflies in his telescope lens. A couple of years later,

Bud Abbott and Lou Costello would spoof the genre in Charles Reisner's *Lost in a Harem* (1944), a slapstick comedy recounting the story of a vaudeville troupe that gets caught up in a political intrigue when a sheik in the Middle East seeks to overthrow his tyrannical uncle, who has imprisoned the blond vaudeville singer and hypnotized her into agreeing to marry him. By the middle of the twentieth century, Hollywood had moved the setting for Orientalist romantic comedies from the desert to the harem. The last of the Orientalist romantic comedies from this era were the joint British-American-Spanish production *Babes in Baghdad* (1952), directed by Jerónimo Mihura and Edgar G. Ulmer, and Gene Nelson's *Harum Scarum* (1965), in which Elvis Presley, dressed in Oriental headgear, is drugged and introduced Don-Juan-like into a harem. Throughout the course of the film, he is abducted by assassins, escapes into the desert, leaps off his horse to battle evil Arabs, rescues a captive woman, and still finds time to sing:

> I'm gonna go where the desert sun is
> Go where I know the fun is
> Go where the harem girls dance
> Go where there's love and romance
> Out on the burning sands, in some caravan
> I'll find adventure, while I can
> To say the least, go on, go east young man
> Go east young man, go east young man
> You'll feel like a sheik, so rich and grand
> With dancing girls at your command
> Go eat and drink and feast, go east young man.

The Middle East largely ceased to be the domain of contemporary Orientalist romantic stories in American films after the Second World War, although historical romances loosely based in biblical times, such as Mervyn LeRoy's *Quo Vadis* (1951), remained popular. The reasons for this were probably the same as for the demise of the sheik novel in Britain a decade earlier: sheer fatigue with the genre, the growing complexity of political events in the Middle East, a growing fascination with international intrigues and thrillers during the period of the Cold War, and preoccupation with the political and economic effects of the Middle East on American society beginning in the late 1960s. Oil politics became increasingly important for Americans in the post-Second World War period, while successive American governments became entangled in the process of decolonization in the region during the Cold War. To support American interest in the Middle East, Lockman points out, the United States

> maintained military bases in several Arab countries; it kept powerful naval forces permanently stationed nearby . . . it funded, armed and trained the military and internal security forces of friendly governments; it sought to draw Middle Eastern countries into anti-Soviet military alliances; and it intervened in the internal affairs of Middle Eastern countries by covert means (starting in the late 1940s with support for *coups d'état* which installed pro-US military dictators in Syria) and on several occasions with military force. (118)

In response to this, and to American support for Israel in the Arab-Israeli conflict, Americans were forced to deal with hijackings, kidnappings, assassinations, and assaults on American-frequented locations throughout the Middle East and Europe in the 1970s and 1980s. The scholarship on Hollywood films engaging with these themes, popular thrillers and crime fiction, and the disturbingly negative ways in which Arabs and Muslims were portrayed through media is abundant (for example, Simon 2010, Bernstein and Studlar 1997, Shaheen 2001, 2003, 2005, 2008, Eisele 2002, Semmerling 2006).

When Hollywood's interest in the Middle East as a site of interracial romance and sensuality was revived in the 1980s, it was to the historical Orient of the early twentieth century that filmmakers looked, rather than to the present-day Middle East. It is difficult to account for the revival of interest in the historicized, romantic Orient of the early twentieth century manifested in American films such as Andrew McLaglen's *Sahara* (1983), John Derek's *Bolero* (1984), and William Hale's *Harem* (1986). Jack Shaheen (2001) argues that in the vast majority of Hollywood films featuring the Middle East since the Second World War, Arabs are not regarded as suitable heroes, especially in the era when images of petrodollar-rich sheiks buying up or bankrupting the United States, or fanatical Muslim/ Arab terrorists hijacking or attacking ordinary Americans, became prevalent. So why resurrect the sheik romance in Hollywood during the 1980s? Perhaps the filmmakers of *Sahara*, *Bolero*, and *Harem* were influenced by the increasing popularity of the Orientalist historical romance novel (discussed in the next chapter) throughout the late 1970s and early 1980s. Certainly, the filmmakers' plots seem to draw from these novels as well as from the earlier tradition of *The Sheik*. Perhaps they were influenced by the "Raj Revival" in British filmmaking, which saw lavish productions about the last days of the British raj in India painstakingly reproduced in films and miniseries such as Richard Attenborough's *Gandhi* (1982), James Ivory's *Heat and Dust* (1983), David Lean's *A Passage to India* (1984), and the U.K. Granada Television series *The Jewel in the Crown* (1984). Or perhaps they simply reflected the private preoccupations of the Israeli-American screenwriter and producer Menahem Golan, who produced *Sahara* and *Bolero*, and whom Clara Gallini accuses of being "heavily involved in the construction of the image of the Arab terrorist and his counterpart, the 'positive hero' determined to defend with all the means available the eternal values of American democracy, as, for example, in the films *Delta Force* and *Sahara*" (176).

Sahara, *Bolero*, and *Harem* all owe obvious debts to *The Sheik*, showing its influence visually as well as in their storylines. *Bolero* particularly emphasizes the legacy of *The Sheik*. It begins with a close-up shot of a poster of Valentino as the sheik, then cuts to the famous abduction scene from the 1921 film. The American heroine of *Bolero*, Ayre (the name is clearly an allusion to Agnes Ayres) "Mac" MacGillvary, played by Bo Derek, is infatuated with Valentino. After graduating from college, she makes plans to visit Morocco to be deflowered by a sheik. She finds her beautiful sheik in a nightclub similar to the casino where Diana first confronts Ahmed. The Moroccan nightclub in *Bolero* is lavish and exotic, with intricately patterned walls, richly textured curtains and carpets, belly dancers, turbaned men lounging on cushions and smoking, acrobats and, bizarrely enough, a llama being paraded around the room. This is obviously the carnivalesque Orientalism of the American world's fairs and Wild West shows, circuses, and department store displays.[7] Unlike the frigid Diana, who scorns men and sex, Mac approaches her sheik and tells him that she has come all this way to give him her virginity, but it has to be on her terms. He wants to take her to his palace immediately but she prefers a tent in the desert, so he flies her out to the Sahara in his yellow biplane the next day. There are nods to the cinematic conventions of the Sahara scene: Bedouins riding over the crest of sand dunes and shooting their rifles into the air. (In Hollywood films, from spoofs like *Bolero* to bombastic action films like *Rambo III*, Muslims in the desert — whether Bedouin or Afghan mujahideen — are always shooting their rifles into the air and whooping like American Indians.) So far, so good. It is when they land in the desert, however, that Mac's fantasies of romantic defloration go awry. First of all, her sheik cannot sweep her off her feet onto horseback because he cannot control his horse. He has never learned to ride properly, and this is only his third time in the Sahara. In fact, he had an English nanny, went to

Oxford, and is a hookah-smoking poet. He smokes so much opium that, despite setting up an elaborate, seductive scene in an ornate tent, he falls asleep on Mac before she can give him her virginity. This scene is a direct spoof on *The Sheik*: filmed silently, spliced with intertitles expressing the sheik's increasingly ludicrous purple prose, and with his detumescence visually linked to his fallen hookah pipe. Mac gives up on sheiks and decides to go to Spain, where she finds an aristocratic toreador to deflower her. The sheik, however, sends men to abduct and deliver her to him, and he then flies off with her in his biplane. "It's a chauvinistic world," he explains, and he has needs. She has needs, too, so she parachutes out of the plane, returns to her Spanish toreador lover, and becomes a bullfighter. If Arabs and Muslims are mocked in this soft-porn farce, so is everyone else.

All three films—*Sahara*, *Bolero*, and *Harem*—feature virginal American heiresses who are, or become, orphans, have a headstrong, tomboyish, independent streak, and transgress gender roles to do things that were the preserve of men in the early twentieth century. They are courted or surrounded by ineffectual and frightfully proper Englishmen. In this respect, they follow in the footsteps of Diana Mayo. Only a Latin lover or desert sheik can seduce them and introduce them to sexual passion. In *Sahara*, Brooke Shields's character, Dale Gordon, is a racing car driver who enters the Sahara World Rally in 1927, takes a shortcut through the desert, gets caught up in tribal warfare, and is abducted. She falls in love with Sheik Jaffar, the leader of a Bedouin tribe, who seduces rather than rapes her. Paralleling the plot of *The Sheik*, Dale escapes into the desert to finish her race, is captured by the leader of the rival Bedouin tribe, and is subjected to attempted rape. She is then thrust into a cave where panthers and leopards are kept, before being rescued by Sheik Jaffar, who frees her to finish her car race to honor her father. Naturally, Dale returns to her sheik after she wins the rally. The half English, half American heiress Jessica Gray (played by Nancy Travis) in the 1986 television miniseries *Harem* goes to Damascus with her English fiancé, makes a trip to see the "pink columns of Palmyra," and is swept up on horseback and abducted by a Turkish rebel who wants to trade her to the Ottoman sultan's harem for the freedom of his captured men. In the harem, her innate love of independence is challenged by the other harem women's passive acceptance of their fate. *Harem* draws from, and luxuriates in, older European Orientalist discourses that feature scheming *kadins* and favorite concubines, poisonings, and brutal executions. The American heroine negotiates her way through all this to end up as the sultan's favorite confidant as well as a spy for the rebels, and she falls in love with the rebel leader Tarik Pasha

(Art Malik), who wants to enact reforms that will lead to democracy in the Ottoman Empire. Tarik rescues Jessica but forfeits his freedom, and she then returns to the sultan's palace from the British embassy to rescue Tarik and save his life.

At first it seems as though interracial relations are of little concern in these movies, since white American virgins desire and have sex with Arab or Muslim men, who are apparently regarded as acceptable substitutes for the Latin lover. Art Malik, the Pakistani-born British actor who plays Tarik Pasha, had previously played Hari Kumar in the 1984 British television series *The Jewel in the Crown*, based on Paul Scott's "Raj Quartet" novels. In the series, Kumar is involved in an interracial relationship with the English Daphne Manners—although the relationship is doomed by Daphne's rape and Hari's subsequent wrongful imprisonment for the crime. In *Harem*, Malik's role as the charismatic freedom fighter who wins the wooden-faced Jessica from her faithful English fiancé (played by Julian Sands) clearly highlights the superior manliness and sexual seductiveness of Oriental men. Malik, however, is the only Muslim actor who plays the hero in these films. The racial and romantic fusion/confusion between the Latin lover and the Arab sheik initiated by casting Valentino as Ahmed Ben Hassan continued with the casting of the French actor Lambert Wilson as Sheik Jaffar in *Sahara*. But this, as well as the substitution of the Spanish toreador (played by Italian actor Andrea Occhipinti) for the sheik (played by English actor Greg Bensen) as Mac's object of desire in *Bolero*, raises questions about whether Arab sheiks need to be sufficiently Westernized in order for these romantic fantasies to work.[8] This certainly seems to be the dominant pattern in historical and contemporary Orientalist romance novels featuring sheiks as heroes, discussed in the following chapters.

When the Orientalist romance novel experienced a revival beginning in the 1970s, the conventions developed by Hollywood's romantic Orient would prove strikingly influential for the subgenre. The film of *The Sheik*, and Valentino's role in it, would be endlessly pastiched, but modern sheik heroes would be patterned after the hybrid lover characterized by Valentino's white ethnic sheik, rather than Hull's brutal, violent, rapist English sheik. The modern Western heroine would tame her Eastern hero and bring him to heel, like the American heroines of these 1980s Orientalist romantic films. The cultural as well as sexual exoticism and eroticism of Hollywood's Orient, with its lush textures and spectacular visual qualities, would be celebrated. The Hollywood emphasis on "Arabian Nights" fantasy, rather than geopolitical realities, would leave its legacy on the fictional sheikdoms that furnished the romantic Orient, particularly in Australian and American romance novels. And the American films' infusion of comedy into the Orientalist romance would feature strongly in modern romance novels that refuse to take themselves too seriously. But before all this could occur in contemporary romance novels, the harem would be revisited and explored within the context of the erotic historical romance novel. The Orientalist romance largely vanished after the 1930s. After a hiatus of nearly four decades, it would reemerge in the form of the historical harem bodice ripper.

FIVE

The Orientalist Historical Romance Novel

Allah loved lovers; he would bring them together when it was His Will and not before.

JULIA FITZGERALD, *ROYAL SLAVE*

In 1998, the president of the Middle East Studies Association commented that "1978 was a very good year for landmark books on the Middle East . . . Edward Said's *Orientalism* also appeared that year. I wonder if there's been a better year since?" (Khoury 5) Philip Khoury's remark was more apt than he could possibly have realized, for coeval with the publication of *Orientalism* came the birth of a cultural phenomenon centering on the Middle East that would have horrified the erudite Said—a well-read, multilingual scholar, who was also an accomplished classical pianist, and who disdained the "lowbrow" tastes of mass-market popular culture. In 1977, historical romance novelist Johanna Lindsey published her first novel, *Captive Bride*, part of which was loosely based on the plot of *The Sheik*. The following year saw the publication of Julia Fitzgerald's *Royal Slave*, Bertrice Small's *The Kadin* and *Love Wild and Fair*, Christina Nicholson's *The Savage Sands*, Julia Herbert's *Prisoner of the Harem*, and Janette Seymour's *Purity's Ecstasy*. The harem historical novel started largely as an American phenomenon. Beginning in the late 1970s, American popular culture was suddenly awash with aristocratic blond heroines being abducted by swarthy Barbary corsairs, stripped naked in slave markets, and sold as concubines into the oppressive harems of Oriental potentates, where they tasted the erotic delights of sex and the exotic indulgence of the senses. At the same time that Said began denouncing Western understandings and cultural representations of the Middle East as imperialist attempts to fix the Orient as its inferior other, claiming them to be "'racist, . . . imperialist, and almost totally ethnocentric" (204), a new subgenre of popular literature began perpetuating the very stereotypes that he so passionately decried. Said was not the only one disturbed by the Western image of the Middle East or the limitations in Western academic approaches to the region. Zachary Lockman provides a comprehensive and insightful analysis of mid-twentieth-century American academic studies of the Middle East against the backdrop of the increasing American entanglement in the region that led up to the publication of *Orientalism* (Chapters 4–7).

The Middle East had dominated international and domestic news since the Six-Day War of 1967. Regional politics affected American consumers directly when U.S. support for Israel during the October War of 1973 resulted in the first OPEC embargo of oil exports to the United States. The embargo was lifted in 1974, but oil prices continued to climb throughout the decade, culminating in another oil shock after the Iranian Revolution of 1979. Stories of revolutionary and terrorist activities also dominated the Western media during the 1970s: from Colonel Muammar Qaddafi's coup in Libya in 1969 and his calls for a Muslim cultural revolution in the region, to the hijacking of British and American airliners by PLO splinter groups, to the overthrow of the shah of Iran by Ayatollah Khomeini, and the American hostage crisis from 1979 to 1980. T. J. Semmerling argues that as American economic and geopolitical anxieties grew in the 1970s, psychosocial unease about the Middle East found expression in Hollywood films mythologizing an assertive, militaristic, and ultramasculine United States threatened by feminized and malevolent Arabs, whose defeat served to "enhance our own stature, our own meaning, and our own self-esteem in times of our own diffidence" (2).

This may well be true; yet the most astounding thing about the Orientalist historical romance novel in all this time was its almost complete lack of engagement with any of the tumultuous upheavals going on in the Middle East. It wasn't oil sheiks but Ottoman sultans who fascinated historical novelists, while Palestinian hijackers were passed over for renegade Barbary pirates. There were certainly loose historical parallels between the 1790s and the 1970s, as Michael Oren (2007) points out, noting the correspondence between North African corsairs who captured Americans for financial gain and the dizzying variety of anticolonial or irredentist terrorist organizations—from the Palestinian Abu Nidal and PLO to the

Lebanese Hezbollah—that kidnapped Americans and hijacked airplanes in the 1970s and 1980s to protest American foreign policy in the Middle East. Like the response in the early American republic, the Reagan administration's response in the 1980s was to use force as well as funding in the form of aid and arms (analogous to the late eighteenth-century "tribute" paid to the Barbary states), which did little to solve America's problems in the region. Historical romance writers, however, did not make connections between their subject matter and current events. Above all, the Orientalist historical romance novel was about the construction of sexual fantasies and sensuous pleasures in their infinite varieties. In the end, it wasn't contemporary events in the Middle East that provoked the revival of interest in the Oriental romance novel; it was the sexual liberation movement's transformation of the tried and true titillations of Orientalist pornographic motifs into a new form of female-authored erotica for women.

In this chapter, I trace the evolution of the female-authored harem historical novel in the Western world, focusing particularly on the eroticization of the historical romance in the 1970s—an extraordinary development that Carol Thurston (1987) has termed the "romance revolution," which followed the sexual revolution and was contemporaneous with second-wave feminism. I examine how and why erotic fiction for women found expression in the historical novel in a way that Orientalized women's sexual culture from the 1970s to the present day. I discuss continuities and changes in Orientalist leitmotifs that historical harem novels have inherited from European culture: abduction, slavery, the harem, and rape. The erotic romance novel has troubled many feminist critics because one of its most common sexual fantasies is the fantasy of seductive rape. In this chapter, therefore, I consider the problem of rape in erotic historical novels, focusing on what rape was supposed to do—and how it was supposed to function—in light of the radical feminist antirape politics of the 1970s. Then, through an analysis of Bertrice Small's *The Kadin* (1978), an Orientalist novel which, in its own way, challenged existing Turkish, women's, and national histories of the 1970s, I look at how, at its best, the harem historical novel engaged with history. I conclude with a discussion of how contemporary readers consume Orientalist historical novels and what issues are of concern to them.

THE RISE OF THE EROTIC ORIENTALIST
HISTORICAL NOVEL IN AMERICA

In 1960, the erotic Orient invaded American bookstores when Searge-anne Golon's French historical novel, *Angélique in Barbary*, was translated into English and published. The book was the fourth in Anne Golon's multivolume Angélique series, the first of which had been published in English in 1957, under the bizarre fusion of Anne and her husband's first names—"Sergeanne Golon"—because the publisher thought that readers would be more comfortable with such a book if they believed a man had written it (an indication, surely, of how much historical romance fiction has been feminized since then). Golon's first novel, *Angélique: Marquise of the Angels*, begins with the eponymous French heroine as a twelve-year-old child growing up during the mid-seventeenth-century French civil war known as the Fronde. Her sexual adventures are the focus of the novel, and subsequent books see her encountering one lover after another as her fortunes rise and fall during the reign of Louis XIV. The fourth book in the series, *Angélique and the Sultan*, was retitled *Angélique in Barbary* for the U.S. market because of American historical memory of the two Barbary Wars fought in the early nineteenth century. *Angélique in Barbary* charts the heroine's escape from the king of France and her journey around the Mediterranean in pursuit of her first husband, Joffrey, who is her true love. She bargains her way onto a ship by trading sexual favors with the captain and is subsequently kidnapped and raped by a renegade French pirate before being taken to the slave market in Crete. There, she is slowly stripped naked on the slave blocks and sold as a sex slave to Mulay Ismail, Sultan of Morocco who, of course, confines her in his harem. After various sexual encounters with the sultan and the leader of the Christian slaves in Fez, she manages to escape from the harem. She continues her sexual adventures in the following volumes.

Within this series which, Golon later claimed, was inspired by the independent and adventurous Scarlett O'Hara in Margaret Mitchell's *Gone with the Wind* (1936, http://www.worldofangelique.com/movies.htm), *Angélique in Barbary* heralded the rise of the historical bodice ripper as well as the return of the sensual Orient to the pages of popular romance. The major motifs of the romantic literary Orient that had developed over the last four hundred years in Western culture were amalgamated in this novel: the feisty, valiant heroine's voyage at sea; her encounter with Barbary corsairs; her abduction by a renegade European pirate; her sale at the slave market; her introduction into the harem of a Muslim ruler; lengthy descriptions of languorous and tragic harem life, including the heroine's complex relationship with the head eunuch; and her escape from the seraglio. As we shall see, all these tropes became standard fare in the erotic historical harem romance novels that began to be produced in the 1970s. The search for Angélique's true love forms the ostensible motivation for the adventures in the Angelique series, but it seems incidental to her lust for travel and sexual experience, while domesticity is dismissed as the appropriate ending to a novel for women. Despite her numerous husbands and lovers who meet unhappy ends, and her children born to various men, Angélique rarely remains for long in the role of mistress, wife, or mother. Rather, she overcomes savage rapes, tragedies, betrayals, and warfare to forge her path as a resistance fighter and leader of men in a variety of contexts — whether among the Huguenots in France or settlers in the New World.

The overt eroticism of the Angélique series (its pornographic possibilities) was blatantly advertised on the covers of the American Bantam mass-market paperback editions from the 1960s to the 1980s.[1] Of all the novels in the series, *Angélique in Barbary* must have been the most popular with American readers, judging by the number of times it was reprinted and the different covers fashioned for it. The covers clearly show a progressive sexualizing of Orientalism in the marketing of this novel in a way that increasingly emphasized violence and sadomasochism within an interracial context. The 1964 edition displays the most sedate of the covers, with a blond Angélique shown only from the torso up flirtatiously holding a transparent blue veil over her face to signify an Oriental tale. The 1966 edition cover of *Angélique in Barbary* introduces a menacing male figure into the background—a sinisterly scowling, dark-skinned man. A white woman dressed somewhat like Barbara Eden in the recently premiered television series *I Dream of Jeannie* (1965–1970), wearing pink pantaloons, a gold waistband, and a low-cut black bra and headscarf, stands in front of a bare-chested, dark-skinned guard wearing a red fez. The cover no doubt draws upon the tradition of nineteenth-century European Orientalist paintings that depict white women juxtaposed against unclothed black bodies in order to sexualize the harem concubines and eroticize white skin (Gilman 1985a: 209). In the United States, however, such an image inevitably conjured postbellum Southern myths of white women's rape by black men (Hall 153). In American culture, the historical reality of black enslavement, white violence against blacks, and white male rape of black women was denied and inverted. White women were constituted as the victims of black men, and they also came to stand in for the "rape" of the South during Reconstruction, thus excusing white retaliation against blacks through lynch violence (Sielke 2). Such images also signaled white women's vulnerability in the public sphere during the first-wave campaign for feminism (Newman 1999), and it is surely no coincidence that this provocative and significant visual cue resurfaced during the era of civil rights campaigns and the women's liberation movement of the 1960s.

The American *Angélique in Barbary* covers became raunchier and more violent or sadomasochistic with subsequent reprintings, and the bare-chested black figure was replaced by fully robed Arabs, thus demonstrating the interchangeability of Arabs and blacks that had become a persistent trope in European imperial culture during the late nineteenth and early twentieth centuries. The 1971 edition presents Angélique on her knees in a blue "harem costume," an ornate bikini bra and short sarong barely covering her hips and the tops of her thighs, her outerwear pulled off and lying around her. Her hands are bound behind her back and her head is yanked back by a sinister-looking, heavily bearded, robed Arab with a scimitar in his right hand. The 1975 edition continues the suggestion of sadomasochistic sex, showing a blond Angélique in a skimpy slave costume complete with a golden cone-shaped bra, on all fours, presenting her bottom to a fat, bearded man in red robes and a turban who is wielding a coiled whip. All the other novels in the Angélique series feature an overtly sexual Angélique on their covers: she is usually portrayed half dressed, her bodice gaping open, and her nipples barely concealed. However, it was only *Angélique in Barbary* that drew on mid-century-American pulp fiction graphics and conflated female sexuality with the iconography of rape and violence, because this was what the Orient connoted.

The Angélique series and subsequent American historical novels were the harbingers of what Carol Thurston terms the "romance revolution" of the 1970s and early 1980s that succeeded the sexual revolution, and they demonstrate the way in which the sexualization of American women's popular culture was also partly an Orientalization of the female erotic imagination. This "romance revolution" encompassed the meteoric rise in the number of mass-market paperback romances published from the 1970s onward and coincided with the women's movement, prompting feminist critics to argue that the destabilization of gender roles by feminism had led conservative women to seek comfort and psychological reassurance in the traditional gender roles and ritualized heterosexual relations depicted in mass-market romance novels (Douglas 1980, Modleski 1982, Mussell 1984). We now know that many romance novel readers were by no means conservative, and that feminists and budding feminists were also avid readers and writers of romance novels (Thurston 1987, Krentz 1992). Diana Wallace speculates that the "number of feminists who later came out as closet romance readers suggests . . . that romance reading answered needs not satisfied or acknowledged by the feminist confessional realist texts" because, as feminist historian Sheila Rowbotham points out, the increased attention to sexual politics did not necessarily translate into an increase in attention to the specific nature of women's sexual desires or fantasies (Wallace 153).

The sexual revolution, as Beth Bailey (1994) explains, was a confluence of movements beginning in the late 1960s that marked the breakdown of congruence between American public sexual mores and private sexual behavior—notably exposed by the mid-century "Kinsey Reports": Alfred Kinsey's *Sexual Behavior in the Human Male* (1948) and *Sexual Behavior in the Human Female* (1953). The "revolution" was characterized as such because two of its most overt expressions were demonstrated by the actions of young people rebelling against the postwar consensus. More young people began openly living together as de facto couples in the 1960s and 1970s, and sex was "*actively claimed* by young people and used not only for pleasure but also for power in a new form of cultural politics that shook the nation" (Bailey 238). In the realm of mass consumption, a sexualization of American culture occurred that decoupled sex from marriage and exempted men from sexual responsibility while reconfiguring sex as a commodity for pleasurable consumption (Bailey 248). Hugh Hefner's *Playboy*, founded in 1953, was at the vanguard of this development and was complemented by *Sex and the Single Girl* (1962) by Helen Gurley Brown, editor of *Cosmopolitan* from 1965 to 1997.

During a short-lived period in the late 1960s and early 1970s, feminists regarded the sexual revolution as an integral part of women's liberation, for they "envisioned sexual pleasure as empowering, as helping men become more human, and as a route out of patriarchal repression of the body" (Gerhard 2). However, feminists—both liberal and radical—quickly became disillusioned with the revolution because it privileged male sexual desire and social needs over women's autonomy (Gerhard 2001). As Sheila Jeffreys points out, popular sex publications from the period, such as David Reuben's *Everything You Always Wanted to Know About Sex (But Were Afraid to Ask)* (1969), J's *The Sensuous Woman* (1969) and Alex Comfort's *The Joy of Sex* (1972), discuss sexual techniques and affirm women's sexuality in heteronormative ways, but implicitly convey the idea that women need to get better at sex in order to service and please men (107–115). "J" and Comfort, for example, explain fellatio to women and insist that they get over their aversion to swallowing men's semen, and they provide suggestions for how women can do this even if they don't want to (Jeffreys 115). "J," who claims to have reinvented herself from a frumpy and unattractive woman into a "Sensuous Woman" who is a "marvellous bitch in bed," encourages women to masturbate regularly so that they can reach orgasm more quickly during intercourse. "Women were instructed that they would need to use fantasies in masturbation and that these could be culled from pornography such as *The Story of O*. Masochistic fantasies were fine, such as 'being kidnapped and raped'" (Jeffreys 109).

The arguments put forward by liberal, radical, and libertarian feminists about the sexual revolution and its supposed benefits or disadvantages highlighted the following problems in Western women's sexual culture. First, as Hera Cook discovered in her research into British women's sexual activities throughout the twentieth century, women felt vastly "ignorant" about actual sexual activity, however much "knowledge" society might have assumed they possessed about sex (167). In addition to reading sex manuals—and perhaps much more commonly, as Thurston suggests—women turned to fiction both to learn about sex and to fulfill sexual fantasies (19). The convergence of the sexual revolution and women's liberation movement produced a flurry of female literature exploring sex: Erica Jong's *Fear of Flying* (1973), Rita Mae Brown's *Rubyfruit Jungle* (1973), Barbara Raskin's *Loose Ends* (1973), Alix Kates Shulman's *Memoirs of an Ex-Prom Queen* (1972), and Margaret Atwood's *Surfacing* (1972), among many others. For women who enjoyed reading romance novels, however, these books were not particularly satisfying and could even be depressing. Kathleen Woodiwiss, whose historical novel *The Flame and the Flower* (1972) is generally credited with sparking the romance revolution of the 1970s, was among the first to recognize that women wanted to read about sex in a way that was escapist, absorbing, and pleasurable. Woodiwiss explains that one of the things that prompted her to write *The Flame and the Flower*, with its pioneering sex scenes, was reading Jacqueline Susann's *Valley of the Dolls* (1966). Although Susann's novel contained sex scenes, Woodiwiss found it "so depressing, I didn't want to finish it. . . . In my frustration to find a novel that was wonderfully romantic and had a happy ending, I decided to write my own" (Bertelsmann Club Interview).

This brings us to the second problem. Novelists faced the challenge of just how to develop a language and fantasy of specifically female erotica when there were no historical precedents for such a genre. Prior to this period, literary and visual pornography catered to an interpretation of male sexuality that, since the advent of industrialization, had been portrayed as mechanical and instinctual—automatic in its response to female genitalia, piston-like in its function, and hydraulic in both drive and orgasm: the buildup of sexual desire had to be released regularly or it would erupt uncontrollably. This idea of male sexuality, together with fantasies of the rape of virgins, had formed the staple plot lines of classic nineteenth-century pornography such as *The Lustful Turk* and *My Secret Life*. Inevitably, they found their way into women's erotic romances of the 1970s and early 1980s.

The historical romance novel became a vehicle through which to explore and create women's sexual fantasies. There were two reasons for this. First, the contemporary romance market (discussed more fully in the next chapter) was dominated by Harlequin Mills & Boon in the 1960s, and the Canadian owners of Harlequin, Richard and Mary Bonnycastle, "wanted straightforward love stories that could be read by young Canadian girls in their teens" (McAleer 122), which invariably meant no explicit sex scenes.

Second, the historical novel had always been a means by which women restored female voices, presences, and historical experiences to male-dominated accounts of the past, as well as a medium for women to engage in contemporary social and political debates that were otherwise considered inappropriate for them (Burstein 2005, Wallace 2005). Since the 1930s, the historical romance novel had become feminized and focused largely on women's experiences of love and life (Hughes 3). By the mid-twentieth century, the historical novel was being used to portray subversive and sexualized women—"wicked ladies" and "wayward women." Diana Wallace argues that novels such as Magdalen King-Hall's *Life and Death of the Wicked Lady Skelton* (1942; filmed in 1945 as *The Wicked Lady*) were a turning point in the historical novel in that they featured female rebellion coded in transgressive or subversive behavior, especially sexual behavior (79–81). These novels' heavy emphasis on luxury goods, travel, food, and glamorous costumes was irresistible to a war-torn and austere society suffering the deprivations of war well into the 1950s (79). The most popular historical romances during the war and postwar years, written by two Americans, were Margaret Mitchell's *Gone with the Wind* (1936; film premiere in 1940) and Kathleen Winsor's *Forever Amber* (1944; film premiere 1947). Mitchell's Civil War epic is, of course, the more famous of the two and is frequently cited by romance writers as an urtext (Zaitchik 2003). However, Winsor's *Forever Amber* arguably had a greater impact on the evolution of the female-authored historical romance, particularly in the genre's later 1970s bodice ripper—or erotic historical romance—incarnation because it featured an orphaned heroine who, like Golon's Angélique, embarks on many adventures and sleeps her way through late seventeenth-century English society, even becoming the mistress of King Charles II. The Angélique series and *Forever Amber* both highlight their heroines' agency and, crucially, they break away from the conventional literary punishment meted out to sexually active and transgressive women: social exile and tragic death.

In the Orientalist historical romance novel of the 1970s and 1980s, women's exploration of sexual fantasies drew inspiration not only from *The Sheik*, but from a vast storehouse of Orientalist characters, plots, and motifs that had accumulated in Western culture over centuries (outlined in Chapter 1) before finding their way into American culture in the late eighteenth century in forms that expressed erotic exoticism as well as female republican rebellion and desire for sexual autonomy and pleasure—the pursuit of happiness. In an era of growing Arab-Israeli tensions in the Middle East, increasingly revolutionary Arab nationalist movements, and strains in the United States' economic and geopolitical relations with various regimes in the region, the female-authored Orientalist historical novel ignored all these contemporary problems to focus on questions of women's adventure, independence, autonomy, and sexual pleasure.

THE ORIENTALIST HISTORICAL ROMANCE NOVEL

The publication of *Orientalism* in 1978 coincided with the rise of the Orientalist erotic historical romance novel, signaling an upsurge of interest on the part of Americans in matters Middle Eastern and Orientalist. The Barbary Coast had formed part of the setting for *Angélique in Barbary* (1960) and Rosemary Rogers's *Wicked Loving Lies* (1976). However, it was with Johanna Lindsey's *Captive Bride* (1977), Julia Fitzgerald's *Royal Slave*, Bertrice Small's *The Kadin* and *Love Wild and Fair*, Christina Nicholson's *The Savage Sands*, Julia Herbert's *Prisoner of the Harem*, and Janette Seymour's *Purity's Ecstasy*—all published in 1978—that the Orientalist erotic historical novel came into its own. The harem historical romances draw from several longstanding Orientalist motifs in European literature: the Crusades; Byronic Giaours, who were also associated with nationalist freedom fighters; abduction by renegade Barbary corsairs; slave markets;

harem life; the similarities or connections between Catholicism and the Oriental harem; escape from the seraglio; and the reworking of the Roxelane theme discussed in Chapter 1, whereby the spirited heroine tames the Muslim despot.

Of the Orientalist motifs listed, the Crusades were the least important and among the latest to be introduced into this subgenre—mostly after the Gulf War, in 1991. The 1970s and early 1980s Orientalist historical romances were generally more concerned with mystifying Islam or demonstrating similarities between Islam and Christianity. The Crusades featured as backdrops to Miriam Minger's *Captive Rose* (1991) and Juliet Hastings's *Forbidden Crusade* (1996). The former, like Middle English epics such as *The Sowdone of Babylone*, features a crusader who is taken captive by Muslims, but the figure of the Muslim princess is replaced by an English heroine abducted in infancy and brought up in the harem. Modern historical romances differ most markedly from pre-twentieth century varieties in that the figure of the valiant Muslim woman—Josian, Floripas, and Gulnare, with all their sensuality, resolve, daring, valor, entrepreneurship, and even capacity for violence—has been replaced by the white "new heroine," (Thurston 1987) who subsumes these qualities.

The new heroine is a descendant of *The Sheik*'s Diana, and in these novels, she is, of course, a historical anachronism. A tomboy as a child, she grows into a well-educated, elegant young lady, who nevertheless finds her greatest pleasure in horse riding. Quite often, she likes to swim and shoot as well. She is a passionate woman but she is not very eager to get married, fearing she will lose her freedom to do as she pleases. She will not marry simply to suit her family and friends. She has a temper and a penchant for getting her own way. She is often a virgin at the beginning of the story, and sometimes she remains one until the end—or is monogamous at least. In some scenarios, virginal heroines only ever engage in sexual relations with the hero even though, in the course of the novel, these heroines might be threatened by rape by other villainous men. Johanna Lindsey's *Captive Bride* is one such novel, as are the novels of Connie Mason, in which the heroine is often placed in situations where it is highly improbable that she will not be raped by the villains around her. Nevertheless, the hero arrives in time to save her from rape—as Ahmed Ben Hassan saves Diana from further rape by the "robber sheik" Ibraheim Omair. Sometimes, the new heroine saves herself through highly ingenious and even involuntary means: vomiting all over the deformed and scabby hypochondriac villains, for instance, in Fitzgerald's *Royal Slave* and Mason's *Desert Ecstasy*.

Her attitude toward sexuality is one of the defining characteristics of the new heroine. She is no longer willing to refrain from sex until she is married, and if her virginity is forcibly taken from her, the experience is traumatic but it does not signify the end of the world for her. The gift of the new heroine's virginity to the hero in many of these novels follows the conventional script of defloration developed in European literature from the thirteenth-century *Roman de la rose* (ca. 1230–1275; see Amans's assault when he plucks the rose) to the nineteenth-century *Lustful Turk* (1828). In Lindsey's *Captive Bride*, the heroine feels "a searing pain as he pushed deep into her," and on the following morning, the hero notices "the deep red stain of blood on the sheet" (69, 71)—the classic topoi of virginal defloration. The post-virginal heroine rapidly develops a voracious sexual appetite. In the words of *Captive Bride*'s Christina Wakefield: "What has he turned me into? . . . I was like a bitch in heat the way I wanted him" (77). This transformation into near-nymphomania occurs even in the historical rape novels, which are plotted around serial sex incidents whereby the heroine is passed from one man to another. It is a classic plotline from libertine pornography, and it is notable that one of the first Orientalist novels to use pornographic motifs to examine socially constructed ideas of love and sexual pleasure was written by a man: Christopher Nicole's *The Savage Sands*, which was published under the pseudonym "Christina Nicholson." This novel is so taxonomically specific and anatomically explicit, and so concerned with the configurations of various sexual positions, that it could be used as a technical manual for sex. Bertrice Small would follow suit in later novels, such as *Love Slave* (1995), and she would become famous among historical romance readers for her explicit sex scenes. However, in her earlier novels, as with other female-authored novels of the 1970s, descriptions of sex mostly focus on fondling the breasts for foreplay, followed immediately by penis-vagina penetration. Only in later novels do more varied descriptions of foreplay and other sexual activities occur. Reading these novels from across several decades, one realizes how difficult it must have been to develop a language to describe female-centered sexual experiences. Ultimately, the erotic historical novelists were focused on celebrating the emotional resilience of the heroine and asserting her right to sexual pleasure.

Many critics have expressed concern over the horrific rape scenes in some of these romance novels, which they assumed to be all the same because the genre was widely regarded as "formulaic." The early scholars of romance novels did not consider that, as with all literature, romance novels might change over time, and that the brutal rapist hero was not necessarily a permanent feature of romantic plots. Readers quickly tired of heroines who are savagely raped, and who then fall in love with the sadistic hero. According to Thurston, by 1981, publishers were warning novelists at the first Romance Writers of America conference in Houston to refrain from rape plots because readers did not like them (22). Because romance writers and publishers are peculiarly responsive to the criticisms and demands of their fans, and because they enjoy a close, symbiotic relationship with readers, the genre evolved rapidly within a short period, particularly in its portrayal of sex and gender relations. However, especially in romance novels of the late 1970s (and even in some novels today), rapes were undeniably frequent occurrences in Oriental harem romances. The burgeoning of the erotic romance novel coincided with increasing feminist attention to the romance novel as well as to the politics of rape. The latter inevitably influenced interpretations of rape scenes in the former and led feminists to fear that romance novels were conditioning women to accept rape and domestic violence in their own lives.

Feminist analyses of rape in the 1970s positioned women as the potential rape victims of all men anywhere, anytime. Kathleen Barry's tract, "The Vagina on Trial: The Institution and Psychology of Rape," published as part of the campaign organized by Women Against Rape in 1971, was among the first radical feminist analyses of the function of rape in patriarchal society. According to Barry (1971), "Rape is the most common and threatening act calculated to induce fear in all women and thereby the means men have chosen to maintain control of women." She argues that in men's eyes, women are pure, sweet, and virginal on the one hand, but subject to an uncontrolled, "raging sexuality" on the other, which means that they desire and enjoy rape. It was precisely this scenario—the innocent virgin raped into nymphomania and romantic love—that dominated the erotic historical romance of the 1970s and made the genre so troubling for feminists. By the mid-1970s, the feminist movement's campaign against rape was beginning to have positive effects, with the establishment of rape crisis centers and "take back the night" marches all over the United States, and with increasing numbers of rape cases being prosecuted in the courts.

Let me be clear about the following: sexually assaulted women are unquestionably the victims of inexcusable male sexual violence. They experience trauma and, unfortunately, only a small percentage of raped women ever see justice enacted in the courts. However, feminist antirape activists positioned all women as potential victims of all men and portrayed every single rape as an almost irreparable rending of the body and a fatal wounding of the soul. This was because, as Foucault argues, in the modern world sex had become "that secret which seems to underlie all we are." Our identity, our very sense of personhood, had come to be primarily understood in terms of sex (Foucault 155). Because rape was viewed as a function of male biology and as the means by which men kept women subjugated in patriarchal society, antirape feminists believed the potential for rape was anywhere and everywhere, from any and every man. In her landmark critique of rape, *Against Our Will: Men, Women and Rape* (1975), Susan Brownmiller argues unequivocally that rape is "the quintessential act by which a male demonstrates to a female that she is conquered." In patriarchal cultures, the possibility of rape functions as "a conscious process of intimidation by which all men keep all women in a state of fear" (Brownmiller 45, 15). Well into the 1980s, Pauline Bart and Patricia O'Brien asserted that "every female from nine months to ninety years is at risk" (1), while Catherine MacKinnon claimed that "rape is indigenous, not exceptional, to women's social condition" (172).

Christine Helliwell (2000) points out that such an understanding of rape is not universal but historically specific and culturally conditioned. There are cultures in which this understanding—not only of rape, but of dimorphic heterosexuality and gender roles, as well as the annihilative power of the penis—does not pertain; cultures in which rape, while certainly regarded negatively, does not have the soul-destroying power to define a woman as a rape victim crushed forever. Yet as a result of the particularly American understanding of the meaning and identity-shattering effects of rape, a 1980s survey showed that American women "subject to rape attempts were more afraid of being raped by their attackers than they were of being murdered and/or mutilated by them." This deep dread was ubiquitous and lifelong (Helliwell 792–793). Understandably, then, feminists responded to descriptions of rape romance in the bodice ripper with revulsion and outrage, rejecting the validity of such fantasies, and fearing that through such popular and widely accessible works, women might be seen to be "inviting" rape (Douglas 25–29). Rape romances, in such readings, could only be regarded as pernicious.

More recently, feminists studying romance novels have posited alternative ways of understanding the function of rape in these novels. Building on Tania Modleski's argument about romance novels being "revenge fantasies" for women (25), Deborah Lutz argues that the "erotic fantasy of being subjugated—terrified and trembling—by an archetypal enemy figure" in a rape romance works for women because it hinges on the fact that the hero is in turn subjugated by her by the novel's end (6). The hero's rape or his savage seduction of the heroine results from a loss of control over his inflexible will because he cannot resist the heroine's sexual attractiveness. In this way, he cedes power to her at the very moment of overpowering her. That some readers decode the rape romance in this way is confirmed by a reader's response to Rosemary Rogers's novel *Wicked Loving Lies*:

> Some people criticize Rogers for her "forceful" sex scenes, saying that rape is not romantic, but to me, it seems as though Dominic, though wary of love, cannot control his feelings when it comes to Marisa and expresses those uncontainable desires by forcing himself on her, but don't get me wrong, she enjoys every moment of it and so do I. I mean, the man is so controlled with everyone else that his inability to control his desires with Marisa makes it even hotter. . . . For those of you that like a sweet, predictable, polite romance reads, stick with other writers. But if you are like me and appreciate love that is dragged through the mud, and lovers that struggle through conflict, who still have an intense burning desire for one another after it is all over then read this book and thank me later. (Amazon.com reader review)

These rape-seduction fantasies do not simplistically influence women's attitudes toward gender and sexual relations. Research into women's sexual fantasies, in the 1990s, revealed that erotic fantasies involving force or coercion against the fantasizer were remarkably common among college-age women in America. Over fifty percent of women surveyed admitted to having engaged in a "force fantasy" set within a romantic narrative, but none of them had ever had actual exposure to sexual violence, nor was sexual violence acceptable to them in real life. The quality of these fantasies, moreover, was markedly different from the flashbacks or memories experienced by women who had been victims of sexual abuse in real life, further demonstrating the difference between fantasy and reality—another point that exasperated readers often make in defense of the novels (Strassberg and Lockerd, 403–404).

Since Golon's Angélique series, historical novelists have exhibited ambivalent attitudes toward rape. On the one hand, rape is unequivocally condemned by the novelist—but it is often described so (porno) graphically that it surely serves the purpose of sexual stimulation. More than this, however, rape fantasies in the historical novel of the 1970s also serve to counter the contemporary feminist argument that rape damages a woman irreparably. From Angélique to the heroines of Small's,

Nicholson's, Rogers's, and Lindsey's novels, nothing breaks the new hero-ine's spirit: not hardship, betrayal, abduction, rape, or even physical and psychological abuse. She may be abused, but *she never remains a victim*. In fact, her experiences of brutal rape, and the fact that she manages to over-come them, strengthen and empower her. Angélique suffers many rapes only to end up in the role of political and military leader in Golon's series. In Christina Nicholson's disturbing novel *The Savage Sands* the heroine, Catherine, is raped by many men; but when she is finally reunited with her true love, who understands and accepts her sexual experiences and continues to love her, it is as though all those rapes have never been. Thinking back on her time with the dey who raped her, she muses that "he had made no mark upon her soul, upon her existence" (249). Signifi-cantly, Catherine realizes that she will never fear sex or rape again. She uses her horrific experiences to empower herself to intervene politically in the traditionally male sphere of anticolonial politics because she be-lieves that, death aside, there is nothing any man can now do to her that she cannot endure or overcome. In this way, the heroine's experiences of rape in *The Savage Sands* are more in the tradition of African American women's rape stories, in which surviving and overcoming are key, rather than in the tradition of white American rape stories that highlight the vic-timization and death of the raped woman (Sielke 17, 143, 184). Heroines in these 1970s rape-romance novels are sometimes subject to what can only be described as truly sickening rapes, but in a move counter to the domi-nant discourse of feminist antirape activism, *they refuse to let the rape define them*. In fact, the counter-fantasy at play is that, far from shattering a woman's identity and destroying her sense of self, the experience of rape leaves no lasting mark on her body or mind.

The importance of not allowing rape to victimize and define the hero-ine is demonstrated by contrasting the Scottish heroine in Small's *Love Slave* with another character: the sheltered, much-loved Muslim princess Iniga, who is abducted and made to be the camp prostitute of bandits. In having no control over her own sexuality, and in allowing herself to be defined by the value men place on a woman according to her perceived sexual status, Iniga's life is ruined through no fault of her own. Like the raped Western heroine, from Lucrece to Tess of the d'Urbevilles, Iniga has no recourse but to commit suicide in order to avoid her shame. The white new heroine, however, is sexually active but she does not allow her-self to be defined according to her sexuality, even if she is raped. The re-versal of the Western European literary tradition of the entrepreneurial Muslim princess and passive Western heroine (Kahf 1999) discussed in

Chapter 1 is thus complete. These historical romances sometimes seem far more interested in the resilience and strength of mind that the heroine discovers within herself than in her relationship with the hero.

Just as Diana Mayo—proud, fiercely independent, awakened to sexuality, love, and "true womanhood" by repeated rapes—is the literary precursor to the new heroine, Sheik Ahmed Ben-Hassan is the archetype for the heroes of these modern Orientalist romance novels. And the sheik, in turn, is largely the descendent of the Byronic hero commingled with the Gothic villain: tall, dark, brooding, mysterious, marked by his compelling eyes and his cruel streak; a physically powerful "rogue," "brute," or "savage" by nature and force of circumstance, he is eventually brought to remorse, repentance, and a change of character by irresistible sex with, if not love of, a good woman. The redemption and domestication of the hero is apparently one of the pleasures of this type of plot: the satisfaction of seeing a powerful man humbled and brought to heel by the force of his emotional attachment to the heroine. The hero in these novels is often culturally, if not racially, hybrid. In Lindsey's *Captive Bride* and *Silver Angel*, Mason's *Desert Ecstasy* and *Sheik*, Diane Dunaway's *Desert Hostage*, and Bertrice Small's *Love Slave*, the heroes are all half English and half Arab. The English heritage, which is often conveniently aristocratic, again follows in the footsteps of *The Sheik* and, like in *The Sheik*, it gives the romantic couple a plausible chance for succeeding in marriage. If it is the "Oriental barbarian" within that leads the hero to abduct, rape, or imprison the heroine, the hero nevertheless also possesses the racial and cultural roots of repentance and redemption that the heroine simply has to discover and nurture. Moreover, the English heritage provides the opportunity of fusing the desert romance with the Regency romance—one of the most popular subgenres of women's historical romance novels. Quite often, an encounter between hero and heroine either at the beginning or at the end of the novel takes place in a ballroom in London, while the landed estate in England provides safe haven and financial security for the "escape from the seraglio" scenarios that are often enacted in these novels.

In a Byronic twist, the hero's descent into temporary villainy is often caused by some injustice experienced at the hands of society or a woman from his youth. Especially in the rape romances, the heroes can be renegades, although it is not entirely clear how some authors regard the term "renegade" since they sometimes use it interchangeably with "villain" or "Muslim." In Miranda North's *Desert Slave* (1989), for instance, the heroine is indignant to discover that the hero, an Englishman, is helping a pirate to hold her captive: "Because he was English she was forgetting he could be as dangerous as any renegade in this part of the world. He dressed as an Arab. Maybe he had adopted Arab ways as well" (49). This particular renegade, however, turns out to be a trader who is also involved in a coup d'état against the sultan of Tripoli. He is a freedom fighter and thus cast in the mold of Byronic heroes such as the Giaour or Lara.

Byron's Giaour can be interpreted as a Romantic incarnation of the medieval crusader and, indeed, the Crusades occasionally form the backdrop to some historical romances. More often, however, the hero's quest is for freedom or nationalism—the twin religions of the modern age—rather than the sacred cause of Christianity. Nicholson's *The Savage Sands* was the first to work the figure of the nationalistic freedom fighter into the Orientalist romance, except that the freedom-fighting *giaour* in this case is actually the *heroine*. In this novel, the heroine, Catherine Scott (who is referred to as a *giaour* by other Muslim women), undergoes unbelievable abuse only to realize that all her sufferings have prepared her to take up her mantle as a freedom fighter and chief counselor to Abd el Kader, leader of the Arab rebels, who unites all Arabs to fight against French colonial incursion into Algeria.

As in Hull's novels, the French are popular targets of anticolonial sentiment in these historical romances. This is not surprising since France was among the first European imperial powers to colonize North Africa. Diane Dunaway's *Desert Hostage* (1982) is centered on a hero whose goal is to unite the warring Arab tribes against encroaching colonization by France and Britain. In Nicole Jordan's *Lord of Desire* (1992), however, the French heroine falls in love with Jafar el-Saleh, the son of an English noblewoman and a Berber sheik who is engaged in anticolonial activities against the French in Algeria. The French are not the only targets of anticolonial sentiment, of course. Nationalism and irredentism are at work against many different countries because so many of these novels are set in the nineteenth century—the age of imperialism and its counterforce, nationalism. In Julia Fitzgerald's *Silken Captive* (1985), the heroine is abducted by a Greek freedom fighter called the Pagan—an obvious allusion to *The Giaour*. Doreen Owens Malek's *Panther's Prey* (1996) also features a hero who turns to the slave trade and abducts the American heroine in order to fund his irredentist ambitions.

The abduction of the heroine by Barbary corsairs, whether renegade or not, is far and away the most popular leitmotif in the Orientalist historical romance—unsurprising, given the longevity of this theme. Captivity narratives were common in Western European literature especially in the seventeenth and eighteenth centuries, and *The Lustful Turk* and

The Sheik obviously exemplify the respective pornographic and romantic ends abduction plots could be made to serve. It is notable, however, that apart from *The Sheik*, British-authored historical romance novels of the twentieth century are far less likely to focus on the abduction narrative than American novels despite the fact that, historically, many thousands more Britons than Americans had been kidnapped and sold as slaves by Barbary pirates because of the longer engagement of British trade in the Mediterranean reaching back to before the British settlement of North America (Colley 2002). However, the Indian captivity narrative is one of the earliest genres of American literature, and as Baepler (1999) shows, these tales were supplemented by Barbary captivity narratives from the late eighteenth century.

Examples of female abduction and captivity by Barbary pirates in Orientalist historical romance novels are almost endless. All the Orientalist novels published in 1978 feature this plot device, as do Bertrice Small's *Skye O'Malley* (1980), Barbara Riefe's *So Wicked the Heart* (1980), Margo Bode's *Jasmine Splendor* (1981), Robin Lee Hatcher's *Pirate's Lady* (1987), Jasmine Craig's *The Devil's Envoy* (1988), Joanne Redd's *Desert Bride* (1989), Bobbi Smith's *Capture My Heart* (1992), Patricia Grasso's *Desert Eden* (1993), Linda Lael Miller's *Taming Charlotte* (1993), and Connie Mason's *The Pirate Prince* (2004). Many of these stories' Barbary corsairs are led by French renegades: Captain D'Escranville, in Golon's *Angélique in Barbary*; Vincent, in Fitzgerald's *Royal Slave*; and David Ricimer, in Nicholson's *The Savage Sands*. Some of these renegades are eventually transformed into heroes, but others remain the evil villains who betray race and faith to persecute the heroine. Significantly, during the 1970s, when Arabs were increasingly demonized in American popular culture, these novels often show Europeans to be even more perfidious than Muslim villains.

After her abduction by Barbary pirates, the long-suffering heroine often undergoes the indignity of being sold in a slave market. Golon's *Angélique in Barbary* was probably the first romance novel to include a lengthy episode in which the heroine is slowly stripped naked and auctioned off in a slave market while men bid furiously against the head eunuch of the Grand Turk's harem for her freedom. So erotic did readers and writers find this scene that variations of it were replayed in Small's *The Kadin* (1978), Fitzgerald's *Royal Slave* (1978), Dunaway's *Desert Hostage* (1982), Lindsey's *Silver Angel* (1988) and Mason's *Sheik* (1997), among many others. Descriptions of such scenes often conjured up images similar to Jean-Leon Gérôme's famous Orientalist painting *Slave Market*

(1886), in which fully robed Arab men and a black eunuch stand around a naked white slave whose head is bowed and whose eyes are downcast while they check her teeth and other physical attributes. As Joan DelPlato observes, the eroticism of unveiling depends upon Western understanding of the Muslim instruction for women to cover themselves modestly. In the nineteenth century, "this Muslim exhortation to veil, constructed by Westerners as dramatically different from Christian customs, constitutes a major reason for the great British and French interest in pictures of harem slaves being unveiled" (73). Scenes of unveiling suggest the promise of colonial penetration and possession of both the female body and the Oriental culture it represents (73).

These heroines are then offered as sex slaves to the various leaders of the Ottoman Empire: the Grand Turk himself or his regents in the North African Barbary states (the dey of Algiers, the bey of Tunis, and the pasha of Tripoli), or the sultan of Morocco. Except for the forced nudity in the slave market, authors emphasize that women are covered—even smothered—from head to toe under heavy black *burqas* (or "purdahs," as the costume is termed in *Royal Slave*) as they are transported through the streets to their various destinations. *The Lustful Turk* was the first romance novel to introduce this costume detail, which reminded Europeans of both the imprisonment and oppression of all women under Islam, and of the purpose of their enslavement: for the sexual use and gratification of the men who owned them. Lady Mary Wortley Montagu had argued that the *burqa* offered women freedom and anonymity in the public sphere, imagining that they might even meet their lovers with no one the wiser (Letter XXIX). Some novelists have picked up this point, as well. In a throwaway line in *Silver Angel* (1988), Lindsey writes: "It was the bane of all men that on the streets, every woman looked alike. A princess could visit the bazaar unnoticed. A wife could walk down the street with her lover, and if her husband passed, he would never know it" (47).

Generally, however, the purpose of the *burqa* scene is not only to add Muslim cultural "authenticity" to the tale, but primarily to emphasize the exclusive sexual use of the concubine by her master. This is done by juxtaposing her nakedness in the slave market and the harem with her opaque invisibility in all other public contexts. It also serves to emphasize the barbarism of the men around her. Time and again, the heroine is told that the *burqa* is for her own safety. If the Muslim men around her—often sailors, or of the working or artisan classes—should see her face and form unveiled, even though she would still be clothed, they would lose all self-control and sexually assault or abduct her, like the European renegade corsair. The *burqa* thus functions as a symbol for the Muslim harem and all it represents in the European imagination.

Unsurprisingly, descriptions of the harem are mandatory in these novels. To varying degrees of detail, novelists describe the courtyards that make up the palace and symbolize access to the sultan's person and power. Because the harem is traditionally understood as an ahistorical, unchanging space in the European imagination, little distinction is made between the politics of the harem in different eras, or between varying cultures or classes of harems. In these novels, the Ottoman imperial harem represents the domestic arrangements of the rulers in the Barbary states as well. A number of writers attempted complicated explanations of the hierarchy of women within the harem. There is some shared recognition, among their novels, of the seniority and power of the *valide sultan* (the sultan's mother), but otherwise, there is considerable confusion over the exact ranking of women in the harem. In Nicholson's *The Savage Sands*, Catherine is told that the *guizde* constitute the lowest rank, the *ikbals* are in the second rank because they have become regular sex companions of the sultan, and the *odalik* are "at the very top" of the hierarchy. "Only a wife ranks higher than an *odalik*, and from a sexual point of view, indeed, a wife often ranks much lower" (104). Fitzgerald's *Royal Slave* affirms that when the sultan chooses his bedmate, "all his family come to watch, Kadines, daughters, past favourites (they are called Ikbals) and the Guzdehs." (234). Lindsey's *Silver Angel*, however, reverses the status of the *odalik*. The heroine is instructed that there are the "concubines, or odalisques, on the bottom of the ladder, those women who have not caught their lord's notice. On the next rung you have the *gozde*, a woman who has caught his notice." Above them are the "*ikbals*, those women who have been 'summoned to his presence,' past and present favorites." Above them are "the *kadines*, his official wives" (163). So many women, so many ranks, and so much confusion over so many terms![2] Whatever the factual inaccuracies in these novels, one thing the novelists do manage to convey well is the sense of formal structure, hierarchy, and protocol within Ottoman life, and they emphasize that these are centered on sexual and reproductive politics. In this respect, Western female novelists' representations of harem politics and fantasy differ from men's representations of the harem in that they place women's experiences of domestic life and sexuality at the center of palace life, integrating women's roles into the politics of the Ottoman state.[3] Nevertheless, much historical male fantasy of harem life is incorporated into their descriptions.

In Orientalist historical novels, descriptions of the Muslim palace and harem focus on opulence, luxury, and sensuality. This had been a literary tradition since Middle English epics such as *The King of Tars*, and it was revived in the late eighteenth century by Beckford's *Vathek* and Byron's calculating use of Oriental "costume" to sell exotic poetry. Marbles, carpets, lattice work, Arabic furniture designs, lush and colorful gardens with water features, and exotic Ottoman or North African feasts are painstakingly described. Many of these depictions conjure up the French Romantic Orientalists' paintings of the bathhouse or the bagnio Lady Mary Wortley Montagu visited. Marble, steam rooms, hot and cold baths, and attendants are all carefully represented along with scented soaps and perfumes. Often, the descriptions of the *hammam* in these novels could be the written equivalents of Gérôme's many airy, light-infused paintings of Turkish baths. The bathing practices of Muslims are often favorably contrasted with the lack of hygiene in Europe at that time. This is a significant point of difference contrasting with contemporary mass-market romance novels and *The Sheik*, in which hygiene is almost always a sign of white identity. In Fitzgerald's *Royal Slave*, the heroine muses on these cultural differences and concludes that where social and climatic conditions preclude bathing in Britain, "cleanliness was a part of . . . Muslim religion" (221). Small's *Love Slave* (1995)—a novel set largely in tenth-century Moorish Spain—makes a deliberate point of contrasting the sordidness of the heroine's dirty, rapist Scots brother-in-law with the cleanliness and courtesy of Muslims, whether slavers or not. At the novel's start, we learn that "Ian Ferguson smelled of horses and sweat. He had obviously not bathed in some time." After Ian Ferguson marries her twin, the thirteen-year-old heroine, Regan, is sent by the Fergusons to a convent so that her offspring will not pose a threat to their land. From there, Regan is sold to slavers in Dublin before being transported to al-Andalus. She learns hygiene from the Muslims, including washing her hands in warm water before she eats, and bathing, of course. The bathhouse attendant tells her that "bathing is an art" in Eastern countries, and that the "Moors like their ladies, both young and old, as smooth as silk" (61). Such comparisons allow a degree of criticism of the West, and remind readers that there was a time when the Muslim world was far more "civilized" than the West.

One practice that is not found in earlier accounts of the harem or the *hammam*, but that became another obligatory Orientalist detail in these historical novels, is the depilation of all body hair, especially pubic hair—a process sometimes accompanied by descriptions of the application of henna, kohl, and other forms of cosmetics. It is puzzling where this emphasis on the denuded pubic zone originated. It could not be from eyewitness accounts of the Ottoman imperial harem since surviving harem records deal with financial accounts rather than customs or cultural practices, and no Ottoman lady would have talked about such an intimate detail to European visitors. It is possible that nineteenth-century French Orientalist paintings might be the source of this convention: the very few concubine women who appear full frontal in Gérôme's slave market or bath paintings (*The Slave for Sale*, 1873, *Slave Auction*, 1884, *The Slave Market*, 1886, *The Great Bath at Bursa*, 1885) all seem to be denuded of pubic hair, as do the concubine women in Ingres's *Odalisque with Slave* (1842), and the famous *tondo* of *Le bain turc* (1862), in the Louvre museum. If the modern romance novel's emphasis on the waxed harem woman was taken from French paintings, then this is reflective of a European artistic convention for representing nudes—following the tradition of the Botticelli and Titian Venuses—rather than an actual Oriental custom. Yet its inclusion in these novels as a "historical detail" is often misinterpreted as a sign of the authenticity of the novel's Orientalist fantasy.

Whatever its origins, depilation of the pubic region in these novels rapidly became a convention to signify Oriental sexual difference and greater sexual availability. Perhaps this is not surprising during an era when Helen Gurley Brown was advising women, in *Sex and the Single Girl*, that "clean hair is sexy. Lots of hair is sexy too. Skimpy little hair styles and hair under your arms, on your legs and around your nipples *isn't*" (Jeffreys 107). In Lindsey's *Silver Angel*, the heroine, Chantelle, fights ferociously to keep her pubic hair as a sign of her European difference from other Muslim women and concubines in the fictitious dey of Barikah's harem. Chantelle is "natural" in her femininity, unlike the other harem women who go to unnatural lengths to beautify themselves for their master. Chantelle's natural beauty and her independent spirit are, of course, some of the things that attract the half English, half Oriental dey to her. The dey's English mother notes with some measure of pride that it is precisely because Chantelle is English that she will not conform to the usual harem rules of grooming (240).

Bathing and grooming scenes often provide the opportunity for the physical individuation of the heroine through an emphasis on her hair or her white skin, which has long been fetishized in Western culture. In addition to the complex meanings of white female skin discussed in Chapter 1, Sander Gilman shows how, beginning in the eighteenth and nineteenth centuries, the white-skinned woman was taken as the ultimate standard of beauty while, at the same time, white women were sexualized by being juxtaposed with black pages or black women. This association of white women with black sexuality can be traced back to twelfth-century representations of black people as concupiscent. Gilman argues that

> by the eighteenth century, the sexuality of the black, both male and female, becomes an icon for deviant sexuality in general; as we have seen, the black figure appears almost always paired with a white figure of the opposite sex. By the nineteenth century, as in [Manet's] *Olympia* . . . the central female figure is associated with a black female in such a way as to imply their sexual similarity. The association of figures of the same sex stresses the special status of female sexuality. (1985a: 209)

The contrast of the luminous white skin of the harem concubine with the black skin of the servant is evident in most of Gérôme's paintings of Turkish baths and in Édouard Debat-Ponsan's *The Massage: Turkish Bath Scene* (1883), in which the black servant, breasts unbound, massages the white concubine lying stomach-down on a marble bench. In novels such as Lindsey's *Silver Angel*, the figure of the black female servant or black eunuch is also juxtaposed against the white concubine in the harem baths.

The historical romance novels follow seventeenth-century travelers' harem accounts and Montesquieu's *Persian Letters* in assigning a cruel, despotic Chief Black Eunuch to oversee the harem. The *Kislar Agha*— the Chief Black Eunuch—exercised tremendous power over the harem women's lives, meting out punishment, such as the bastinado or whipping, as he saw fit. Accounts such as N. M. Penzer's *The Harem* (1936) seem to be the basis of the Chief Black Eunuchs in historical harem romances.[4] However, Penzer had an almost pathological dislike of eunuchs, describing them as "unproductive, sterile, unnatural, and altogether unwholesome member[s] of society" (140). He describes the *Kislar Agha* as a "crude, ignorant and corrupted man," and most novelists seem to have followed suit. The exception is the *Kislar Agha* in Small's *The Kadin*, in which, unusually, the Chief Black Eunuch is an honorable man of integrity, loyalty, patriotism, and great political wisdom and astuteness. Otherwise, the character of the Chief Black Eunuch in the romance novel is drawn from the same Western Orientalist tradition that produced the barbaric splendor of Nubian guards in nineteenth-century paintings: Gérôme's *The Guard of the Harem* (1859) and Ludwig Deutsch's various versions of black palace guards.

White skin, like virginity, is associated with beauty and purity, but it is also the object of erotic obsession and possession in the novels. The fetishization of white skin in the Orientalist tale occurred as early as *The King of Tars*, in which the king's daughter has skin as white as a swan's feather (l. 12), while the Muslim sultan's black skin turns white upon his baptism and conversion to Christianity (ll.928–930). The first Orientalist novel to fetishize white skin overtly was *The Lustful Turk*, in which the bey of Tunis writes to the dey of Algiers about his newly acquired European slave: "What most struck my fancy was the beautiful whiteness, roundness and voluptuous swell of firm flesh of her love buttocks and thighs." The bey, unlike the dey, is into sadomasochism. His arousal is achieved at the thought not just of rape, but of marring his new concubine's white skin: "Soon shall this lovely whiteness be mixed with a crimson blush!" White skin does not only appeal to these Oriental men. The sensual value of whiteness is universal. The perverted, slave-peddling abbot Pedro writes to his fellow monk Angelo about the convent novice he deflowers, taking care to create a tableau evocative of numerous painted Venuses and odalisques: "The unrivalled whiteness of her skin was emphasized by the black velvet of the sofa on which she was laid," he tells Angelo; "Every part of her body was ivory whiteness, firmness and delicacy" (64, 79, 84).

White skin, blond hair, and blue eyes are usually prized in Orientalist romance novels (although redheads are sometimes featured). In Johanna Lindsey's *Captive Bride*, the heroine despairs over her abduction for she knows that "she would make an unusual attraction, with her long blond hair and slim white body." Chantelle in *Silver Angel* has "platinum" hair and violet eyes, while blue-eyed Catherine Scott in *The Savage Sands* has hair "so pale it was almost white" (Nicholson 7). These features are emphasized prominently on the covers of these novels.[5] Catherine becomes known as "*Ya Habibti*, the darling" to the harem master, and "her rivals could only watch, and wait, for him to grow tired of the long ash blonde hair, the long white legs, the flat belly, the high, full breasts" (145). The renegade French corsair in *Royal Slave* "supplied the Sultan with the pick of the women whom he abducted from every coast in Europe, putting into Constantinople every four or five months with one dozen or more voluptuous, white-skinned women to titillate the Sultan's sexual appetite" (Fitzgerald 71).

In this novel, Cassia is told that the sultan is "always eager for new concubines, and although he has some five hundred women, he is always in readiness for more. White skins, maidenheads, intrigue him above all" (74). The association of virginity with white skin is also made in *The Kadin*, in which, after the heroine's abduction and prior to her auction, she had been kept secluded from the sun while her body was bathed in perfumed waters and bleached with lemons to restore its true whiteness. She had been massaged with sweet-smelling creams until her skin was like silk to the touch. Her tan, under this treatment, had gradually given way to its natural Celtic white. (32)

At the same time, her virginity is also examined and certified by three doctors. Both conditions increase her value as a sexualized woman for sale. *Royal Slave* makes it clear that it is not only Middle Eastern men who prize white skin. When Cassia is trussed into a sack and dropped into the Bosphorus to drown, she is rescued by a seemingly chivalrous Englishman, Leo, fourth Earl of Marchington, who came to Istanbul to sketch and paint. He is particularly taken by her complexion when he saves her. He sees that she is "deathly white," and unconscious, but even as he looks at her face, which "gleamed whitely in the dusk," he is "gripped by a feeling of possession" because his "artist's eye had seen and appreciated the ivory skin, the voluptuous curves" (301, 303).

"Voluptuous curves" in these novels refers mainly to white women's breasts, for the women's physiques are otherwise unrelentingly slender. The ideal of beauty that prevails in these novels is an anachronistic, late twentieth-century American ideal of the big-busted but lithe and athletic female body. Historically, of course, such a body would not have been considered beautiful prior to the twentieth century, when the modern woman's emphasis on exercise and physical culture meant that slenderness became prized. Lindsey makes a point of contrasting her heroine's slim, boyish figure in *Silver Angel* with the fatness of the other sweetmeat-eating concubines. In *The Kadin*, the Scottish heroine and her two close friends in the harem exercise regularly so that they will retain their youthful slenderness and not grow fat like the other harem women. This disciplining of their bodies matches the disciplining of their minds, and it serves to set them apart from the Muslim concubines. The criticism of Muslim harem women for being lazy, fat, and frowsy had its origins in nineteenth-century British female travelers' accounts of the harems of the ordinary households they visited. The inertia of the harem women contrasted with the physical as well as mental freedom and energy of the British travelers. Beyond this, however, there was also an association of fleshiness with the excessive and commercial sexuality of the prostitute in nineteenth-century Western European culture. As Gilman points out, the French writer A. J. B. Parent-Duchatelet, who studied prostitutes in Paris, mentions that prostitutes have a "peculiar plumpness" which is attributed to "the great number of hot baths which the major part of these women take"—or perhaps to their lassitude, since they rise at ten or eleven in the morning, "leading an animal life." They are fat as prisoners are fat, from simple confinement. (1985a: 223)

In a culture that historically misunderstood concubines as prostitutes and the harem as a whorehouse, the supposed physical and culturally induced attributes of concubines were applied to prostitutes. The fact that Arabs and Ottomans frequently bathed might have elicited modern approval for hygiene on one hand, but it also signified the stifling boredom of the harem, where there was nothing else for concubine-prostitutes to do but wait to be called to sexual service.

However, the harem was not always a space of negative contrasts that worked in favor of the Western heroine. It could also be a space where cross-cultural, interracial, and interreligious relationships among women were built, and where comparisons were made between Islam and Christianity. One notable difference between women's Orientalist historical romance novels and similar fare produced in popular culture in response to American-Middle Eastern affairs in the 1970s and 1980s is the treatment of Islam. While American popular culture had reverted to a longstanding view of Islam as cruel and perverted (Oren 154), increasingly demonizing the religion and its "fanatical" adherents, in romance novels, Islam is mystical and Allah exists to predestine and ensure the union of romantic heroes and heroines. Islam usually functions as "costume" to adorn these tales with easily identifiable references to the Orient and to create a sense of cultural authenticity. In other words, readers know that they are reading about Muslim males when these men give way to such utterances as "kismet" or "inshallah." Islam is regarded as both a childish religion of superstition and an alluring, mystical religion of the desert. This latter interpretation was especially attractive beginning in the 1960s, when counter-cultural values and alternative religions were celebrated. Mystical Islam did not conjure up violence or jihad in the 1970s and 1980s; rather, it evoked the romantic idea of kismet, which became associated in these novels with fate, destiny, and star-crossed love. Therefore, heroes and heroines took comfort in Islam, whether or not they had converted.

The issue of conversion was strongly linked to individuality and cultural identity rather than to national betrayal and religious apostasy for the sake of lust, as had been the case in the seventeenth and eighteenth centuries. In *The Savage Sands*, Catherine Scott wonders whether she should convert to Islam. Doing so would enable the dey to manumit and marry her, thus securing her precarious position in the harem, which is based solely on her ability to sexually satisfy the dey and maintain her status as his favorite. Wealthy Muslim wives had greater financial security because they were given property that was theoretically inalienable even if they were to be divorced, and because they accrued status and power through any sons they bore. Catherine's maid converts and advises her to do so. However, Catherine decides not to in the end because "to change one's religion, without a total loss of faith in it, was surely the lowest of human acts. . . . Do that and you have lost your very last individuality. Then truly will you sink into the depths of the *harem*, to be forgotten" (Nicholson 140). There are two interesting points here. First, that it is one of the "lowest of human acts" to convert because of convenience and self-advancement is a longstanding idea dating back to the seventeenth-century distaste for, and condemnation of, renegades and "convertites" who abandoned their Christian faith for the social advancement possible in the Ottoman Empire. Since it was usually people from the lower classes who did this, there was something of an aristocratic disdain for such conversion.

Second, the point is made that to become a Muslim woman is to sink down among the indistinguishable hordes in the harem. As Kahf (1999) argues, modern Western culture has lost the stock character of the strong, independent, assertive Muslim princess found in medieval Orientalist discourse. The Western heroine of modern romance novels has subsumed these characteristics, while Muslim women occupy a lower level in the hierarchy of gender, race, and religion. The less savory aspect of Islam for 1970s novelists pertains to the rule that while a Muslim woman may have only one living husband, a Muslim man may have up to four wives and as many concubines as he can afford. Muslim women are therefore understood to be oppressed victims whose lot in life—partly a result of their culturally conditioned mindset, which accepts their inferiority and the patriarchal status quo—contrasts vividly with that of the Western heroine. Muslim women are ignorant, uniform, and interchangeable, whereas the Western woman is uniquely individual and possesses a rich and rigorous intellectual life. Over and over again, the romantic heroine rails against her plight of abduction and cannot accept life in the harem because, being Western, Christian, and highly individualistic, she does not have the slave mentality that is ultimately associated with Muslim women, nor will she passively accept that it is her fate, kismet, to be imprisoned in a harem as only one sexual partner among many.

Nevertheless, Islam is not always unfavorably compared with Christianity. British novelist Julia Fitzgerald's *Royal Slave* (1978) presents one of the most positive and sympathetic views of Allah in romance fiction, and makes a careful distinction between the cultural institution of religion and the deity who is worshipped. The heroine, Cassia, is moved by the devoutness of the Muslims she meets: "Although Allah was a strange God in every way to a girl reared as a Christian, Cassia could not help thinking that such faith and trust put many Christians to shame" (129). Although she had initially regarded Islam as "far removed from the English creed," she comes to realize that "fatalism was also part of true Christianity. Trusting absolutely in whatever God brought" (166). This view of the two religions is, of course, highly anachronistic and ill-informed. The late twentieth-century culture in which both Christianity and Islam can be reduced to mystical "destiny," romantic "kismet," and melancholy "fatalism" is a culture that does not understand the significance of theological distinctions that drove Protestant and Catholic nations to war with one another and among themselves during the sixteenth and seventeenth centuries, or that motivated the Ottoman sultan Selim I to embark on a jihad against Safavid Persia in order to stamp out the heresy of Shiism and restore the Sunni tradition after the Battle of Chaldiran, in 1514. Reductiveness, however, makes for excellent antiracist, anti-Orientalist politics in the 1970s romance novel, as do comparisons between the cultural institutions of Christianity and Islam.

When Cassia initially rejects any similarity between the Christian God and Islam's "Allah," the Muslim woman Xenobe proceeds to draw an unflattering picture of Christianity and Christian practices, telling her: "It does not automatically follow that because men are followers of your prophet Christ they treat women gently, you know. Nor men, either." Though the harem eunuchs are castrated, so did the Catholic popes castrate young boys for the Vatican choir.

> And what of the way you treat witches, my dear? They are hounded and tortured and burned at the stake, they are stripped and searched for marks where Satan has suckled them, and if so much as a mole is discovered, the women are condemned. One hundred years ago, the Archbishop of Salzburg sent ninety-seven women to the stake because cattle were dying in large numbers. In 1630, the Bishop of Bamberg had nine hundred witches and sorcerers put to death, and, about the same time, the Bishop of Wurzburg was responsible for twelve hundred dying

similarly. At Wittenberg, in 1591, it was still being debated by a Christian council whether or not women are really human beings at all. (203)

This is a remarkable denial of both Christian and European superiority over the Muslim world. It is also a demonstration of how historical understandings of religious culture and the treatment of women have transformed since the mid-twentieth century. Even more, it is an example of how relativistic attitudes toward religion, and a concern for women's rights, found their way into a "bodice ripper."

Fitzgerald's novel, like Bertrice Small's *The Kadin*, portrays different kinds of women sympathetically and shows the support women could offer each other in the harem. However, more commonly, boredom, petty politics, jostling for status, and jealousies among women characterize the harem in these historical romance novels. Again, this is a European Orientalist motif dating back at least as far as Racine's *Bajazet* and finding voice through later writers such as Montesquieu. These were longstanding male fantasies about the harem that late eighteenth- to early twentieth-century eyewitness accounts by women failed to displace. Again and again, European women who visited the harem tried to desexualize, domesticate, and normalize it as a space homologous to the bourgeois home (Lewis 2004, Melman 1995). These women's eyewitness accounts made little impact on Western popular conceptions of the Oriental harem. The female novelists discussed in this chapter all continued to perpetuate male Orientalist fantasies instead, conflating sexual depravity with violence.

In *The Savage Sands*, the harem women try to inflict the bastinado on Catherine when she becomes the dey's favorite, while in Lindsey's *Silver Angel* and Small's *Love Slave*, jealousy on the part of the other concubines leads to attempts to poison the heroine. In *Royal Slave*, the watchful surveillance of a jealous concubine discovers the heroine having sex with the hero when he breaks into the harem, with the result that the heroine is thrust struggling into a sack and thrown over the palace parapet into the Bosphorus. This method of execution had first been referred to by Byron in the Advertisement for *The Giaour*. It was taken by Orientalist historical romance authors as a standard form of execution. Lindsey writes in *Silver Angel* that "to be trussed up alive in a weighted sack and dropped into the sea was the Sultan's favorite mode of doing away with the women of his harem who had displeased him, women kept veiled from other men in life—and so in death as well" (90). *The Savage Sands* saw the heroine suffering a similar fate when she refused to marry the dey of Algiers.

Drowning was clearly one form of release from the harem. More popular, however, was the leitmotif of "escape from the seraglio." American men are particularly resourceful in helping abducted European women to escape in these novels. The American hero in Sarah Edwards's *Fire and Sand* (1989) helps the heroine to break out of the harem, as do the American captain in Joanna Redd's *Desert Bride* (1989) and the American adventurer in Evelyn Rogers's *Wanton Slave* (1990). Englishmen sometimes get a chance to play the role of liberator, of course—the English heroes in Victoria Holt's *The Captive* (1989) and Carola Dunn's *Scandal's Daughter* (1996) being cases in point. In Connie Mason's *Desert Ecstasy* (1988) and *Sheik* (1997), however, the tables are turned and the female characters rescue the imprisoned heroes. Occasionally, the heroines have no desire to be rescued from the harem. They take on the role of Marmontel's and Favart's Roxelane, teasing and taming the harem master until he becomes a suitable hero and mate. This plot is more commonplace in contemporary mass-market romance novels, but there are a few examples among the historical romances as well. In novels such as Catherine Coulter's *Devil's Daughter* (1985), Doreen Owens Malek's *The Panther and the Pearl* (1994), and Anne Herries's *Captive of the Harem* (2002), the respective beys and sultans are intrigued by the rebellious and independent blond-haired "hellions," whose courage, spirits, and love of freedom are never broken. Malek's and Herries's novels follow the Roxelane plot most closely in that the sultans are determined to seduce the heroines but find themselves becoming Westernized and domesticated instead. By the end, they have become the de-Orientalized heroes that these Western women can truly love and be loved by in return. Such a transformation can also be found in the contemporary mass-market romance novel, discussed in the following chapters.

HISTORY AND THE ORIENTALIST ROMANCE NOVEL: BERTRICE SMALL'S *THE KADIN*

If the Orientalist historical romance novel allowed women the opportunity to negotiate sexuality and changing gender relations after the sexual revolution and second-wave feminism, at its finest, it also served as a vehicle through which women's history and the history of the Orient—particularly the age of Muslim expansion and interaction with Europe—could be explored.[6] This is best exemplified in Bertrice Small's *The Kadin* (1978),[7] a remarkable novel that not only introduced Western women to the late fifteenth- and early sixteenth-century Ottoman court, but also posed several challenges to existing traditions of male historiography. *The Kadin* tells the story of Janet Leslie, the daughter of a Scottish earl who is sent by James IV of Scotland as an ambassador to a mythical duchy in Italy in order to secure better Mediterranean trade relations with Venice and the East. In the tried and true traditions of Orientalist romance, Janet is kidnapped by pirates, her name is changed to Cyra, and she is sold as a slave to the Ottoman sultan. However, she refuses to be a victim of her fate and, together with two other newcomers to the harem, vows to become the most powerful woman in the Ottoman Empire. "If we must be slaves," Janet declares, "let us be powerful ones," that "we may someday rule not only the harem but the sultan as well" (53–54). Trained in the harem of sultan Bajazet II, Janet rises to become the favorite *kadin* (a concubine who has born the sultan a son) and true love of Sultan Selim I, with whom she shares a romantic, companionate relationship despite the existence of his other concubines. Upon his death and the accession of her son Suleiman (the Magnificent) to the throne, she is renamed Hafise and she becomes the *valide sultan*—the king's mother, who is the most powerful woman throughout the Ottoman Empire. However, her unrivaled rule of the harem and, consequently, her influence over Ottoman imperial politics, is challenged by her son's new favorite concubine, the Russian slave girl Roxelana, who is renamed Khurrem. Out of love for her son, Janet decides to bow out of Ottoman life after Khurrem attempts to poison her. However, before she stages her own death and returns to Scotland, she reminds Suleiman of the great debt that he owes to her and her sister *kadins*:

> From the moment you were born, I have guided your destiny. Others have helped me. Without Firousi, Zuleika, and Sarina, would your childhood have been safe? They, too, bore your father sons. . . . Yet always our efforts were for you, and you alone. . . . When the Persian campaign was won, I was responsible for seeing that you were sent to Magnesia to learn how to govern. Who warned you not to follow your father into Syria and Egypt? I did! When my beloved Selim died, who held Constantinople in check until you had safely arrived? I did! Without my help you would have faltered a thousand times. . . . I solved your problems. (357–358)

In other words, this Scottish-born harem concubine ushers in the greatest age the Ottomans will ever know, under the reign of Suleiman the Magnificent; an age when the empire is at its zenith as Suleiman builds on his

TABLE 5.1. FACT AND FICTION IN *THE KADIN*

Fact	Fiction
Selim I seized the Ottoman throne, deposed of his own father, Bajazet II, possibly by poisoning him, and then killed his two brothers, Ahmed and Korkut, in a civil war over the succession.	Bajazet II renounces his fat, dissolute, and pedophilic elder son, Ahmed, in favor of Selim. Korkut commits suicide because he is a scholar—not a ruler—and doesn't want to present rebels with an alternative ruler to Selim.
Selim came to be known as "Selim the Grim" or *Yavuz*—"Selim the Terrible."	Selim is initially called "Selim the Just" by his people. Stomach cancer causes him to become "grim" later in life.
Hafsa Sultan (Hafise in the novel) was one of Selim's many concubines and the mother of Suleiman the Magnificent. We don't know whether she was Selim's favorite *kadin*.	Scottish Janet Leslie becomes Cyra/Hafise, Selim's favorite *kadin* and the mother of Suleiman.
Hafsa, like Selim's other concubines, was only permitted to bear him one son, thus following the Ottoman reproductive principle of one son per mother.	Selim's four principal concubines—his *Kadins*—bear him many sons.
Complying with Ottoman tradition, Hafsa was sent away from court with Suleiman when he came of age (i.e., fourteen years old).	Selim keeps Janet at court because he has a romantic, companionate relationship with her and she is his most trusted adviser.
Selim probably murdered all his sons except Suleiman to give Suleiman clear accession to the throne.	Suleiman's brothers and half brothers conveniently die in battle or by disease and are mourned by Selim.
Suleiman the Magnificent was a warrior sultan who, building on Selim's conquests, expanded the Ottoman Empire and ushered in its greatest age. He was known by his people as "Suleiman the Just" or "Suleiman the Lawgiver" because he rectified many of his father's unjust laws.	Suleiman is a weak, easily influenced, and uxorious man, who is ruled first by his mother and then by his favorite concubines, and who has to be almost bullied into going to war.

TABLE 5.1. CONTINUED

Fact	Fiction
Suleiman became monogamous and broke important Ottoman traditions for Hürrem Sultan. He: • married off other concubines in the harem • allowed Hürrem to bear more than one child • manumitted Hürrem • married Hürrem, and the wedding was marked with lavish public celebrations	Suleiman's furtive, secret marriage to Khurrem is at her instigation. Janet convinces Suleiman to divorce Khurrem.
In 1651, Turhan, the favorite concubine of Sultan Ibrahim (r. 1640–1648), successfully poisoned his mother, the *valide sultan* Kösem Mahpeyker.	In *The Kadin*, a scheming, ambitious, and vengeful Khurrem tries to poison Suleiman's mother, Janet (Cyran/Hafise).

father's conquests, and when the classical culture and architecture of the Ottomans flourish under the patronage of the court.

In the final, rather disjointed section of this novel, Janet establishes her own landed property back in Scotland, is raped by a neighboring aristocrat who had an eye on her when she was a young girl, and ends up taking him as her lover, although she refuses to give up her independence to marry him. She is also raped by King James V of Scotland when he stays overnight at her castle. In return for sexual services rendered, the king confers an earldom on one of her sons who was sent back to Scotland to keep him safe from harem politics. Janet's brother, son, and many other clansmen are eventually killed while fighting for the king of Scotland against England, and so instead of the quiet, peaceful old age she had imagined, she spends her last days raising up her brother's and son's offspring to continue their Scottish dynasty. Janet thus generates two dynasties: the imperial Turkish dynasty, through Suleiman I, and a Scottish aristocratic dynasty whose exploits are recounted in Small's subsequent novels. *The Kadin* ends with Janet's grandson visiting her grave and reflecting on the thought that "in the years to come, those who read her epitaph, 'Born a Scot, she died a Scot,' would think her a poor, sad, spinster. They could never even begin to imagine those fantastic years between her birth and her death" (441).

Three historical sultans are portrayed in *The Kadin*: Bajazet II, Selim I, and Suleiman I. Of the three, Bajazet is depicted fairly accurately, but Selim and Suleiman are deliberately distorted to fit the conventions of romance fiction. The previous table sets out the accepted historical facts and the fictional elements in *The Kadin*.

The main point is that in order to fashion Selim the Terrible into an acceptable (if not ideal) romantic mate for Hafsa Sultan—the concubine upon whom Janet Leslie is based—aspects of Bajazet's and Suleiman's characters and rule are attributed to Selim, while the deaths of all his sons, apart from Suleiman, are explained away through an improbable series of accidents and deadly diseases. The conjugal, companionate relationship that actually existed between the historical Suleiman and Hurrem Sultan is attributed instead to Selim and Hafsa Sultan in order to enhance the romantic aspects of their story.

The Kadin also contains a number of inaccuracies based on the flaws of its historical sources, particularly Penzer's *The Harem*. The late sixteenth- and seventeenth-century structure of the imperial harem and the power struggles of the harem between *valide sultan* (the sultan's mother) and *haseki* (the favorite concubine) during the "sultanate of women"—a period when women were prominent in Ottoman politics—are anachronistically transposed to the late fifteenth- and early sixteenth-century Ottoman harem. This confusion over the complexity of changing harem politics throughout the centuries is entirely understandable, for it was not until Leslie Peirce's *The Imperial Harem* was published in 1993 that the historical nature of the harem and the politics of reproduction in the Ottoman court were closely analyzed in the English language.[8]

In obvious ways, then, *The Kadin* represents what many historians have always found objectionable in historical fiction: primarily, the emphasis on historical personages over processes, and the bending of historical fact to suit romantic fantasy. Nevertheless, *The Kadin* raises significant questions about traditional Western historiography. Women's historical novels may often play fast and loose with the known facts of history—the primary felony in historical fiction which, together with the slightly lesser misdemeanor of being romantic and escapist, outrages historians; but they present an unsettling view of the past that forces the reader to think about the historical gender and social orders that precluded possible alternative lives and choices for women. They make us think about the many women in history who have been silenced, their stories ignored or prevented from being told. According to Wallace, the very excesses of historical fancy—the highlighting of sentiment and the concerns of the domestic sphere with its different rhythms and cycles that contrast with the approved chronology of political history—"all work to disturb accepted accounts of 'history' and suggest that what it offers as 'truth' is in fact equally fictional, and damaging to women" (17). It is in this light that Bertrice Small's Orientalist bodice ripper challenged extant historiographies in the 1970s.

First, *The Kadin* presents an early, mid-1970s challenge to traditional Turkish understandings of the Ottoman imperial harem in a way that was not explored by female historians until ten to fifteen years after the novel was first published. It was not until the early 1990s that Peirce's pioneering work on women in the imperial harem transformed earlier understandings of the "sultanate of women" and the way historians have conventionally attributed Ottoman imperial decline to the period of female rule. Peirce observes that

> modern historical accounts of this period have tended to represent the influence of the harem as an illegitimate usurpation of power that resulted from a weakening of the moral fiber and institutional integrity of Ottoman society and that in turn contributed to problems plaguing the empire toward the end of the sixteenth century. (viii)

By contrast, Peirce argues that far from being illegitimate, royal women's sources of power were based, like royal men's, on family relationships and dynamics—a model that was postulated and carefully explored in *The Kadin*. Moreover, Pierce's *The Imperial Harem* challenges the idea that "gender segregation, so widely accepted as one of the hallmarks of traditional Islamic society, precluded women from playing anything more than a subordinate role within the household," demonstrating instead the myriad ways in which various women in the harem accrued or exerted power (ix). These ideas are already evident in *The Kadin*, even though, as mentioned above, the structure and dynamics of harem politics are anachronistic in the novel.

The Kadin also presents a challenge to European historical understanding of the harem as a place of bored and oppressed women, degraded sexual slavery, vicious jealousy, and pointless lives (Yeazell 2000). In *The Kadin*, the imperial harem is a complex, hierarchically organized place of ritual and relationship where women have agency and can accrue power. The novel demonstrates that the most relevant relationship in the harem is not between sultan and slave; rather, the crucial and most powerful relationships are between the harem women and their family, friends, associates, and others, like the black eunuchs or the Jewish *kiras* (agents of the *valide sultan*), who mediate between the inner sanctum of the harem and the world outside. Janet has power in the novel because she is Selim's favorite; but she also has power because she is Suleiman's mother, so she enjoys the advantages of seniority in the harem after Selim's death. Her exercise of power is demonstrated through her firm rule over Selim's harem, and also in the way she builds factional power with other senior harem women and the Chief Black Eunuch. Yet another basis of power is her wealth, accrued through her position as *haseki*—favorite concubine—as well as *valide sultan*. Historically, the wealth of high-ranking Ottoman women far outstripped that of the majority of women in Europe during the early modern period, and in this novel, Janet's wealth, gathered over her career in the harem, later becomes the basis for building landed power in Scotland. *The Kadin* therefore emphasizes women's agency rather than simply focusing on women's oppression, as Mary Ritter Beard had accused first-wave feminists of doing, and which radical feminists were still doing in their accounts of "victim" history in the 1970s (Spongberg 131, 190–191).

Small's novel is thus also part of the feminist challenge to extant historiographical practices up to the 1970s. Mary Spongberg argues that "at the heart of feminist criticism of masculinist historiography was concern about its overt focus on the public sphere" (187). Beginning in the late 1970s, feminist historians presented a revisionist challenge to such historiographical practice by shifting the focus of research to the cultural history of women and the domestic sphere. This focus on "women's private experience of marriage, religion, romantic friendships and family life" was done in order to "delineate the distinctive nature of women's rituals, values and beliefs." Feminist historians insisted that "the domestic realm and other women's spaces were just as important historically as the public realms of men" (Spongberg 195). In particular, Carroll Smith-Rosenberg's article "The Female World of Love and Ritual" (1975) generated what Spongberg calls a "paradigm shift in women's history" (197). Smith-Rosenberg explores the possibilities of companionship, support, and deep and intimate love between women whose lives were largely confined to the domestic sphere in the nineteenth century. She argues that in a patriarchal society, the relationships women built with one another were just as important, if not more important, than their relationships with men. In *The Kadin*, love is indeed possible in the harem, not merely between sultan and slave, but among women who support and are loyal to one another. This is a break with the British tradition of romance novels, in which the pre-1970s bifurcation of women into the chaste heroine and the sexually aggressive "other woman" often precluded depictions of strong female friendships or sisterly solidarity (Thurston 36). Instead, in *The Kadin*, the bonds of sisterhood—especially among Janet, Firousi, and Zuleika—are the basis of the women's power and advancement in the harem. It is significant that such an interpretation should have come from an American novelist, for as Spongberg comments, "the idea that the private sphere nurtured a sense of sisterhood" was particularly marked in American women's history; "in other countries the emphasis on women's culture was less pronounced," particularly in Britain, where "the emphasis on class within women's history meant that 'the notion of universal sisterhood' was only rarely broached" (199).

By focusing on the "domestic sphere" of the harem, *The Kadin* teases out how Ottoman imperial relationships and dynastic ambitions were based on familial as well as sexual relationships. The novel shows that these relationships form an important foundation for the sultans' and princes' power—something that Peirce confirmed in her 1993 work. The public sphere is thus closely imbricated with the world of the harem and men's relationships with women. This is shown in Janet's claims that despite their names being absent from the historical record, she and other harem women helped Suleiman attain the throne. Indeed, the closing lines of *The Kadin*—the simple epitaph on Janet Leslie's tomb that reads "Born a Scot, she died a Scot," and that hides "those fantastic years between her birth and her death"—underscore the fact that many women's lives have been omitted from the historical record or glossed over as insignificant, without posterity realizing the enormous impact these women had on their worlds through their relationships. The epitaph, moreover, obscures the transnational nature of Janet Leslie's life and identity, and this presents the final revisionist challenge that *The Kadin* posed to historiography of the 1970s.

The vast body of feminist historical work that appeared in the mid-1980s as a part of what has become known as the "new imperial history," analyzing the dynamics of gender, race, and culture in European imperialism, has influenced substantial biographies on European and colonial women's lives. These biographical works have highlighted the inadequacy of the nation as a framework for understanding many people's lives, especially in the context of the international mobility that followed European colonial expansion (Deacon, Russell, and Woollacott 2010). *The Kadin* demonstrates that the nation is an inadequate prism through which to understand women's lives and loyalties. Janet Leslie is undoubtedly a pawn in patriarchal political alliances in Europe and the Ottoman Empire even though she discovers ways of overcoming her circumstances. The intertwining of domestic and public spheres, the life of the emotions and the politics of the wider world, is revealed in Janet's loyalty and forty-year service to the Ottoman Empire, which arises not only from a strong sense of survival, but also from her love for Selim and her son Suleiman, and her friendship and loyalty toward others in the harem. Her return to Scotland, however, shows that it is not the nation that determines her allegiance, but her ambitions for her family. To understand this character primarily as a Scotswoman or thoroughly Turkish concubine (as many in the novel say she becomes) is to misinterpret who she is, for the nation or empire is always subordinate to the claims of family and dynasty. Bertrice Small was therefore remarkable in penning this novel that encompassed such a varied, transnational, cross-cultural life at a time when female historians were still inserting women into a national framework of historiography, and cultural historians were busy constructing an edifice of national identity.

READER RESPONSES TO ORIENTALIST HISTORICAL ROMANCES

All this is interesting to historians, of course, but how much do ordinary readers care about the historical content of these novels? How do readers understand "history" and the romance novel? How do they consume fantasies of Orientalism and sex? What do they look for in these novels? In the final section of this chapter, I look at readers' responses to Orientalist historical romance novels. I do not present a systematic sociological survey of reader responses à la Radway or Thurston, but simply a brief discussion of reader reviews culled from Amazon.com. The development and growth of the Internet has seen significant changes to the ways in which readers interact. Innumerable niche websites have mushroomed catering to the specific hobbies and interests of web users. Among these are romance reader websites and blogs dedicated to Orientalist romance novels, such as "Sheikhs and Desert Love," "Historical Romance Authors of Sheiks and the Exotic," "Romancing the Desert—Sheikh Books," and "Shabby Sheikh: Romance Novels & Oriental Others." More general romance websites and blogs such as "Teach Me Tonight," "Splumonium," "Romancing the Blog," "Smart Bitches Trashy Books," and "Mrs. Giggles" also discuss romance novels, including the Orientalist subgenre (see bibliography for URLs). These websites have permitted romance readers to become far more assertive in voicing their likes and dislikes, to pass on tips about good reads, and to create an online community of contemporaries who share an interest (though not necessarily the same tastes) in Orientalist romance novels. What these websites demonstrate, above all, is the utter futility of talking about the generic "romance reader" because there simply isn't one. These readers vary in every conceivable way, and the only thing that is certain is that a novel that appeals to some groups will not appeal to others.

For my purposes, I have found it illuminating to read the Amazon.com reader reviews of some of the books discussed in this chapter. This is because the site permits readers to post their own views on particular books so that, unlike on many romance blogs, where the discussion is more general and about the subgenre as a whole, readers posting on the Amazon.com website are responding to a particular novel. This is helpful in ascertaining precisely what readers liked or disliked about a novel. Furthermore, blog discussions are often limited by time—the topic generates discussion only for a few weeks—before readers move on to something more current. The Amazon.com site, on the other hand, shows all reviews from the first post, hence some novels have discussions that span more than a decade. (See the bibliography for URLS of reviews.)

There are obviously a number of methodological problems with this approach. First, authors have been accused of accessing the Amazon.com website to post positive reviews of their own novels (or getting friends to do so) in order to boost sales. On reading some of the excoriating and sometimes excruciatingly funny reviews given by readers, however, it is clear that this is not a huge problem where this subgenre is concerned. Second, the sample is self selected and not representative of anything but romance readers—and almost overwhelmingly American romance readers at that—who feel strongly enough about a novel or about other people's reviews to post their responses on the site. In this respect, it is interesting to note that there are some novels that generate so many more reader reviews than others that the discussion dates back to a decade prior, when reader reviews first began appearing on the Amazon.com site, around 1997. When this is the case, the novels seem to be considered important, landmark books even if they elicit critical reviews. Finally, the reviews only tell us what a small, self-selected group of readers has thought about the novel in recent years, not what the contemporary reception of a novel would have been if it were published in the 1970s and 1980s. With these limitations in mind, then, let us turn to what readers have made of these novels. I have used whatever names have been provided on the Amazon.com site; some of them are real, some are monikers.

Generally speaking, the novels that have generated the most heat and discussion, as of July 2011, are Johanna Lindsey's *Captive Bride* (ninety-five reviews), Bertrice Small's *The Kadin* (seventy-six reviews), and Small's *Love Slave* (fifty-four reviews). Most other popular novels in this genre have accrued between a half dozen and two dozen reviews. Lindsey's *Captive Bride* is the novel most criticized for its lack of literary quality, and for its "rape and spanking scenes." The main reader complaints, however, are that the hero and heroine are unappealing, two-dimensional characters. Two reviewers comment on the similarity of the plot to E. M. Hull's *The Sheik* and recommend the original. To a 2005 reader who calls the novel the "Captive Bride of Frankenstein," the violence detracts from the romance and makes the characters, if not the novel, seem pathological:

> Somehow rape, beatings, threats and fear just don't seem to be the stuff of this woman's dreams. Philip needs to do time, and the woman (what was her name again? She was such a wimpy non-entity that it now escapes me) needs therapy and a restraining order. Some of the reviewers state that this sort of thing was acceptable in the 70's. I was around then . . . and I can tell you that treating a woman like dirt and actually enslaving her was no more acceptable then than it is now. Let's not romanticize violence, and excuse abuse towards a woman by calling it love. Unless you're the kind of woman who trolls for dates at a maximum-security institution, I'd give this one a miss.

Lindsey has a huge and loyal fan club, however, and many of the reviewers defend the novel. Some concede that this, being her first, is not one of her best novels, and they go on to suggest her others, particularly *Silver Angel*, for those who like harem historical romances. Others declare fierce enthusiasm for all aspects of the novel ("For all of you other reviewers who thought this book was awful, let me tell you something — YOU DON'T KNOW A THING ABOUT ROMANCE!!!") and excuse the violence because it is "like Arabia or something for Christ's sake; they have different traditions there, it's not thought as 'degrading' when a man spanks his wife. I mean, come ON ppl! [*sic*]." K. Warren of Clarkston, WA, on the other hand, excuses the violence on the grounds of history rather than Orientalism, urging people to "Remember this is a HISTORI-CAL romance!"

I agree that this is far from JL's best. Taking into consideration that it was a first book, it really wasn't as bad as some have said. One problem many have is rape, beatings, and other unacceptable behaviors. If you are any kind of a student of history you should know that many of these behaviors were common in historical context. While they were no less horrible for the women, they happened. It is wrong to apply current sensibilities to historical fiction. We should remember that women were treated differently before the 20th century.

The same response is elicited by Rosemary Rogers's part-Orientalist bodice ripper, *Wicked Loving Lies* (forty-one reviews), for which some readers impatiently write: "Yes we know that violence against women is wrong no matter the time period. This book contains several rapes scenes. If you know that this kind of material offends you then don't read this book."

It is interesting that those who enjoy the rougher sex or rape scenes make a distinction between their own open-mindedness and what they perceive to be the insipidity of other romance readers whom they sneeringly classify as Harlequin readers. SlippersLadd writes of *Wicked Loving Lies*:

> This is a fictional piece we're discussing, not yesterday's front page headline of events that happened to a young girl down the street!! Lighten up & enjoy this novel as it's intended to be. However, pay close attention to negative remarks if you are faint of heart & prefer Harlequin or simpleton short stories from a romance magazine.

For most readers who enjoy reading about this kind of rough usage, however, the important criteria are usually whether the hero is somewhat likeable and whether the heroine experiences sexual pleasure or even orgasm in the midst of rape. Laurie E. Baker of New York objects to *Wicked Loving Lies* on these grounds:

> Too much abuse, not enough love. . . . Don't get me wrong. I am not one of those people who can't stand novels unless they are totally PC. There have been some romances I've enjoyed where there have been rape scenes, but at least the rapist gave the heroine a good orgasm or two. Nothing [of] that kind in this book.

On the other hand, in discussing the rape scene in Lindsey's *Captive Bride*, Avezbadalova of New York writes that she likes the hero Philip, and "[despite] what anyone else says, I loved the part where he had to spank her. I don't think I'd mind getting spanked by him myself ;-)." Where Rogers's *Wicked Loving Lies* is too dark to be read humorously, Lindsey's *Captive Bride* elicits ironic readings that provide much fun and pleasure. This contrapuntal, comedy-skewed angle of reading comes through most clearly in the tongue-in-cheek review of the book on the "Sheikhs and Desert Love" website:

> This book, written in 1977, is a delicious romp completely unburdened with political correctness. Not only does Sheik Abu rudely snatch Christina away from her life, he orders her to stay inside his sparsely furnished tent, spanks her with frequency, and physically overpowers her in his bed. Only in an historical romance novel written in the 1970s could this be considered really really hot. . . .
>
> Abu, ever the Neanderthal, has a rather unconventional exchange with his beloved as he is asking her to wed him:
>
> Abu: "If I ever catch you looking sideways at another man, I will beat the daylights out of you!"
>
> Christina (surprised): "Will you really?"
>
> Abu: "No. You won't be out of bed long enough to give me reason."
>
> Now who could possibly turn down a proposal like that?

These reviews demonstrate a number of things that do not align with traditional psychoanalytic or sociological analyses of "the romance reader." First, it is obvious from readers' comments that literary quality—the construction of plot, pacing, character, use of leitmotifs, and language—is important to romance readers even if the standard required is different from that of "high" literature, and even if it differs from one reader to another. Second, there is no consensus among reader attitudes or responses to violence, but none of the readers mistake fantasy for reality. Those who find rape fantasies acceptable or enjoyable make it clear that rape is unacceptable in real life. Third, while critics such as Snitow, Modleski, Radway, and others have assumed that romance readers are reading these novels "straight," reader reviews show that this is by no means always the case. Readers sometimes approach these novels from the skewed angle of bathetic humor and with the same ironic distance as the critic (a position that they assume in these reviews), noting the flaws but enjoying the fun and the purple prose. One reader writes of Small's *Love Slave*: "Small is so graphic when it comes to sex. Is it tittilating [*sic*]? Nope. It's funny and disturbing. The prose are [*sic*] so purple that you'll need sunglasses to protect yourself from the ultraviolet light they practically emitt [sic]." Some readers certainly obtain emotional fulfillment, satisfaction, and escape from reality through these novels; for others, reading romance is simply about the sublimely ridiculous and wonderful fun of reading an outrageous, improbable story. This attitude toward reading works with novels such as Captive Bride, but is less successful with The Kadin.

Small is a polarizing novelist but her work is considered innovative and important by most Amazon.com reviewers. In the reviews, The Kadin is highly praised by most readers for its historical content, although this praise is by no means unanimous. Many readers comment that the book is well researched and gives them a fascinating insight into the Ottoman Empire—something about which they had known very little when they first began reading the novel. All reviewers take for granted the accuracy of the historical information offered in the novel. This is because, in comparison to other harem historical novels, Small's work is anchored in actual historical personages and events, and is meticulously detailed with extensive descriptions of costumes, architecture, and furnishings, and allusions to obscure and exotic customs and historical facts. She skillfully creates the "reality effect" of a different historical and cultural world that Helen Hughes refers to in her work on historical fiction, The Historical Romance (18–20). An early 1997 review simply states: "This book paints a very different picture of Sultan Selim I, usually called the Grim. It shows his love for his wives and children, his sense of fairness of the law, and the truth of his father's abdication of the throne. . . . A must read for anybody interested in Turkish history." Michelle Slaughter of Orlando agrees, over a decade later, that The Kadin provides "a fascinating glimpse into what the private lives and motivations of Selim I and Suleiman/Suleyman the Great might have been." Reading the novel prompted greater curiosity and interest in the Ottomans for some readers. Terra Chadwick of Panama writes: "The Kadin explained so much about the Sultan [sic] way of life, not known today. So much so, that I re-read certain parts of the novel today, and looked up on the internet all that I could find on Sultan Selim." Erika Overton of Poughkeepsie agrees: "It made me extremely interested in Turkish history and harem life in that time period." One reader, who was not particularly enthused by history, concedes that "Bertrice teaches you about history, and you don't even mind!"

Not all readers, however, are enamored with the historical aspect of the novel because they feel that it gets in the way of a good romance. Hanna Bagai expresses disappointment that "it focused more on politics of Ottoman Empire, rather than on love or romance," and N. Pandit agrees that "The beginning was great . . . But I don't like politics at all. . . . This book made me think about it and the characters so much when it was done that I had to remind myself that it was just a story. Gave me a heart-ache." A number of readers mention the emotional pain they felt reading this particular novel, much of their concern centering on the fact that so much of the heroine's life is marked by tragedy: she loses so many members of her family, and she has to deal with the polygamous nature of Ottoman culture and share the love of her life, Sultan Selim I, with his other wives. An anonymous reviewer warns readers: "I cannot really recommend this book unless you can stand the pain of the story. Some may see it as one woman's triumph over whatever life threw at her, but it was more than I could handle." The reviewer concedes that "Small is a great writer and her sense of history is fantastic but I am a romance novel reader not a history buff." In its historical accuracy and superb achievement of verisimilitude, the novel had failed as an escapist, feel-good romance novel for this reader.

Whether the polygamous plot is acceptable, and whether it allows the novel to still be categorized as a romance, is fiercely debated among readers, as well. For some readers polygamy kills the romance even though "from a historical perspective it was very enlightening and interesting." An anonymous reviewer complains:

> I'm sorry, but I just can't get past the idea of four women sharing one man—and then actually liking each other, too! Yes, I have a Western bias and I'm not ashamed to admit it. Slave auctions, spouse splitting, isolation, harem intrigue . . . Color me clueless, but how romantic is any of that? A 13 year-old girl sold naked on a slave auction block may have been in vogue for those times, but I think it should thoroughly repulse the modern reader.

Interestingly enough, one reader acknowledges that the expectations of genre played a part in determining her response: "Had I set my expectations for a history lesson, my review may have been different." Generally, those who can accept the polygamous storyline and still view the relationship between Janet and Selim as romantic excuse it because it happened "in other cultures and other time periods"—the same justification given for the rape and spanking in Lindsey's *Captive Bride*. Similarly, Orientalist assumptions shape readers' acceptance of such practices, as in the following comment: "Wow. The historical detail in this novel was excellent, rivaled only by the love story between Cyra and Selim. For those who point out that they can't imagine sharing one man, please open your minds! This happened regularly during that time period, and it still goes on today in the Middle East."

Readers of *The Kadin* who were familiar with Small's other historical fiction often expressed surprise at the restraint shown in depicting sex scenes in this 1970s novel, for they had come to expect highly graphic scenes and multiple sex partners for the heroine of a Bertrice Small novel. *Love Slave* met these expectations but, at the same time, it also generated a torrent of warnings from readers that "this story is NOT for everyone. Bertrice Small has always been extremely graphic in her stories, and if you don't like highly detailed erotic scenes, stay away from this story." Many reviews of *Love Slave* are very enthusiastic, praising the book for its conscientious historical research into the reign of Abd ar-Rahman III, Emir and Caliph of Cordoba (r. 889–961), and into Moorish culture, as well as its "hot" sex descriptions. It is clear from these reviews that Small has a loyal and devoted fan base who follow her work closely. Some readers are frank about enjoying *Love Slave* mainly as erotica. S. Quevedo of San Diego writes: "I didn't like this book so much for the romance . . . as I did for the SIZZLING love scenes. Boy, I thought I was in a sauna!" Reader enjoyment of sexual explicitness, however, could also meld with amusement at its purple prose. One review reads: "Wonderfully Trashy. . . . Parts of the book [were] explicit and disgusting but I loved it. I never knew there were so many ways to describe sex without actually saying the word 'sex.'"

However, the enthusiasm shown by some readers is counterbalanced by confusion and distaste from other readers who cannot decide whether or not this is a romance novel. In 1999, an anonymous reviewer addicted to alliteration denounced *Love Slave* as "Sleazy, skanky, slutty sex! . . . I needed a shower after reading this potpourri of porno, pillage and pretense! . . . There is no romance—just sex ad nauseum [*sic*]." The issue of sex in this novel raised two problems for readers. First, some readers criticize the novel for confusing sex with romantic love, as the previous comment demonstrates. For other readers, contemporary social issues intrude on the fantasy of the story. F. Orion Pozo from Raleigh, North Carolina, feels that *Love Slave* romanticizes the serious global problem of sexual slavery which, considering the victimization of "hundreds of thousands of women and children subjected to this horror every year," is "not a problem to be taken lightly." An anonymous reviewer condemns the book as "kiddie porn," questioning how some reviewers can rate highly "a story of a young girl . . . and a 28 year old man then a 50 year old man who use her sexually," and insisting that the "fact that so many find it 'erotic' that a man would insert silver balls, use dildos rectally on a (age range in this story) 13–15 year old girl is sort of creepy." In response, another reviewer falls back on "historical accuracy," once again, to mount an impassioned defense of *Love Slave*:

> The review who thinks this is all "Kiddie Porn" is missing the point. I am a faithfull [*sic*] reader of Small's work in part because of the lush love scenes, but more importantly [*sic*] as a historian I appriciate [*sic*] the HISTORICAL ACCURACY of her work. IF the "Kiddie Porn" reviewer had bothered to look at ANY crediable [*sic*] history book she would know that women were married young throughout most of history. . . . The historical accuracy Small presents is what keeps me coming back for more, I can make the distinction between REALITY, FICTION and HISTORY.

By the turn of the twenty-first century, however, violent sex, especially when it involved young adolescent girls, was generally considered highly disturbing and could not be easily justified on the grounds of historical or cultural difference. "Audrey the librarian" from Boston complains that

> what I was most disturbed by was the violence, and to me it's amazing that even those who are critical of the author's efforts here have not even mentioned it, whereas I would go so far as to say it ruined this book for me. I can enjoy brutes and naughtiness right along with the next person when it comes to reading a romance, but there is some disturbing violence here in the form of a mass murder, a suicide, graphic torture and the death of children. I need escape from my escape literature! C'mon, Bertrice, lighten up!

The solution to this problem is suggested by J. Dirpaul: "Despite the shocking rape scenes in the novel, it is quite a very good read. I just skip along the sex and continue reading as the plot thickens." Here, as with all the other reviews, it is clear that one of the pleasures of reading is that it is an active, reader-directed process, and each text is experienced and enjoyed differently by individual readers.

Perhaps the most surprising thing arising from these reviews, finally, is the fact that the al-Qaeda attacks on the United States on September 11, 2001, have scarcely made a dent on the popularity of cross-cultural historical romances. Among all the Amazon.com reviewers, there is only one reader, Elizabeth Cook, who brings up September 11. Writing about Small's *Love Slave*, Cook acknowledges that

> she delivers a hot and spicy erotic novel that will keep the pages turn-
> ing. . . . [But] the biggest problem I have with this book, is it was writ-
> ten pre-September 11th back when being abducted by a sheik and
> carried off into the desert was favorite fodder for all of us romance
> buffs. I don't know about you, but my enjoyment of reading romances
> with Arab hero's [*sic*] and harems . . . came down with the twin towers.
> I know it isn't really fair, but somehow being abducted and carried off
> to the middle east as a captive or "love slave" has lost it's [*sic*] romantic
> appeal. Now all it does is remind me of the way things have changed for
> us all and the huge gulf that divides us.

It is certainly possible that there are other readers who feel the same way and who have simply stopped buying these novels without leaving comments on any romance website. However, the steady output of this subgenre and its climbing sales figures in the years after September 11, 2001, tell a different story. It appears that readers *want* to know more about Middle Eastern culture and history, and the harem historical novels are an enjoyable and accessible way of learning about these things within an environment that is recognizably structured according to the conven-tions of Western Orientalist literature and romance novels. The impor-tance of a well-researched historical background to the Oriental romance is demonstrated by the popularity of Bertrice Small's novels (*The Kadin* remains in print more than thirty years after its first publication) despite the strong reactions provoked among some readers. That the subgenre of harem historical novels is "Orientalist," in Edward Said's pejorative re-definition of the term, is undeniable. The reiteration of Orientalist "facts" is certainly problematic and fails to add to a greater understanding of contemporary Middle Eastern politics, society, or culture. In the novels, the East is sensual, violent, barbaric, despotic, debauched, and patriar-chal to the point of misogyny. But then again, so is the West, according to these novels, in which the greatest villains are often not Muslims or Arabs or Ottomans, but other Europeans. "History" was like that, as so many readers' reviews make clear. These readers have an instinctively pro-gressive sense of their own history, whereby the primitivisms of the past have evolved to the enlightened present of Western modernity, whereas the Middle East still seems to be snared in the Middle Ages—yet another

Orientalist perception. But surely it counts for something that readers of mass-market popular fiction continue to be interested in other cultures and other times (however misrepresented) in an age of Islamist terrorism and a global retreat from multiculturalism; that readers acknowledge their own history to contain many of the "Orientalist" qualities of the Middle East; and that the novels continue to affirm the possibilities of communication and relationship with the Oriental other, not only in the purple-prosed past of the harem historical, but also in the modern-day sheik novels that form the subject of the next three chapters.

SIX

The Contemporary Sheik Romance Novel: The Historical Background

Lighthearted escapism is the supposed raison d'être *of the romance genre, so what happens when such novels are set in the present day, in a part of the world that we see on the nightly news? What is it that makes these swarthy princes of the desert so hot now, capturing the imagination—and dollars—of the American romance audience at a time when the Middle East seems more perilous than ever?*

CHRISTY MCCULLOUGH, "DESERT HEARTS"

Romance fiction constitutes the largest segment of the American consumer book market today. In 2007, estimated earnings reached just under $1.4 billion. American publishers released around 8,090 titles that year, with fourteen percent of Americans buying twenty or more novels for themselves (RWA statistics, 2009). In 2008, one in four Americans—74.8 million people—read at least one romance novel, while 29 million read romances on a regular basis. Of these readers, 9.5 percent were men (RWA readership statistics, 2007). The statistics for turn-of-the-century sales of romance fiction outside the United States are just as remarkable. In 1999, Harlequin Mills & Boon claimed 32 percent of the paperback market in the United Kingdom, totaling eleven million readers, or four out of every ten women (McAleer 3). In Australia in 2000, 36 percent of all mass-market paperback sales were romance novels. Harlequin Mills & Boon sold more than five million copies in Australia that year, or more than 400,000 books a month: one-fifth of all paperbacks sales (www.eharlequin.com 2000). Sales figures were also high in non-

Western countries such as India—the largest market for Harlequin Mills & Boon outside Britain and North America (Parameswaran 1999: 84). The sheer size of this market, combined with the fact that readers often enjoy armchair travel and the "facts" they glean from romance novels set in exotic locations, means that we need to take seriously the Orientalist discourses reproduced in these novels (Mann 13, McAleer 99–100, 258).

The Sultan's Bed, The Sultan's Bought Bride, The Seductive Sheik, The Sheik's Revenge, The Sheik's Reward, The Sheik's Captive Bride, The Sheik and the Kidnapped Bride, The Sheik and the Princess Bride, The Sheik and the Virgin Princess, The Sheik and the Virgin Secretary, The Sheik and the Vixen, The Sheik's Seduction, The Sheik's Temptation, The Surgeon Sheikh's Proposal, The Solitary Sheikh, Secret Agent Sheik . . . . These are just a few of the titles beginning with "s" on the "Sheikhs and Desert Love" website database of Orientalist romance novels published since the 1970s—a list that runs well into the hundreds. The contemporary romance fiction genre is divided into two forms: "category" romances, which are released on a regular basis, focus almost exclusively on the unfolding romance between hero and heroine and are sold under particular publisher imprints or series lines, such as Harlequin Presents, Harlequin Intrigue, Silhouette, and so forth; and "single-title" or mass-market paperbacks, which are longer and looser in plot, structure, and focus, and are marketed by the author's name rather than the publisher's category imprint (Frenier 5). In this chapter, I concentrate on category romances because the modern sheik romance is a phenomenon almost wholly within category romance fiction. Also, unless keywords such as "sheik," "sultan," or "desert" feature in the title, it is very difficult to determine which single-title novels are actually Orientalist romances featuring cross-cultural, interracial relationships, with one partner having a Middle Eastern background. There may well be other single-title romance novels featuring interracial couples of Islamic or Arabic descent that were published in the second half of the twentieth century, but I have not been able to locate them, and they do not appear on the websites devoted to Orientalist romance novels, which focus on historical and category romances.

That the sheik romance novel should have enjoyed such popularity at the end of the twentieth century would have been unthinkable in the 1930s, when the modern-day desert romance petered out. The reasons for its decline have already been discussed in Chapters 2 and 3. Readers began to tire of the glut of sheik and desert romances produced throughout the 1920s, especially when these became the source of ridicule and satire in popular culture. The onset of anticolonial unrest in the Middle East made

it difficult to imagine the region as a setting for romance, although it became increasingly popular as a location for male thriller and adventure
novels (Simon 1989 and 2010). Furthermore, writers also struggled with
the problem of achieving a happy ending in an age acutely conscious of
the taboo of transgressing hierarchical racial divides. "Sheiks" were charismatic, sexy, romantic heroes, but unless romance novelists continually
unveiled them to be European, the novel endings were shadowed with the
prospect of interracial union and its implications for the white heroine,
her mixed offspring, and the imperial race. Although the genre labored
on in American films, it fell out of favor with British romance publishers
in the ensuing decades. For example, an attempt by the British-born Australian author Nerina Hilliard to submit just such a story set among the
North African Tuaregs to romance publisher Mills & Boon in 1959 met
with a flat rejection and the declaration that the genre had been mocked
so much it would be "hopelessly unfashionable" (McAleer 208). A mere
decade later, however, Mills & Boon would publish Violet Winspear's *Blue
Jasmine* (1969), the book that marked the revival of the contemporary
sheik romance novel. It was a trend that began with a slow and intermittent trickle of desert books throughout the 1970s and early 1980s, but
turned into a deluge of largely North American-authored novels after the
Gulf War of 1990–1991. By 2005, the modern sheik romance was such
a notable phenomenon that it attracted serious attention from political
bloggers and *Time* magazine, which inquired sarcastically: "As the genre's
51 million readers pump gas this summer, will they be dreaming of oil
sheikhs in exotic kingdoms or eternal supplies of fuel in the arms of a gas
station owner?" (August, "Sheiks and the Serious Blogger").

What caused the revival of the modern sheik romance novel, particularly in the United States? Was it triggered by a growing awareness
of political events in the Middle East, as was so much other postwar Orientalist American popular culture? As scholars enumerating the various
negative images of Arabs and Muslims in American novels, comics, cartoons, films, and songs have noted, these cultural forms were often responsive to crises in the Middle East: the establishment of the state of
Israel in 1948 and the Arab-Israeli War; the CIA-assisted overthrow of the
democratically elected Iranian prime minister, Mohammed Mossadegh,
in 1953, after he tried to nationalize Iranian oil; American intervention in
Syria and Lebanon during the civil war of 1957; the Six-Day War of 1967;
the beginning of PLO splinter-group hijackings of European and American jetliners starting in 1968; the massacre of Israeli Olympians in Munich
in 1972; the October War of 1973; the OPEC oil embargo against countries

that had supported Israel in the war, which subsequently sent oil prices skyrocketing in an already stressed American economy suffering from the effects of the Vietnam War; the paranoia that petrodollar-rich Arabs were "buying up Wall Street" and acquiring American businesses, agriculture, and political influence;[1] the overthrow of Mohammed Reza Pahlavi, shah of Iran, in 1979; and, of course, the Iranian hostage crisis of 1979–1981, whereby fifty-three Americans from the embassy in Tehran were held hostage for 444 days.

Male adventure fiction and thrillers thrived on such exciting international events. Reeva Simon (2010) examines how, from the First World War onward, the Middle East formed the backdrop to British spy intrigues such as John Buchan's *Greenmantle* (1916), Sax Rohmer's *The Mask of Fu Manchu* (1932), Eric Ambler's *Journey into Fear* (1940) and *The Levanter* (1972), and, later, Cold War thrillers such as Ian Fleming's James Bond novels. American novels such as Leon Uris's *Exodus* (1958) and *The Haj* (1984), Mark Helprin's *Refiner's Fire* (1977), Benjamin and Herbert Stein's *On the Brink* (1977), "Trevanian's" *Shibumi* (1979), and British author John le Carré's *The Little Drummer Girl* (1983) were all inspired by, or written in response to, events in the Middle East: attacks on Israel; Palestinian displacement and desire for self-determination; revenge attacks on the Palestinians who had killed the Israeli Olympians; and international oil intrigues involving OPEC (Orfalea 1988, Christison 1987). Melani McAlister argues that as a result of the twenty-nine Palestinian-related airliner hijackings between 1968 and 1976, terrorist attacks in various places between 1974 and 1975, and the Iranian hostage crisis, "the rescue of hostages taken by Middle Eastern terrorists became a near obsession in U.S. cultural texts, inspiring films, novels, and true-story narratives" (181–182, 223–224). Hollywood action films such as *Iron Eagle* (1986), *Delta Force* (1986), *True Lies* (1994), *G.I. Jane* (1998), and *The Siege* (1998) incorporated motifs of Arab hostage-taking and Middle Eastern terrorism into their violent plots about (usually white) American families who needed to be rescued.

Such popular discourses conflated "Arab" with "Muslim" and "Middle Eastern," ignoring the dizzying variety of languages, cultures, religions, and various ethnic and national identifications to be found in the Middle East: Jewish, Sunni, Shi'a, Druze, Sufi, Catholic, Maronite, Greek Orthodox, Coptic, Protestant, Baha'i, Moroccan, Algerian, Libyan, Eritrean, Egyptian, Sudanese, Lebanese, Syrian, Israeli, Palestinian, Jordanian, Kurdish, Turkish, Iraqi, Kuwaiti, Yemeni, Saudi Arabian, Bahreini, Qatari, Dubaian, Tunisian, Assyrian, Chaldean, Berber, Bedouin, and others.

Furthermore, as many Arab Americans complained, the anti-Arab images presented by the media generated a homogenized category of the "Arab/ Middle Eastern/Muslim" enemy, which was particularly pernicious during times of specific U.S. government interventions in the Middle East. The images provided a cultural justification for American foreign policy as well as for increasingly discriminatory domestic measures against Arab Americans in the late twentieth century (Naber 49–50).

In contrast to these forms of popular culture, however, the modern sheik romance novel seems to bear little direct connection to Middle Eastern politics. The reasons for this are obvious. The modern mass-market romance novel focuses on the relationship and growing love between the hero and heroine; it must have a happy ending where readers can imagine its protagonists setting up a viable new family unit. As Peter Mann's commissioned reader surveys for Mills & Boon in 1969 and 1974 show, although romance readers came from a surprisingly diverse background as far as education and occupation were concerned, they were emphatic about wanting feel-good escapism in their romance reading (Mann 1969 and 1974).

The wars, oil crises, international intrigues, hijackings, and hostage traumas of Middle Eastern affairs were hardly the stuff of love, and optimistic endings. Reality was not at all romantic. This is not to say that there was no connection at all between romance novels and what was happening in the Middle East. Violet Winspear's *Blue Jasmine*, for example, was published at a symbolically significant time for British–Middle Eastern relationships: Aden's achievement of full independence, and the revoking of British protection and withdrawal of British troops from the Trucial Persian Gulf territories of Abu Dhabi, Dubai, Sharjah, Arjman, Umm al-Quwain, Ras al-Khaimah, and Fujarah, which all federated to become the United Arab Emirates in December 1971. The plots of subsequent sheik romance novels penned by British authors often relied on the background of Britain's good trading and political relations with these Gulf states throughout the 1970s and the fact that British professionals secured lucrative development contracts in these states (Brenchley 273, 280). However, the withdrawal "East of Suez" aside, these were hardly headline-grabbing events compared to the humiliation for the British and French during the Suez Crisis in 1956, or during any of the other Palestinian- or Iranian-related upheavals throughout the 1970s. And most significantly of all, although American romance novelists were writing single-title Orientalist historical novels, as discussed in Chapter 5, no American romance novelist engaged with the contemporary sheik novel at this time despite the fact that American interests and involvement were rapidly eclipsing British ones in the region.

This was because the revival of the modern sheik romance novel had more to do with the vagaries of the international romance publishing industry than with Middle Eastern politics. In this particular scenario, the dominance of the British publishing company Mills & Boon in the international romance industry was central, as was its decision to publish only one American romance author prior to the 1980s despite the fact that the British publishing house had merged with the Canadian paperback company Harlequin in 1972. By 1975, the Canadian media giant Torstar Corporation had taken over Harlequin Mills & Boon. Since the United States was a huge and lucrative market for paperback romances, one might have expected a greater proportion of American romance authors to be included in the Mills & Boon "stable" after the 1970s. However, editorial decisions were made in the London office, and Peter Mann's surveys for the publisher had shown that British readers preferred British or Commonwealth stories to American settings (Mann 1969 and 1974). As Pamela Regis observes, although Harlequin Mills & Boon recruited the American novelist Janet Dailey in 1975, they made no effort to contract any other American romance novelist, content with Dailey as their sole American representative until the 1980s (158–159).

This meant that although American readers were consuming romance novels throughout the twentieth century, it was not until the establishment of rival New York-based American romance publishing imprints, such as Silhouette, Candlelight, or Loveswept, that American writers contributed to the field of category romance fiction in significant numbers. And when American-authored contemporary romance novels first entered the market in the early 1980s, they were almost exclusively focused on American settings. Janet Dailey emphasized her Americanness to carve out a niche for herself in the romance fiction market, setting a novel in every state in the union and romanticizing the genre of the Western novel (Grescoe 120). "Exotic" romantic settings in Dailey's case referred to the cowboys and ranches of her "Calder" series — *This Calder Sky* (1981), *This Calder Range* (1982), and others—with the occasional incursion in the Western hemisphere, as in Dailey's Mexican novel, *Touch the Wind* (1979). By the 1990s, though, American novelists were beginning to write about countries other than the United States. This, together with the fact that Harlequin Mills & Boon had acquired its main New York-based rival, Silhouette, in 1984, meant that American authors were beginning to produce sheik romance novels in ever greater numbers. The Gulf War of

1990–1991 seems to have been the watershed for this interest in modern American love stories about the Middle East.

The final chapters in this book are about Orientalism and the generic mass-market romance novel in the twentieth and twenty-first centuries. This extensive focus on the mass-market romance novel is due to the sheer scale of numbers in category romance as far as publications and readership are concerned. During the "first wave" of scholarship in the 1970s and 1980s, scholars and critics often assumed that because category romances are fairly short (usually just under two hundred pages), and because their plots generally stick to the "formula" of a hero and heroine meeting, conflicting, falling in love, and finally living happily ever after, these books are unchanging and interchangeable. They are not. They clearly show change over time as far as historical background, social issues, heroes and heroines, and national specificities are concerned. In this chapter, I trace the rise of the contemporary sheik novel within the romance publishing industry throughout the twentieth century, exploring the publishing possibilities as well as the circumscriptions that authors of modern Orientalist romance novels experienced when they first started writing sheik love stories. I look at changing ideas of race and ethnic identity resulting from civil rights campaigns and the onset of multiculturalism; then I compare and contrast British, Australian, and American historical ties to the Middle East in an attempt to determine when and why the sheik romance novel was revived. In the following two chapters, I explore characters and themes more fully. In Chapter 7, I examine the development of heroes and heroines, and the role of the harem in mediating East-West and male-female relationships. In Chapter 8, I analyze the changing contours of the sheik romance novel from the 1970s to the present day, focusing on themes of travel, tourism, and place, and continuities in Orientalist topoi. I consider new discourses on development, modernization, and political conflict that were introduced into the sheik romance in the late twentieth century, and I evaluate American romance novelists' responses to the al-Qaeda terrorist attacks on September 11, 2001 and to America's subsequent war on terror.

"RACE" AND THE RISE OF THE HARLEQUIN MILLS & BOON SHEIK NOVEL

The history of category romance novels in the early to mid-twentieth century is largely the history of Mills & Boon, founded in 1908 by Gerald

Mills and Charles Boon. Mills & Boon had started as a general publishing company producing all kinds of fiction and nonfiction, but it soon began to focus on romance fiction written by unknown authors, publishing early desert romances among the various subgenres ("town," "country," and "colonial") then in their nascent state of development. These novels from the 1910s to the 1930s are longer, less formulaic, less predictable, and more like today's single-title romances than their successors in the post-Second World War period. They are often more adventurous, but also more rambling, than their present-day counterparts, frequently given to lengthy descriptive passages rather than the contemporary trend for short paragraphs with a heavy emphasis on dialogue. One of the earliest such novels published by the company was E. S. Steven's *The Veil: A Romance of Tunisia* (1909), which portrayed on its dust jacket sheiks wandering through a street in North Africa, and advertised a story about British protagonists falling in love in the French colony (McAleer 21). Before the 1920s, such stories were part of a broader subgenre of British imperial romance novels set in various European colonies or in the newly formed British dominions, particularly South Africa, Australia, and New Zealand. The popularity of these novels sprang not only from the pervasive culture of imperialism in Britain at the time, but also from the fact that the British Commonwealth formed an important and lucrative market for the London book industry.

In 1896, British publishers had formed a cartel known as the Publishers Association of Great Britain, which was responsible for the regulation of book prices and trading margins for all books produced and distributed throughout Britain and its colonies and dominions. The power of the cartel rested largely on the fact that, according to the Berne International Book Copyright Agreement of 1886, the Anglophone book trade was divided into two distinct spheres: British and American. This meant that British publishers controlled the book industry of more than seventy countries throughout the British Commonwealth, which became a dumping ground for cheap colonial editions of British books. This state of affairs was reaffirmed in the 1950s, when British and American publishers signed a Traditional Markets Agreement that remained in place until the rise of multinational publishing corporations and Internet bookstores began to undermine the two traditional blocs at the end of the twentieth century (Teo 2004: 722–723). The consequences of this arrangement for romance fiction as it developed throughout the twentieth century were significant and meant that although American romance novels were published in the United States and distributed in Britain, few American ro-

mance novelists were published directly in Britain and almost none participated in the shaping of the Mills & Boon variety of category romance
that came to dominate the better part of the twentieth century and made
the name "Mills & Boon" synonymous with "romance novel" in much
of the English-speaking world.[2] Other British colonies and dominions in
turn became "part of an imperial cultural space, dominated and defended
by London publishers, and shared with Canadians, South Africans, New
Zealanders and other readers of the Empire" (Lyons 22).

In Mills & Boon's colonial romances, Arabs were minor but significant characters, particularly in the stories of Louise Gerard, who made
her mark with novels set in African and Middle Eastern colonies. Gerard's
desert romances for Mills & Boon were typical of stories by other British
authors at the time in that, while they tacitly acknowledged the appeal of
the Arab male, they strongly upheld the color bar and shied away from
miscegenation. These stories sometimes told of the fruitless attempts of
Arabs to become "white" so that they could win the heroine, as in Gerard's
Flower-of-the-Moon (1915). Despite the ostensible failure of Arabs, with
their "dark blood," to breach the barrier of race and to marry white women,
Gerard's novels—like other desert romances of the 1920s—demonstrated
inadvertently that white men were by no means wholly distinct or distinguishable from Oriental men. Rather, as far as both the physical appearance and the behavior of men were concerned, white masculinity formed
one end of a continuum of colored masculinities that shaded into each
other: white (British or French), white/brown European (Latin or Mediterranean), and brown Oriental (Arab and sometimes Indian). This is
most clearly shown in Gerard's romance novel *A Sultan's Slave* (1921). The
hero of the novel is actually the son of a French colonel but believes his
father to be an Arab sultan killed by the British. Physically, he passes as
Arab, French, Italian, or Spanish since his biological father, like romantic desert sheiks, was a "big, handsome man with a swarthy complexion,
coal-black hair and dark, fiery eyes, by nature impetuous and reckless"
(Gerard 1921: 1). There is no clear physical difference here between continental European men and Arabs, and the ambiguity in appearance turns
out to be a metonym for moral and racial character. The troubling moral
of the story is that a white man can ignore the "white ideals" of his "white
side" and become just as "barbaric and savage" as any Arab. Just as European men's physiognomies are not always clearly distinguishable from
Arab men's, so, too, European men's values and behavior are not always
sharply defined against that of Orientals. What is needed, therefore, is a
pure white heroine to stop the hero from "going native," and to help him

to "grope back to . . . white ways" (243–245). While the racial *character* of white women is always clearly demarcated from Orientals, the *physiognomy* and sexual appeal of Arab men is closely identified with popular Latin heroes in these early romance novels. The difference, of course, is that white British women could marry Latin European men with impunity since these men were still part of the "white race" despite their swarthy appearance. Yet the near-interchangeability of Arab with Latin men meant that although "ethnic heroes" fell out of favor during the Second World War, their resurgent popularity during the countercultural 1960s brought a rekindling of interest in the sheik hero and the Middle Eastern desert romance novel.

By the Second World War, the romance novel was a recognizable literary genre produced by all the major British publishing houses of the day, but with Mills & Boon in the ascendant. Through standardizing its hardcover books with their easily recognizable brown bindings and highlighting the Mills & Boon imprint rather than the author's name, in addition to maintaining consistent production values, the firm had created a brand associated with a certain type of contemporary romance novel. The war years, moreover, effected a change in the length and format of these stories because of paper rationing, which was an issue in Britain until 1949. The "Mills & Boon" novel became shorter, more streamlined, and written to specific editorial guidelines. Thus was the "category romance" born as standardization continued throughout the 1950s in terms of length (188–192 pages), dust jackets, titles, blurbs, and the prominence of the Mills & Boon logo (McAleer 65–85).

Romantic novels of the 1930s and 1940s had focused largely on the experiences of women within Britain, but this began to change in the 1950s. Although the fifties were characterized by plots with a strong domestic emphasis, they also saw the introduction of new authors from the British dominions, and a turn toward travel abroad, especially after British government restrictions on overseas travel were lifted in 1949. As in the early 1900s, romance novels became vehicles for armchair travel, and included descriptions of exotic landscapes, fauna, flora, and people. They catalogued luxurious fashions, enticing *objets d'arts*, and a plenitude of rich, fresh food. In many novels from the 1950s to the 1970s, the focus is as much on these elements of foreign lifestyle as on the developing romantic relationship between the hero and heroine. The appeal of escapist fantasies abroad is obvious, considering the bleak economies of wartime Britain: the bombings and rationing; the shortages of consumer goods; the drab, postwar jerry-built housing; the lack of fresh food; the prevalence of ersatz tinned goods; and the restrictions on travel during the war—not just abroad, but to the south and east coast of Britain as well (Middleton 18). "Rosalind Brett" (Lillian Warren), one of the most popular postwar authors for Mills & Boon, tapped into a growing trend when she wrote stories about independent young women who went out to the sunlit plains of Africa, where they met, conquered, and civilized the pioneering hero. Another Mills & Boon novelist commented that she "loved Brett's foreign backgrounds" because "I always longed to travel. The English people did not travel much after the war" (McAleer 99).

In addition to the exotic element of travel abroad, Jay Dixon argues persuasively that cultural changes in the postwar years increasingly wrought changes in British perceptions of masculinity that made ethnic men desirable as alternative heroes in romance novels. In her century-long survey of Mills & Boon novels, Dixon contends that the postwar years were characterized by a shift from the wartime hero to the tame and domesticated "boy next door" as romantic hero (70). This was fine for romance novels set in Britain, but in novels set abroad, such British types often fared poorly against their rough and rugged, aggressively masculine, pioneering colonial counterparts. The rise of the macho, "angry young man" in Britain during the 1950s provided little inspiration for romance novelists in Dixon's view, "perhaps because this type of brutal working-class masculinity was too close to reality to fantasize about" (71). With their aggressive and overtly sexist masculinity, their hostility toward women, and their defiant championing of drunken nights out with the boys, bar brawls, and freedom from the ties of emasculating domesticity, these were hardly men with whom heroines could dream about living happily ever after. The same applied to the androcentric worlds of the Teddy Boys and the skinhead bovver boys during the 1950s and 1960s, when youth culture became dominant.

Dixon argues that in response to these expressions of British masculinity, romance novelists "developed the Alpha man—a hero placed, not against a background of home, but against the world" (71). The alpha male was powerful, masterful, competent, and resourceful in all situations. He was ruthless against his enemies (and therefore an effective protector of the woman he loved), a high achiever, a leader of men, and, above all, he was sexually dynamic. With the advent of hippie culture in Britain during the 1960s, if the alpha male wasn't from the colonies or former colonies (Australia, McAleer asserts, was "definitely 'Alpha' country," 203), then he was Latin or Arab, for British romance novelists attributed to these conservative cultures "the machismo they [could] no longer find in British masculinity" (Dixon 72). The renaissance of the Arab sheik as romance hero and the revival of the modern-day desert romance therefore have more to do with changes in British domestic popular culture—particularly certain perceptions of British masculinity—than with Britain's actual relationship with the Middle East. Quite often, the character traits supposedly distinguishing the Arab sheik hero overlap with those of the Latin lover (who could be Spanish, French, Greek, or Italian) because of the continuum of colored masculinity mentioned above. These men are patriarchal, and physically and verbally domineering to the point of harshness. They maintain a strong sense of differentiation between masculine and feminine gender roles, but they also possess a strong attachment to the idea of the traditional family. They are gentle with children, and they show profound respect to their elders, both male and female. It is the tenderness and dutiful care they demonstrate to familial dependents—the willingness to assume the responsibilities of adulthood—that also distinguish them from the "angry young men," Teddy Boys, and hippies.

Still, because of the association of Arabs with Africans (discussed in Chapters 2 and 3) in British culture during the age of empire, the Arab male had been roundly rejected as a lover and marriage partner in early twentieth century romance novels, even if he had European blood. Having European blood, in fact, made his situation all the worse since he was then considered a "half-caste," acceptable to neither Europeans nor Arabs. How and when did British romance novelists overcome the racial barrier, or decide that the Arab sheik was in fact white enough for the heroine?

The racial politics of Mills & Boon novels began to change slowly as a result of the Second World War, which had demonstrated the barbarous ends of racism taken to its extreme, not only in the form of the Holocaust, but also in the racial war conducted on the Eastern Front, and perhaps even in the racially segregated armies the United States sent to fight Nazism in Europe after 1941. Some British authors had always manifested signs of a troubled conscience as far as the treatment of "natives" was concerned. Although miscegenation was taboo in the early twentieth-century romances, novelists sometimes took it upon themselves to argue for greater tolerance and the just treatment of racial others, possibly out of a sense of imperial noblesse oblige. In Gerard's *A Sultan's Slave*, for example, the heroine intervenes in an Arab slave's whipping. She throws herself in front of the slave and takes the lash upon her own back, forcing the hero to stop the punishment, and filling him with remorse. Thus she keeps the hero "European" and halts his "Oriental" behavior. McAleer argues that from the 1940s onward, Mills & Boon authors began to depart from the overt racism of earlier novelists. The firm began to publish novels urging "greater tolerance for foreigners," while racial "prejudice and jingoism" began to be condemned during the war years. In Elizabeth Hoy's *Proud Citadel* (1942), for example, the heroine is angrily censured by the hero for referring to Moroccans as "childish savages" who have no manners and who have never heard of Oxford or the Sorbonne. (Her racist views were particularly troubling during the war years since the British and the French were partly relying on colonial troops to combat Nazism.) In the end, the heroine learns to value Muslim culture from an Arab teacher who tells her: "We who are Moslems are interested only in the progress of the spirit. For the Western peoples progress is measured in terms of cruelty and might" (McAleer 185). In the midst of the Second World War, this seemed irrefutable. And it was certainly a far cry from the image of cruel and fanatical Muslim terrorists that would come to dominate Western popular culture in the last third of the twentieth century.

The popularity of postwar stories set in foreign locations, especially the colonies or former colonies, and the recruiting of novelists from the British Commonwealth, raised the issue of how authors were to deal with race relations, particularly during the 1950s and 1960s. Such an issue was salient in the era of decolonization and increasing immigration to Britain by subjects from its former colonies in the West Indies and South Asia. Until the passage of the Commonwealth Immigration Act of 1962 (followed by subsequent acts in 1968 and 1971), Britain had an open-door policy toward its Commonwealth subjects that facilitated immigration. Increasingly restrictive policies toward immigration were prompted by British fears that there were, in Chris Water's words, "dark strangers in our midst," and that "deviant" white women were having sexual relations with these men (Waters 229 and Collins 406–407). Racial tensions accompanied nonwhite immigration, and in 1958, the British experienced their first race riot since the 1920s, when white thugs went on a "nigger hunt" in London and Nottingham, attacking West Indians with knives and broken bottles (Hansen 28). By 1964, a Tory politician was campaigning against a Labour Member of Parliament with the slogan "If you want a nigger for a neighbour, vote Liberal or Labour" (Hansen 29). The British Labour Party responded to such racism with antidiscrimination legislation in 1965—the same year that student protests were held in London against both the Vietnam War and the racism of Ian Smith's white apartheid government in Rhodesia. By the end of the decade, however, racist and Far Right anti-immigration supporters were galvanized by Enoch Powell's "Rivers of

Blood" speech in 1968, in which he denounced the forthcoming Race Relations Bill and prophesied that immigrants would "organise to consolidate their members, to agitate and campaign against their fellow citizens, and to overawe and dominate the rest with the legal weapons which the ignorant and the ill-informed have provided" (Powell 1968). Nevertheless, antiracism and civil rights activists persisted with their campaigns, eventually winning mixed gains. Although the government was alarmed by the rising tide of right-wing, anti-immigration sentiment and the formation of the British National Front, responding with further restrictions to primary immigration in 1971, some concessions were made to those nonwhite Britons already living in the country. By 1976, antiracist activism resulted in the passage of the Race Relations Act as well as the establishment of the Commission for Racial Equality and the de facto adoption of multiculturalist policies.

Although primarily responding to specific local conditions of decolonization and Commonwealth immigration, civil rights activism in Britain was part of a larger global movement inspired by events in the United States. Opposition to "Jim Crow" laws and discrimination against blacks had been mounting since the 1930s, becoming particularly acute when black Americans were transported in segregated ships to fight against the Nazis. The National Association for the Advancement of Colored People led the way. The dismantling of the United States' various apartheid institutions began in the 1950s with the landmark legal case *Brown v. Board of Education* (1954), which ordered the desegregation of schools. From 1955 until his assassination in April 1968, Martin Luther King Jr., led a series of nationally publicized nonviolent protests against various Jim Crow practices in the South. In the 1960s, he was joined in this endeavor by the Student Non-Violent Coordinating Committee and the Congress on Racial Equality, while the summer of 1963 saw a quarter of a million Americans marching peacefully through Washington, D.C., to gather at the Lincoln Memorial, where King gave his famous "I have a dream" speech. The culmination of such efforts to redress racial discrimination through the legal and political system was the Civil Rights Act of 1964, which prohibited discrimination or segregation on the basis of "an individual's race, color, religion, sex, or national origin" in public spaces and in public life (CRA 1964 Title VII—Equal Employment Opportunities—42 U.S. Chapter Code 21). White Americans formed a significant minority of activists in these movements, which were also notable for instances of interracial or ethnosexual relations between black men and white women. As Joanne Nagel explains:

The movement's challenge to the racial order contributed to an atmosphere in which blacks and whites were allowed and sometimes expected to have sex with one another. Both blacks and whites began to view one another as potential sexual partners through lenses colored by the sexual fantasies, stereotypes, and meanings associated with skin color. For both blacks and whites interracial sexual contact was pregnant with sexual, political, social and cultural meanings. (119)

Yet for many romance readers of the time, discussions of interracial relations were deeply uncomfortable, if not offensive. Racial conflict was ugly and surely had no place in an "escapist" romance novel. Still, race was the ubiquitous and unavoidable issue of the day, and as Joseph McAleer shows, a significant number of Mills & Boon novelists were eager to take progressive, activist positions on the depiction of nonwhite people, although these nonwhites were never seriously considered for the role of the romantic protagonists (268–269). Reform-minded writers who championed civil rights wanted to tackle issues such as apartheid and the treatment of black people. They were always reined in by Alan Boon (nephew of founder Charles Boon) and the Mills & Boon editorial team, who were mindful not only of the South African and southern United States market, but of racial sensitivities in other nonwhite Commonwealth markets as well (McAleer 269–270). Boon liked his romantic countries and characters to be "uncolored." In the midst of the Tory "nigger for a neighbor" campaign against Labour M.P. Patrick Gordon Walker, Mills & Boon received a manuscript from Alex Stuart, vice president of the British Romantic Novelists Association, set in the fictional African country of Lehar, where the heroine's father is a civil rights, antiapartheid activist. Stuart acknowledged that the "Colour Question" would be a problem in the South African and southern United States market, but asked provocatively:

> Do we care about American sales? Personally I think that having the book banned in S. Africa because it was anti-apartheid ought to increase its sales elsewhere but this is your province, not mine. . . . This is the sort of "romantic" novel I am now hoping to be able to write . . . as I believe it to be the kind which *must* come in the future, if the romantic novel is to hold its new, young, readers and go forward, rather than backward. (269)

Boon disagreed, for he cared not only about the South African and southern American market, but about the British one as well. "There is no doubt today," he wrote in reply to Stuart, "that when even a prospective Labour cabinet minister is supposed to be in danger of losing his seat because of the ramifications of immigration, that the subject is dynamite." He instead advised her to make her fictional country "an uncoloured nation in the history of Israel, Cyprus, Malta, and X others" (McAleer 270).

Such considerations dogged the submission of Nerina Hilliard's 1959 manuscript about the Tuaregs in Algeria. Hilliard was a British-born author who lived in Sydney, Australia, and who published eight romance novels with Mills & Boon from the late 1950s to the mid-1970s. According to McAleer's summary of Hilliard's original manuscript:

> The hero is Muslim, raised by Frenchmen, but secretly a nobleman and a member of the Tuareg tribe, descendant of a lost European Crusader army. He has, Hilliard noted, "a 'lord of creation' air which would fit in well with the aloof and somewhat infuriating type of hero you seem to like." The English heroine travels to Algeria with her fiancé to seek out her mother's Tuareg roots. She meets the hero, falls in love, is released from her engagement, and they marry. (207)

In some ways, this was hardly a radical story for the firm, for in this version both hero and heroine turn out to be Tuareg and of the same racial stock which, Hilliard hastened to add, "are supposed to be a Caucasian or 'white' race" (although "deeply suntanned"), and they did not, in any case, take Islam seriously (McAleer 208). Thus no interracial boundaries are transgressed in this plot. Boon's reader rejected Hilliard's manuscript on the following grounds:

a) Colour bar. Miss Hemming's [*sic*] account of this race as originally Caucasian would do for English readers, but we have to think of our South African market, too, and I don't believe they'd stand for it.

b) Religion. If the hero is a Moslem, I don't think it helps much that he is a lax one! The Eire readers would find much matter of offence here. If, on the other hand, he is made an R[oman] C[atholic] (because of his French upbringing) then we must expect roars of rage from the manse.

c) However carefully the scene is set, the story is surely bound to recall the sheikery of the *Garden of Allah* and *Desert Song* period. This is hopelessly unfashionable, and so much mockery has been slung at that particular genre that I very much doubt whether it will ever share in the revival that other vogues of the 20s and 30s have been enjoying.

d) Algeria. This link-up is the reverse of an advantage. Our readers have shown over and over again that what they like about romance is that it takes their minds off the troubles of real life. Algeria is one of the nastiest things happening today, and fortunately it is one that we can put out of our minds with a clear conscience. This does seem to me a most excellent reason for *not* writing about it. (McAleer 208)

The book was unacceptable in 1959 but it was eventually published post-humously by Mills & Boon in 1976 with small but significant changes to the plot.[3] In the novel, titled *Land of the Sun,* the heroine is unquestion-ably British; it is her Welsh fiancé and his sister who discover that their mother is Tuareg, and they journey, with the heroine, to Algeria to explore their mother's roots. Little is said about the Algerian War of Independence, which had lasted from 1954 to 1962, and which had caused Mills & Boon so much concern. Instead, despite its contemporary setting, the racial focus is on the distant past. Much is made of the myth that the Tuareg are a warrior tribe who "could be descendants of a Roman legion which managed to get itself lost in the desert," or who are perhaps "descendants of Crusader ships wrecked on the coast of Africa." (The "descendants of shipwrecked Crusaders" theory was used not only for the Tuaregs, but for Violet Winspear's Berber and Moroccan heroes as well.) In any case, the Tuaregs are "whites" of some sort. Hilliard's fair-minded and unprejudiced heroine in *Land of the Sun* falls in love with an aristo-cratic Tuareg man, disregarding claims of his savage "desert raider" heri-tage as well as the fact that some Europeans consider him a "native." She is rewarded by the revelation that he is, in fact, a Frenchman, who was adopted into a Tuareg tribe when his father, a French army officer in Alge-ria, died in the war. Although he considers himself "actually a Tuareg by upbringing, if not by birth," no racial or ethnic bodies intermingle to pro-duce "half-breed" children in this novel, either.

Therefore, the revival of the desert romance novel utilized the mas-querading Middle Eastern hero's racial sleight of hand made famous in *The Sheik* and mimicked in dozens of novels and films during the inter-war years. As in the early twentieth century, the contemporary desert romance novel catered to British women's hunger for exotic travel and erotic heroes. It teased women with "dark" fantasies of potentially violent, interracial sex, but reassuringly unmasked at the end a European hero who would make for good husband material. This unease with the hybrid hero was a legacy of colonialism. Miscegenation and hybridity were deeply subversive and destabilizing for a colonizing system justified by racial hierarchies. In early twentieth-century romance novels, as we have seen in Chapters 2 and 3, the sexual desirability and potency of the Arab male could not be uncoupled from the tangible result of his sexual union with the white woman: their "half-caste" children. Racial hybridity remained troubling even until the 1970s, hence the prevalence of "white sheiks" in these novels, or Spanish grandees who have cultural ties and own property in Morocco, as in Margaret Rome's *Bride of the Rif* (1972) and Violet Winspear's *The Sun Lord's Woman* (1985).

By the 1980s, however, this was beginning to change. Sheik novels began to feature Middle Eastern men who claimed mixed European biological or cultural heritage. They were hybrid and happy about it. When Australian and American novelists began writing sheik romances in the mid-1980s, they took not only the sheik's racial hybridity for granted, but the heroine's white ethnic hybridity as well. No longer was the heroine simply "English," with all the connotations of racial, ethnic, national, and cultural identity that Wendy Webster (2007) argues were encompassed by this term. Australian and American heroines were "white," but not necessarily of English or even British descent. Two factors contributed to this new assumption that hybridity was to be celebrated in the romance novel's protagonists. First, Australia and the United States were both immigrant countries. Both had a history of restrictive white racial immigration policies in the early twentieth century, and both moved toward dismantling these policies after the Second World War even though immigration and settlement policies were still strongly assimilationist in the postwar years. The civil rights movement had an undeniable impact, too. By the time romance novelists began contemplating hybrid heroes, ethnosexual barriers between white women and all sorts of men had already been breached in American society. After all, the most famous of such interracial relationships, represented by Sidney Poitier and Katherine Houghton on the silver screen, in *Guess Who's Coming to Dinner*, had appeared in 1967.

The 1970s also saw the birth of the multicultural period in Britain, Australia, and America — the second factor contributing to the acceptance of hybridity in these novels, as well as to the celebration of the culture and heritage of white ethnic groups. The turn toward a celebration of multiculturalism was spurred by the civil rights movement and its various offshoots of ethnic identity movements as well as by the counterculture's embrace of alternative ethnic cultures in the 1960s and 1970s. Ethnic cultures, including Oriental cultures, were fashionably exotic; they provided the middle classes with new and interesting products for consumption and new modes of self-creation. By the time Australian and American romance writers began producing sheik novels in the mid-1980s, therefore, one of the most difficult battles over the racial or ethnic makeup of the hero had already been resolved. Arabs, because of their perceived continuity of physiognomy with Mediterranean Europeans—Spanish, Italians, and Greeks—were acceptable as either "pure-blooded" or hybrid heroes in the mainstream, mass-market Harlequin Mills & Boon novel. (Interestingly enough, other groups of men—blacks, Jews, and Asians among them—still do not seem to be, and are featured in very few mainstream interracial category romances as romantic protagonists. Black American novelists have developed their own romance lines—something that I will discuss in Chapter 9.)

THE MODERN ORIENTALIST ROMANCE NOVEL AND THE MIDDLE EAST

Throughout the 1970s and 1980s, British romance novelists began to produce desert romance novels set in Algeria, Morocco, Kuwait, and fictional simulacra of the Trucial or Gulf states. As mentioned before, the timing of this revival of the Orientalist romance novel lacked tangible connections to events in the Middle East, but perhaps it could be linked to the growing visibility of Arab immigrant communities in Britain, especially from the 1970s onward. Britain's heyday of influence and engagement with the Middle East was from the end of the nineteenth century to the early 1970s, when protectorates and mandates over various Middle Eastern states were acquired and slowly lost again. Certainly, Britain suffered from the oil crises of the 1970s, which made newspaper headlines during a sometimes dismal decade. Saudi Arabia was Britain's largest supplier of oil by this time, followed by Iran and Kuwait. In return for oil, Britain supplied exports and services to these countries (Brenchley 258–263). These prosaic economic relations were accompanied by opportunities for British expatriates, especially in the Gulf states, as well as by immigration of people from the Middle East to Britain.

Yemenis were among the earliest people from the Middle East to migrate to Britain after the Second World War, and they set up the first mosques, Islamic schools, and the first Arabic newspaper, *Al Salaam*, by the late 1940s (Halliday xiii). They were followed by Palestinians after

1948. Iraqis, Egyptians, Sudanese, Algerians, Somalis, and Gulf Arabs im-migrated to Britain throughout the 1970s and 1980s (Halliday 1–3). The number of Arab immigrants in Britain reached half a million in the mid-1980s, and accounted for about ten percent of Britain's immigrant popu-lation (*The Economist*, 1988). Many of them were professionals: doctors, teachers, academics, and businessmen. The presence of Arabs in London was given symbolic significance when the Egyptian businessman Moha-med al-Fayed—the father of Princess Diana's last lover, Dodi—bought the famous British department store Harrods in 1985, amidst much con-troversy and xenophobic fears that wealthy Arabs were buying up British assets and iconic institutions. Certainly, Saudi Arabia and the Gulf states were major investors in Britain during the 1980s. The Kuwaiti Investment Office in London, for example, invested fifty-five billion pounds in Brit-ain in the 1970s and 1980s, while the Kuwaiti-owned St. Martin's Property Group was responsible for developing London Bridge City as a Thames-side commercial and residential area. Saudis, meanwhile, purchased busi-nesses, banks, hospitals, and mansions in Britain during the 1980s, and the Arab elite became highly visible in the horse-racing world. As Fred Halliday notes, Arab tourists also began to visit London in increasing numbers during the 1970s, averaging 200,000 per year, and "larger num-bers of Arabs began to establish some kind of residence in Britain." By the late twentieth century, "half a million Arabs lived most or part of the year in Britain" (3). The majority of Arabs in Britain were not from these wealthier classes, of course, but it was the elite who contributed to "anec-dotes about huge houses, retinues of servants and a limitless supply of cash" that came to be synonymous with Arabs in Britain by the mid-1980s (*The Economist*, 1988). This, together with the longstanding exoticism of the Orient, female dreams of feudal fairy tales featuring benevolent Ori-ental rulers bent on modernizing their backward states, the charms of exotic travel, and the rise of the alpha male hero, probably also contrib-uted to the revival of the sheik romance in Britain.

More difficult to explain, however, was the Australian contribution to this genre, beginning in the early 1980s. For most of its history, Australia had little direct engagement with the Middle East. As David Walker points out, Australia's other was found in East Asia—the "teeming hordes" and "yellow peril" of China and Japan waiting to overrun Australia's empty northern lands (22). What little direct experience Australians had of the Middle East was gleaned through military expeditions. The colony of New South Wales sent a contingent to aid the British in the Sudan during the Mahdi-led revolt in 1885. Australian expeditionary forces were stationed in Egypt on their way to fight in the Gallipoli campaign during the First World War, while the Australian Light Horse also saw action in Sinai and Palestine. During the Second World War, Australian forces again fought in the Middle East, while expeditionary forces were sent to guard British air bases there during the Cold War, in the 1950s. As David Lowe argues, "Australians and New Zealanders knew the Middle East through the lesson of civilizing imperialism" wrought by battle on behalf of the British in the first half of the twentieth century (35–40, 50). More recently, Australian military forces were part of the United Nations coalition—led by the United States but also comprising Saudi Arabian, British, and Egyptian forces—that expelled Saddam Hussein's Iraqi forces from Kuwait during the Gulf War of 1990–1991. Australia again formed a small part of the "coalition of the willing" supporting President George W. Bush's invasion of Iraq in 2003, on the pretext of Saddam Hussein's ongoing production and maintenance of "weapons of mass destruction," which contravened UN Resolution 687—a resolution that had brought the Gulf War to a close by calling for the destruction or removal of nuclear, biological, and chemical weapons and their components in Iraq.

Australia's engagement with the Middle East has thus been mediated through its relations with, and adherence to, the foreign policies of first Britain then the United States, and through war. Its views of Islam, meanwhile, have been filtered through Asia (primarily through Indonesia) despite the fact that Islam was introduced to Australia with the first Afghan camel-driver immigrants in the mid-nineteenth century. The dismantling of the "White Australia" policy in the early 1970s and the acceptance of immigrants and refugees from the Middle East, particularly Lebanon, during the civil war, have brought more Australians into contact with Middle Eastern cultures and with Islam, while the turn of the century has seen an aggressive pursuit of lucrative trade relations—largely the exchange of livestock and agricultural products for oil and petrochemical by-products—between the two regions. Nevertheless, Australia's direct engagement with the Middle East is still quite recent. The first visit by an Australian foreign minister to Saudi Arabia was made in 2001, while only in 2004 was an Australian embassy opened in Kuwait (Mansouri and Wood 2).

What this means, then, is that Australia's understanding and interpretation of the Middle East has been mediated through British and American relations with the Middle East, and through Orientalism in popular culture. Put simply, Australian romance novelists probably wrote sheik novels because they comprised an already-established subgenre of the category romance market—like medical romances or romances featuring ethnic Latin heroes—and this exotic subgenre was commercially profitable and exciting for writers. This piggybacking onto an established genre or subgenre was not unique to romance novelists. As Toni Johnson-Woods (2004) shows, Australian writers of pulp fiction, such as Gordon Bleeck and Carter Brown, produced knockoffs of American dime novel genres, such as Westerns and detective fiction, at prolific rates during the mid-twentieth century. This does not mean that Australian novelists have not brought anything new to the genre. However, this second-hand Orientalism resulting from a lack of sustained national engagement with the Middle East may go some way to explaining why—apart from a few novels such as Mons Daveson's first sheik romance, *My Lord Kasseem* (1982), set in Egypt; Miranda Lee's *Beth and the Barbarian* (1993), which has a Moroccan hero; Helen Bianchin's *Desert Mistress* (1996), set in Riyadh; and Emma Darcy's *Traded to the Sheikh* (2005), which takes the reader on a whirlwind armchair tour of Zanzibar, Kenya, Zambia, and South Africa—Australian novelists were among the first to produce sheik romance novels set in entirely mythical Middle Eastern states: the oil-rich states of Bayrar or Cassar, the sheikdoms of Zubani and Xabia, and the desert kingdoms of Duhar and Jamalbad clustered along the coastline of the Arabian Sea. Here is late twentieth- and twenty-first-century Orientalism as the blatant production of simulacra. No longer bound by any relation to, or consideration for, Middle Eastern geopolitical realities, the Australian romantic Orient is largely a confection of popular Orientalist discourses transmitted through Orientalist romance novels of the late twentieth century. Although Australian novelists such as Emma Darcy and Miranda Lee sometimes connect their sheik stories to the reality of Arab sheiks' prominence in the Australian horse-racing scene, many Australian sheik novels feed off others in the subgenre and do not purport to be anchored in any existing Middle Eastern reality.

The same is true with regard to American sheik romance novels, despite the Moroccan and Tunisian settings of Barbara Faith's mid-1980s novels. The overwhelming majority of American sheik romances also feature mythical Middle Eastern or Central Asian states: Sedikhan, Manasia, Kaljukistan, Marakite, Bahania, Tamir, El Zafir, Beharrain, Al Ankhara . . . . There is no end to the proliferation of these imaginary fairy tale sheikdoms superimposed over, and obliterating, the complex geopolitical realities of the Middle East. While American authors had begun writing about the Middle East in increasing numbers after the Second World War, American romance novelists engaged with the Orient primarily through historical harem romances in the 1970s and 1980s, until after the Gulf War. As mentioned, American writers entered the category romance genre rather belatedly, in the 1980s, because of the dominance of Harlequin Mills & Boon throughout most of the century. The new American category romance writers generally followed Dailey's lead in celebrating the vast variety of American settings. There were only a handful of authors, such as Barbara Faith and Iris Johansen, who published contemporary sheik or desert romances in the 1980s.

Indeed, there seemed to be little reason for American romance novelists to turn to the Middle East as a setting for romance during the 1980s. The decade had begun with the humiliation of the Iranian hostage crisis; a humiliation in no way ameliorated by the subsequent bellicose announcement—in response to the Soviet invasion of Afghanistan in 1979—of the Carter Doctrine in January 1980, stating America's intention to use force to defend its interests in the Persian Gulf against Soviet attempts to assert geopolitical hegemony in the region. Even after the release of the American hostages in Iran following the Algiers Accords in January 1981, hostage-taking continued in the 1980s, with the Lebanese Shi'a group Hezbollah systematically kidnapping Westerners between 1982 and 1992, during the Lebanese Hostage Crisis. This led to the American political scandal of the Iran-Contra affair in 1986, when it was revealed that senior American officials had approved the sale of arms to Iran in exchange for American hostages, and to fund anticommunist Contra rebels in Nicaragua. The sordidness of such dealings and the complexity of the scandals no doubt made any engagement with the contemporary Middle East undesirable for many romance writers and readers in the mid-1980s. So did the suicide bombing of the American embassy in Beirut in April 1983 by Islamist groups; the ongoing civil war in Lebanon; the Iran-Iraq War lasting from 1980 to 1988; the ongoing Arab-Israeli conflict; the hijacking of the cruise ship *Achille Lauro* off the coast of Egypt by the Palestinian Liberation Front in 1985; and the outbreak of the First Intifada in Gaza and the West Bank. There was nothing romantic about any of this and, moreover, these events had the potential to alienate various groups of readers in the international romance market. Yet Americans were certainly engaged in the production of Orientalist romances during this time—but in the format of the 1980s harem films and historical harem novels discussed in the last two chapters.

The Persian Gulf crisis, precipitated by Saddam Hussein's decision to send Iraqi forces to annex Kuwait in August 1990, appears to be the turning point for American romance writers' and readers' interest in the Middle East—an interest that persists to the present day. The Gulf crisis—including the war that broke out on January 16, 1991, and lasted until February 28, 1991—was the most heavily televised conflict involving American troops since the Vietnam War. CNN provided twenty-four-hour news coverage of the entire crisis from August 1990 until March 1991, with nightly programs on the "Crisis in the Gulf" emphasizing U.S. troop deployment, but also with special reports on various aspects of the Middle East because, as Douglass Kellner wryly points out, "they had so much air time to fill" ("The Persian Gulf TV War"; see also Kalb 1994). The other major American networks—ABC, CBS and NBC—also provided extensive coverage, as did all the major international news presses. Through the coverage of the Persian Gulf War, the Middle East was brought into American living rooms on a daily basis in a manner reminiscent of blockbuster movie trailers. Reports displayed the banner headline "America at War" over montages of battle scenes, and figured various political and military leaders as "action heroes" (Shohat 140).

Despite the Orientalist portrayals of uncivilized, fanatical, American-flag-burning Arab "mobs" in the Middle East that were popular during the Gulf War, American audiences were also shown that there were "good Arabs" on "our side."[4] However brief the time the media coverage accorded them, the long-robed, burnoose-wearing Kuwaiti leaders were portrayed with dignity and respect, in contrast to the snide sexual innuendoes about Saddam/Sodom Hussein, and attempts to associate him visually and verbally with Hitler (Norton 27–28). Much was made of the fact that Saudi Arabia and Egypt were part of the United Nations coalition bent on ousting evil Iraqis from a ravaged Kuwait. This did not stop the swell of anti-Arab sentiment in the United States, of course, or the abuse meted out to Arab or Muslim Americans. In this regard, it is both fascinating and significant to see how American romance novelists began to engage with the Middle East in such a way that modified the region and made the people assimilable to American social and gender norms. Whatever the representational failings of sheik romance novels, no other genre of American popular culture has determinedly and repeatedly attempted to humanize the Arab or Muslim other—even if, out of ignorance or incomprehension, imaginary Orients had to be created in order to do so.

SEVEN

Harems, Heroines, and Heroes

*The heroine—a feisty, brassy American woman, representing
hundreds of thousands of female romance readers—is irresistibly
drawn to the Arab sheik. He's dark, brooding and incredibly
wealthy, ruling everything he surveys in his desert kingdom. They
have exotic adventures and eventually make hot, feverish and often
graphic love. The End.*

PATRICK T. REARDON, *CHICAGO TRIBUNE*, APRIL 24, 2006

In the late 1960s, Lorna Morel, a cool, blond, middle-class English woman brought up in a convent school travels to Morocco
and has to explain to an eager young Englishman that she doesn't
care to dance or get married, can't bear to be touched by a man, and is
not at all romantic by nature or inclination. She scoffs at fanciful warnings culled from romance novels about "ardent and dangerous Arabs who
carry off lonely girls to their *harems*" (Winspear 1969: 9). And, of course,
that is precisely what happens to her. Violet Winspear's *Blue Jasmine*, published as Mills & Boon's first postwar desert romance in 1969, paid self-
conscious homage to Hull's novel and its ilk, borrowing heavily from the
storyline of *The Sheik*. Lorna is rescued from the "bad Arab" abductor by
the "good Arab" sheik, who we know will turn out to be European because
he "spoke like a Frenchman and used his hands in a Gallic way." Like
Hull's Ahmed Ben Hassan, he has spotless clothes, sumptuous furnishings, and a small library of French books. His mother, as it turns out, is a
Spaniard from Cadiz who worked as a nurse in a Moroccan hospital, married an emir, and cuckolded her husband with a French traveler when the
emir took a second wife. Being of Latin parentage, the hero can naturally

pass as an Arab. Further references to Hull's novel are scattered through-out the text. Like Diana Mayo, Lorna likes to ride; she is intrigued by the "eternal mystery of the East" that she feels in the desert; she is moved by the sound of a haunting Eastern melody that she hears while in a garden; she is forced to wear "harem clothes" and to accept the sheik's gift of a pearl necklace; she fights fiercely with him; and she is afraid that if she re-sponds to his lovemaking, he will grow tired of her. The hero, meanwhile, is harsh and autocratic; he is a ruthless leader of men and possesses the ability to tame wild horses—and the heroine—by sheer brute strength and force of will. The publication of *Blue Jasmine* heralded the revival of the British-authored sheik romance in the last quarter of the twentieth century. In this chapter, I examine continuities and changes between the modern sheik novel and its 1920s counterpart, focusing particularly on issues of feminist independence, cultural conversion, hybridity, and mas-culinity in the portrayal of Western heroines, Muslim women, and sheik heroes from the 1970s to the present day.

HAREMS

Beginning in the 1970s, contemporary desert romance novels over-lapped in many ways with *The Sheik* and with their historical counterparts examined in Chapter 5. References to abduction, rape, white slavery, and incarceration in the harem were rife. In Barbara Faith's *Bedouin Bride* (1984), the heroine is kidnapped by the Moroccan hero, carried into the desert, and seduced through rape, as is the heroine in Australian writer Miranda Lee's *Beth and the Barbarian* (1993). In Emma Darcy's *The Sheikh's Revenge* (1993), Leah Marlow is abducted by the sheikh of Zu-bani in revenge for her brother eloping with the sheikh's betrothed. The novel begins with allusions to abduction and rape. When the sheik first meets Leah, she is in her garden working on a tapestry of a Rubens pic-ture of the rape of the Sabine women. However, no rape occurs in this novel, or in Canadian writer Alexandra Sellers's *Bride of the Sheikh* (1997), in which the heroine is romantically abducted by her former sheik hus-band—rather in the manner of Walter Scott's Laird of Lochinvar in his epic poem *Marmion*—when she tries to marry someone else after her di-vorce. Unlike in *The Sheik* and 1970s erotic historical romance novels, and in notable contrast to the targets of early feminist criticism about violent sex in romance fiction, actual rape does not feature often in the postwar Mills & Boon sheik novel. The threat of its occurrence is certainly present:

heroines are spoken to savagely, misunderstood, mocked, and derided for being ice cold or mercenary. They have their wrists cruelly bruised and their lips brutally kissed . . . but they are rarely raped. If rape does occur, the author generally makes it clear that sex is secretly desired—albeit reluctantly—by the heroine. In Emma Darcy's *The Falcon's Mistress* (1988), the heroine realizes that she is completely in the sheik's power and that he is determined to have sex with her. This eases "the burden of responsibility from Bethany's heart. Her conscience was appeased" since she is still a virgin. "Did he know that he had just released her from the need to keep fighting him? Did he know that she wanted him to love her . . . just a little?" (101). From the threat of rape to seduction, consensual sex, and then love—the pattern of the plot is as old as *The Sheik*.

Because captivity features so prominently in many of these novels, as Emily Haddad (2007) shows, many modern heroines find it obligatory to pass some time in the harems of their sheik heroes, even if only as tourists or guests. In between her quest to find her missing anthropologist father, believed to be the hostage of Marxist guerrillas, the Australian heroine of Emma Darcy's *The Falcon's Mistress* (1988) whiles away her time in the harem and ponders "the age-old question": "Did Arab sheikhs practise monogamy, or did they have many wives and mistresses? How many times had a woman been prepared for him in this way?" (95–96). British romance novelist Charlotte Lamb made the point first raised by Lady Mary Wortley Montagu in the eighteenth century: that the pampered lives of wealthy Western women might not have been that far removed from their Oriental counterparts. In *Desert Barbarian* (1978), the spoiled heiress, Marie, whom the hero abducts for a few hours just for fun, is told that her "life in the harem would not be hard; it would be as filled with luxury, as idle and spoilt, as your life has always been. You would merely exchange one indulgent owner for another" (17). The harem thus highlights the inequality between the sexes and signals that the resolution of this inequality is an important theme in the novel. As Jessica Taylor notes, where nineteenth-century Orientalist paintings "pictured a harem full of women, waiting for the European man to enter," contemporary sheik romance novels "create an Orient with harems empty of women" (1041, 1034).

The empty harem symbolizes the emotional and sexual vacuum in the contemporary sheik hero's life; a vacant space waiting for the white woman to enter, to succumb to the pleasures of this place and of the man who owns it and, eventually, to dominate both through her emotional and sexual power. Far from merely signifying the Western woman's captivity, enslavement, and submission to traditional femininity, the harem in modern romance novelists' writings can also symbolize the space of the heroine's triumph and power. However, since her domination of this space occurs at the expense of the Oriental woman (more on this later), it can be read as a neo-imperialistic Western female fantasy, as well.

Sometimes the harem also serves to emphasize the Western heroine's Orientalist misunderstanding about the contemporary Middle East. Nerina Hilliard's heroine in *Land of the Sun* has her misconceptions about Tuareg women being "made to wear a veil and tucked away in some old man's harem" gently corrected. She learns that among the Tuareg, it is the men who veil themselves and the women who enjoy a remarkable degree of freedom (17). In Mary Lyons's *Escape from the Harem*, the "medieval harem" that the heroine fears she will be incarcerated in has actually been closed down by the hero. When Barbara Faith's American heroine wants to help the archconservative Lord Ali Ben Hari to organize an important international conference in *Lord of the Desert* (1990), he tells her that if she comes to his country she will have to live in the palace harem. The American woman's indignant objections to being a prisoner are waved aside with the explanation that there are no concubines in the harem. "The women in the harem are wives, sisters, daughters, relatives of our family and the families of the ministers. They all live very well" (32). But her fears are not dispelled until, instead of the "odalisques in flowing gossamer, sad-eyed veiled ladies reclining on velvet chaises" that she imagined from European Orientalist paintings, she finds ladies "dressed in colorful kaftans . . . with children in their arms or clinging to their long skirts" (52). Harem life, she discovers, has its attractions after all, especially for the overworked modern Western woman. It is a vacation or a form of early retirement. "What would it be like to live her days in this exotic setting?" she wonders:

> To never again have to whistle down a taxi, make a mad rush for the subway or try to eat a sandwich at her desk in between telephone calls? What would it be like to awake when she chose? To sun and swim, to have someone draw her bath and prepare her for the evening to come? (56)

Like their historical romance counterparts, Western heroines in the modern romantic Middle East luxuriate in massive and ornate marble bathrooms where they can indulge in scented water strewn with rose petals. The more hardy women who travel out to the desert can expect to find a convenient oasis where they can enjoy a bath, be assisted by a submissive Muslim woman, or be lustfully observed by the sheik hero who, in the tradition of Ahmed Ben Hassan, is always immaculately clean himself. Especially in the novels of the 1970s and early 1980s, the hygienic hero signals to the Western heroine his European racial or cultural heritage—the thing that makes him a suitable mate for her.

HEROINES AND HOURIS

Continuity with Hull's novel is in some ways strongest where the construction of feminist-influenced heroines is concerned. Contemporary sheik novels present a strong-willed and independent heroine who wants to earn her own living and forge ahead with her career. Often, she initially regards love and marriage dubiously, if not with outright scorn. This attitude is summed up by Elizabeth Mayne's American heroine Haley Bennett in *The Sheik and the Vixen* (1996), who mourns the fact that

> of all the dumb luck, [she had] to fly halfway around the world and land in a war zone to find her Prince Charming . . . . What could she possibly do with a man whose idea of chivalry meant locking a woman away in a desert place? Nothing. Absolutely Nothing.
>
> She was a career woman. She had worked hard to achieve her place at Bennett Industries. Was she going to throw away all those years of working like a dog to match the standards of excellence her father and her eldest brother set? The competition was tough in aeronautics . . . She'd had to prove herself over and over again by being better than everyone else. Was she going to throw away her education because she finally found a six-foot-three hunk with bedroom eyes that hit all her warp-speed buttons?
>
> Not likely! (78)

Yet unlike Hull's novel, contemporary sheik romances do not require the sacrifice of a fulfilling career and financial independence for a happy resolution to interracial desire. On the contrary.

From the British novels of the 1970s to the present-day Australian and American novels, heroines are independent women, undaunted by threats of abduction and incarceration alike. In Winspear's *The Burning Sands* (1976), the Berber hero threatens the heroine with the fact that she is now in the realm where not so long ago prisoners were fed to tigers, and decapitated heads leered on spikes from the walls of a despot's palace. Slave sales were public occasions, and lovely female captives were held to ransom. This is Barbary, where the last of the corsairs have their *kasbahs*, and care very little what goes on in the world beyond their own kingdoms. (65)

The heroine is momentarily cowed at the thought that she might be considered "white ivory" to be sold "into terrible vice dens in the Middle East," but she does not remain intimidated for very long. Not only is she English, she is also of Cockney heritage. She is "a determined girl from the Bow Bells area, not one of those elegant daddy's girls who stroll about Sloane Square" dabbling in boutique work "until a nice boy with a nice rich dad comes along" (13).

Here, then, is a fundamental difference between the heroines of the 1970s and early 1980s and their historical romance counterparts discussed in Chapter 5. The heroines in both subgenres share many similar traits, including their independence and their innate sexuality, which needs to be awakened by the hero's forceful kisses that would, in all other contexts, be considered serious sexual harassment. However, heroines in the contemporary desert romance novels are usually from the middle or working classes, and they possess a strong work ethic and a keen sense of pragmatism (Dixon 55). Their professional aspirations soar as the decades pass. They are not the spoiled aristocratic adolescents of the historical Orientalist romance novel. The British heroine in *Tawny Sands* (1970) begins as a secretary to a Barbara-Cartland-style romance novelist, but her ambition is "to open a tea-shop, or take training as a beautician" (77). Hilliard's heroine in *Land of the Sun* (1976) is "efficient at her work and would be able to earn herself an income that . . . would enable her to live quite comfortably" (152). Leonie in Lyons's *Escape from the Harem* (1986) supports herself and her young daughter by selling Oriental rugs and carpets in London, while Jeannie Bennett in Sara Wood's *Perfumes of Arabia* (1986) possesses "single-minded ambition" as an educator who travels to the Middle East to help modernize the schooling system. From the mid-1980s to the present day, Australian heroines range from being secretaries and teachers to hotel managers, scuba diving instructors, and veterinarians. American heroines are diplomats, television journalists, public relations consultants, photographers, aeronautic engineers, and one is even an earnest university professor, whose "dissertation was on the changing face of society as demonstrated by feminist writers in the last quarter of the twentieth century" (Mallery 2002: 152). In the twenty-first century, these women are female soldiers, bodyguards, and leaders of oil companies. The fragmenting of the contemporary romance novel at the end of the twentieth century into different cross-genre "lines," including romantic suspense, crime, and thrillers (represented by Harlequin's Intrigue and MIRA lines), has permitted the emergence of very different types of heroines and heroes who do not conform to traditional gender roles or gender-typical occupations. These women are all financially self-supporting and are in no need of a husband. It is precisely their independent streak, however, that flings them headlong into heated battles with the sheik hero. The sheik hero has to learn—like Soliman with his Roxelane, in Marmontel's and Favart's eighteenth-century comedies—that the Western heroine must "never again be made to do anything—anything at all that you don't wish to do" (Winspear 1976: 181).

In novels of the 1970s and 1980s, the independence of the Western heroine is established through a description of her working life and her initial lack of passion (in the tradition of Diana Mayo), but also by contrasting her with Muslim women. Drawing from an earlier historical discourse on virginity (discussed in Chapter 1), the virgin/virago heroine's autonomy is connected to her bodily integrity and her control over her physical desires. This autonomy comes under assault from both within and without as the heroine struggles against her own awakening sexual desires and the desire of the sheik hero to master her sexually and socially. The romance novel recounts the Western heroine's triumph as she is rewarded with love, sex, power over the hero, and a surprising degree of independence and intellectual or professional fulfillment at the novel's end. This triumph, this reward, is a consequence of the Western woman's refusal to submit to the veil and to arranged marriages, in contrast to the cowed, passive, silenced, and submissive Muslim woman. Especially in the late twentieth-century novels (though less so in novels of the twenty-first century), Muslim women are often completely absent, erased from their own space and stories and replaced instead with the white Western heroine who transgresses both female and male Muslim spaces. Where fleetingly present, Muslim women are a collective, undifferentiated mass against which the white woman's individuality, modernity, liberation, and control over her self and her destiny can be seen more clearly (Naber 44–45). Clever, resourceful, pragmatic, and passionate Josian, the Muslim princess of the late medieval *Bevis of Hampton* tales, has been replaced by the white Western middle-class woman.

This is not particularly new in the Western discourse of Orientalism or in the Orientalist romance. The Western woman has been displacing the Muslim woman as the center of the Oriental story since the eighteenth century, relegating the latter to the inferior status of the scheming "other woman"; turning her into a supplicant for the white woman's help, or into a passive bystander functioning as Oriental furnishing. As Elizabeth Shakman Hurd notes, Islam historically "plays the role of the 'alien' in the construction of Western modernity" (27). Within Western liberal feminist discourse of the late twentieth century, this tendency manifests itself in what Chandra Talpade Mohanty calls the production of "third world difference," where "third world women" are constructed as "ignorant, poor, uneducated, tradition-bound, domestic, family-oriented, victimized," and generally powerless in comparison to the empowered Western feminist, whose obligation is to help the "third world woman" become like her (337). This is a manifestation of feminist colonial discourse of the kind explored by Antoinette Burton (1994), whereby first-wave feminists in the United Kingdom used their efforts on behalf of oppressed Indian women to argue for equality for themselves in Britain, and for a role in the British Empire. Similarly, Louise Newman argues that in the history of American liberal feminism, white women empowered themselves as "central players in civilization-work during the late nineteenth century" by claiming to "uplift" and represent the interests of nonwhite, non-Christian others, thereby consolidating an "imperialist rhetoric that delegitimized dissent" from these other women. By the early twentieth century, the discourses of race and Orientalism were conflated by white women to show the degradation of nonwhite, non-Western women, who were associated with "zenanas and harems; the seraglio and the bagnio, female infanticide and suttee, concubinage and polygamy; bride sale; foot-binding and ear and nose boring, consecrated prostitution and sacrifice; bastinado; child marriage and slavery" (7). When white women championed the abolition or reform of such nonwhite practices, they increased "their own authority, both in relation to other groups of women . . . and in relation to white men" (8). As Joanna Liddle and Shirin Rai (1998) argue, Western liberal feminism in the late twentieth century sometimes revived this discourse by positioning Western women as the global leaders of universal feminism while reproducing imperialist images of colonized women to justify white women's status and identity.

Muslim women thus act as foils for the independent Western heroine in sheik romance novels of the 1970s. Time and again, the Western heroines tell their sheik abductors to let them go because "I am not an Arabian girl and I resent being held a prisoner to your whims. I have rights and you can't altogether ignore them. I am not a *thing*" (Winspear 1969: 74). Muslim women are bewildered that the Western heroine will not submit to a forced union with the lordly sheik. The Western woman has to explain kindly and patiently: "You . . . were brought up to this kind of life. . . . Your gilded prison suits you . . . from small girls you have been taught that men are your masters and your place in life is to please them" (Winspear 1976: 175). Muslim women are dolls or other sorts of possessions "to be put away in a cupboard when not required," "pampered, kept in seclusion, and greatly cared for" should they bear sons, and sent away if they don't, always "bowing down to the lordly male" and blamed for "every petty fault in the book" (Winspear 1976: 35, 43). Downtrodden, ignorant houris, they marvel when Western women courageously defy the sheik's wishes and are amazed when the sheik treats the modern white woman as his equal (Winspear 1969: 111).

Although many current American romance novelists describe themselves as feminists and pursue a recognizable feminist agenda in their novels (apart from abortion rights, which hardly any romance novelist will touch), it would be going too far to describe the British authors of the 1970s and early 1980s or their heroines as feminists—yet the influence of the women's liberation movement is certainly evident in their novels. Women demand to be treated as men's social equals and sometimes demand the same economic opportunities as men. Often, it seems as though it is not the demands for equality heralded by the liberation movement that alarm British novelists so much as the sexual revolution, and this is, of course, ironic since it is precisely the advent of the sexual revolution that increasingly moved romance novelists to portray the heroine as a woman with a strong sexual appetite. What British novelists depict, therefore, is the paradoxical heroine: chaste, but innately sexual; stubbornly independent, but willing to submit to the sheik hero once he gives her her own way; professionally competent and successful in her career, but willing to subordinate this aspect of her life to the demands of motherhood; egalitarian and democratic, but willing to marry into a feudal order. If her individuation as the heroine takes place in contrast to passive Muslim women, it takes place in contrast to promiscuous Western women as well.

More recent romance novels, particularly the American ones, tend to shy away from the subplot of the seductive "other woman"—be she Eastern or Western—who is a rival for the hero's affections. American novelists, in particular, presented other women as the heroine's friends, mother figures, mentors, and support networks soon after they started publishing in the 1980s. In British novels of the 1970s and 1980s, however, other Western women apart from the heroine are often shown to be vain, shallow, silly, scheming, mercenary, and willing to trade sex for social advancement. They rarely serve as friends for the lonely heroine; rather, they let her down, betray her, or try to steal the hero from her. British women have a bad reputation among the Arabs, Penny Jordan states in *Falcon's Prey* (1981). The heroine knows "what the Arab community thought of the British girls who gave their favours so freely in return for a diamond bracelet or a fur, and she wondered if those same girls had the slightest idea of the contempt in which they were held by their erstwhile escorts" (20).[1] In the same novel, the hero vents his poor opinion of the British: "My friends are amused by the low price your women put upon themselves. The British were once greatly respected, but who can respect a race that allows its women to sell themselves for so little?" (35) Just as well, then, that the British heroine in these novels is usually a passionless virgin, disgusted by the touch of a man—any man—until quarreling with her sheik hero over women's liberation arouses her fury; until his "punishing kiss," which he administers to shut her up, arouses her sexual passion.

Courtship and sexual drama in these 1970s and early 1980s British novels are almost always cast as a battle of the sexes, as well as an internal battle within the protagonists. The heroine resists her growing attraction to a man she believes would strip her of her independence while treating her as one of many other women, and the hero struggles against his own overpowering attraction to a Western woman whom he finds (mistakenly, of course) morally contemptible but sexually irresistible. During this period, romance novelists evidently found it difficult to describe or narrate the course of sexual arousal between hero and heroine. Temper and fury served as the transition point into passionate lust. In Winspear's *The Burning Sands*, the heroine feels a "flash of temper" and a "sheer awareness of the sex warfare between men and women" that the sheik has aroused "to an alarming degree" (54). For the heroine, the most exhilarating struggles take place over quarrels about the equality of men and women; particularly the freedom and independence British women are permitted in modern society. As Evelyn Bach wryly notes:

> The main bulk of the desert romance is devoted to her struggles as
> she pits her intelligence, her Western supremacy, her verbal weaponry
> and any other resources she can muster against the sheik's implacable
> power and, increasingly, against her own love and desire for him. The
> narratives of these vain attempts to win back her freedom and independence are larded with unaccountable tremblings, quiverings, scorch-

ing sensations and, in the more recent publications, erect nipples and swollen manhoods. (21–22)

The novels generally end with both parties compromising, but in the more recent novels Western heroines retain their independence and sense of purpose in life as their sheik husbands come to realize the value of their professional skills and abilities. This is particularly the case for novels that reiterate narratives of modernization and development—something that will be discussed in greater detail in the next chapter.

Australian and American heroines are eager to claim equality with men, and independence of spirit, too, again attributing these to national characteristics. In one of Australian author Emma Darcy's novels, *Traded to the Sheikh* (2005), the hero is annoyed that the heroine keeps defying his wishes. The sheik cannot understand her attitude until a helpful minion explains her reluctance to "bend to his will":

Perhaps it is because they are from a country which is detached from everywhere else . . . I have found Australians to be strangely independent in how they think and act. They are not from an authoritarian society and they think they have the right to question anything. In fact, those who have been in our employ at Dubai have bluntly stated we will get a better result if we let them perform in their own way . . . . This may be an endemic attitude amongst both men and women from Australia. (29)

Nevertheless, the heroine trades obedience and sex in return for the sheik's influence in rescuing her sister's family from Zimbabwe, where they are being kept under house arrest by Robert Mugabe's regime. When she suspects the sheik of reneging on his part of the bargain, she erupts into yet more nationalistic rhetoric, telling him off and insisting on being treated with equality and justice because, "Where I come from we have a saying that every Australian understands and respects. *Fair go!* It's an intrinsic part of our culture—what we live by" (146).

American culture and society are held equally responsible for fostering such character traits in American women. Nora Roberts's *Sweet Revenge* (1989) is one of the very few single-title, mass-market romance novels (that I am aware of, at least) partially set in a fictitious Middle Eastern country. Roberts's Arab-American heroine is a jewel thief who seeks revenge against her tyrannical sheik father, the ruler of an ultraconservative country who fell in love with an American actress, married her, then raped and rejected her when she failed to deliver a son and heir. Perhaps more than any other contemporary romance novel, *Sweet Revenge* rehashes every racist and negative Orientalist stereotype about barbaric, despotic tyrants and backward, oppressive Muslim cultures where women are raped and confined to the harem before being sold off in marriage. In contrast to this oppression stands the modern American woman in all her stubborn independence and her truculent insistence on equality with men. In a New York subway station, the heroine overhears two American women complaining about their husbands:

> "So I says to him, you got a wife, not a goddam maid, Harry. I promised to love, honor, and cherish, but I didn't say nothing about picking up your slop. I tell him the next time I find your smelly socks on the rug, I'm stuffing them in your big mouth."
>
> "Good for you, Lorraine."
>
> Adrianne wanted to second that. Good for you, Lorraine. Let the bastard pick up his own socks. That's what she loved about American women. They didn't cower and cringe when the almighty man walked through the door. They handed him a bag of garbage and told him to dump it. (131)

American culture is inherently liberating in this novel. Even the heroine's Arabic/Muslim half sisters, who grew up in the oppressive atmosphere of her father's harem, find freedom when they are married off to American men; a freedom symbolized by the substitution of their burqas for bikinis.

Judging from her other romance novels (of which there are over two hundred) written before and after *Sweet Revenge*, Roberts is one of the most progressive and politically liberal romance novelists writing in the United States today. Her witty and well-written novels portray strong, feminist-influenced women; successful interracial relationships; a celebration and inclusion of characters from different ethnic groups in America, many of whom are in positions of power and authority; a consistent respect for working-class values and culture; and a championing of the disadvantaged and marginalized. Her "in Death" crime fiction series, written under the pseudonym J. D. Robb, features a futuristic America where prostitution has been legalized and guns have been banned. Reading many of these other novels, Roberts is clearly not a racist, and I believe that were she to write *Sweet Revenge* today, it would be a very different book indeed. Her desire to include Arabs (along with other ethnic groups) in American society in *Sweet Revenge* is shown by her deliberate choice of an Arab-American heroine—one of the few in the 1980s, apart from those in Barbara Faith's category romances discussed below. It is therefore greatly significant that such a liberal, progressive, feminist writer would (unwittingly) reiterate such Orientalist topoi that demonize Arabs and Muslims. It speaks to the pervasive power of Orientalist discourse in American culture that these assumptions, attitudes, stereotypes, and plot devices seem authentic and not racist to an antiracist writer who would undoubtedly be disturbed to have her oversight pointed out to her. It is a clear example of how, in discourse theory, "discourse speaks the subject": preexisting Orientalist discourse creates the position the writer takes and thereby shapes the text. And since the age of empire—as so much feminist historical scholarship has shown—white women's modernity, agency, and feminist agendas have depended on the creation of a discourse of helpless, nonwhite women who need to be saved by them.

American writers go beyond the need to assert the independence and equality of their heroines with any and every man. Many seem determined to bring the feminist crusade to the Oriental world and liberate their unenlightened Muslim sisters. Such a determination is certainly not confined to American novels; in British author Penny Jordan's *Falcon's Prey* (1981), the hero scolds the heroine for lecturing Muslim women on "the rights of the liberated woman" (78). This becomes more common in the later novels. The American heroine in *The Sheik and the Vixen* (1996) insists on flying an airplane she has designed to Kuwait because of a personal "vendetta," a "strike back at purdah." She explains to her father:

> Dad, these planes are my design, and mine alone. Nobody but me touched a single one of the designs that over-rich oil prince fell in love with. He's paying you enough money to float a couple of third-world nations for a year, just to have a fleet of them. One for each and every one of his spoiled, male chauvinist sons . . . .
>
> Do you realize that all of Sheik Haaris's sons were educated at Oxford, Harvard and Yale? . . . None of his daughters have been . . . .
>
> I want just one conservative Muslim sheik to have to face up to the fact that a woman can do as fine a job as a man. That's why I'm flying this plane today. (11–12)

Conversion has always been a prominent plot device of the romantic Orientalist tale since the medieval verse romances of the twelfth to the fifteenth century. Rather than religious conversion, modern sheik romances are concerned with cultural conversion. One of the earliest such attempts at converting conservative Muslims to the feminist cause can be seen in Barbara Faith's *Flower of the Desert* (1988), in which the Arab-American heroine, Jasmine Hasir, visits Marrakech and follows her family out into the desert so that she can learn something about her Bedouin ancestry. The Bedouins' lifestyle initially appalls her: the "women spoke only when they were spoken to. Otherwise they remained silent, with downcast eyes" (109). Once she gets to know them, however, she realizes that their dreams, aspirations, conversation, and behavior are "like women everywhere," and she is determined to change their lives. She foments feminist rebellion in the desert, telling them that challenging the fact of their oppression isn't antithetical to Moroccan culture:

> You're out here on the desert, away from big cities like Casablanca or Rabat or Marrakesh, so you don't know what's going on in your own country. Some Moroccan women wear modern clothes today. They go to universities and many of them work. A lot of them aren't even veiled. . . .
>
> Women in Morocco and in almost every country in the world have demanded and received equality with men. They are lawyers and doctors and heads of state, engineers and astronauts. They . . . we, all of us, can be anything we want to be. Soon one of us will go to the moon. (134–135)

When the thrilling possibilities of a feminist-inspired moon mission fails to convince them, Jasmine recounts the story of Aristophanes's *Lysistrata*, and encourages the Bedouin women to go on a sexual and labor strike until their menfolk treat them with respect and include them in the decision-making processes concerning their families and the tribe. Significantly, she says that the worst that can happen is that their husbands would "get angry" or "yell." "Don't tell me they'd beat you because I don't believe it. I've been here for almost two weeks and I've never seen any of your husbands raise a hand to you" (136). It is noteworthy that American female novelists almost invariably insist that Muslim men are generally non-violent and do not mistreat women; rather, they show the men to be gentle, if authoritarian, with their families. Jasmine makes the women understand that "they had the power to change their own lives" and in the end, one of the Bedouin women tells her, "I remember all the things you told us about America and how free American women are. We have spoken up and things are better, but it will be a long time before women in Morocco will be as free as women in your country" (246). This desire to change Muslim men and women is as much for Jasmine's sake as for the Bedouin women's; in the course of her feminist campaign, the hero comes to understand Jasmine's needs as a modern American woman. While the sheik had once considered sequestering Jasmine in the harem with the other women and children of his extended family, he grows to support her wish to return to the United States to continue her studies while he runs his business empire out of New York. He assures her that even if she becomes pregnant during her studies, "We'll work something out about your classes . . . We're a team . . . I intend to be as much a part of caring for our children as you will" (250).

While there are hopes that Western women can be the agents of liberal change in the Orient, especially in novels concerned with modernization and development, there is nevertheless considerable ambivalence about the extent to which traditional Oriental cultures can in fact be changed. This explains the popularity of the resolution of escape, not just from the harem, but also from the Oriental country. Re-invoking the Orientalist trope of an escape from the harem, the Western heroine and the converted sheik often escape to the Western world at the end of the novel. The hero in Faith's *Lord of the Desert* (1990) gives up his position as heir to the throne to become his country's ambassador to Italy, just so that he can marry "Genevieve Jordan from Ann Arbor, Michigan, vice president of one of the most prestigious public relations companies in New York. A today woman who could hold her own with any man anywhere in the world" (57)—although not necessarily with the men in the Middle East. And this brings us to the problem of casting Orientalist sheiks as modern romantic heroes.

HEROES

These modern sheik novels begin with stereotypical Orientalist representations of traditional, patriarchal, authoritarian Arab men and submissive Arab women who are second-class citizens. This pattern of gender relations, the novels implicitly argue, is the legacy of regressive interpretations of Islam, which is represented as a hierarchical, sexist, and deeply unequal religion. (Unlike in the Orientalist historical novels in Chapter 5, comparisons are rarely made between Islam and Christianity in these contemporary novels.) The arrival of the Western, liberated, independent, career-minded heroine on the Islamic scene initially gives rise to chaos and confusion because she is so different from traditional Arab women, and the deeply chauvinistic, despotic Arab men simply cannot deal with this. In Australian author Lynne Wilding's novel *The Sheikh* (1991), the schoolteacher heroine, Lindsay Pentecost—a significantly androgynous as well as Christian name—clashes with the sheik hero on their first meeting because he cannot believe that a woman could be as good a teacher as a man. Wilding emphasizes the blatant inequality between the sexes, stressing that it arises from Arabic/Islamic culture. "Why did he have something against women?" Lindsay asks herself, only to come to the conclusion that

> the United Emirates [*sic*] in the Persian Gulf was male dominated— politically, economically and culturally. So perhaps it was too much to expect him to have empathy toward equality of the sexes . . . There was no way a man with his background would consider anything a woman said worthwhile . . . Nor would she demean herself further by arguing her merits with such a horrid sexist. (18)

But she does, of course, and ultimately converts him to her point of view through her sexual, moral, and cultural power; the power of a liberated, liberal, Western woman.

Female power, romance writer Jayne Ann Krentz argues, is the fundamental theme of category romance novels. "The woman always wins. With courage, intelligence, and gentleness she brings the most dangerous creature on earth, the human male, to his knees. More than that, she forces him to acknowledge her power as a woman" (5). By getting the hero to give in and fall in love with her, and admit it, she brings him into the "feminine" worldview. In the sheik novel of the late twentieth century, these gender politics are played out through what Joyce Zonana calls "feminist Orientalism." Zonana argues that although eighteenth and nineteenth century female writers reproduced in their writings the standard tropes of Orientalism, the primary function of such representation was *not* to "secure Western domination over the East, though they certainly assume and enforce that domination." Rather, by "figuring objectionable aspects of life in the West as 'Eastern,' these Western feminist writers rhetorically define their project as the removal of Eastern elements from Western life" (594). Thus gender reform was cast as a "de-Orientalizing" of European men, and their restoration to a civilized European norm. In the same way, modern sheik novels deploy feminist Orientalism to insist on women's equality with men, and on women's right to a fulfilling career outside the domestic realm. Modern sheik heroes also have to "de-Orientalize" themselves, to learn to respect women's independence and treat them as equals before they are deemed suitable partners for these romantic heroines.

In many modern romance novels, the romantic plot is sustained, and the reader's desire elicited, through conflicting ideologies, interests, practices, and other problems that keep hero and heroine apart despite the fact that they may love each other. The central problem to be solved in modern sheik novels (and also other romance novels featuring "traditional," patriarchal heroes, such as Mediterranean men) is the question of how modern career women who value their independence, life experiences, and career choices can ever find love and happiness with despotic, authoritarian men—those desirable alpha males!—who have not been brought up to treat women as their equals. The resolution to this problem rests in the education of the sheik hero. If many modern, independent heroines need to be taught to place more value on their femininity, sexuality, and family life, sheik heroes need to be taught to acknowledge—theoretically, at least—that women should be treated as men's equals, that they have a right to a fulfilling working life, and that their confidence and independence contribute to their sexual desirability. The modern heroine understands this all too well, and one of her main functions in the sheik novel is to educate the sheik about women's rights. It is no coincidence, therefore, that so many of the Australian sheik novels have teachers as their heroines. It may be argued that such a career choice is essentially conservative, especially compared to American heroines' professions, but the pedagogical capabilities of the heroine are of crucial importance in resolving the central problem between her and the sheik. For both the hero and heroine to be happy after the declaration of love, not only must the declaration end in marriage, but the marriage must be a companionate one between equals. No lasting happiness can result otherwise, nor can the sheik hero be assimilated into modern Western society until this occurs.

When feminist scholars first began to research women's popular romances in the early 1980s, they generally disapproved of mass-market romances. Feminists agreed that such romances "rarely challenge the social order, and they do not urge women to recognize oppression or to revolt; instead, they reinforce the value of traditional roles in a changing society" (Mussell preface). While not wishing to posit the mass-market romance as a feminist text, I would certainly question such an assessment. During the era of increasing political and cultural conservatism in America in the 1980s and 1990s, when the demise of liberal humanism was periodically mourned and the backlash against feminism made headlines, these novels insisted on the importance of women's rights to a good education and a fulfilling career as a fundamental part of the stability of marriage and family life. Why have a sheik hero at all when he is ultimately de-Orientalized and made to look so much like a reconstituted Western man who is sensitive to women's needs, and a good husband and father figure? Because if *even sheiks*—who, in the tradition of Orientalist representation, are despotic, domineering, patriarchal leaders, and intolerant of women's rights—can be brought to understand the importance of women's independence and right to fulfilling careers, and to adjust their attitudes toward women accordingly, then how much more should Western men do the same? The story of the sheik in the contemporary romance novel from the 1970s to the present is therefore the story of a hero who, from an original position of alien Islamic otherness becomes de-Orientalized, Westernized or Americanized, and incorporated into the Western body politic. It took a number of years for this to occur.

Despite the determination of 1970s British novelists to take activist positions where race relations were concerned, they still caved in to the idea that a completely Arab hero, let alone one who was also Muslim, would not be acceptable to their more conservative readers. Category romance novels have always catered to the lowest common denominator because of the breadth of the domestic and international markets. The sheik hero in the British novels of the 1970s and 1980s was therefore either wholly European or a hybrid mix. In Winspear's *Blue Jasmine*, the hero has a Spanish mother and a French father, while the Tuareg hero in Hilliard's *Land of the Sun* turns out to be completely French, as does the gifted surgeon sheik in Pargeter's *The Jewelled Caftan*. Other sheik heroes, such as those in Lamb's *Desert Barbarian* (1978), Mather's *Sandstorm* (1980), Jordan's *Falcon's Prey* (1981), Lyons's *Escape from the Harem* (1986), and Wood's *Perfumes of Arabia* (1986) are of English descent, their racial heritage reinforced by education in English public schools, universities, or training in the British army. They are handsome, arrogant, harsh, frightening, sometimes sexist to the point of misogyny, and always sexually exciting, of course.

Unlike the desert romances of the 1920s (apart from Hull's *The Sheik*), the foil to the sheik hero in British novels is not the villainous Arab but the weak and inadequate British man who loses the heroine because he is incapable of courting or keeping her. In *The Land of the Sun*, the heroine's Welsh fiancé acts like a "sulky boy wanting to smash up a toy that he at the same time still wanted to play with," because he cannot accustom himself to the harsh desert and the nomadic life of the Tuareg (44). The heroine concludes that he is a man of weak character. The heroine in

Desert Barbarian is bored by all the British men vying for her attention: "Nigel with his bland smile and passion for cars, Daniel who talked obsessively of cricket and danced like a rogue elephant, Stephen, the shortest man she had ever met, who was aggressively masculine and carried a chip on his shoulder the size of a tree" (47). Meanwhile, the half Spanish, half Arab sheik hero in *The Sun Lord's Woman* "looked as if he could wipe off the tennis court every member of the Kingswood Country Club" (47). How can these tennis-and-cricket-playing Englishmen with two left feet on the dance floor possibly compete with an autocratic sheik hero who informs the heroine that "a real woman likes to feel that she is mastered," (Winspear 1969: 87), or that "in my veins runs the inclination to treat women as if they are pomegranates to be plucked from the wall of an enclosed court"? (Winspear 1970: 15) The heroine might be outraged, but she is also aroused by such purple prose linking the sheik to the villainous heroes of Hull's *The Sheik* or of the Orientalist historical novels discussed in Chapter 5.

In the 1990s, Australian and American sheik novels also constructed an arrogant, domineering, chauvinistic, seemingly callous but sexually potent sheik hero who is an amalgam of Western and Oriental race and culture. Almost all these sheik novels feature as their heroes an Arab man who either has European blood, or who has been so thoroughly acculturated to the West through its educational institutions—Oxford, Harvard, Yale—that his mentality is split between East and West. These are schizophrenic sheiks, who move through two disparate worlds and seemingly belong to neither. Yet it is this very hybridity that makes them suitable heroes and potential husbands for Western heroines. For unlike in sheik novels of the 1920s, issues of religious difference, race, skin color, hybridity, and miscegenation no longer matter. In fact, racial and cultural difference, as symbolized through skin tone and clothing, is often emphasized and celebrated on the covers of novels such as Alexandra Sellers's *Bride of the Sheikh* (2002) and *The Solitary Sheikh* (1999), Carol Grace's *Fit for a Sheik* (2002), and Isabel French's *Beauty and the Sheikh* (2005)[2] The continuing plot device of Western parentage and hybridity matters only insofar as it provides enough common cultural ground between the sheik and heroine, along with sufficient Western tendencies for the sheik, to let the heroine hope that he may indeed be redeemed to become more "Western" in his outlook and in his treatment of women. The hybridity of the sheik ultimately guarantees his socialization and incorporation into Western culture.

In these particular narratives, the love of a Western woman who is the sheik's equal in every way heals the cultural schizophrenia arising from his hybridity. When the half English sheik in *The Sheikh's Seduction* turns the rule of his county over to his fully Arab half brother, because he loves the Australian heroine and realizes that his people will never accept her as their sheika, he feels elated and liberated. More than that, he finally feels whole. He is "free of the duality that had plagued him since early boyhood, free to take new paths, . . . free to choose how to live." "I was brainwashed from childhood to accept and fulfill a role I didn't choose," he tells Sarah. "There were times I railed against it. My English half rebelled. I felt burdened with duties I was not in tune with." By choosing love over his duty as sheik to his people, he is now "a man no longer divided" (183). Similarly, when the hero of *How to Marry a Real Live Sheikh* (1998) finds the strength to choose a life of love with an American woman, instead of an arranged marriage, the internal conflict between his Eastern and Western selves is ended. Together, they would "create their own reality, one that encompassed two cultures and two personalities" (251). "True love," Catherine Belsey writes, "promises to bring mind and body back into perfect unity, to heal the rift in experience which divides individuals from themselves . . . Love dissolves the anxiety of division in the subject, and replaces it with a utopian wholeness" (23). But the fulfillment of love between the Western heroine and the sheik hero promises more hybridity, not less: a new, hybrid life of two personalities, hybrid progeny, and a new, hybrid culture. Even the heroine is culturally hybrid because she is attracted to and becomes increasingly drawn into the sheik hero's world, as Amy Burge (2011a) points out, often displaying her hybridity through the harem clothing she adopts. Hybridity is the hallmark of modernity in contemporary sheik novels, and this constitutes a distinct reversal of the racial resolution to the novels of the 1920s, whereby the sheik is ultimately revealed to be a "pure-blooded" European.

By the 1990s, fully Arab and Muslim heroes were appearing in the pages of the contemporary sheik romance novel. Australian author Emma Darcy's *The Sheikh's Revenge* (1993) features just such a sheik, but they were more commonly found in American romance novels, perhaps because in America, Arabs had been regarded as officially "white" since the early twentieth century. Arab heroes are found in Iris Johansen's *Strong, Hot Winds* (1988), Barbara Faith's *Lord of the Desert* (1990), and Elizabeth Mayne's *The Sheik and the Vixen* (1996), in which the hero proclaims that he is neither Saudi nor Kuwaiti. Rejecting geopolitical boundaries, he proudly asserts: "I am nomad. I am Muslim. I am my father's son. I am Bedouin and my home is Summan, the Rub' al Khali, Mecca, Baghdad, Al Kuwait, Cairo, the Sinai, Jordan. No matter where I go, my heart faces Mecca and I heed the Prophet's call" (69). This sheik might be a devout Muslim (he is, in fact, a *haji*—one who has made the pilgrimage to Mecca), but the most notable change in the American sheik hero of the 1990s is his transformation from the arrogant Arab autocrat to the "sheik daddy" of Barbara McMahon's eponymous novel of 1996—prefaced by a cutesy letter written by the sheik's daughter, in which she tells her best friend:

> When I found out that Ben was my daddy, I was scared at first that he would be too busy with his sheik work and my mom to pay me much attention, but he's not. He spends time with me every day. . . . The best part is when he tucks me into bed every night. He says Mom had the first nine years, he gets the next. Then he tells me stories about when he was a little boy, or we just talk.

The covers of novels such as McMahon's *Sheik Daddy*, Jacqueline Diamond's *How to Marry A Real-Live Sheik* (1998) and *Captured by a Sheikh* (2000), and Kasey Michael's *The Sheikh's Secret Son* (2000) are telling: they show the suntanned face of a Western man dressed in a *thawb*, his head covered with a *keffiyeh* or *ghutra* and secured with the black-corded *igal*, holding a toddler. These men are not only potential lovers and husbands, but they are good father material as well. They are companionate rather than cruel, and they are boyish, playful, and affectionate toward children, who form an important part of the plots. Even in turn-of-the-century American sheik novels in which children do not feature, the playfulness of the Americanized sheik endures. He is a sensual lover as well as a fun and loyal friend to the heroine. In novels such as Teresa Southwick's *To Catch a Sheik* (2003) and Lucy Monroe's *Hired: The Sheikh's Secretary Mistress* (2008), the heroes are charmingly self-deprecating and they can take a joke against themselves. The sheik hero has come a long way since E. M. Hull's Ahmed Ben Hassan.

It is certainly not the case that the stern, traditionally garbed sheik disappears. Rather, he is joined in both the covers and the contents of these recent novels by a proliferation of modern sheiks who appear in tuxedoes, business clothes, dinner dress, casual shirt and trousers, ornate and vaguely Central-Asian-looking embroidered jackets, and one even appears bare-chested and jeans-clad, but still wearing his *thawb* and *igal* to reassure readers that this is indeed a sheik romance. These men are not only the dictatorial rulers of desert tribes, but they are surgeons, busi-

nessmen, diplomats, owners of race-horse farms, pilots, and secret agents
(working in tandem with the United States government, of course). In
other words, by the turn of the century the sheik hero has become Americanized and assimilated, indistinguishable in features—and sometimes
in dress—from other types of heroes of category romances. He has been
transformed into a suitable hero, friend, and father for the modern Western heroine and her children. When he is not the potentate of a resource-
rich desert kingdom—when he is based in the United States—he can be
incorporated into the American body politic through his relationship
with the heroine. In turn, the heroine is incorporated into a larger extended family: his.

One of the things that makes the sheik a desirable contemporary hero
to romance writers and readers is the Western perception of the strength
of family ties in traditional Arab countries. In this respect, the Anglo-
American culture from which these heroines come fares badly in comparison to the Orient and, indeed, to other Western ethnic cultures perceived by Anglo-Americans as more "traditional" and "patriarchal," such
as Greek, Italian, or Spanish societies. As I argue in Chapter 6, the sheik
hero in contemporary romance novels exists along a continuum of darker
Mediterranean heroes in terms of his physical appearance and behavior.
The same applies to gender and familial relations. The emotionally dam-
aged heroines in these types of novels, who scarcely believe in romantic
love, and who are often cynical about marriage, come from cold, distant,
deeply dysfunctional families. This motif of the broken, emotionally if
not physically abusive family can be found in *The Sheik*. In this novel,
Diana Mayo's mother died giving birth to her, and her father subsequently
shot himself. Her cold, effeminate, and utterly selfish brother, Aubrey, is
left with the burden of her upbringing, and he decides to treat her as a
boy so that he can be saved the trouble of socializing her. This results in
the heroine's unfeminine and androgynous behavior as well as her aversion to love and marriage. When taken to the extreme, one of the mani-
festations of Western modernity—individualism—destroys families and
leaves children, heroines, and heroes lonely and maladapted to society. If
Diana's English family is dysfunctional, Sheik Ahmed Ben Hassan's biological English family is no less so. His mother ran away from his father,
the Earl of Glencaryll, because he "had a terrible temper that was very
easily roused, and . . . he also periodically drank a great deal more than
was good for him, and when under the influence of drink behaved more
like a devil than a man" (247–248). She left her son with the Bedouin sheik
who became his foster father because she was convinced that the Arab

sheik would treat her son better than his alcoholic English father had. It was only in the desert, among the Bedouins, that Ahmed found the family that he needed, and of which Diana would eventually become a part. Thus these novels contain an implicit criticism of the extreme individualism and anomie characterizing Western modernity, even as the heroine seeks to incorporate the sheik into her modern Western world.

This theme of lonely heroines from fragmented dysfunctional Western families who eventually find love, acceptance, and affectionate family ties through their sheik husbands is common in contemporary sheik novels. Orphaned heroines have been very popular with British novelists from the 1970s to the present day. In Pargeter's *The Jewelled Caftan* (1978), not only was the poor British heroine orphaned, but she was also made to work as a virtual slave for her aunt. Her hapless half brother then swindled her of what little savings she had before abandoning her to bandits in the desert. In a more recent novel, the orphaned British heroine of Sarah Morgan's *In the Sheikh's Marriage Bed* (2005) undergoes a similar ordeal when her brother sends her to explain to a desert crown prince he has defrauded that he cannot pay his debts on time. She is then held hostage in her brother's stead. Chantelle Shaw's *At the Sheikh's Bidding* (2008) features yet another lonely English heroine who grew up as an "unloved child and rebellious teenager who had been dumped in a care home after her mother's final and fatal heroin fix" (13). When heroines are not orphans, their parents are often cold and distant. Absent fathers are particularly mourned in these novels. Lynne Wilding's Australian heroine in *The Sheik* (1991) finds herself falling in love with Sheik Karim El Hareembi because he "became another person when he was with the children." The sheik is a "loving, affectionate father," and "[Lynne] could barely recall her father ever playing with her as Karim did with his children whenever he could" (88). Emma Darcy's Australian heroines in *The Sheikh's Revenge* (1993) and *The Sheikh's Seduction* (1998) are children of messy divorces, unwanted and neglected by both their parents. Such indifference on the part of the parents—such a lack of traditional roots and familial bonds—is incomprehensible to the sheik heroes of these novels. Not only do they have strong and affectionate family ties, but they also have a strong sense of their cultural heritage— something that is appealing to the heroines of white settler nations—like Australia or Canada—with brief histories of colonization and immigration. Darcy's heroine in *The Sheikh's Revenge* wonders

what it would be like to belong to a family and tradition that had continued unbroken for centuries. She had no sense of roots at all. Glen [her brother] had been her only mainstay in a life marked by shifting loyalties and relationships. It was one of the things she had admired about the Arab way of life, the security of close family where doubts about one's position were never harboured. (72–73)

Similarly, Canadian writer Alexandra Sellers's *Bride of the Sheikh* (1997) presents a heroine who feels lost and without roots because she had been brought up by nannies as she followed her formal and distant diplomat parents from one country to another. "What was her culture? Who were her people? Where was her home?" she wonders as she views her sheik husband's strong familial and cultural ties with envy. "She had links with half a dozen cultures, but she had none to yearn for" (49).

The modern romance that readers vicariously participate in is thus not merely a romance of sexual, emotional, and intellectual attraction between the hero and heroine that ends happily ever after in marriage; it is also a romance about the idealized Middle Eastern families and close-knit communities that these heroines find when they marry their sheiks. They are no longer alone or lonely, with or without the sheik. They are valued by the sheik's family and lavished with affection. The Arab and Muslim men in these novels are often portrayed as doting and loyal fathers, brothers, husbands, sons, and grandsons. If gender conflict over equality of the sexes is a battle the heroines have to fight with the sheiks, the prize is the power they have over the Muslim males once they are accepted as part of the family. In Faith's *Flower of the Desert*, the daughter of the Moroccan sheik and his American wife acknowledges that her father and grandfather "could turn a grown man pale with a look," while "all she'd ever had to do to get her own way was let her lower lip start to tremble" (17).

Meanwhile, the Muslim women—mothers, sisters, aunts, and grandmothers—in American novels such as Teresa Southwick's *To Catch a Sheik* (2003) and *To Kiss a Sheik* (2003), Barbara McMahon's *Her Desert Family* (2004), and Lucy Monroe's *Hired: The Sheikh's Secretary Mistress* (2008) welcome these heroines into the extended family. The older Muslim women in these novels can be loving, warm, supportive, and maternal . . . and they take the heroine shopping for glamorous clothes as the final seal of their approval of her as a prospective daughter-in-law. These early twenty-first century novels are obviously no longer the desert romances of rolling dunes, oppressed women, and the threat of rape in goat-hair tents. This is the modern Middle East, whose wealthy classes are integrated into, and at home in, a global economy. It is a Middle East that has been transformed by modernization and development.

EIGHT

From Tourism to Terrorism

It seems that an Arab man can now get on the cover of a romance novel in the United States almost more easily than he can get past airport security.

CHRISTY MCCULLOUGH, "DESERT HEARTS"

In Chapter 6, I made the point that the gradual revival of interest in the modern sheik romance novel beginning in the 1970s had less to do with events in the Middle East than with a confluence of other factors: a desire for alpha male heroes in Harlequin Mills & Boon romance novels; gradually changing social mores regarding multicultural, interracial relationships from the late 1960s onward; and an "armchair tourist" desire to read about travel to exotic lands and Oriental cultures. In this chapter, I focus on significant ancillary themes in the sheik romance novel since the 1970s. I discuss travel and tourism in the sheik novel: the representation of exotic space and place and the gradual "Disneyfication" of the Middle East that occurred by the end of the twentieth century. I then examine the introduction of new discourses about development, modernization, nation building, and—after September 11, 2001—terrorism. Although the revival of the sheik romance novel was not a direct response to Middle Eastern affairs, and despite the prevalence of a Disneyfied, "Arabian Nights" East, certain novelists have used the medium to mount subtle critiques of British and American foreign policies in the Middle East.

Like its 1920s predecessor, the revived sheik romance novel was initially grounded in the real, if Orientalized, Middle East. North Africa was a popular setting for desert romance novels in the 1970s and 1980s. Nerina

Hilliard's *The Land of the Sun* (1976) was set in Algeria, while Violet Win-spear's *Tawny Sands* (1970) and *The Burning Sands* (1976), and Margaret Pargeter's *The Jewelled Caftan* (1978), were set in Morocco. Barbara Faith, the only American novelist apart from Iris Johansen writing contempo-rary desert romances in the 1980s, also set two of her novels in Morocco: *Bedouin Bride* (1984) and *Flower of the Desert* (1988). Interest began to move from North Africa to the Arabian peninsula by the 1980s, with Penny Jordan's *Falcon's Prey* (1981) set in Kuwait, and Mary Lyon's *Escape from the Harem* (1986) set in the fictional state of Dhoman, but clearly modeled on an amalgam of Gulf states. Many varied and sometimes im-probable reasons take these heroines out to the Middle East, but their de-light and absorption in travel is constant in these novels.

Indeed, like many of Hilliard's other 1950s romances, *The Land of the Sun* (1976) is taken up with a delight in tourism. The novel describes care-fully the passage to Algiers: the heroine, her fiancé, and his sister must take a liner to Marseille before their onward journey to Algiers. Tourist ports and towns are described along with the tourists' expectations about their various destinations. Touggourt is represented as the fulfillment of tourist dreams of the Orient: "Here were some of the things she had read about . . . palm trees, the curved beauty of a minaret against a brazen blue sky, the silk robes of some desert sheik brushing the tattered and filthy rags of a beggar, every variety of impression one could hope for" (22). There are tourist brochure descriptions of "fabulous El Golea with its fountains, palms and cypresses" and of an exotic and spectacular camel race "like a scene from some Arabian film" (68).

Yet travel through Algeria also pricks conventional romantic ideas about North Africa. The characters do not simply encounter hot desert towns and wind-swept sands, but also, cold mountains, "good roads," and "impressive" tunnels and railway bridges that represent the inexorable march of modernization and development in the region. Reassuringly, however, they find that "simple and charming Tuareg customs, such as the drinking of strong and sweet peppermint-scented tea" (31) are retained. The novel instructs readers on how to partake in this ritual:

> You will usually be offered three cups of tea. Always drink them. To refuse the second or third would be to cast a slur on the teamaker and, indirectly, the hospitality received, but . . . if you are ever offered a fourth, it means you have overstayed your welcome. You very politely get up and leave. (31)

These tidbits of information about foreign customs, scattered throughout the romance, provide the "authenticity" expected by readers, serving to anchor the fabulous romance to an exotic but "real" destination. As Billie Melman comments about the 1920s desert romance subgenre, "The desert novelist seeks to validate her fantastic fabrications by an almost obsessive attention to scenic actuality. Accuracy in geographical and ethnographical details is the primary requirement of the genre" (96). Such a judgment held true for the sheik novels of the 1970s and early 1980s but this was not necessarily the case by the turn of the twenty-first century, as we shall see.

Little distinction was made between the categories of "traveler" and "tourist" in Hilliard's 1950s novel. By the 1970s, however, the terms were no longer synonymous. The 1960s had seen an increase in global travel, so much so that the United Nations had declared 1967 the "international year of the tourist." The growth in global and local tourism brought anti-tourist invectives from social commentators and authors such as Daniel Boorstin and Paul Fussell in the 1960s and 1970s. Boorstin was among the first to draw a firm, status-ridden distinction between the traveler (often figured as male) and the tourist, and he argued that Americans had lost the art of travel: "The traveler was active; he went strenuously in search of people, of adventure, of experience" (85). The tourist, on the other hand, was an inferior agglomeration of all things that were spoiling travel for the affluent middle classes in the jetliner age of modern mass tourism. The tourist was depicted as a passive spectator who goes sightseeing and is provincial and unappreciative of the "authentic . . . product of foreign culture," preferring caricature instead (Boorstin 106). Fussell agrees that "the tourist moves toward the security of pure cliché" (39). If this was a mid- to late twentieth century elite American reaction to the democratization of international travel, it had deep roots in nineteenth-century British culture. Self-styled British travelers had been denigrating "vulgar tourists" since the advent of Thomas Cook's tours in the mid-nineteenth century, while the Reverend Francis Kilvert had infamously opined in the 1870s that "of all noxious animals, the most noxious is the tourist" (Boorstin 40). These were British class-bound attitudes, as James Buzard (1993) has shown, and they appear in the attitudes toward tourism in British sheik romance novels.

Charlotte Lamb's *Desert Barbarian* (1978) presents an example of the traveler/tourist distinction being applied in the desert romance. The novel begins with the upper-middle-class heroine, Marie Brinton, on holiday in the Middle East, where she is bored senseless because the luxury hotel might as well be another holiday resort in the south of France. With its "soft beds, expensive food that managed to taste the same every time, the relentless monotony of comfort and idleness," the hotel is one of Fussell's "pseudo-places," trapping Marie in a tourist bubble, making her feel as though she is "wrapped in transparent plastic, hygienically protected from the dangerous world beyond" (7) She is disappointed by her travel experience:

> The brochure had promised her a world more ancient, more mysterious than her own, and it had been in search of that that she had flown here, only to find herself imprisoned in her own world of air-conditioning, hot water and fitted carpets, unable to reach the teeming, enthralling secret world she had glimpsed in her visit to the Kasbah. Their visit had been a brief one, closely supervised by a nervous guide who had not permitted them to wander far from the path he chose and who had constantly looked over his shoulder with visible anxiety as if expecting every moment to be attacked. From the main street they had followed, Marie had seen dark huddled alleys leading away into a tortuous maze of tiny dwellings; women in dark veils shuffling away with lowered heads, olive-skinned, striding men moving arrogantly through the crowds, their dark eyes passing over the little huddle of excited Europeans without interest. For a brief moment she had felt her imagination kindle, only to be led away by the guide, whispering to her of unimaginable dangers lurking in the shadows. (6–7)

It is clear that the traveler/tourist distinction serves not only to distinguish the romantic traveler from the commonplace tourist, but to assert class distinctions as well. In contrast to Marie's growing sense of frustration at her touristic experience, her fellow tourists, "Mrs. Brown and her quiet husband, Don," had "never been out of England before and were ecstatic over their trip. They had won two weeks at the hotel in a competition, and could not get over their good luck" at this change from their usual "sedate English holidays" (7). What is good enough for Mrs. Brown does not satisfy Marie, who yearns to get "off the beaten track" in order to "see the desert, the wild, empty spaces of the world" (10). The sheik hero overhears this wish, obligingly abducts her, and introduces her to the sordid realities of poverty in a "real" Middle Eastern town, before carrying her away to the desert she wants to experience.

Despite the growing consciousness among these authors of the distinction between real travelers and herd-like tourists, desert romance novels of the 1970s and 1980s abound in tired clichés about the "mysterious" desert that symbolizes freedom and encapsulates the "eternity" of the East and the "insidious enticement of the senses" (Pargeter 1978: 111). This is because, as Melman suggests, "the explorer's voyage to unknown places is . . . analogous to the discovery in the desert romance of the heroine's hitherto repressed sexuality" (1988: 95). Yet these frigid, virginal heroines' desire for the desert betrays not only their desire for sexual awakening, but also for a life of adventure unavailable to them in Britain. British novelists were well aware of the history of British imperial travel and adventure in the Middle East. This is made clear in Winspear's *The Burning Sands* (1976), when a Moroccan man asks the heroine whether she knows anything about the desert and she replies: "I imagine most women have read about the desert . . . one way or another, in sultry novels or in articles by journalists who have travelled there. I think I read about it in a book by Burton the explorer. He lived like an Arab for a time, didn't he?" (27). A mention of T. E. Lawrence, who "slew his enemies as the Arabs slew them, straight across the throat and without mercy," brings to mind Peter O'Toole in David Lean's 1962 film, *Lawrence of Arabia*. The heroine imagines

> Lawrence in his white robes with fanatical blue eyes sweeping the desert ranges he had conquered with an army of brigands riding fast horses and camels across the limitless spaces that smoked in the sun. The legendary Arabs, who sleep upon the sands and follow the stars. (27–28)

These heroines yearn to experience just such an adventure. The romance, then, is not simply about finding love; they can do this back in England. It is about traveling through a space made exotic by Orientalist literature, historical myth, and Hollywood film. It is about the opportunity Orientalism presents women to escape the dreariness of Britain.

For in these British novels of the 1970s and early 1980s, unlike in the later American novels of the post-Gulf War era, which celebrate American life and the centripetal pull of its culture, Britain fares badly in comparison with North Africa and the Middle East. The Britain of these novels is a place of endless rain and enervating grayness. It is stifling in its middle-class respectability, which turns its denizens into dullards. In Winspear's *The Sun Lord's Woman*, the heroine wishes to escape the limits of her aunt's suburban world, neatly encompassed by the privet hedge of the mock-Tudor house with the coach-lamp hanging in the porch. A house that was a twin to every other dwelling in the quiet, self-contained neighbourhood where the offspring learned to ride and play tennis at the Kingswood Country Club and intermarried with each other. (25)

The Britain of these novels is a class-ridden land, short of opportunities for ambitious working women, as the heroine in *The Burning Sands* explains after a horse riding accident leaves her lame and unfit for her job as a model:

I have no option but to use what resources I have in order to live and not become a factory drudge like my poor mother. She couldn't afford to stay away from work even when she was ill, and coming home late from work one night she collapsed on the bus and was rushed to hospital with a bad dose of 'flu. She never recovered, and I'll do anything rather than follow in her shoes. (13)

And so she accepts a job as a governess/companion to an unknown and unseen family in Morocco rather than return to her job as a low-paid "machinist in the East End."

The Britain these heroines wanted to escape from was no longer the Britain of imperial might, but the Britain of economic decline and social crisis during the 1970s and early 1980s.[1] In the very one-sided view of these novelists, this was a Britain faced with the sterling crisis and the unprecedented problem of "stagflation"—price inflation accompanied by high unemployment and the three-day work week for many workers. It was a Britain where the energy crisis created by the oil shocks after the Yom Kippur War of 1973 was compounded by random strikes by dockers and oil tanker and road haulage drivers. Various public sector workers in schools and hospitals also organized random stoppages for pay increases to an admittedly low minimum wage. It was a Britain of industrial disputes, union militancy, and wildcat strikes by dustmen and electricity workers that saw piles of rubbish rotting in the streets, a veritable smorgasbord for rats, and power cuts during the "winter of discontent," from 1978 to 1979, when Britons were urged by ministers to share their bathwater and brush their teeth in the dark. Postal workers' and funeral workers' strikes left the mail undelivered and the dead unburied for a time. It was a Britain that saw the Callaghan Labour government ignominiously defeated in the 1979 general election by the Conservatives, led by Margaret Thatcher, who campaigned with the slogan "Labour isn't working." The subsequent social stress resulting from the Thatcher government's economic liberal reforms, compounded by reduced expenditure on social services and the ruthless reining in of militant unions—particularly Thatcher's confrontation with the National Union of Mineworkers—resulted in growing civil unrest and even violence along the picket lines in the early 1980s. Against such a backdrop, it was understandable that British romance heroines felt, in the words of the hero in *The Sun Lord's Woman*, "a basic need to escape . . . life in England," to go abroad "in search of something you were unable to find in your own country" (56). By contrast, "Africa and the Sahara, golden land of the sun, where there were strange customs and alien peoples" (Hilliard 1976: 25), had probably never looked so good to the British since the end of the Second World War.

Generally speaking, Australian and American sheik romances lack both this overwhelming desire to escape abroad and the acute awareness of the traveler/tourist distinction. An unabashed sense of jingoistic nationalism often pervades these books. For example, Australian author Mons Daveson's novel *My Lord Kasseem* (1982) clearly has tourism on the agenda. Daveson's librarian heroine accompanies her employer to Athens and Cairo, ticking off the tourist spots especially in Egypt: Luxor, the temple at Karnak, the Valley of the Kings, the Aswan Dam, and "Shepheards Hotel, remaining from when Britain ruled in Egypt" (26).[2] Because these characters are unabashed tourists, there is no sense that Australia is necessarily disadvantaged in comparison to North Africa or that, without the powerful incentive of the heroine's relationship with the sheik hero, she would prefer to stay there rather than return to Australia. Daveson brings the women to the Orient via Qantas Airways, patriotically making sure her readers know that Qantas—an Australian icon—is superior to every other airline. In Australian authors Lynne Wilding's and Emma Darcy's sheik novels, the heroines travel to the Middle East on personal or familial quests, or in search of professional opportunities. They are not usually refugees fleeing a dreary life or dismal weather. Darcy, in particular, celebrates Australia as a space of the exotic in her other category romance novels (interview with Thomas 2008: 121). The same generally holds true for American sheik novels. Authors such as Barbara McMahon, Jacqueline Diamond, Linda Winstead Jones, Lucy Monroe, and Dana Marton move their heroines between San Francisco, Los Angeles, Texas, New York, and their imagined worlds of the Middle East without giving any sense that a desire to escape the United States motivates these women.

It might be argued that the disparagement of Britain in comparison to North Africa and the Middle East was a feature of the particular socio-economic circumstances of Britain in the 1970s and early 1980s. Certainly, more recent British authors of sheik novels, such as Susan Stephens (2005 and 2007), Chantelle Shaw (2008), and Kim Lawrence (2008), do not portray Britain negatively, or as a dreary, stifling place from which to escape. Yet in *The Sheikh's Virgin Bride* (2003), Penny Jordan paints a highly unflattering picture of drunken British louts abroad making "loud-voiced demands" of the locals, while Sharon Kendrick presents a damning portrait of modern British youth culture in *The Desert King's Virgin Bride* (2007), in which the ruler of Kharastan travels to Brighton to find his British ward, only to discover her hosting a party that seems to have gotten out of control. The heroine's apartment is a mess, young couples are making out everywhere, and people are smoking pot on the balcony! He can't believe that she gave up the culture, luxury, and dignity of life in his Central Asian palace for this "debauchery":

> Food lay congealed in silver containers—some of it spattered on the surfaces—and half-empty bottles stood in warm puddles of beer. In his country food—even when it was simple—was always served with a certain amount of ceremony and respect . . .
>
> His eyes flicked to where a spoonful of rice lay coagulating on the side. And now Malik's lips curved with distaste—never in Kharastan would there be such an undignified mess daring to masquerade as entertainment.
>
> Was this what Sorrel had wished for when she'd demanded to leave Kharastan? This was the destiny she followed—the dream she chased? This casual and rather depressing sight of excess combined with little elegance or formality? (68)

Little wonder, then, that these heroines wanted to escape abroad. And yet, perhaps this disparagement of Britain—which naturally finds no echo in other non-Orientalist category romance novels set in Britain—is less about the country itself and more of a lingering legacy of the discourse of travel and tourism that has shaped British literary understanding and representation of travel abroad since the nineteenth century. It is certainly noteworthy that this particular aspect of the British sheik novel has not emerged in its American, Australian, and Canadian counterparts.

"Strange customs and alien peoples" were naturally an intriguing part of the travel experience, as were the plenitude and variety of exotic foods presented especially in British sheik novels of the 1970s and 1980s. Mariam Darce Frenier, in her attempt to draw a sharp distinction between American and British romance novels of the 1980s, argues that British heroines tended not to have much of an appetite, whereas American heroines thought more about food, got hungry more often, and actually ate (65). This is certainly not true when we look at the sheik romances of the 1970s and 1980s. Winspear's novels abound with roasted quails, vegetables, couscous, the "spicy aroma of rissoles," roasted lamb served with "small sultana pancakes," pink melons with a "sweet cool taste," butter melting on corn cobs, "rice in which chicken had been baked with raisins, onions, and chopped eggplant," caramel custards, squeezed passion fruit juice, and the "ripe, almost purple coloured figs" that tasted like a "blend of nuts and honey." Hilliard's, Pargeter's, and Wood's novels similarly tantalize the taste buds, and the end of Penny Jordan's *Falcon's Prey* presents the reader with a recipe for "Delicious Shish Kebab" and an explanatory note from the editor:

> When Felicia travels to Kuwait, she encounters a host of new experiences, and perhaps not the least of these is the local cuisine. We thought readers might enjoy the following recipe for shish kebab, which is a traditional Arabic dish that in recent years has become popular all over Europe and North America. (189)

These novels are not merely about the heroine's sexual arousal, but about the awakening of all her senses. In this regard, they continue a long-standing tradition from the late medieval verse romances that celebrated the luxury and opulence of the Islamic world in poems such as *The King of Tars*. Thus, the lavish banquet of exotic food laid out for the reader was accompanied by the dazzling spectacle of Oriental commodities available at the *souk*, or bazaar, piled high and jumbled together in a display of bright colors and contrasting textures. In Winspear's *Tawny Sands* (1970), for example, the heroine experiences a growing wonder as her senses are aroused in the *souk*. She sees "handwoven silks of every colour and so soft to the touch. Rugs in bright Arabian designs. Hammered jewellery and strings of beads. Silver bird cages. Heaps of symbols in the shape of fish, stars, and the Hand of Fatima." In a nearby stall,

> mounds of mint sent out a tang that mingled with smoking *kebab*. Pumpkins towered over purple figs and sweet lemons. Apricots and henna were piled besides slippers of soft leather, and gorgeous stuffs for bride dresses

were surrounded by chattering women. The scent-sellers displayed their
wares in the tiniest phials, and the most ornamental flagons. (83)

The detailed description of non-Western markets was a traditional part of
the repertoire of travel writing. The heroine of the modern British desert
romance is heir to this tradition and all it signifies, particularly as far
as British women's independence and freedom of movement, and their
ability to sample cultural difference is concerned.

Yet if the market represents the space of exotic otherness, it also displayed Western women's vulnerability abroad, for the *souk* could also be
a claustrophobic place where white women were accosted, subjected to
violence, and even abducted. This metamorphosis of the *souk* from the
mysterious to the menacing occurs in Alfred Hitchcock's film *The Man
Who Knew Too Much* (1956), in which the middle-class American Mac-
Kennas (played by James Stewart and Doris Day) are enchanted by the
exoticism of Djemaa el-Fna—the famous square lined by *souks* in Marrakech—only to be plunged into intrigue and dangerous adventure when
a man dies in front of them after being stabbed by an assassin. While the
goods on display in the market are enchanting, the Arab people milling
about in the *souk* are unknowable, easily excitable, and threatening. They
are, after all, Orientals. Sometimes they barely seem human, reduced to
sinister eyes and grasping limbs, hands clawing at the romantic heroine's
white body. Winspear's heroine in *Tawny Sands* spends too long wandering in the bazaar and suddenly the mob seems to "press in upon her,"
and "their eyes seemed hostile, and the musk of their robes caught in
her throat" (83). Hilliard's heroine in *Land of the Sun* is swept away by a
"flood of dirty humanity that made her feel faint with its nearness" (35).
"Rude" hands reach out to touch her and "all the stories she had ever read
of people vanishing without a trace returned to put further terror in her
heart" (35). These female tourists are out of their element; they need to be
rescued by the sheik hero in all his wrathful glory.

The *souk*, especially Djemaa el-Fna, also features in Barbara Faith's
novels set in Marrakech, but an interesting transformation takes place
in these American novels. The *souk* becomes not only a marketplace,
but a fairground offering carnivalesque entertainments as well as exotic
foods for consumption. Here is Faith's description of Marrakech's Djemaa
el-Fna in *Bedouin Bride* (1984):

The mammoth square was crowded. There were monkey trainers, trick
cyclists, jugglers and magicians, even a flame eater who called to her as

she went by. A variety of musicians each trying to drown out the others,
added to the hodgepodge of noise and confusion. There were whirling
dervishes and acrobats, dancers with henna'd hands dressed in folds
of cobalt blue and black, their hair bound with silken cloths decorated
with jingling silver coins. (57)

In *Flower of the Desert* (1988), Faith embellishes this scene with the
addition of acrobats, fortune-tellers, and "snake charmers with flat-
headed cobras swaying to the high, keening music of a flute" (26). The
point is not whether the description of the Djemaa el-Fna is accurate or
inaccurate; instead, it is the emphasis the author places on the *entertainment* value rather than the food. In this, we see the differing strands of
Orientalist discourse woven into the desert romance, for where British
authors seemed to draw from earlier British travel accounts, American
Orientalist discourse in Faith's novels alludes to its roots in the 1893 Chicago World's Fair and its offshoots in turn-of-the-century amusement
parks with their "hoochy-coochy" exhibitions, fakirs, and fortune-tellers;
the department store decorations and advertising; and, of course, lavish
Hollywood productions featuring dancers, acrobats, flame eaters and the
like discussed in Chapter 4.

Beginning in the late 1980s, attempts to portray real locations in the
Middle East had given way to make-believe locations drawing on these
"Arabian Nights" sources of American Orientalist discourse (Nance
2009). This transition to mythical places occurred in British and Australian as well as American sheik novels, despite the occasional novel set
in a real Middle Eastern country. Orientalist discourse has always been an
imaginary construct of the fantasy space of the Orient, but in the nineteenth and twentieth centuries it had functioned in tandem with realism.
By the turn of the twenty-first century, a "Disneyfication" of Orientalism
was occurring in contemporary sheik novels. Not only are most of the recent settings fictitious, but many modern heroines almost cultivate ignorance of the region and blatantly and blithely declare their ignorance to
the reader. Haley Bennet, pilot extraordinaire in Elizabeth Mayne's *The
Sheik and the Vixen* (1996), concedes that "what she knew about Saudi
Arabia she could stuff in a thimble . . . Everything . . . she knew about
the Mideast was media gleaned, via telecasts of terrorist bombings, ongoing internal wars, propaganda and coup attempts. None of which she'd
ever followed" (33). The same probably applied to many of the readers of
these novels as well. As Michael Oren notes, even as the Reagan administration's incoherent and contradictory foreign policy in the Middle East

lurched from crisis to crisis, increasingly alienating different groups in the region, and even as the threat of specifically anti-American terrorism built throughout the 1990s, Americans were distracted by other global occurrences, entertainments, and domestic problems, and "were scarcely of a mind to monitor these events" in the Middle East (580). Instead,

> movie audiences cheered as Michael J. Fox in *Back to the Future* (1985) and Tom Cruise in *Top Gun* (1986) handily dispatched Libyan assailants, and as Indiana Jones (Harrison Ford) smirked and shot a scimitar-wielding Arab in the 1981 blockbuster, *Raiders of the Lost Ark.* They delighted as a winsome Brooke Shields, cast as the naïve American ingénue in *Sahara* (1983), was swept away by an Arab horseman in black. They laughed at the bumbling Muslim terrorists who, in the 1982 comedy *Wrong is Right*, experimented with suicide bombers and plotted to blow up New York's Twin Towers.
>
> Hollywood was once again indulging in Oriental fantasies and conflating them with Middle Eastern facts. (562–563)

Jacqueline Diamond's *How to Marry A Real-Live Sheikh* (1998) is quite extreme in its disregard for "Middle Eastern facts," but not particularly unusual for this subgenre. At no point in the novel does Diamond attempt to connect her sheik and his Islamic background and Muslim nation to any recognizable people or place in the Middle East. To the Americans in these novels, the East—undifferentiated and homogeneous—is a "place of legends rather than real flesh-and-blood people. China was a place you could dig a hole to, India resembled a scene from *The Jungle Book*, and Aladdin flew through Arabia on his magic carpet" (69). Diamond's reference is, in fact, not to the Middle East or the Orient of European historical construction, but to Hollywood. Scattered throughout the novel are references to films and film scenes. The heroine's first glimpse of the hero, with his "high cheekbones and dark, burning eyes of a desert warrior" has her picturing him "astride an Arabian stallion, leading a charge against impossible odds." When he walks up the driveway of her hotel, his white robes flapping in the wind, "the sight reminded Cathy of a scene from *Lawrence of Arabia*." She tells her mother: "He's like something out of an old movie." "That movie wouldn't be *The Sheik*, would it?" her mother coyly teases. "Just because he dresses like Rudolph Valentino in *The Sheik* doesn't mean he's going to sweep me off to his tent in the desert and ravish me!" Cathy says (30). Finally, Cathy's daughter, seeing pedestrians in robes and *kaffiyehs*, in *thawbs* and turbans, and with the occasional "curved dagger tucked into a richly embroidered belt," asks: "Is this place Disneyland?" No, it is not Disneyland, she is told. "There is no Mickey Mouse." But it may as well be Disneyland, this postmodern pastiche of Oriental film clips haphazardly juxtaposed with what Jean Baudrillard calls "the pure baroque logic of Disneyland . . . a magnificent stroke of cynicism, naivety, kitsch, and unintended humor—something astonishing in its nonsensicality" (101). There is, in the final analysis, something profoundly imperialistic in the way Western romances are played out against a vague, sanitized simulacrum of the Middle East, which has expunged not only the countries, but the very reality of people's lives in this region.

The contrast between attempts to depict a realistic Western setting in contemporary romance novels and a complete disregard for the same where the Middle East is concerned is striking. Indeed, readers can garner basic tourist information about many different Western settings in other contemporary romance novels. Novelists take care with their descriptions of various American, British, European, Canadian, South African, New Zealand, and Australian localities because they realize that some readers will be familiar with these places, and others will expect basic accuracy of information. The indifference of authors toward the realities of the Middle East is potentially problematic for romance readers because these romance novels are read not only for entertainment but for education as well. In the 1980s, Margaret Ann Jensen claimed:

> Readers often choose to read a specific romance on the basis of its setting. They feel that while they are enjoying themselves, they are also learning about other countries, the people and their customs. The "educational" aspect of the books is sometimes used by readers to justify their reading to outsiders or skeptics. (148–149)

The readers interviewed by Janice Radway in the mid-1980s also believed that "[romance] novels teach them about faraway places and times and instruct them in the customs of other cultures" (Radway 109). Harlequin Mills & Boon certainly fostered this idea, for its guidelines for authors even in the late 1990s emphasized that "the books are contemporary and settings can be anywhere in the world as long as they are authentic" (quoted in Bach 13). More recently, *Chicago Tribune* journalist Patrick Reardon reported that the sheik romance readers he interviewed explained that "when they read about sheiks, they're learning about the exotic world of the Arabian Desert" (2006).

Authors from the 1970s and early 1980s show evidence of some research into the backgrounds of their desert romances, and some contemporary authors such as American writer Lucy Monroe and Australian writer Emma Darcy continue this trend. Darcy sometimes lists the places she has traveled to in order to do her research (see the author's note at the end of *Traded to the Sheikh*, 2005). However, meticulous research is no longer strictly necessary in the make-believe world of the mythical Middle East. After all, these books are not really about the Middle East or Muslim cultures; they are about romantic love. This attitude is displayed in Kathleen Creighton's *Virgin Seduction* (2002), a book she was commissioned to write as a sequel to Linda Winstead-Jones's *Secret-Agent Sheik* (2002). In the foreword, Creighton tells her readers:

> I was thrilled to be asked to participate in this wonderful new series, ROMANCING THE CROWN, but I must confess that when I learned I would be writing about the princess of a mythical Arab kingdom, my first thought was, "Who, *me*? But I don't *do* Arab sheik books!" How, I wondered, would I ever be able to write convincingly of a people and a culture I knew absolutely nothing about?
>
> But as I began the research for *Virgin Seduction*, it suddenly came to me: "This isn't a book about sheikdoms and Arabs and Eastern Mediterranean culture; it's the story of two complete strangers who don't even know they're in love yet, struggling to find a way to make a life together."

This does not mean that Creighton did not do any research for her novel. On the contrary; she learned enough to scatter Arabic terms throughout the novel, giving it an illusion of exoticism and Islamic authenticity. Thus she describes the *Nikah* (marriage) ceremony and the *Walima*, or marriage feast; and she refers to the *Khutba-tun-Nikah* and the "words of the *eshedu*," which the hero has to recite. But these details are simply there to give a flavor of the Orient and Islamic culture, rather than to depict any place or culture conscientiously.

Other writers who make up their own sheikdoms acknowledge that the books are simply "broad fantasy" and "not based in reality," in the words of writer Susan Mallery: "I don't deal with anything icky. [Readers] are not going to learn anything about the Middle East from me" (Reardon 2006). Yet perhaps readers no longer expect verisimilitude or an allusion to reality. On her blog, sheik romance reader Marilyn Shoemaker, who had been interviewed by Reardon about the sheik romance phenomenon, muses about the al-Qaeda attacks on the United States on September 11, 2001, and sheik romances:

> He asked me interesting questions and one I actually did not think about, 911 [*sic*] and how reading books concerning sheikhs affected me? 911 was personally horrific for me and my country and mostly importantly for the city of New York.
>
> Quite honestly, when I read these stories I don't think about 911, nor religion, nor where they take place, I think about falling in love, about romance and hopefully all of this craziness going on in the world will someday resolve itself and there will be peace! I pray this happens for all because in my heart it's all about LOVE.

This is an astounding comment in many ways. As Norman Denzin and Yvonna Lincoln wrote soon after the al-Qaeda terrorist attacks on the United States:

> The world changed on 11 September 2001. For Americans, not since Pearl Harbor and Hiroshima . . . had there been one global symbolic event of the force of 9/11 . . . The global repercussions of 9/11 are still being felt today, from the Middle East to Afghanistan to Washington, D. C. Indeed, the 9/11 event is taking on the aura of history, an apocalyptic moment, a turning point in the history of America and its relationship with the world." (xiii)

The impact of 9/11 (discussed more fully in the Conclusion) reverberated throughout American society through deep grief and emotional distress, an increase in post-traumatic stress disorder,[3] a backlash against Arab and Muslim Americans, a disruption of public life, the curtailment of civil liberties and the increased power of the state and its agencies, the "war against terror" carried out in Afghanistan and then Iraq, and a pervasive sense of fear and insecurity about enemies within and without. Yet for Shoemaker, although sheik romances are acknowledged to be about the Middle East, the books do not help her to understand anything about American relations with the Middle East, or why the United States might have been a target for Islamist terrorism. Because these recent books have little correlation to the reality of Middle Eastern geography, regimes, peoples, or cultures, turmoil in the region and terrorism against the United States are reduced to "religion," and "all of this craziness going on in the world," which will magically resolve itself some day. As the Beatles sang, "all you need is love, love is all you need."

MODERNIZATION, DEVELOPMENT, AND POLITICAL CONFLICT

However, an indifference toward, and cultivated ignorance concerning, the Middle East has not always characterized the writers of sheik romance novels. If the authors of sheik romances made use of centuries-old Orientalist tropes such as exotic bazaars, kasbahs, harems, bagnios, and the "timeless" and "mysterious" desert, they were also at pains to point out that times were changing, and so were Middle Eastern countries as they underwent modernization, development, and nation building. Much of this was linked to the European or American presence in the Middle East. However, modernization and development have historically signified different things to different Western countries. To Australians, they meant lucrative professional as well as trade opportunities in the Middle East—particularly in wheat and live agricultural exports—toward the end of the twentieth century. To the British, they were a legacy of the civilizing mission and a justification of past imperial rule in a decolonizing or postcolonial world. To Americans, however, development and modernization were key weapons in the Cold War struggle for the allegiance of the Third World.

The British and French decolonization of North Africa and the Middle East took place in the midst of the Cold War. The Truman Doctrine—and every subsequent American presidential foreign policy "doctrine"—had emphasized that communism could be contained specifically by curtailing the expansion of Soviet influence in the decolonizing world. Americans had relied on the British to act as proxies and guardians of their interests in the Middle East since the early twentieth century, but the Suez debacle of 1956 prompted the United States to focus on its own bilateral relations with the region, and this meant renewed attention to development. The utopian ideals and revolutionary fervor that swept the region were to be channeled into the more moderate path of economic development and political and social reform, thus ensuring the creation of U.S.-friendly polities with a semblance of democracy—or so it was assumed, according to the theories of modernization popular with sociologists and political scientists writing especially about Latin America and the Middle East in the mid-twentieth century (Lockman 133).

The 1950s saw the publication of influential books in America, such as Daniel Lerner's *The Passing of Traditional Society: Modernizing the Middle East* (1958), that urged the American government to give more aid for developmental purposes in the Middle East on the condition that this would be accompanied by democratization and reform. Such policies were considered necessary to stave off the popular appeal of the Egyptian president Gamal Abdel Nasser's calls for revolutionary "Pan-Arab socialism." In the 1960s—labeled as the "crucial decade of development" by President John F. Kennedy—John Badeau, the U.S. ambassador to Egypt, argued that the United States needed to work more closely with "moderate" Arab rulers, such as King Hussein of Jordan, to foster modernization via "progressive movements and liberal institutions." This would prove to the Arab world that "an Arab country can pass into the modern world and solve its basic problems without the destructive upheaval of revolution" (Little 194–196). In the context of the Cold War, the American political and scholarly classes focused on modernization and development as a teleological pathway to Americanization because they believed the alternative would be revolution and communism. The U.S. government made economic and military aid available to pro-Western leaders such as Iraqi prime minister Nuri Said, Libya's King Idris, and the shah of Iran in exchange for assurances of political and social reforms, only to be stunned, according to Douglas Little, "when modernization brought xenophobic nationalism and revolutionary Islam instead" (194). In Iraq, the Hashemite monarchy was toppled in July 1958 by an army coup led by Abd al-Karim Qasim; the anti-Western Colonel Muammar al-Qaddafi overthrew King Idris in Libya; and Shah Mohammad Reza Pahlavi's top-down "White Revolution" was brought to a halt when he was ousted from power by Ayatollah Ruhollah Khomeini. As Little argues, "America's attempt to modernize the Middle East backfired, igniting the very revolutions it was supposed to squelch" (6).

The United States' role in Middle Eastern affairs since the Second World War has been very complex. We can hardly expect writers and readers of romance fiction to understand the intricate histories and politics of this region (although other genres, such as thrillers and espionage novels, make attempts, however biased or inaccurate, to do so). Nevertheless, it seems plausible that there would be some cultural awareness of the failures of modernization and development, and of conflicts at least partially wrought by U.S. interests in the region. Despite the tenacious belief of the United States in the universal efficacy of development, modernization, and progress, there is less focus on these issues in the American sheik romances than in the British and Australian romance novels, in which it is taken for granted that it is the civilizational responsibility of the heroine to assist in the program of modernizing the Middle East. From the 1980s to the twenty-first century, the themes of modernization and development have been connected to Middle Eastern conflicts, often providing an easy explanation for war and terrorism, because the pro-Western forces of modernization in these countries are believed to clash with backward-looking elements in Muslim society. As articulated in Sandra Marton's *The Sheikh's Rebellious Mistress* (2008), conflict in the sheik's country escalated as the "ugly philosophical battle between those who wanted to remain in the past and those who wanted to step into the future . . . became an actual war" (150). This battle between modernization and regression is played out in British novels that touch on historical and political events in the Gulf states from the 1950s to the 1980s, and in the few American romance novels that engage with America's involvement in the Middle East since the 1990s, through the Persian Gulf War, the Iraq War, and Islamist terrorism.

British sheik novels of the 1970s and 1980s emphasize the importance of development, congratulate their sheik heroes for bringing it about, and suggest an important role for the heroine in furthering such programs, especially where Muslim women and children are concerned. Modernization is equated with Westernization, and the Oxbridge-educated sheik is a conduit of both. In Hilliard's *Land of the Sun*, the Tuareg leader's "Western education" is the basis of his enlightened view toward crime and punishment as well as toward the presence of Europeans in his capital city, where "there was a small hospital and even a school, staffed by Europeans of varying nationality" (116). Despite the backwardness of his people, he had decided that

> if the Tuareg were to become a nation again, instead of a lot of squabbling tribes, something would have to be done about the rut of superstition and outmoded customs into which most of them were deeply sunk. The school was at least a start and there was even talk of bringing in engineers to build a small generator—but such very advanced ideas were looked on so far with a rather jaundiced eye by the majority of the population, who had a suspicion of anything savouring even remotely of machinery. (116)

The reluctance of the ignorant masses to embrace modernization and development is sometimes an implicit justification for the benevolent dictatorships or enlightened absolute monarchies that characterize the vast majority of these novels. Democratization is supposed to be one of the principal results of Western development, but apart from the feminist issues of women's rights and gender equality discussed in the previous chapter, the novels have surprisingly little to say about democracy. Indeed, part of the appeal of the sheik romance novel is that it offers the opportunity—so rare in the modern world—to indulge in feudal fantasies of powerful "Sheik Charmings" sweeping modern-day Cinderellas into a life of luxury, power, and authority in the Oriental palace. Many of the recent sheik novels, both British and American, have in fact upgraded the sheik hero to a prince or crown prince: Sarah Morgan's *The Sheikh's Virgin Princess* (2007), Sharon Kendrick's *The Desert King's Virgin Bride* (2007), Chantelle Shaw's *At the Sheikh's Bidding* (2008), and Kim Lawrence's *Desert Prince, Defiant Virgin* (2008), among the British novels; Susan Mallery's *The Sheikh and the Virgin Secretary* (2007) and Sandra Marton's *The Sheikh's Wayward Wife* (2008), among the American novels.

Beginning in the 1970s, the sheik's attitude toward social and economic development was as important as his final attitude toward women's independence in determining whether he would be a suitable match for the Western heroine, for both indicated the extent of his enlightened modernity. If he is going to be an autocrat, then best he be a benevolent and incorruptible one devoted to improving the lot of his people in the modern world. In fact, the sheik hero is everything that the West wished King Idris, the shah of Iran, and all the other toppled monarchs in the Middle East had been. The sheik's attitude toward modernization is sometimes contrasted with that of his peers or forebears. Mary Lyons's *Escape from the Harem* (1986) features a heroine who escapes to London after living in a southern Arabian kingdom called Dhoman—a "backward, hopelessly archaic country," (16) which the old sultan ruled despotically,

> banning such items as sunglasses, the live playing of music and radios, cigarettes, dancing, all travel between towns without a permit, and even the wearing of trousers by men. . . . However, it was his fierce, obdurate refusal to spend any of his vast oil revenues on important and necessary items such as schooling or medicine that had led to the present unrest and rebellion in the western part of the country. There were, apparently, only three small primary schools in the whole of Dhoman, and no hospitals or health service other than that offered by a small clinic in Muria, run by a dedicated group of American doctors. (59–60)

Because of underdevelopment, preventable or treatable diseases such as malaria, tuberculosis, and trachoma were rife, and the sultan's subjects lived in abject poverty. This created the perfect conditions for Marxist propaganda to take root and flourish, especially in the climate of the Cold War. Consequently, the country faced a civil war when "Marxist rebels," who were "heavily supplied with men and weapons from both Russia and China," (32) seized hold of regional areas. It took all of the sheik hero's efforts—aided by troops sent by the British government—to quell the rebellion, oust his father from the throne in a popular coup, and begin developing the country.

Dhoman may be a fictional country, but the author's familiarity with recent Middle Eastern history is evident in the parallels with the Buraimi dispute of the mid-1950s and the failure of the rulers of the Trucial Gulf states of Abu Dhabi and Oman to develop their sheikdoms, which eventually led to their overthrow. In 1952, Saudi Arabia attempted to assert claims of sovereignty over the newly discovered oil fields in Abu Dhabi, sending Saudi troops to occupy the nine villages in the Buraimi oasis, six of which belonged to Abu Dhabi, and the other three to Oman. Abu Dhabi was then a British protectorate, while Oman had a Treaty of Friendship and Commerce with Britain. Sheik Shakhbut of Abu Dhabi and Sultan Said bin Taimur of Oman therefore requested help against the Saudis from the British government. In October 1955, British troops aided the Trucial Oman Levies and the Omani army in expelling the Saudis from the Buraimi oasis, thus bringing the dispute to an end (Brenchley 79–81).

The real-life parallels with Lyons's novel did not end there. After the crisis and the exploitation of oil in Abu Dhabi, Sheik Shakhbut's family ousted him from power in 1966 and instated his brother Zaid in his place because of Shakhbut's miserliness with Abu Dhabi's oil wealth and his failure to develop the country. Sheik Zaid was subsequently responsible for developing Abu Dhabi and creating the welfare system as well as strengthening both military and commercial ties with Britain, thus increasing the Gulf state's importance to the United Kingdom as an export market (Brenchley 159). The same thing occurred four years later in Oman, when Sultan Said bin Taimur was overthrown in a coup by his son Qabus, who then proceeded to develop the country's infrastructure. As with Abu Dhabi, development brought closer ties with the United Kingdom and fresh opportunities for British firms because of historical connections dating back to the days when these Gulf states were British protectorates (Brenchley 279).

Lyons's sheik hero, who mounted a coup d'état against his miserly and rather mad father who hoarded oil wealth and refused to develop the sheikdom of Dhoman (the conflation of Abu Dhabi and Oman), therefore had a basis in Middle Eastern reality. Similarly, the threat of Marxist gue-rilla forces mentioned in the novel was certainly real in places like Yemen and the Dhofar, West Oman, in the 1970s. In subsequently embarking on a program of rapid health, educational, commercial, and infrastructure development and modernization, the sheik hero creates conditions under which his English wife can return and play an important role in mod-ernizing the country. In fact, he gives the heroine "the opportunity to do something useful with her life" (109), not because she is necessarily the best qualified throughout the region, but because she is a British-educated woman and his wife. There are notable limits to the idea of meritocracy in this enlightened absolute monarchy. This scenario is a reprisal of the days of British colonialism, when, because of their status as white women man-aging subordinate "natives," British women found far more professional opportunities abroad than they had in Britain (Sharpe 94–95).

The neocolonial implications of the British heroine's role in mod-ernizing a Middle Eastern country are recognized by Sarah Wood in her remarkable book *Perfumes of Arabia* (1986), which presents the most sustained critique of the history of British imperialism as well as British people's Orientalist and racist assumptions in the novels from this period. Other novelists had occasionally demonstrated an awareness of such issues. In Winspear's *Blue Jasmine* (1969), for example, the heroine is gently mocked for her incredulity and indignation when she is abducted. She finds it almost impossible to believe that this is happening to her be-cause she is a British subject. In Pargeter's *The Jewelled Caftan* (1978), the heroine angrily informs the sheik hero, after he rescues her from her Bed-ouin abductors, that she is English, to which he replies: "I thought you might be, but that is no excuse to feel superior, or imagine you have the sole right to speak your mind" (32).

Wood's *Perfumes of Arabia* goes beyond such passing references. In this novel, the rather aggressive and obnoxious British heroine Jeannie Bennett travels to the desert sultanate of Riyam to take up a position re-forming primary education. She is rude and suspicious toward the locals, assuming that they are trying to steal her bags, but she is subsequently embarrassed by their dignified courtesy and hospitality toward her. On the way to the capital, she is driven through a village where she witnesses a brawl over what she assumes to be the right of ownership and sexual ac-cess to a fourteen-year-old girl. She is in fact greatly mistaken, continu-ally led astray by her Orientalist and racist assumptions concerning the "differences between East and West," the lechery of Muslim males, and their pedophilic sexual practices (22). "How very Arab" and "barbaric," she thinks, to fight "like a dog for the favours of a fourteen-year-old girl" (25). The winner of this brawl, the sheik hero, is someone she feels she can handle because "she was almost certainly more intelligent than he" (18). She accuses him of trying to hinder her professional appointment because he wishes to impede the progress of Riyam, particularly of Riyami women and children, to which the sheik replies sarcastically: "Such fire! Such impressive desires to civilise the natives!" (31).

In the first half of this novel, then, the function of the sheik hero is to undermine the discourse of Orientalism as well as of white women's assumption that they can "civilize the natives" by bringing progress to a backward land. It is the British who are shown to be uncivilized and even unhygienic here, for they are out of their element and too arrogant to ask for help in dealing with the desert and local custom. Their gaucheness is contrasted with the Arabs' general patience and graciousness in the face of continuing British arrogance and condescension. Nevertheless, the sheik bluntly informs Jeannie, resentment against the British still exists in some quarters because the "British sometimes tread heavily with their clumsy feet. My people look out for someone of your race—anyone—to avenge insults, whether real or imagined" (46). When she tries to interfere in a local tradition, he tells her, "I don't want to hear your opinion. We've held such traditions for thousands of years—before you British formed primitive tribes" (47). He openly mocks the tradition of the sheik romance novel, telling her: "You Englishwomen think you're so desirable to us" (32). Yet she is of course desirable and irresistible to him. In the face of her outrage when he kisses her, he remarks that "the rough native defiles you with his greasy hands" and mockingly apologizes: "I forgot. I must return to my place at your feet, bowing low in the dust" (57). The heroine is continually shown to be in the wrong, frustrated to the point where although "she'd never thought of herself as racially prejudiced before" (57), such underlying attitudes and assumptions are forced into the open. The fact that the sheik hero is attracted to an English woman and that, as it turns out, he has a very personal reason for disliking the English (his English mother abandoned him and the pattern was repeated with his brother's English wife) ultimately undermines, in the second half of the novel, the early critiques of Orientalism, imperialism, and racism, but it is still significant that such sustained critiques were made at all through the medium of the sheik novel.

What characterizes many of the British sheik romances from the 1970s and 1980s, and differentiates them from their counterparts from the turn of the twenty-first century, is the anchor to some sort of geographical, historical, and political reality in the Middle East. This faithfulness to place is evident in the discourse of travel and tourism discussed above, as well as in specific details of development, allusions to the history of British imperialism, and references to the actual text of the *Qur'an*. Winspear, Pargeter, and Jordan, for example, were familiar with the *Qur'an* and incorporated quotes from it into their novels. Islam was an actual religion with a specific set of beliefs for them, not a vague matter of "culture" as it would be for later novelists.[4] In *The Jewelled Caftan* (1978), Pargeter explains that the *Qur'an* is "the Islam[ic] equivalent of the Christian New Testament and about the same length," with an emphasis "laid on charity and justice" and on Allah as a forgiver (106). This is hardly the stuff of Islamic Studies 101, of course, but it shows that at this stage novelists had not become wary of any mention of Islam or Muslims, nor were these equated with "terrorism," as was gradually occurring in other forms of Western popular culture.

The attempt to ground these sheik romances in some sort of Middle Eastern reality can also be seen in vague and oblique references to contemporary events in the region. Lyons's *Escape from the Harem* refers to the 1979 Iranian Revolution, which has forced the heroine's father, "a senior executive with an oil company based in Tehran," to relocate to England. The heroine works as an Oriental carpet broker, and she tells an American client that carpets from "the holy city of Qum in Iran" are increasing in value because "the political climate in that country is not too good at the moment and so these pieces are becoming increasingly rare" (7). Winspear's *The Sun Lord's Woman* features an English woman whose developing relationship with the half Spanish, half Arab sheik is marred on her wedding night, when he discovers that she is of Jewish descent. "My mother's relations were almost wiped out by the Nazis," she confesses, and "only her father survived by escaping from a labour camp in Holland where he joined a resistance movement" (114). The sheik is appalled by this revelation, and tells her: "I am an Arab on my father's side! . . . How do I justify to myself and my compatriots a wife who is related to those who were part of the fighting in which my father was brutally killed?" (115). Unsurprisingly, few details are given regarding the Arab-Israeli conflict, which is presented as simply a tragic but vague case of "Judaic ideals" clashing "with those of the Moslem," (138) rather than enmity arising from territorial claims or any specific action or event. Inchoate historical forces seem to be at work, producing hostility between the two sides:

> It didn't seem possible that they could have been so close, and now were pushed apart by the enmity that raged back and forth across the desert sands, erupting every so often into fierce clashes of temperament and ideals at cross purposes. People got caught up in the middle of those outbursts and it had happened to Karim's eminent father and the [Spanish] mother who had never recovered from the shock of seeing her husband battered to death [by Israelis]. (117)

It is precisely because of the indistinctness of the Arab-Israeli conflict as delineated in this novel that the Spanish-Arab hero and British-Jewish heroine can finally put aside such differences and focus on their romance instead. Still, this is the only novel I have come across that even mentions the conflict. In this respect, the genre of the contemporary sheik romance is markedly different from all other forms of popular fiction dealing with the Middle East, in which the Arab-Israeli conflict often provides the basis of the plot.

British Mills & Boon novelists seemed to lose interest in the sheik romance after the mid-1980s. Few British sheik novels were produced from the late 1980s until after 2000. Unlike the earlier sheik romances of the 1970s and 1980s, the recent turn-of-the-century British sheik romance novels show little understanding of, or interest in, the geopolitical realities and cultural differences of the Middle East. Real geographical locations have given way to fairy-tale simulacra of the region, and the recent British sheik novel has lost any connection, however tenuous it may have been, with Britain's historical engagement with the Middle East. The twenty-first century novels of Penny Jordan, Susan Stephens, Sharon Kendrick, Sarah Morgan, Chantelle Shaw, and Kim Lawrence are all set in fictitious Middle Eastern or Central Asian Muslim states. They often feature the usual misunderstood and orphaned virgins battling against overbearing sheiks. There is little development since these novels' predecessors. Indeed, the attitudes of some authors seem to have regressed. Sarah Morgan's *In the Sheikh's Marriage Bed* (2005) is a particularly pernicious novel that represents all Muslims, apart from the sheik hero, as cowardly, incompetent, or stupid. The Muslim nanny tells the sheik's toddler nephew frightening bedtime tales about being mauled to death by tigers, then refuses to leave him with a night light, causing him to have terrifying nightmares. When the toddler ventures into an enclosed courtyard where the sheik's fractious stallion is tethered, none of the Muslim men will risk his life or limb to save the child. Only the British heroine, Emily, has the courage to dash into the courtyard, rescue the child, and magically calm the horse down. Later, when the sheik's household is camping in the desert, the child rides off into a sandstorm and not one of the Arab attendants is brave enough or cares enough to venture after him. Again, only Emily has the courage to risk her life to save the child.

Such novels seem remarkably retrograde for the twenty-first century, not only rehashing Orientalist discourses, but also emphasizing the English heroine's virtue—her right to be the heroine and to be rewarded with wealth and a wedding at the novel's end—at the expense of all racial and working-class others in the novel. In Kim Lawrence's *Desert Prince, Defiant Virgin* (2008), nobody in the kingdom, apart from the sheik hero, seems to care about development and the people's welfare. The sheik's father is a selfish tyrant who berates him for exchanging the country's "mineral rights for a water-treatment plant instead of new yacht" (8). His playboy brother is little better. Only the sheik is concerned with a "training programme for our people" and with "improving transport links and dragging the medical facilities . . . into the twenty-first century" (12). Such depictions reinforce the idea that the backwardness of the Orient is due to the greed, corruption, and mismanagement of its rulers. But there are still no calls for democratization or for the monarchy to be overthrown and a republic established in its place.

American sheik romances today are also concerned with modernization and development. In many cases, however, they show that these processes are already well underway because of the efforts of the Westernized sheik hero and his education at Eton, Oxford, Cambridge, Harvard, Princeton, Yale, or MIT. Sometimes development is apparently as simple as the throwaway line in Sandra Marton's *The Sheikh's Rebellious Mistress* (2008)—that the sheik "had formulated a plan to take the funds now pouring in from Senahdar's oil fields and use them to make better lives for his people" (150). In Marton's *The Sheikh's Wayward Wife* (2008), the story is set in Al Ankhara, a country that is "part of an alliance known as The Nations," which are all "rich beyond all measure," and where the modernity represented by "skyscrapers in their cities" coexists with a "traditional way of life." The crown-prince sheik in this novel has personally "seen to it that children were being educated, that hospitals and clinics were built, that the wonders of the Internet were reaching even the smallest village" (87).

In some novels, the dreams and aspirations of the heroine merely articulate another progressive aspect of ongoing social and economic modernization in the Middle East. For example, the heroine in Teresa Southwick's *To Catch A Sheik* (2003) comes to work in the Middle East in order to fund her ambition to open "preschools in [American] corporate environments so that women can work while having good care for their children." She has no support from American institutions to finance this goal, so she has to raise the money herself. She explains to the sheik that: "As long as women are part of the workforce, and I don't see that changing anytime soon, quality care for children will be an issue" (38). He recognizes this as a necessity for women's careers and as an opportunity for social and economic progress, so he urges her to open childcare centers in his country instead. Astonishingly, an important goal on the feminist agenda—affordable and accessible childcare for working mothers—is sooner achieved in a culture that is traditionally portrayed in popular culture as misogynistic, rather than in the United States. Perhaps this is an implicit critique of American political leaders' willingness to raise concerns about the position of women in the non-Western world while neglecting or even winding back the domestic women's rights agenda in the United States at the turn of the century (Eisenstein 158).

These twenty-first century novels present a notable contrast to the sheik novels of the 1990s, in which heroines had to argue their case for both equality and participation in the social and economic development of the country. In Canadian author Alexandra Sellers's *Bride of the Sheikh* (1997), for example, the heroine divorces her sheik husband because he treats her like a woman who could be of no other use to him than as decoration. Not until the sheik is able to work alongside her in rebuilding his war-torn country, and admit that he needs her help as a social policy developer and government administrator, is their marriage harmonious. The adjustment of these sheiks' attitudes toward women is of greater social import in the novels than romantic happiness between the couple. Often, an entire tribe's or nation's well-being in the modern world is at stake! Thus Emma Darcy's Australian heroine in *The Sheikh's Revenge* (1993) informs her sheik that: "I care that girls be given as much opportunity to develop their capabilities as boys . . . And what's more . . . you're going to need them to help run this country of yours, if you don't want to depend on the expertise of foreigners forever and a day" (151). This lesson has obviously been learned by sheik heroes in the twenty-first century, and yet it needs reinforcing time and again, not only in the mythical Middle

East but, more pertinently, in contemporary Western societies as well. Here, then, is yet another instance of feminist Orientalism at work, urging gender equality in the public as well as the private realm, characterizing inequality as an Oriental practice that should not exist in the West. The modern sheik novel is nothing if not a vehicle for liberal feminist concerns.

The Orientalist assumptions underpinning liberal feminism have not gone entirely unchallenged in American sheik romance novels. One of the most remarkable novels in this subgenre is Elizabeth Mayne's *The Sheik and the Vixen* (1996), which is set during the Iraqi invasion of Kuwait in August 1990. The novel is notable for its critique of American arrogance and neo-imperialism in its dealings with the Middle East. It features an engaging, entrepreneurial, and highly intelligent Texan heroine who comes from a family of macho men and feminist women. She is an aeronautical engineer, pilot, and computer programmer. *The Sheik and the Vixen* begins with the heroine, Haley Bennett, and her father and uncle flying her custom-built planes to Kuwait to deliver them to an impossibly wealthy Kuwaiti family—the hero's family, in fact. Unfortunately, they arrive on August 2, 1990: the day that Saddam Hussein's forces invade and bomb Kuwait City, and seize its airport and two air bases. Haley manages to escape but her father and uncle are trapped by Iraqi forces. While fighting off Iraqi MiGs in the air, she is aided and forced to land in Saudi Arabia by a skilful Kuwaiti pilot flying an F-15. The pilot is the hero, of course, whom she labels "Omar the Magnificent," with casual racism. Because war has just broken out and she is a foreigner in the country, she is detained. Her nationalistic chauvinism erupts at this point, and in an outcry similar to British heroines' in the 1970s and 1980s, she declares: "You're not going to imprison me! I'm an American citizen, you barbarian!" (19). Her protest and the reasoning behind it are meaningless, of course, given that American and other hostages were seized by Saddam's regime and used as human shields around potential military targets during the Gulf crisis. American citizenship was certainly no automatic guarantee of safety overseas, or immunity from the consequences of political crises, as Americans abroad have known only too well since the 1970s.

Through a constant switching of narrative perspective between the American heroine and the Kuwaiti hero, Mayne sets up an intriguing tension in this novel between the feminist heroine's undaunted courage and pragmatic "can-do" attitude in the difficult circumstances in which she finds herself, and the fact that her supreme self-confidence arises from an Americanness which comes across as ignorant, overbearing, and arrogant to others. She is determined to enter Iraqi-occupied Kuwait to find and rescue her father and uncle. Regardless of the fact that Saudi Arabia is at war, she hotwires a jeep and drives out into the desert, toward the airbase where her plane is kept. This scene gives Mayne a further opportunity to describe in considerable detail the aftermath of the Iraqi invasion. Haley encounters refugees fleeing Kuwait and trying to bribe Saudi guards at the border. The guards simply toss fistfuls of Kuwaiti dinars into the desert because the currency is now worthless. This small detail points to the amount of research that has gone into this novel, and its attempts at realism[5] stand out against the Disneyfied sheikdoms that have come to dominate the genre in the 1990s and twenty-first century. In this vein of realism, the heroine's classic "escape from the harem" is shown to be an ignorant and foolhardy move. She is caught by the sheik and reprimanded because the airbase is at the Saudi-Kuwaiti border where Iraqi Red Guards are amassed. "Can you comprehend that this base is now a closed fortress, sitting in the path of the biggest army my world has ever seen?" the sheik roars at her.

> I'm yelling at you because your stupidity has landed you where no woman belongs! It isn't safe! I don't need the worry of keeping watch over some reckless, blundering American woman. I've got the lives and welfare of thousands of my people to look out after, and you keep preventing me from doing the job I must do . . . .
>
> Americans never understand anything. You would have died in the desert. I diverted ten patrols from their necessary duties to search the desert for you. Can you understand that? (129)

In contemporary sheik romance novels, the white Western heroine usually steals the scene and saves the day through her valiant actions, particularly where Muslim women and children are concerned. *The Sheik and the Vixen* incorporates this motif, then turns it upside down, revealing it to be an Orientalist and neo-imperialist topos. Haley eventually gets to Kuwait by marrying the sheik. In the Saudi embassy in Kuwait, she overhears panicked Australians and Canadians clamoring to leave because all Kuwaiti borders will be closed in twenty-four hours. She immediately jumps to the conclusion that everyone in the Saudi embassy will be stuck there unless she steps in and does something. She arranges for Kuwaiti women and children to be delivered to her family's hangar at the airport, where she then flies them to safety in Saudi Arabia before returning to

Kuwait to rescue her husband. When he doesn't seem in the least grateful for what she has done, she says defensively:

> I haven't caused any trouble . . . I found a way to get people out of this country, which is something nobody else in this godforsaken place has managed to do in days. I cannot believe that people just stand around, wringing their hands, doing absolutely nothing, letting those goons with rifles take everything they have. (179)

Far from appreciating or applauding her initiative, the sheik replies sarcastically:

> Oh, I understand now. You got a rush, didn't you? A great big ego boost to your head all because you flew a forty-year-old plane jammed with a hundred frightened children out of Kuwait. How fortunate we *third worlders* are to have Americans to our rescue! . . .
>   I want you to know . . . that over ten thousand people, and more than half of those, very young children, have passed through this embassy in the past five days. All have been transported safely out of Kuwait and into Saudi Arabia without risking a single life. . . . You listened to gossip and came to your own conclusions. (180)

In doing so, in being a gung ho American hero, she has unnecessarily put all lives in the embassy in danger.

The Sheik and the Vixen is by no means a complete critique of the dominant discourse of Orientalism in popular culture today. That is certainly not the purpose of any sheik romance novel, not even this one. Muslim women are still largely absent from the Middle East in this novel and when they appear, they continue to be represented as homogeneous, silent, and submissive masses who need direction from the strong-willed Western heroine. Yet apart from Sara Wood's British novel *The Perfumes of Arabia*, I have not come across another sheik romance novel that shows such an acute awareness of the problems of liberal feminist assumptions in the production of Orientalist romantic discourse, or of the unthinking attitudes of superiority and the displays of condescension shown by the women of the West toward the East.

Mayne's novel was most unusual in utilizing a "real" historical setting; the requirements of the romance genre and the complexity of ongoing problems in the Middle East do not easily lend themselves to realist romantic fiction. However, the growing popularity of Harlequin's Intrigue

series—first established in 1984—seems to have created new possibilities
for sheik romance novels to engage with contemporary problems con-
fronting the United States and the Middle East. According to Harlequin's
own description on its website, the Intrigue novels are

> taut, edge-of-the-seat contemporary romantic suspense tales of in-
> trigue and desire. Kidnappings, stalkings, women in jeopardy coupled
> with bestselling romantic themes are examples of story lines we love
> most. Whether a murder mystery, psychological suspense or thriller, the
> love story must be inextricably bound to the mystery where all loose
> ends are tied up neatly . . . and shared dangers lead right to shared pas-
> sions. As long as they're in jeopardy and falling in love, our heroes and
> heroines may traverse a landscape as wide as the world itself.

American writer Dana Marton has been most innovative in pushing
the boundaries of the sheik romance novel, dealing with issues such as
the war in Iraq, terrorism after the September 11, 2001, al-Qaeda attacks,
and even the problems of being Arab-American in her Harlequin Intrigue
novels. Her third novel for Harlequin Intrigue, *The Sheik's Safety* (2005),
is striking for its reversal of gender roles and for its setting, which parallels the American-initiated Iraq War that began on March 19, 2003. The
casus belli for the Iraq War was ostensibly the suspicion that Saddam Hussein was harboring "weapons of mass destruction" (WMD)—agents of
chemical, biological, and nuclear warfare—as well as terrorists with connections to al-Qaeda, none of which could be proven in the end. In *The
Sheik's Safety*, Morton skirts around such a contentious event in American
society by setting up her story's own Middle Eastern war.

The half Native American heroine, Dara Alexander, is part of the
United States Air Force but is involved in covert operations for the fictional Special Designation Defense Unit. She and a few other American soldiers are parachuted into a Middle Eastern country to intercept a
weapons smuggler (shades of the WMD issue here), but a surface-to-air
missile attack kills all except for her. On the ground, she is rescued by a
sheik whose cousin is the tyrannical mad monarch of the country. When
she manages to contact her commanding officer, she is reassigned as the
sheik's bodyguard. The sheik is not surprised to see a female soldier because he knows that the Israelis have female soldiers in their army, as does
the United States. Indeed, until the court martial of Lynndie England in
2005 for the torture and abuse of prisoners at Abu Ghraib prison, during
the American occupation of Iraq, the highlighting of female soldiers in

the media was a prominent part of the Iraq War, with American female soldiers in uniform contrasted against the usual images of veiled (read: oppressed) Muslim women (Norton 28).

Many single-title American romance novels now combine the romance genre with the thriller or adventure novel to produce resourceful heroines in every sphere of life, including war and covert operations outside the United States. American writers such as Cindy Gerard, Tara Janzen, Suzanne Brockman, and JoAnn Ross, among others, produce cross-genre novels combining romantic plots with war in Afghanistan, SEAL operations, CIA-inspired missions against drug lords in South America, and so on. Within contemporary *category* romance novels, however, few authors have challenged traditional gender roles for their heroines or pushed the liberal feminist argument for equal opportunity in every sphere of life, including the military, as much as Marton does in *The Sheik's Safety*. Dara comes from a military family and "she'd grown up around military men, talking trash, wearing bravado as a uniform, everybody vying for the position of the biggest badass on the team" (86). Her father always insisted that she had to be "toughened up to be fit for the military," though "he hadn't meant it disparagingly. He merely saw the difference between the sexes as a weakness" (79). Her masculine upbringing, which lacked tenderness, echoes the upbringing of heroines in earlier sheik romance fiction, but unlike the heroines in the other novels, Dara is not abducted or imprisoned in a harem. On the contrary, when the sheik is arrested by his cousin and imprisoned in the castle, Dara breaks in and rescues him, casually noting that the "trouble with this country was that nobody believed a woman could be dangerous" (113). In one respect, we have come full circle as far as the history of interracial or cross-cultural relations is concerned, for if we go back far enough in Western literature, this is a variation of medieval verse romances, such as *The Sowdone of Babylone* and *Bevis of Hampton*, in which the crusading hero is imprisoned by his enemies, then rescued by the heroine. Except, of course, that the medieval hero is Christian and European, and the resourceful female who rescues him—the dangerous woman—is Muslim.

Marton, who admits she does a lot of research before writing her novels (*Coffee Time Romance* interview, 2009), presents in *The Sheik's Safety* a thoughtful and interesting perspective on U.S. involvement in Middle Eastern wars. Her soldier-heroine tells the sheik that the United States is intervening because "My government wishes to see your country stable. . . . Instability in this region is not a good thing." The sheik replies cynically, "You are here to ensure I live, so I can take the throne and will be grateful enough to your government to sign an economic treaty"—a point the heroine acknowledges as true. "She wasn't so naïve as to think money didn't come into play when it came to politics" (63). Is it too fanciful to read into this an indirect allusion to accusations that the United States had invaded Iraq for access to its oil reserves, which were among the largest in that region, after Saudi Arabia's and Iran's?

The Iraq War had begun surprisingly well for Americans, with Baghdad falling on April 9, within twenty days of the invasion, and Saddam Hussein himself captured on December 13, 2003. By spring 2004, however, Iraqi resistance had been joined by other militias and sectarian groups, and the conflict escalated into full battles in Najaf, Fallujah, and Mosul, alongside other skirmishes and insurgencies. In early 2005, insurgent attacks against U.S. and other coalition occupation forces, and suicide and roadside bombings, increased. Marton's novel was published in the midst of the deterioration of the Iraq War in 2005. In *The Sheik's Safety*, the American soldier-heroine asks the sheik why he does not want to ask for American assistance in overthrowing his tyrannical cousin, who is bent on attacking the American Air Force base in Saudi Arabia. Here is the sheik's explanation, which implicitly refers to the U.S. government's stated intentions of giving freedom and democracy to the Iraqi people through "Operation Iraqi Freedom":

> Freedom must be paid for—sometimes in blood—but nobody can pay the price for us. The people must know that they are strong enough to control their own destinies. Some things cannot be given on a platter as a gift. They must be earned. (175)

Marton tries to present the Arabic point of view as far as the U.S. invasion and stationing of American troops in Middle Eastern countries is concerned:

> The Cold War has been over for more than a decade. Russia is a friend to the US, right? . . . And after your dark days of terror when your country was in great pain and upheaval, would you have wanted friendly Russian forces to be deployed in your cities to help keep your country safe? How would American citizens have reacted to seeing armed Russian soldiers on their streets? . . .
>
> What would any foreign country want for their [American] help? . . . Because know this, nothing is free in this world, especially not

when given to a country rich in oil. Would our [American] rescuers
want more influence in regulating the industry my nation depends on?
Would they want to dictate policies and politics? (175–176)

This is a striking passage for a romance novel: the acknowledgement of
the mistakes in American foreign policy in the Middle East, the allusion
to the ongoing American occupation of Iraq—that American troops did
not leave after the overthrow of Saddam Hussein's regime, and how Iraqis
might feel about this—as well as the blunt reference to American oil interests in the region.

Americans ride to the rescue at the end when they are ambushed, and
Dara leaves the U.S. military to marry the sheik and become the queen
of the country of Beharrain. In obvious ways, her freedom to transgress
gender roles and her freedom in her personal life have been curtailed. She
must content herself with the usual civilizing and modernizing projects
"aimed at women and children," which "even the religious fanatics tended
to overlook . . . as long as she didn't involve herself in things they considered strictly men's territory" (248). However, her pet project, through
which she defines her role as queen, can be read as yet another subtle
critique of the American-led invasion of Iraq. She spends much of her
time finding and preserving Beharrain's cultural heritage, and opens a
national museum to save "a large part of Bedu history" (248). It is difficult
to read this without being reminded of how the National Museum of Iraq
was looted and vandalized during the Iraq War in April 10–12, 2003, despite the American Council for Cultural Policy's and other international
archaeologists' urgent petitions to the Pentagon and the Bush and Blair
governments as early as January 2003 to protect the museum from just
such an occurrence during the war. Although the looting was not as extensive as initially reported, and many items were later returned or recovered, at the time, the media criticized the U.S. military for securing oil
wells, dams, and the oil ministry without making an attempt to guard the
National Museum in the days immediately after the fall of Baghdad (Jehl
and Becker, *New York Times*, 2003; Poole, 2008). If the sheik novels are in
part a wish-fulfillment fantasy of how Americans would like Middle Eastern leaders to behave, Mayne's and Marton's novels are also wishful fantasies of how they would have liked Americans to have behaved, in turn.

Marton turned her attention to terrorism in the Middle East in her
novel *Sheik Protector* (2008). The American heroine travels to a fictional
country to inform her Arab lover that she is pregnant, only to find that he

has been murdered by terrorists. His twin brother is attempting to hunt down the Islamist terrorists and bring them to justice. Together with the sheik, she becomes a target of this group. Escape to the United States is not an option; when she mentions she might be safer there, the sheik asks: "Will you? Because religious extremists never went to the US to do their dirty business there?" She then realizes that "if these maniacs had set their sights on her, there'd be no hiding from them" (121). Where *The Sheik's Safety* had attempted to think through U.S. foreign policy in the Middle East and the reaction of people in Islamic countries to the prospect of American occupation, *Sheikh Protector* does not go far in analyzing the motivations of Islamist extremists. Even Art Malik's portrayal of Aziz, the Crimson Jihad Muslim terrorist in Arnold Schwarzenegger's *True Lies* (1994), links his terrorist attacks on the United States to American foreign policy in the Middle East and the destruction of civilian lives, dismissed by Americans as "collateral damage." *Sheikh Protector*, however, makes no attempt to connect the goals of Islamist terrorism (see Payne 30–31) with American policies or military actions in the Middle East. Instead, in the following portrait, the Islamist terrorist is represented as akin to deluded psychopathic serial killers in American crime fiction:

> All his life he wanted to be a holy man. He had even changed his name to Mustafa, which meant *chosen*. And he indeed knew that Allah had chosen him when the only God trusted this most important task to him. Old evil had returned into this world—old evil that offended the faith of his people and threatened their souls. He had sworn to destroy it and all who had come in contact with it, all who had been contaminated. And the One God had been gracious and had given him followers, a tight sect of righteousness and light. They were all happy to die for the cause. (48)

The "old evil" that he wants to rid the world of refers to pre-Islamic idols, "statues of ancient gods" that used to be in the Ka'ba, and that Muhammad was supposed to have destroyed when his armies conquered Mecca (112).

According to this novel, then, terrorism arises from ignorance, superstition, and extreme beliefs directed toward purifying other Muslims. It has nothing to do with American foreign policy in the Middle East—particularly the covert arming of its enemies (Iraq, Iran, the Taliban) during the Cold War struggle against the Soviet Union—even though certain American scholars had been warning for years that these policies would eventually result in "blowback" for the Unites States. As Douglas Kellner wrote soon after the 9/11 attacks:

> The events of the September 11 terrorist attacks should be seen in the context of several US administrations and CIA support for the per- petrators of the monstrous assaults on the United States from the late 1970s, through the Reagan-Bush years, to the present. This is not to simply blame US policy in Afghanistan for the terrorist assault of Sep- tember 11, but it is to provide some of the context in which the events can be interpreted. There are, of course, other flaws of US foreign policy during the past decades that have helped generate enemies of the United States in the Middle East and elsewhere, such as excessive US support for Israel and inadequate support for the Palestinians, US support of authoritarian regimes, and innumerable misdeeds of the US empire during the past decades that have been documented by [Noam] Chomsky, [Edward S.] Herman, [Chalmers] Johnson, and other critics of US foreign policy. (2003: 16)

Little of this entered the political or popular discourse on terrorism or the war in Iraq and Afghanistan. Instead, Islamist terrorism was con- tinually portrayed as a Manichean struggle between good and evil, and the American-led war on Iraq was explained by President George W. Bush as a quest to "eradicate evil from the world," to "smoke out and pursue . . . evil doers, those barbaric people" (Kellner 2003: 11). Islamist terror- ists attacked the United States because, according to Bush's address to the joint session of Congress on September 20, 2001, "They hate our free- doms—our freedom of religion, our freedom of speech, our freedom to vote and assemble and disagree with each other." This explanation circu- lated widely in American popular culture in the years following the war. In Suzanne Brockman's single-title novel *Into the Night* (2002)—the fifth in her "Troubleshooters" series of Navy SEAL romance novels, which fea- ture the war in Afghanistan and terrorism in the United States as part of their plots—the SEAL hero fights in Afghanistan to preserve America's freedom (64).

> Every one of us . . . every single man, is sitting here waiting for a chance to go back into action and do what we do best. Which is to protect our country from people who take their my-way-or-the-highway views of religion and politics to such an extreme that they'll intentionally tar- get and kill innocent civilians. We're dying to get back out there and to

protect you and all your family and friends and coworkers . . . We want
to protect you from the people who proclaim that all Americans, including the tiniest newborn infants, are their sworn enemies and de-
serving of death. (51)

Their opponents in Afghanistan are simply terrorists who "had pledged to
die defending Osama bin Laden"; who "trained their boys to hate and kill,
and enslaved their girls by forbidding their education"; and who "supported a killer who fought his war against unarmed men, against women
and children" (7). I am not arguing that there is no truth in some of these
assertions; I am simply pointing out that in American popular culture,
and particularly in romance novels that deal with this topic, this narrative
has become the *whole* truth, ignoring the other complex explanations for
terrorism against the United States relating to American foreign policy in
the Middle East, including the reasons given by Osama bin Laden himself (Payne 2008).

Suzanne Brockman's *Into the Night* (2002), Linda Winstead Jones's
Secret-Agent Sheik (2002), and Dana Marton's *Desert Ice Daddy* (2009) are
some of the very few contemporary sheik novels to consider Islamist terrorism within the United States after September 11. Brockman's novel was
written in the immediate aftermath of the 9/11 attacks, when the American
war in Afghanistan was justified as a means of finding Osama bin Laden.[6]
The novel features an Islamist terrorist plotline revolving around a con-
spiracy to assassinate the American president, but it simultaneously seeks
to disarm hostility and suspicion toward Muslim and Arab Americans.
One of its secondary romance plots involves a redneck, racist, abused,
alcoholic working-class woman, Mary Lou, who falls in love with a gentle,
Saudi-born Muslim American. Ihbraham [*sic*] Rahman had "embraced
the American Dream," owned a business as a gardener and handyman,
and was "making it pay off" (322). Ihbraham has assimilated into American culture, but he still faces considerable discrimination because of his
color and religion. As Mary Lou realizes:

When most people looked at him, unless they looked closely, they
wouldn't see his eyes or his smile. And if those people were anything
like her, they'd cross to the other side of the street when they saw him
coming. They'd assume, from the color of his skin and from the way he
looked, that he was dangerous.

She remembered all those nervous phone calls she'd made to her sister when he'd first started caring for the Robinson's yard, and she was ashamed.

"I'm sorry," she told him, although she was certain it didn't make up for all the shit he'd no doubt been through since 9/11.

"It's okay," he said. "I have T-shirts that I sometimes wear when I go out. They say 'I am an American, too.' It's helped a little." (125)

Brockman's novels are well-known for their progressive, feminist, and antiracist politics, in addition to their jingoistic patriotism. Her Navy SEAL novels feature multiracial romantic unions. It is significant that, so soon after 9/11, this romance author tried to present a sympathetic portrait of a Muslim Arab American whose life is successfully integrated into American society, but who has suffered because of Americans' suspicions of all Arab and Muslim Americans. Nevertheless, *Into the Night* ends with Muslim terrorists attempting to gun down the president, thus confirming the dominant narrative in popular culture. It reiterated that Muslim terrorists are the enemies of the United States, which is why the American military, like the SEAL hero, is justified in waging war on Afghanistan.

Also published just after 9/11, Linda Winstead Jones's Harlequin Intrigue novel *Secret-Agent Sheik* (2002) is interesting in that it features an Arab-American CEO of an oil company as the heroine. Her father turns out to be the terrorist leader of the "Brothers of Darkness," whom the "secret-agent sheik" hero from a Middle Eastern country is tracking down. Her father has been using his oil refinery as a front to raise money for smuggling arms to fund terrorist activity in the Middle East, and to house terrorists in Texas. A complete degenerate, he murdered the heroine's mother and tries to kill the heroine when she gets in the way of his evil plans. Once again, the motivation for terrorism is located purely in arcane power struggles in the Middle East; there is no direct causal relationship between U.S. foreign policy or actions abroad and Islamist terror. Marton's *Desert Ice Daddy* posits an even more ignoble cause for the act of terrorism and the abduction of the heroine's son: a criminal desire for money and diamonds.

What is unusual about *Desert Ice Daddy*, however, is that it does not feature a Middle Eastern sheik. The hero is the grandson of a sheik, but he identifies primarily as an Arab-American businessman. The novel opens with the scene of a massacre at a Texas ranch, and the suspicion that the hero, Akeem Abdul, is a terrorist since one of his business associates might have been involved. Unusually for this subgenre, except for the heroine's brother, most of the white American men in this story are redneck rubes, while the heroine's ex-husband is an abusive drunk whose sulky incompetence contrasts markedly with the Arab American's hard work, success in business, chivalry toward the heroine, and competent determination to protect her and get her son back. Nevertheless, the Arab American is the one regarded suspiciously by other characters as a possible terrorist. "Being Arab-American, he was pretty much used to that of late, even if he had been born and raised in Texas" (15). It is not the first time he has been discriminated against simply because he is Arab-American. We learn that just after 9/11, his girlfriend broke up with him because, she told him, "I just don't feel safe around you" (117). Little else is said in this novel about the impact of September 11 and the Iraq War on the lives of Arab Americans, but despite the popularity of sheik romance novels in the twenty-first century, few writers apart from Brockman, Winstead Jones, and Marton have yet defended or incorporated Arab Americans into their plots. Those who do so deserve recognition.

While there are certainly distinct continuities in Orientalist leitmotifs in the contemporary mass-market sheik romance novel, a survey of British, Australian, and American novels from the 1970s to the present day reveals significant differences in themes, and fluctuating levels of engagement, with the Middle East or Western foreign policies. The independent Western heroine has remained a constant throughout this time, mainly just upgrading her professional status as the years have progressed, her modernity and confidence contrasting with the Muslim woman's timidity, submissiveness, and even erasure. The sheik hero has undergone a transformation from a Heathcliff-like villainous hero to the playful, boyish Americanized sheik of recent years, and he has sometimes lost some of his Orientalist qualities along the way, becoming indistinguishable from other ethnic heroes as he is assimilated into American culture. While the vast majority of sheik novels are set in an imaginary Orientalist fantasyland disconnected from the geopolitical realities and cultural complexities of the Middle East, some authors have attempted to grapple with issues relevant to the region and to their countries' foreign policies as well. In the end, however, it is not the purpose of the romance novel to explore foreign policy or American Orientalist attitudes, but to provide a good love story. This is what readers overwhelmingly look for, but the issues raised and responses elicited by sheik novels can sometimes be most surprising.

NINE

Reader Responses to the Modern Orientalist Romance Novel

Quite honestly, when I read these stories I don't think about 911, nor religion, nor where they take place, I think about falling in love, about romance and hopefully all of this craziness going on in the world will someday resolve itself and there will be peace! I pray this happens for all because in my heart it's all about LOVE.

MARILYN SHOEMAKER, BLOG

At the start of this book, I raised the question of why so many readers in the early twentieth century found it romantic to read about a white woman being raped into love and submission by an apparently Arab sheik. In this chapter, I consider why, in the wake of the Islamist terrorist attacks in the United States on September 11, 2001, and in Britain on July 7, 2005, readers still want to escape into fantasies of white women falling in love with Arab men. What is the appeal of the sheik romance novel for contemporary readers? What are they looking for, and how do they respond to different novelists and to the issues raised in this subgenre? Amazon.com reader reviews, blogs, and online discussions about the sheik romance novel, carried out on specialist romance websites, provide us with some answers to these questions.

There are several cached websites that contain discussions about the appeal (or lack thereof) of sheik romance novels. One of the most popular romance readers' websites, "Smart Bitches Trashy Books," held a forum on the sheik(h) romance in May 2007, and asked readers to explain the fascination of these novels (URL provided in bibliography). The forum is not particularly helpful in revealing the attractions of the subgenre, for most participants—themselves avid romance readers—profess in their comments an intense, visceral dislike of the sheik novel. The most frequently voiced objection is made on the grounds of writers' and readers' ignorance about the Middle East, which participants argue leads to a "butchering of the culture" and the perpetuation of Orientalist stereotypes. Both Muslim and non-Muslim readers who participated in the forum raised these concerns. They, by contrast, "know too much" or are too "[well-]informed on current events and ME culture" to buy into the sheik fantasy. A range of statistics and facts, and a reference to a Human Rights Watch article on women in Baghdad, are offered up as evidence supporting their views. Men from such a culture could not possibly be "romantic."

Interestingly, non-Middle Eastern contributors' objections to other readers' and writers' willful ignorance and misunderstanding of "the culture" also tend to perpetuate Orientalist ideas of the oppressed Muslim woman. The Malaysian-born moderator of this discussion thread, Candy Tan, was quick to draw attention to the stereotypes and generalizations perpetuated by those who claimed to "know too much" about a huge region encompassing disparate peoples, languages, and cultures. Tan also pointed to parallels between the oppression of women in Middle Eastern countries, and in the United States, where domestic abuse and illegal trafficking of women and children still occur. The "Smart Bitches" discussion of Orientalism, American assumptions, Middle Eastern culture, and the problems of the sheik subgenre is one of the most insightful that I have read, and it provides a very clear picture of the different ways readers consume the romance genre, as well as showcasing their own critical voices. It does not, however, offer much clarity on why certain readers enjoy the sheik romance so much, because the few fans of the subgenre who participated in the forum merely stated their dislike for it without explaining its appeal.

Two subsequent online discussions led by sheik romance writers were more promising in this regard. In November 2008, sheik romance novelist Annie West convened a discussion on the "Down Under Desirabelles" website on "The Lure of the Sheik Hero," and a year later, in December 2009, fellow sheik novelist Liz Fielding ran a forum for the Harlequin website on "The Appeal of the Sheikh" (URLs provided in bibliography). These discussions were more illuminating, for the participants were mainly fans of the genre, although some confessed to reading sheik romances out of author loyalty: West or Fielding were "must buy" romance authors for them, whatever the type of romance story written. The most common reason participants gave for liking the sheik romance was that the subgenre usually features an alpha male hero who is, in Fielding's words: "a man totally in control of his world, at one with his environment. Commanding, dynamic . . . and yes, passionate. He is like a Latin or Greek lover squared" (here again we have the continuum of sexy, patriarchal "brown heroes"). According to these discussants, romances that feature such a hero actually enhance the white heroine's power, which is exercised primarily through the hero falling in love with her, but in other ways as well. Annie West explained: "He rules his world with absolute power. He has utter dominion over the woman he's lured/seduced/kidnapped/rescued/found. We sit on the edge of our seats wondering whether he'll use that power for his own ends, or will he refrain, and meet her on her own terms? Will he relinquish that power for love?" Of course he will! Because the sheik romance (perhaps more so than most other romantic subgenres) is about the white heroine's empowerment in any variety of ways: sexually, emotionally, financially, and socially. These heroines "stand toe-to-toe" with the heroes and "always bring them to their knees." In falling in love with the Western heroine, the powerful sheik is humbled, reformed, and, most pleasurably for readers, he ends up groveling to the heroine.

Readers also enjoyed the exoticism and Orientalism of the stories. One contributor, Lois, explained this appeal for her:

> Well, I'm still pretty new to sheikhs myself, but what I think makes them popular is they are exotic and just down right different. In the end, the Greeks and Venitians [*sic*] and Londoners and Italians, they are exotic, but still 100% Western, so not a whole lot different. But the sheikhs, even if the written ones are more westernized and not what we might think of in the real world, it's still different enough for us to be fascinated and want to read them. And there is an air of royalty in it without being your usual Prince/esses and the like . . . so, in really short, it's the fact that they are different. ("Appeal of the Sheikh" website)

According to Annie West, the tradition of Orientalism in Western culture was directly responsible for the popularity of the subgenre:

> For centuries sheikhs, sultans and pashas have intrigued audiences, perhaps in part because of Western perceptions of the sexual power play associated with harems. Maybe too because they just seem so exotic! Think of Mozart's 'Escape from the Seraglio', Edith Maude Hull's 'The Sheik', Peter O'Toole and Omar Sharif in 'Lawrence of Arabia'.

She also mentioned the settings:

> Desert strongholds, romantic oases, sprawling palaces with hidden
> treasures, or perhaps a penthouse apartment in the heart of an exciting
> metropolis. . . . For background colour there are silk carpets, souks,
> glittering jewels and an exotic 'Arabian Nights' aura. Other sheik fans
> agreed that they loved "the palaces, the passion and glamour."

Many of these discussants were familiar with Orientalism in popular culture, having watched films with Oriental themes or read E. M. Hull's *The Sheik*, Johanna Lindsey's *Captive Bride*, Patricia Ott's *Bitter Passion, Sweet Love*, or "any Barbara Cartlands with Arabian heroes."[1] This cognizance of older forms of Orientalist romance made contemporary sheik novels attractive because the participants were used to the form. In the words of Ann Wesley Hardin on the "Smart Bitches" site: "the sheik is still around simply because we love tradition."

Fans of the sheik novel who posted on these sites were careful to emphasize that they realized the stories were only fantasies. Liz Fielding wrote: "I'm never, as I'm writing, snagged by the fear that I've overstepped the boundaries of reality. This is pure fantasy and I can let my imagination take wings." Another reader agreed with Fielding: "In real life do I want a sheikh? Nope, but the fantasy stories make wonderful modern fairy tales. So I'm a convert!" These fantasies were not just about exotic, alpha males and strong women. They were also "fun" fantasies about royalty, wealth, and consumption. Fielding loved the fact that she could incorporate "anything" into her stories, including "private jets, helicopters, fabulous cars, [and] palaces." Two other readers on "The Lure of the Sheikh Hero" site agreed: "The clothes, setting and the passion all combine to make a spectacular story," wrote Dina, while Gina confessed that "I especially like to read it when they have shopping included in them. Oh the description alone is worth the money paid for the book." Here is a clear indication of the continuing strength of American "Arabian Nights" Orientalism as a mode of consumption, as discussed in Chapter 4. However, these "fantasies" are not unanchored in what writers and readers believe to be the reality of the Middle East. A sheik hero conjures up such dreams of limitless wealth and consumption because Western readers are aware of the personal wealth and power of the elites from countries in the Middle East. Furthermore, the erotic "Arabian Nights" images on the romance covers are juxtaposed with photographs of real desert scenes on the websites, indicating that the boundaries between fantasy and reality are not always clear. The Orientalist misrepresentations that the "Smart Bitches" discussants complained about therefore cannot be waved away with the explanation that they are "merely fantasies" with no connections to, or ramifications for, American understandings of the Middle East, even though this is not recognized by the contributors to the above three online discussion sites. For everyone who posted on these sites, the "problem" was the inaccurate portrayals of Muslims, Arabs, and the Middle East, and whether these depictions suited the romance novel and the modern American heroine. Despite the ongoing wars in Afghanistan and Iraq, and the still-present threat of Islamist terrorism, no one—including the Muslim or Arab discussants—considered the ramifications of American foreign policy in the Middle East and whether this issue might constitute "problems" for romance novels focusing on Arab and/or Muslim romantic relations with Americans.

It is clear, though, that sheik novels are not all alike and interchangeable for fans of the subgenre. Readers profess clear preferences for certain novels and allegiance to particular authors. The novels may appear "formulaic" to outsiders, but seasoned romance readers are aware of the specific differences among them. Unlike with the Orientalist historical romance novels discussed in Chapter 5, it is much harder to gauge the popularity of contemporary sheik romance novels, especially individual novels, from reading Amazon.com reviews. There are so many novels in this subgenre that individually, they do not rate many reviews: few novels have garnered more than a dozen reviews; many average from four to six reviews (as of November 2009). Comments tend to be brief, and usually describe the plot and mention whether or not the reader liked the characters, plot, and sexual tension. One of the more unusual reviews came from Steven Augart of Lexington, Massachusetts, who loved Barbara McMahon's *Sheik Daddy* (1996), calling it "a fun heartwarming read." This was the first romance novel he had ever read, and he notes disarmingly that

> It was fun, with a real plot. A page-turner; I stayed up an extra hour
> late just so that I could come closer to finishing it. The ending was
> touching as well. If you're a man looking for a good read, I highly
> recommend it.

That a man should enjoy these romance novels should come as no surprise. As mentioned previously, research conducted by the Romance Writers of America has shown that just under ten percent of romance readers in North America are male.

The novels of Canadian Alexandra Sellers and American Susan Mallery have perhaps generated the most positive, as well as typical, comments for this subgenre. Readers enjoy these authors' novels for their complex stories and emotional resonance, although they come in for their fair share of criticisms as well. For example, readers' comments on Susan Mallery's *The Sheikh's Secret Bride* (2000) range from the gushing enthusiasm of "I adore sheik books and this is one of the best," to complaints about being "talked down to" because "it's like the author got bored with the story line before she finished her contract . . . Mallery's sex scenes are so contrived and overblown that I could not stand to read them." The novel even prompted one reader to ask the searching question: "How many sheiks does the Middle East have?" Generally speaking, however, Mallery is acknowledged to be a master of this genre. One reader's comment about Mallery's *The Sheikh's Kidnapped Bride* (2004) sums up the average response of readers to her work: "I loved the heroine, I loved the desert, I especially loved the clueless hero who has to learn to love! Susan Mallery understands the appeal of the sheik romance and creates a special world where men are men and women are witty and everyone gets to win." This is the enduring attraction of the romance novel, of course. American writer Lucy Monroe has commented that the role of the romance novel—as writers and readers understand it, at any rate—is not to campaign on issues such as the oppression of women, or American foreign policy in the Middle East; nor is it to focus on disturbing stories in the news, but to "feed hope in the world—the hope that those we see as our enemy can also be our friend" (Reardon 2006).

Thus mainstream contemporary romance novels do not seem to provoke readers to think much about the Middle East, Muslims, or Arab Americans. It is the Orientalist details that readers enjoy in these novels. The fact that authors are obligingly serving them up to the public is nothing new. Modern Orientalism sells. One Amazon.com reviewer comments appreciatively on Alexandra Sellers's *Solitary Sheikh* (1999), saying the author "has the knack of capturing the mystery of the Middle East in a way that is [sic] sweeps you right up in it. Her characters are so recogniseable [sic] that you relate to them completely. . . . Her eye for detail brings these foreign worlds alive." Evelyn Bach argues that the Orientalist motifs in sheik novels that conjure the "mystery" of the Middle East render these works intriguingly foreign but reassuringly familiar. The leitmotifs in nineteenth-century paintings that confer upon them their "Orientalist" qualities consist of exotic costume, furniture, food, the intricate latticework of windows and doorways, or the interiors of harems and bagnios.

These are still to be found in sheik romance novels, accompanied by the "bath scene, the abduction, the sandstorm, riding through the desert on magnificent horses and the heroine's futile attempt to escape." These topoi "act as small oases of familiarity, reassuring the reader that, for all its wild, exciting barbarism, this is, after all, recognisable terrain" (15). Stripped of these motifs, the stories and characters are interchangeable with contemporary romance novels featuring almost any other type of "ethnic" hero.

It is largely left to the contemporary romantic suspense novels to engage with Middle Eastern politics, but the Amazon.com reviewers seem ambivalent about this. Of the various lines of contemporary sheik romance novels, the Harlequin Intrigue novels appear to produce extreme reactions: readers either love them or hate them. Dana Marton's stories have so far generated only positive comments on the site. The few readers who have commented on her work find the plots riveting, and one reader states: "I love that Ms. Marton writes her heroines to be equally as brave and strong as her heroes." Marton's comparatively extensive research is generally acknowledged by her readers, with one of Amazon's regular reviewers, Judith Conklin, from Texas, writing that in Marton's novels "you get a true 'feel' for the Arab way of life, their value system and of the tensions there that rule their lives." But other sheik romantic suspense novels have not fared as well, especially when they have engaged with current events such as the Gulf War or terrorism after 9/11.

Elizabeth Mayne's *The Sheik and the Vixen* drew a very critical comment from a reader who pans the book because "modern romance should follow some semblence [*sic*] of reality and I cannot buy an independent Texas girl genius falling for any guy who believes that women are subservient to men. He may be a Kuwaiti prince, but I do not see it happening." However, another reader responds that: "This is one of the more realistic romances based in the Middle East I have ever read. Having traveled there myself, although I am an American, I can tell you that the differences in male/female relations are very real. . . . The backdrop of the 1991 Gulf War is also very realistic." Realism seems to be the problem, though, especially with Linda Winstead Jones's *Secret-Agent Sheik*. Again, readers' responses are polarized. While some proclaim this novel "one of the best" in the sheik subgenre (one reader even goes so far as to write: "Believe it or not it made me want to be a chemical engineer, just like the main characters!"), other readers did not find the story romantic at all. A-M complains that "the things in [the heroine's] life that happened, were just too horrible for me to really enjoy this book. It is so close to not being a romance novel, I would have enjoyed it more if it wasn't something I had certain expectations for, which it fell short of."

Reader expectations of what an ideal romance novel ought to be certainly play a large part in determining responses on the Amazon.com site. Nora Roberts's contemporary Orientalist romance novel/jewel-thief thriller, *Sweet Revenge* (1989), has garnered the most reader reviews on the site—seventy-nine, as of July 2011. Greater attention has been paid to this novel because it is a single-title mass-market romance and is therefore more substantial in length; the plot and characters are more memorable; and Roberts is one of the most popular romance writers of the late twentieth- and twenty-first centuries. Many reviewers discuss whether or not they like the somewhat clichéd fairy tale/fantasy of international jewel thieves wanted by Interpol who fall in love and plan a daring heist, and the rape and physical abuse of the heroine's mother at the hands of the Muslim king of Jaquir. From the first Amazon.com reader review of this novel in 1997, until 2006, reviewers' comments tend to focus on the romantic plot and the characters. Complaints were directed against the Arab king's rape of his Hollywood actress wife, and a Hollywood agent's attempted rape of the heroine when she was a teenager. Little thought was given to the portrayal of Muslims and Islamic culture. If they were mentioned at all, reviewers tended to assume that Roberts's representation of Muslim culture is accurate; certainly, it draws from, and is aligned with, prevailing stereotypes of Muslims and Arabs in American popular culture. Thus one reviewer complains that although she was disappointed by the story, "Roberts shows what it is really like living inside a harem. . . . She did excellent field work on it." Terry A. Benedict praises the author because

> Nora Roberts takes us behind the walls of Jaquir and the Muslim way
> of life. Women [are] protected within their harem, however, their sole
> purpose in life is to please their King—who by the way is permitted
> four wives—and bear sons. . . . This was an enticing and endearing
> story as well as an informative one as to the ways of a world completely
> outside of what we know. A story told in only the way Nora could tell it
> and a complete gift to the reader.

This "gift" to the reader includes a nationalistic reinforcement of the idea that American women are by definition free, because in these novels their lives and situations are always contrasted with Muslim women's servitude, as discussed in Chapter 7. A reader from Alabama states simply: "It gives you some insight on how Muslim women live. It literally is a Gilded Cage they live in. This book reminded me how truly lucky I am to live in America!"

However, from mid-2006 to 2011, readers became increasingly critical of the racist and Orientalist discourses recycled through *Sweet Revenge*, which have become the main targets of reader complaints about the novel. These reviewers are mostly, but not all, Muslim. The earliest such critique of *Sweet Revenge* is from Avid Reader, of California, who condemns the novel for perpetuating "Typical, Eurocentric Stereotypes About Muslims."

> I couldn't read past the second chapter. Roberts is just perpetuating the same old stereotypes about Muslims. It really steamed me that she used a verse of the Quran out of context for the title page of "The Bitter." "Your wives are your fields, so go to your fields as you like" isn't meant as a justification of sexual abuse and has never been interpreted as so by real scholars of the Quran. I'm not going to finish this book, because I'd rather not be reminded of how much I am viewed as some sort of exotic, oppressed "other" type of woman, thanks.

This is probably one of the first Amazon.com reviews by a Muslim woman about a contemporary Orientalist romance novel, and it reveals a degree of hurt, anger, and disappointment that is not uncommon among other readers who stigmatize the novel as "propaganda against Islam." "Before reading this book, Nora Roberts was one of my fav [*sic*] writers," writes one reader, but "not anymore. I never thought anybody could use a romantic fiction novel to badmouth Islam. I wish I could list the absolutely wrong things that she has written about Muslims, but I'm afraid the list is too long." Similarly, Mehvesh Khan also used to be a Roberts fan but the "whole completely evil, abusive and narrow minded portrayal of a Muslim country seriously turned me off. I doubt she has actually visited any Muslim country to begin with. I used to love her books but after reading this one I can't bear to pick up another one of her books."

These criticisms about unthinking regurgitations of negative stereotypes of Muslims strike at the heart of the contemporary Orientalist romance novel written by authors with little knowledge and poor understanding of the variations of religious practice, or the diversity of cultures and peoples in the Middle East. They may be "harmless fun" and simply enjoyed as fairy tales by non-Muslims (which is the rebuttal of most authors and readers) but, collectively, they reinforce Orientalist ideas that vilify Muslim culture while justifying discrimination against Muslim and Arab Americans, as well as U.S. foreign policy seeking to "save" oppressed Muslims—represented by the sexually abused Muslim woman or, more recently, the Afghani or Iraqi woman—from their violent and misogynistic leaders. The point is not to deny that certain groups of Muslim women are oppressed by their governments and societies, but that this is used as an excuse for Western military intervention to support Western interests. Meanwhile, other groups of oppressed women (e.g., women and girls in certain parts of rural India or China) are simply left to languish, invisible and "unrescued," when it does not suit American, British, or Australian foreign policy objectives to intervene militarily on their behalf. This is something that at least one non-Muslim reviewer, rawreader, finds deeply disturbing and uncomfortable. Rawreader's review is fascinating because it is a thoughtful reflection on the practice of reading and rereading at different points in life, and reveals how the significance of a novel to an individual changes over time, and how rereading is tinged with nostalgia as well as with the sadness that the first experience of a favorite book cannot always be relived. *Sweet Revenge* was the first Nora Roberts book read by this reviewer, as a teenager. After twenty years of reading Roberts's novels, rawreader had this to say about the novel:

> Nora's prolific writing habits result in a diversity of settings and professions for her books, but no human being could know enough to portray the complexity of all of her subject matter in a competent way. I have often been annoyed at her unrealistic portrayal of people in a variety of professions at the top of their fields at impossibly young ages, but that, of course, is part of the fantasy. Here, the absence of complexity is more disturbing and damaging, because the depiction of the despotic, harem-owning, Middle-Eastern leader is pretty over-the-top (the frequent over-the-top villain is another one of her less than fabulous plot features). Please don't write this off as a "PC" critique. This is only a warning for people who, like the reader from Alabama, comments that this teaches her about the Middle East, or for readers like the one who picked the book up and was understandably offended by the cartoonish depiction of the evil Arab father. I am not denying that there is misogyny in the Middle East (there is all over the world). But there's no doubt that this feeds into a representation of the Middle East that, if we read more widely, is far from the complex histories and social structures in a variety of different countries. As my first Nora, it

holds a special place in my heart, but it does not hold up for me almost twenty years later because of the stereotyping.

This is yet another timely reminder to academics that it is impossible to generalize about readers or their responses to novels, especially because their perspectives evolve over time, and because many of the criticisms made by scholars are also shared by readers. One group is not necessarily more "enlightened" or "aware" of potential problems than the other.

One of the most surprising and fertile online discussions about specific sheik romance novels has focused on the topic of "race" from an African-American perspective. According to Romance Writers of America industry statistics from 2002, 77 percent of romance readers were white, 11 percent African-American, 9 percent Hispanic, and 2 percent Asian or Native-American. The racial makeup of the romance market goes some way in explaining the predominance of white heroines in contemporary mass-market romance novels, but it does not satisfactorily explain the popularity of stories with Arab sheiks or Native Americans as heroes—something that has become so common that it has developed into its own subgenre. These are white racial or interracial fantasies that do not correlate to market segmentation, for were they to do so, we might expect to see many more mainstream contemporary romance novels featuring black Americans as protagonists.[2]

The first mainstream African-American romance novel, Rosalind Welles' *Entwined Destinies*, was contracted by a black American editor at Dell and published as part of its Candlelight romance series in 1980. Harlequin followed belatedly in 1985 with the publication of Sandra Kitt's *Adam and Eva*, but Kitt went on to write romances mainly featuring white protagonists (Osborne 50). At a time when Hispanics, Native Americans, and Arab sheiks were gracing the covers of romance novels, very few romance novels with black Americans made it into the mainstream romance market. As of 2002, Harlequin had only five or six African-American authors among its international "stable" of 1,200 (Osborne 50). The entry of Kensington Publishing into the romance fiction scene changed the publication prospects for African-American romance writers with the establishment of the black American romance line, Arabesque, in 1994. Since then, the African-American romance market has grown, with more romance lines being added (for example, Kensington's Zebra and Pinnacle imprints; Harlequin's Sepia, New Spirit, and Kimani Romances; and Parker Publishing's Noire romance lines), but it has become increasingly cordoned off from the mainstream American market and exists largely as a niche market patronized overwhelmingly by African Americans.

Although black romance writers have been publishing category romance novels for over two decades, it was only in 2002 that a sheik romance novel appeared featuring an African-American woman: Brenda Jackson's *Delaney's Desert Sheikh* (2002). Jackson had already published around fifteen romance novels under the Arabesque/BET imprint before she became the first African-American woman to publish in Harlequin's Silhouette Desire line, and many of her own fans crossed over with her into the mainstream category romance market. The response from Amazon.com reviewers—forty-two reviews as of July 2011—has been staggering for this particular subgenre, where books usually merit half a dozen reviews at most, and it has also generated its own blog discussion. The plot itself is banal and insubstantial: an African-American pediatrician has a holiday in a friend's log cabin only to find it already occupied by a conservative sheik diplomat from the Middle East who believes in arranged marriages and mistresses on the side. She is a virgin to boot, and he initiates her into a variety of sexual experiences. Amazon.com reviewers focused primarily on two things: interracial romance, and the sex scenes—"Hot! Hot! Hot!" according to many readers. Janina from Ypsilanti, Michigan, enthuses that the "heat between these two characters made me turn my ceiling fan on to cool off," while P. B. Hall from Louisiana comments: "Delaney did not have a chance against a man that can make her climax with a kiss. Goodness. I have to research that."

There is considerable ambivalence about the desirability of interracial relations as well as the authentic portrayal of blackness. One of the earliest reviews on the Amazon.com site applauds Jackson for breaking through Harlequin's "color barrier" but regrets that "some editor at Silhouette got a hold of this and tried to wipe out the references to black culture. The language tends to be very formal at times and slang terms like 'da bomb' have become 'the bomb'." However, the topic of interracial romance triggered many more comments. One reader expresses concern about the interracial relationship, stating that it is "hard to identify with Jamal [the sheik] because he was not a 'true brother'." Another reader from Florida comments that "Brenda Jackson is a master at celebrating black love which is the reason I almost didn't buy this book . . . . I'm not big on interracial dating and didn't care to read about it. It was refreshing to read that the characters where [*sic*] people of color but hailed from different ethnic backgrounds."

The significance of having nonwhite people as the central protagonists of a mainstream romance novel cannot be underestimated. Because the story involves an African American and an Arab, readers acknowledge that it is not just a "great African American romance novel," but a "great romance read period." One reviewer notes approvingly: "For those of you looking for a romance book that deals with racism since both the heroine and hero are not of the same race then this is not the book for you. In fact, the author did not make it an issue in the book and what a sigh of relief!" The aspect of the novel that is universally applauded is the fact that

> Jackson validates African American women as encompassing the same personal concerns and professional tenacity that women of all races do. *Delaney's Desert Sheik* is refreshingly void of concentrating on the differences between persons with diverse backgrounds, but celebrates those distinctions instead.

After reading *Delaney's Desert Sheikh* and an article on romance novels in the feminist popular culture magazine *BITCH* in 2007, romance blogger Gwyneth Bolton wrote a short piece on "Reading and Writing African American Romance." Her commentary, posted on June 12, 2007, prompted an extensive discussion on race and the romance novel. For Bolton and the other discussants on the site, the popularity of the sheik romance novel merely serves to emphasize the marginalization of black people in the nation's mainstream romantic imagination.

> We have been having this discussion based on the things that most white romance readers won't read—African American romance novels. But what happens to the conversation when we really interrogate the ever-so popular reads: the sheiks, the Native Americans, the Latin Lovers. What happens when we really interrogate how men of color are objectified and made into the exotic other? What does this tell us about racism in romance? Is it particularly telling that we have so many captive by the savage other stories in romance land? And what does it mean that we seldom see black men in this savage other role, with the exception of perhaps MANDINGO many years ago? (Bolton 2007)

Discussants on Bolton's blogsite agree that the romance market is skewed toward white readers and writers, and they question why, even in the era of Islamist terrorism, when "the media portrayal of Middle Eastern men . . . paints them as the most dangerous and brutal out to kill 'innocent' US citizens," Arab sheiks should still be regarded as highly desirable sexual and romantic "alpha male fantasy" partners for white women, while black men are not. There are, in the words of one discussant, "no brothers in romanceland." Opinions on why this is the case vary. The Cinderella fantasy was posited as a reason by many. Ann Aguirre writes:

> I think it's more the money factor, to be honest. Harlequin Presents embodies escapism fiction at its pinnacle. So we have the stereotypes of the rich man, coming in to sweep the heroine off her feet. Taking her away to exotic climes, so she can roll around in his big ole piles of loot, and live happily ever after.
>
> Well, who does the American woman think of as being well off? Well, there's the Greek tycoon billionaire, of course. And the oil-rich Arab sheikh. Anyone else? Well, occasionally you get a European playboy.
>
> I'm not saying there aren't rich men in America, but they lack the "take me away" quality. A book about a black man who made his money on Wall Street just isn't as exotic. Maybe he can afford to take you to Monaco, but he wasn't *born* there.

Extending the argument along the same lines, another discussant points out that "blacks aren't seen as financially secure . . . so how could a general romance reader be 'taken away' [by] the fantasy of a black man with tons of money when they think it is pure fantasy?"

Other African-American discussants disagree, arguing that racializing stereotypes are more important factors because they make black men desirable only if they are athletes or celebrities. "In general," one discussant observes, "most white women are not interested in losing white skin privilege, a fact of life that comes with being with a black man." Another argues that "African-American men are feared more by American Caucasian women because of the media's depiction of them as violent, brutal sexual predators, players or pimps." In reality, white American women came into contact with African-American men, whereas they did not come into contact with Arab sheiks. Argues one reader, a sheik is simply "a white man wearing a turban . . . . You have the fantasy of the rich exotic sheik, without dealing with the reality of how a real Middle Eastern man would behave with a female." This last comment shows that these discussants—some black, some Hispanic, and some white—were no more immune to existing stereotypes about Muslims and Middle Easterners than the general population. The same points were raised about women's rights in America in contrast to the perceived lack of them in the Middle East, although at least one discussant was aware that this was a clichéd motif in sheik romance fiction.

Race in the romance novel is always a contentious topic; many discussants disagreed with the above arguments, often reverting to personal experiences to counterclaims of blind and endemic white racism. Contributors' posts were vetted by other contributors for underlying attitudes of racism, but even these could be ambiguous. For instance, the topic of sheiks being white men in turbans is accompanied by a sarcastic comment by a black woman that "black men as romance heroes would be very popular if they could somehow not be so . . . black. You know, have all the flavor and mannerisms, and the cool cache [*sic*], but for the love of Goddess don't make them so . . . black." This comment points to an underlying issue that the discussants do not fully explore: is it desirable to nonwhite readers to have nonwhite protagonists in a romance novel if they are then culturally stripped and "whitened" or made to conform to mainstream, mostly white American values and ideals, whether physical, economic, social, or cultural? The historical dominance of white readers and writers in mainstream category romance fiction means that people of other races or ethnicities are invariably cast as the exotic other in category romances. Is this what black American readers want to see: African-American protagonists contorted to fit the common plots and character types of category romance novels? Discussants appear confused about the issue, and never engage with this question directly.

Bolton argues that Brenda Jackson's *Delaney's Desert Sheikh* "doesn't play into the captured by the savage sheik stereotypes that a lot of these novels have. It is different and I think the fact that it has a black woman as the lead has a lot to do with that difference. The stereotypes have to be reworked when you change the players." But the sexist, patriarchal, authoritarian desert sheik who is tamed and transformed into good husband material by the strong, independent American heroine is nothing if not a stereotype, even though this heroine is black. In commenting on the lack of black heroes in "romanceland," one discussant hastily adds, "Not that I'm saying we should objectify and make brothers into the exotic other for some taken by the savage fantasy [*sic*] . . . But it does say a lot that they aren't there." Another discussant agrees that "it seems sad that multiculturalism is expanding in the romance genre for every race except African Americans," before acknowledging: "But then again, the depiction of Native American, Middle Eastern and even Asian men in the romance genre has probably been more of a parody or stereotype than anything else." In the end, for these discussants, there seems to be only two choices for nonwhite protagonists in the contemporary category romance: invisibility or stereotype.

Of course, readers do not always take the sheik romance novel seriously or read it "straight." One of the most insightful and acerbic readers and reviewers of sheik romance novels is the Malaysian blogger "Mrs. Giggles," who, "in real life" is a "retired biochemist and demure, nice, agreeable granny," but whose purpose online is to "keep making everyone in the romance industry irritated" (Amazon.com profile). Mrs. Giggles regularly reviewed for Amazon.com but now maintains her own blogsite, mrsgiggles.com, where she reviews romance novels and other books, movies, and music. Cultural howlers, stupid or clichéd plotlines, liberal feminists, neo-imperialist assumptions, sloppy editors and publishers who peg "the most embarrassing titles onto their books," heroines who "make me want to take an ax to the book," and "jackass" heroes all come in for deliciously vicious verbal lashings by this reviewer. I conclude this discussion of reader responses with a quote from Mrs Giggles's review of Diana Palmer's *Lord of the Desert* (2000), which touches on many of the issues raised in the last few chapters on modern sheik romance novels:

> It feels like a romance right out the early 1900s, complete with *Casablanca* name-droppings and Anglo-Saxon Sheikh imageries. Middle-Eastern romance readers may get offended by the patronizing idea of a Christian, French ruler bringing Democracy and Enlightenment (Western style) to rural dark Middle Eastern lands, so exercise your discretion. . . . Gretchen the sad no-life no-personality heroine is still in mourning about her mother, whom she has devoted herself to caring for until old mum croaked from cancer. Even pre-mommy's-cancer, Gretchen has no life, and is content to stay at home, arms folded, eyes down. In short, she is just perfect for the life of a Middle-Eastern consort to some royalty. Enters Phillippe, our Enlightened Sovereign who brings Peace and Feminism to rustic backward Qawi. . . . Think of all the bad sheikh romances where the actors playing the sheikhs never look remotely Middle-Eastern . . . . Still, really, *Lord Of The Desert* is great inane fun. It's not high art, it's not even decent romance, but it sure is a bloody campy hoot of a read.

And that, no doubt, explains the enduring, and even escalating, popularity of sheik romance novels in the age of Islamist terrorism and American-led wars in the Middle East.

Conclusion

*The job of a romance novel is to feed hope in the world—the hope
that those we see as our enemy can also be our friend.*

SHEIK ROMANCE NOVELIST LUCY MONROE (REARDON, 2006)

The al-Qaeda terrorist attacks on the United States on September 11, 2001, have had an enormous impact around the world. Two wars in Central Asia and the Middle East have resulted, embroiling the United States, Britain, Australia, and other members of the "Coalition of the Willing" in long-lasting battles, producing massive numbers of coalition casualties, and leaving thousands of Afghani and Iraqi men, women, and children—combatants and the innocent—dead, wounded, radicalized, or as refugees from the war on terror. In the United States, Americans have endured mounting body counts from these wars; erosions in civil liberties and modifications to habeas corpus (Giroux 2003); inconveniences from increased security, especially in air travel; and fear of further terrorist attacks. It no longer matters that until the World Trade Center bombing of February 1993, the Reagan and George H. W. Bush years were characterized by terrorist attacks from organizations other than Muslim ones, according to FBI statistics:

> Puerto Ricans, 72 attacks; left-wing groups, 23 attacks; Jewish groups, 16 attacks; anti-Castro Cubans, 12 attacks; and right-wing groups, 6 attacks (FBI 1995). An analogous pattern can be seen with regard to anti-U.S. terrorist attacks abroad: In 1994, 44 took place in Latin America, 8 attacks in the Middle East, 5 in Asia, 5 in Western Europe, and 4 in Africa. (U.S. Department of State 1995, 67; quoted in Gerges 80)

In the years following September 11, the terrorist became synonymous with the Muslim/Arab extremist. The effect of this on Arab Americans, Muslim Americans, and others mistaken for them—especially
South Asians—has been profound. On September 12, 2001, an angry
mob of largely white Americans, partially armed and sometimes shouting
"kill the Arabs," marched to a predominantly Arab mosque in Chicago,
and 125 police had to be called to protect the mosque and the surround-
ing Arab-American homes from being stormed by the mob. On September 15, 2001, Sikh-American Balbir Singh Sodhi was gunned down outside
his gas station in Mesa, Arizona, with the killers bragging that they were
going to "kill the ragheads responsible for September 11." On the same
day, Pakistani-American Waqar Hasan was shot in his convenience store
in Texas by Mark Stroman, who then went on to murder Vasudev Patel
and blind a Bangladeshi man. After he was caught, Stroman boasted to
police: "I did what every American wanted to do after September 11th
but didn't have the nerve." Also on September 15, Adel Karas, an Egyptian Christian, was killed at his grocery store in San Gabriel, California.
On September 21, a Yemeni American, Ali Almansoop, was murdered in
his Detroit home. In October, Swaran Kaur Bhullah, a Sikh, was stabbed
in the head while waiting at a traffic light in California. He survived only
because the attackers fled the scene when another car pulled up. By the
end of the year, the Chicago Commission on Human Relations had recorded more than one hundred hate crimes against Arabs and Muslims,
including Muslim women being spat at in the streets and having their
hijabs violently torn off. On October 5, 2003, a Muslim woman wearing
a *hijab* in Springfield, Virginia, was stabbed in a supermarket parking
lot. The white male teenage assailant allegedly shouted out, "You terrorist
pig!" before fleeing. The Council on American-Islamic Relations (CAIR)
recorded 1717 reports of "bias incidents and hate crimes" against Arabs
and South Asians in the first six months after September 11—an increase
of more than 1600%—with another 325 incidents in the following six
months. Mosques as well as Assyrian churches have been repeatedly vandalized or subjected to arson attempts. As of 2008, more than 3000 hate
crimes had been committed against Arab Americans, Muslim Americans,
or people who simply looked "Middle Eastern" (Cainkar 2004, Bakalian
and Bozorgmeh 2–3).

Government initiatives enacted to respond to the real threat of Islamist terrorism have also affected Arab and Muslim Americans inordinately.
As Louise Cainkar (2004, http://www.ssrc.org) elucidates,

measures have included mass arrests, secret and indefinite detentions, prolonged detention of "material witnesses," closed hearings and use of secret evidence, government eavesdropping on attorney-client conversations, FBI home and work visits, wiretapping, seizures of property, removals of aliens with technical visa violations, and mandatory special registration. At least 100,000 Arabs and Muslims living in the United States have personally experienced one of these measures. Indeed, of thirty-seven known U.S. government security initiatives implemented since the September 11 attacks, twenty-five either explicitly or implicitly target Arabs and Muslims in the United States.

Opinion polls conducted since September 11 have consistently shown a significant measure of public support for the exceptional, discriminatory treatment of Arab Americans (Cainkar 2004).

Sadly, there is nothing new about these responses after September 11. Since the mid-1980s, the FBI has subjected Arab Americans and their friends, colleagues, and neighbors to harassment in the form of phone calls and visits to "obtain non-criminal information about pro-Arab political activities; to obstruct interaction and cooperation between Arab political activists and other segments of North American society; and to diminish support for Arab-American causes by creating an atmosphere of fear, suspicion and isolation" (Naber 49). After the 1985 TWA hijacking in Lebanon, Alex Odeh, the regional director of the American-Arab Anti-Discrimination Committee (ADC), was murdered, and some ADC offices were forced to close because of threats to staff and attempted arson or bombing of their premises (Naber 47). After the first Persian Gulf War in 1991, a taxi driver in Fort Worth, Texas, was killed, shots were fired into the homes of Arab Americans, Arab-American schools and mosques were vandalized or bombed, and incidents of hate calls increased dramatically. In the aftermath of the 1995 Oklahoma City Bombing, perpetrated by Irish-American U.S. Army veteran Timothy McVeigh, more than two hundred attacks against Arab Americans were recorded before the findings of the investigation were made public (Gerges 80). Since the 1980s, therefore, following domestic crises and during times when the United States has been engaged in war in the Middle East, there have been increases in violence and discrimination against Arab and Muslim Americans, as well as people who simply look like these groups (Akram 2002).

In Britain and Australia, government responses to September 11 have resulted in the erosion of civil liberties, temporary suspensions of habeas corpus, and increased measures in security, especially in the wake of the July 7, 2005, bombings in London, which were followed by attempted terrorist attacks on July 21, 2005, and attempted car bombings at Glasgow and London airports on June 29, 2007. Australia has not thus far experienced an Islamist terrorist attack on home soil, although eighty-eight Australians were victims of the October 12, 2002, bombings in Bali, along with thirty-eight Indonesians and seventy-six other people. In early August 2009, Australian Federal Police claimed to have foiled a homegrown Islamist terrorist plot to stage a military shoot-out at an army barracks (*Sydney Morning Herald* August 4, 2009). The situation of Muslims and Arabs in both countries, however, differs considerably from their situation in the United States.

In Britain, public perceptions of Muslims have been partially shaped by South Asian settlers who have been telling stories about their own culture through commercial film, theater, literature, and television since the 1980s. As Pnina Werbner (2004) argues, these artists tell "a story of cultural hybridity and cosmopolitanism, of intergenerational conflict, inter-ethnic or inter-racial marriage, family politics and excesses of consumption; a cultural arena that makes its distinctive contribution to British and South Asian popular culture by satirizing the parochialism and conservatism of the South Asian immigrant generation." This is evident in films such as *My Beautiful Laundrette* (1985) and *Sammy and Rosie Get Laid* (1987)—both directed by Stephen Frears and based on screenplays by the novelist Hanif Kureishi, whose prize-winning novel *The Buddha of Suburbia* (1990) also features problems of identity and racism in multicultural London of the late twentieth century (Werbner 897). Werbner points out that in Britain, Muslims were subsumed within a general "South Asian" migrant/settler identity until the Rushdie Affair of 1989, when the Iranian Ayatollah Khomeini issued a fatwa directing Muslims to assassinate Salman Rushdie for perceived blasphemy in his prize-winning 1988 novel, *The Satanic Verses*. Protest letters were written to Rushdie's publisher, Viking, and violence was directed against bookstores carrying the novel. Bombings or attempted bombings carried out at many different bookstores resulted in Rushdie's novel being withdrawn from shelves. This, rather than terrorist attacks, was the incident that began to galvanize British public opinion against Muslims, who were nonetheless not automatically synonymous with "Arabs" in Britain because the majority of British Muslims were from countries that were part of the Asian subcontinent, such as Pakistan and Bangladesh. Muslim immigrants in Britain arrived in the post-Second World War period, and especially after the

1960s. In comparison with the United States, the higher concentration of Muslim immigrant settlers in particular cities, and their (generally) lower educational achievements combined with greater disadvantage, has meant that social problems associated with "Muslims"—such as the Old- ham race riots in May 2001—have been interpreted as arising from socio- economic conditions such as poverty, high youth unemployment, lack of opportunity, racism from both white and nonwhite Britons, and the fail- ure of authorities—both local and national—to address these problems.[1] Therefore, the radicalization of British Muslims has been recognized to result from issues other than religion; issues that are compounded by British foreign policy responses to the confrontation between India and Pakistan over Kashmir, the first Persian Gulf War, September 11, and the wars in Afghanistan and Iraq, for example. The radicalization of young Muslims is not simply sheeted home to a rather vague and generic root- cause of "Islamist terrorism."

In Australia, the rallying of public opinion against Muslims did not originally result from Islamist terrorism so much as from local problems, particularly the Sydney gang rapes of 2000, in which Bilal Skaf led up to fourteen Lebanese Australian men in at least four confirmed incidents of rape against women and teenage girls. Interracial tensions exploded in Cronulla, a beachside suburb south of Sydney, in December 2005. Five thousand white Australians gathered to protest the intimidating behavior of mostly Lebanese-Australian young men on the beach during the previ- ous weeks. In the course of a drunken afternoon of protests, a few Middle Eastern and Indian Australians were attacked. The rioting by white Aus- tralians was then followed by retaliatory attacks, forcing the unprece- dented closure of some Sydney beaches in December 2005. These inci- dents were largely blamed on certain groups of Middle Eastern Muslim males, rather than all Muslims in general, but tensions between Lebanese Muslims and the wider Australian community were further strained when the imam of a Sydney mosque, Sheikh Taj el-Din Hamid Hilaly, seemed to suggest in a Ramadan sermon of October 2006 that women who wore provocative clothing in the public sphere were responsible for their own sexual assaults (Kerbaj 2006). A straw poll of the mosque's members con- ducted by the *Sydney Morning Herald* showed widespread disagreement with the sheik's comments, but the damage was done (Malik 2006).

Further interracial and interreligious controversies between Muslim Australians and the wider community erupted over the proposed building of Muslim schools in southwest Sydney, and took a nasty turn when pigs' heads were rammed onto metal stakes on one of the sites in 2007 (Murray

2009). Certainly, war in the Middle East and Afghanistan has exacerbated Australian fears of Muslim immigrants, particularly Muslim refugees, and hate crimes against Muslim Australians have been perpetrated in the wake of the Persian Gulf War (for example, a mosque in Brisbane was bombed, while women wearing *hijabs* reported having their headscarves yanked off), September 11, and the war in Iraq. Because of local conditions, however, "Muslims" are often not treated as an all-encompassing, undifferentiated group in Australia. Muslim groups such as Pakistani, Turkish, and Indonesian Australians elicit far more complex and varied responses than do "Lebanese Australians" (from which group Lebanese Christians ["Maronites"] often seem to be omitted).

All three countries have made efforts to address the victimization of Muslims after 9/11, while sympathetic responses from the wider international community have also been recorded. In the United States, as Evelyn Alsultany (2007) notes, the Ad Council ran the "I am an American" campaign, attempting to portray an inclusive image of Americans of various ethnicities in response to the hate crimes perpetrated against Arab and Muslim Americans. An informal 2006 survey of Muslim Americans showed that some felt they were supported by their fellow Americans in the aftermath of 9/11. Meanwhile, American interest in Islam has grown, with soaring sales of the *Qur'an* as well as demands for Arabic language lessons (Hoke 2006). Throughout the first decade of the twentieth century, interest in Middle Eastern culture—particularly belly dancing—has also increased, especially in places like the San Francisco Bay Area, where there are significant Arab populations (Maira 2008). Attempts have also been made to incorporate Muslim and Arab Americans into the polity at an official level: Zalmay Khalilzad, a Muslim Afghani American, was appointed as an ambassador to the United Nations and was the highest-ranking Muslim American under President George W. Bush; Arif Alikhan, a Pakistani Sunni, was appointed Assistant Secretary for Policy Development at the United States Department of Homeland Security in 2009 and previously held the post of Deputy Mayor of Homeland Security and Public Safety in Los Angeles from 2006 to 2009; and Houston appointed its first Muslim councilman, Pakistani-born engineer Masrur Javed Khan, in 2003, after he won an election in which the majority of his support came from his district's Catholic Latinos (Hujer and Steinvorth 2007).

Despite these efforts, however, the reflexive connection between terrorism and Arab and Muslim enemies has been strengthened by media reports as well as by the entertainment industry. Since the late 1970s, this connection has been made in films such as *Black Sunday* (1977), *The Black*

Stallion (1979), *Back to the Future* (1985), *Iron Eagle* (1986), *Death Before Dishonor* (1987), *Wanted: Dead or Alive* (1987), *Navy SEALS* (1990), *Delta Force* (1991), *Patriot Games* (1992), *True Lies* (1994), and *Executive Decision* (1996). After September 11, as Jack Shaheen notes, in television series such as *24*, Arab Americans are demonized and depicted in various seasons plotting to "nuke Texas," "nuke Los Angeles," or simply to "nuke our country, killing neighbors in the process," while the protagonist, Jack Bauer, guns down hundreds of "Muslim American 'fanatics'" (2005). Although some television dramas have made attempts to portray Arab and Muslim Americans sympathetically in the wake of 9/11 (Alsultany 2008), Shaheen claims that

> "Family Law," "Judging Amy," "The District" and "The Practice" have
> had storylines that imply that airlines should discriminate against us,
> that we should be jailed without due process, and that we burn down
> our own mosques and abuse our children. "Third Watch" has shown
> us making radioactive bombs, and pitted us against the NYPD. "JAG,"
> "Navy NCIS," "The Agency," "Sue Thomas FB Eye" and other shows
> have portrayed us as traitors and terrorists who run sleeper cells in
> mosques. (Shaheen, "Network TV demonizes American Arabs")

ABC correspondent John Cooley noted in 1983 that "Arabs are probably still the only group in the U.S. that anyone dares to portray in pejorative terms . . . This kind of thing would never be tolerated by any other group in the United States—Italians, Jews, Blacks, Irishmen, whatever" (Christison 397). The same still holds true today.

Arabs and Muslims have fared no better in American literature. Reeva Simon (2010) has documented the rise of Arab and Muslim villains in Western literature, and the increasing preoccupation with *jihad* and global terrorism. Michael Suleiman observes that "Arabs and Muslims are usually depicted as inherently violent, religiously fanatic, hopelessly backward, dirty, lazy and anti-Western, particularly anti-American. They are people who mistreat and suppress their women, who are supposedly no more than sex objects" (35). Other peoples and cultures may also be subjected to such stereotyping and demonization, but the point is that the representation of Arabs and Muslims is overwhelmingly negative in both popular and high culture, and that this has significant social effects for these groups as well as for others, such as South Asians, especially in times of crises. Arabs and Muslims are simply not usually portrayed as "normal" or "human." As Susan Akram points out, the most significant thing about "portrayals of Arabs and Muslims is the omission of Arabs as ordinary people, families with social interactions, or outstanding members of communities such as scholars or writers or scientists" (63).

In this respect, the modern-day sheik novel stands out as a significant exception. Of course, the novels are Orientalist in the leitmotifs they invoke; they are part of a centuries-long Western tradition that has represented the Orient and Orientals in a multitude of conflicting ways, often demonizing Muslims and Islamic culture even as it emphasized the sensuous appeal and romance of the East. Certainly, within the subgenre of the sheik romance, there is still the figure of the angry, vengeful, menacing sheik who kidnaps the Western virgin and locks her up in the harem for various reasons before succumbing to the overwhelming force of his love for her, ceding a good measure of his power to her, "de-Orientalizing" himself to a certain extent, and marrying her so that together, as an interracial, interreligious couple, they can rule over some desert kingdom or be incorporated into Western society. But this is not all there is to the sheik novel. Arabs and Muslims are also represented as "ordinary people" (although usually wealthy beyond the dreams of most), who are businessmen, surgeons, soldiers, diplomats, entrepreneurs, and many other things. Such portrayals show Arabs and Muslims as "outstanding members of communities." Romance novelists depict Arab and Muslim men as having close-knit, loyal, emotionally warm and caring families that are often far superior to the heroine's dysfunctional Western family. These ameliorative representations are vital in the current climate.

The modern-day sheik romances present an alternative Orientalist discourse to the current vogue for biographies of women oppressed under Islam. This vogue began with Betty Mahmoody's *Not Without My Daughter* (1987) and has since become a distinct genre focused especially on female slavery and honor killings: books such as Zana Muhsen's *Sold: One Woman's Account of Modern Slavery* (1994), Jan Goodwin's *Price of Honor: Muslim Women Lift the Veil of Silence on the Islamic World* (2002), "Souad's" *Burned Alive: A Survivor of "Honor" Killing Speaks Out* (2005), Ayaan Hirsi Ali's *The Caged Virgin* (2006), Unni Wikan's *In Honor of Fadime: Murder and Shame* (2008), Rana Husseini's *Murder in the Name of Honor* (2009), and countless others so often feature fully veiled women on their covers as a symbol of their oppression. I am not suggesting that all such biographies are not true (although, as critics have pointed out, many are not without their representational problems, cultural misunderstandings, and sensationalist exaggerations). Honor killings do take place, each and every incident is abhorrent, and these women should be free to tell their stories. However, collectively, these books present an unrelieved picture of Arab and Muslim men as the barbaric oppressors of all Muslim women—an image that not only confirms existing Orientalist stereotypes, but is used as an excuse for Americans and others in the Western world to save Iraqi and Afghani women from Muslim men through war and "regime change." Given the scarcity of alternative representations of Muslim men in Western popular culture, therefore, the existence of the sheik novels, with their panoply of Muslim heroes, is significant.

I don't want to claim too much on behalf of these novels. They are often inaccurate in their historical, cultural, or geopolitical information; they are often set in fantasy sheikdoms rather than in real countries; and they often feature what are essentially white men performing in "Arabface." Even more disturbingly, over and over again these novels show white Western women displacing Muslim women in their own lands and lives. Muslim women are silenced and infantilized, while condescending white women strive to save them through education about liberal feminism, or through modernization or development projects that are not only a legacy of British imperialism, but that also align with the mid-twentieth-century American political establishment's beliefs about how to stave off radicalization and revolution in the developing world.

Nevertheless, the sheik novels affirm readers' willingness to believe in the power of romantic love to breach cross-cultural, interracial, and interreligious boundaries and to integrate the Arab or Muslim other into modern Western societies. They signal a sustained and growing interest in the non-pathological, non-terrorist Middle East on the part of American women, however misguided or inaccurate the women's sources of information might be. In light of the enduring negative and hostile portrayals of Arab and Muslim males in Western popular culture, surely their humanizing—their representation as attractive and intelligent potential lovers, partners, husbands, and fathers, as well as active participants in strong and intimate family units—represents the ability of this particular form of women's popular culture to temper negative stereotypes that seem ubiquitous today. In the novels of authors such as Sara Wood, Elizabeth Mayne, and Dana Marton, we even see the attempts of women to think through the impact and legacy of British and American foreign policies in the Middle East, to position themselves in the place of the (neo) colonized Oriental other, and to present some kind of critique of British and American policies as well as of the very conventions of the sheik novel itself. The problems with these conventions are not ones that readers remain unaware of.

If nothing else, the sheik novel has been most successful in provoking a range of online discussions among romance readers and writers about contemporary social and cultural issues in addition to literary concerns about genre, writing, plot, and character. These issues include sexuality, violence, patriarchy, race and the desirability of interracial relations, the possibility of representing ethnic or cultural others rather than simply "a white man in a turban," the dangers of perpetuating stereotypes of the Middle East, and even the problematic perpetuation of Orientalism in these novels. Nevertheless, while recognizing that sheik novelists have meant well and have not misrepresented different Middle Eastern or Muslim cultures out of ill intent, romance readers themselves are beginning to call for more accountability in this subgenre. As Candy Tan, the moderator of the "Smart Bitches Trashy Books" discussion thread on sheik novels, bluntly complains:

> Sheikh romances (and Native American romances, for that matter) . . . heavily fetishize a culture that's still alive, and I can't help but feel that:
> a) it can't be that hard to do SOME research and attempt to get SOME things right, yeah? and
> b) the culture as a whole has been bastardized and misinterpreted so frequently that seeing a whole sub-genre pretty much dedicated to perpetuating old myths in the 21st century is pretty damn infuriating.
> . . .
> I suspect it has to do with cultural misappropriation, and how much I feel the authors "own" the culture they're portraying. Feel free to butcher and fuck up your own culture as much as you want, but if you want to poach other people's cultural territory, then you better make some kind of good-faith effort to get some things correct.

The romantic Orient has been an integral part of Western culture since the twelfth century. It may be the case that the slow accretion of Orientalist motifs over the course of these past centuries is now too firmly embedded into Western culture to be easily dislodged and replaced. These fantasies of sex, romance, and exotic consumption have simply been too successful, fulfilling, and fun for many writers and readers preconditioned by Orientalist assumptions and ignorance about the complicated realities of the Middle Eastern or the Muslim world. Nevertheless, it is encouraging that there exists an exuberant online community of romance readers who are aware of the Orientalist implications of the sheik novel, and who are willing to question, challenge, ridicule, and demand greater responsibility or even reform in this subgenre. Given the xenophilia, multicultural politics, and responsiveness to their readers that many romance writers espouse—the very conditions that prompt them to write sheik romance novels to begin with—it would be most surprising if we do not see some salutary changes in the years to come.

Notes

INTRODUCTION

1. In this book, I assume that "the Orient" is a Western discursive construct rather than an existing geopolitical reality but, for ease of reading, will omit scare quotes from the term and its derivatives in subsequent references.

2. Novelists increasingly use the spelling "sheikh" these days, but I have retained the original spelling, "sheik," used by early twentieth-century novelists, unless otherwise indicated in the title.

3. For a comprehensive account of the historical, academic, and political context of *Orientalism*, including its reception and its problems, see Lockman (2004), Chapters Five to Seven.

4. For a discussion of male writers of romance fiction, see the forum "Male Authors of Romance/Romantic Fiction," "Teach Me Tonight" blog site: http://teachmetonight.blogspot.com/2006/09/male-authors-of-romanceromantic.html; and "Male Authors of Romance/Romantic Fiction (2)," "Teach Me Tonight" blog site: http://teachmetonight.blogspot.com/2007/02/male-authors-of-romanceromantic-fiction.html. Accessed July 4, 2011.

CHAPTER 1

1. Sections of this chapter were published in Teo 2011.

2. The term "courtly love" (*amour courtois*) was coined by the French scholar Bruno Paulin Gaston in Paris in 1883 and popularized thereafter.

3. The first three romances can all be found in the Auchinleck manuscript, dated around 1340. Bevis also survives in six other English manuscripts, thus attesting to the huge popularity of these verse romances. For an in-depth discussion of these romances and their relationship to modern romance novels, see Amy Burge (2010, 2011b).

4. The spelling in the Auchinleck manuscript, which I used, is "Floris and Blancheflour," but other Middle English versions translate the French tale as "Floris and Blanchefleur."

5. See Amy Burge's discussion of medieval geography in her thesis.

6. For an extended discussion of medieval heroines' agency, see Judith Weiss (1991).

7. See the discussion of Josian's agency in Myra Seaman (2001).

8. For a full discussion of monstrous races, see Debra Strickland (2000) and Rudolph Wittkower (1942).

9. At first, the Islamic population in reconquered areas was left alone, but in 1501 the Muslims in Granada were ordered to convert to Christianity or leave. This edict was then extended to the rest of Spain in 1526. Converted Muslims were known as "Moriscos" and were expelled from Spain between 1609 and 1614.

10. It should have been "Soliman I" since it was following the Suleiman I-Hurrem Sultan story. Suleiman (or Soliman) II ruled from 1687 to 1691 but had spent most of his life imprisoned in the palace cage (*kafes*) and was quite ineffectual as a monarch.

11. That is, the nightingale, a common way to signify the romantic Orient.

CHAPTER 3

1. Parts of this chapter were published in Teo 2010b.

CHAPTER 4

1. See, for example, Pearce (1947), Vaughn and Clark (1981), Vaughn (1983), Van-DerBeets (1984), Derounian-Stodola (1993), Burnham (1997), and Strong (1999).

2. The Ancient Arabic Order of the Nobles of the Mystic Shrine formed in 1872 as an offshoot of the Freemasons.

3. Its only foreign conflict with the North African powers to date resulted in concessions of free naval and merchant shipping passage extracted from the North African "Barbary" powers of Morocco, Algiers, Tunis, and Tripolitania after the two Barbary (or Tripolitan) Wars of 1801–5 and 1815.

4. Much has been written about how Valentino challenged to a duel the author of the infamous "Pink Powder Puff" editorial in the *Chicago Tribune*, excoriating him as the model of American masculinity. See Melman (1988) and Leider (2003).

5. I am grateful to Eric Selinger for pointing this out.

6. Because many of these films are no longer available, I have compiled plot summaries from reviews in contemporary film magazines such as *Bioscope*, *Photoplay*, *Pictureplay*, and *Kinematograph Weekly*, as well as from The Internet Movie Database website, www.imdb.com.

7. The visual style of this, and other American harem films of the 1980s, con-

trasts markedly with a contemporary French effort: Arthur Joffé's *Harem* (1985), starring Nastassjia Kinski as Diane (yet another reference to *The Sheik*, showing its widespread influence even in French cinema), a lonely stockbroker in 1980s New York who is drugged, kidnapped, and imprisoned in the harem of an OPEC oil executive. Visually, Joffé's harem draws more directly from Gérôme's various paintings of Turkish baths and from ethnographic photographs of Moroccan and Algerian life discussed by Malek Alloula in *The Colonial Harem* (1986). They show dim places with light filtered through wooden lattices or apertures in the ceiling, with a rough, rustic, "primitive" feel characterizing the stone walls and floors. By contrast, the harems in American films resemble the brightly colored, brilliantly lit scenes from British Orientalist artist John Frederick Lewis's paintings, such as *The Reception* (1873). Although Joffé's *Harem* is set in the 1980s, the Oriental world of the harem it recreates is deliberately "timeless." Where harem women in American films inevitably feature the gauzy draperies and spangles of belly dancers, or the richly embroidered, heavy silk and damask robes of high-status women, the women in Joffé's harem wear cotton robes and don the *burqa* when prepare to see the harem master, Selim (played by British-born Indian actor Ben Kingsley).

8. It is indeed notable that so many of the principal cast members in these 1980s American harem films were mainstream Western actors, rather than Arab or Muslim actors, or even Arab/Muslim-American actors. Certainly, Omar Sharif played the Ottoman sultan infatuated with the American heroine, Jessica Gray, in the television miniseries *Harem* (1986). But his *kadin* was played by Ava Gardner and there were no other significant Arab/Muslim actors. Similarly, in *Sahara* the main Bedouin characters were played by Europeans. Apart from Lambert Wilson starring as the hero, Sheik Jaffar, the sheik's uncle Rasoul was played by British actor John Rhys-Davies, and the villainous Bedouin, Lord Beg, was played by yet another Briton, Ronald Lacey. Americans were not the only ones to cast mainly Westerners in the roles of Middle Eastern characters, of course. In Joffé's *Harem* (1985), there were only two named characters played by Middle Eastern actors: the Sunni Indian actress Zohra Sehgal as one of the harem women, and Kinski's own Egyptian filmmaker husband, Ibrahim Moussa, in a bit part. The lachrymose master of the harem, Selim, was played by the British-born Gujerati actor, Ben Kingsley.

CHAPTER 5

1. Unfortunately, I have not been given permission to reprint these covers. They are easily accessible on the following website: http://tanzanitesbookcovers.blogspot.com/2009/03/angelique-series-by-sergeanne-golon.html, accessed July 6, 2011.

2. The confusion over the term "odalisque" seems to be due to early modern European visitors to the Sublime Porte who assumed that all women within the harem were sexual partners—or potential partners—of the Ottoman sultan. This was possible in principle, for the Muslim male had the right of sexual access to his

slaves, unless they were already married. As Peirce shows, though, the sexual activity of the sultan and the imperial princes was strictly controlled because the sultan's sexuality was always political, with reproductive and dynastic consequences (ix, 3). The vast majority of women in the household held administrative and service functions, and these women did not have sex with the sultan. The Turkish term *odalik* meant "chambermaid," and these women's function in the harem was not necessarily sexual, although theoretically this could change. However, since Europeans at the Ottoman court regarded all harem women as the sultan's sex slaves, the mistranslation of *odalik* into the French *odalisque* meant that in Western Europe the term became synonymous with "concubine." The strong connotations of the *odalisque* in the nineteenth-century sexual imagination can be seen in the French Romantic Orientalists' swooning depictions of nude women whose purpose is clearly sexual availability: Ingres's *Le Grande Odalisque* (1814) and *Odalisque with Slave* (1842), Gérôme's *Odalisque* (n.d.), Delacroix's *Odalisque* (1857), and even the Spanish painter Mariano Fortuny Marsal's *Odalisque* (1861). These *odalisques* are often represented sprawled supine across couches or beds, naked or semi-naked and apparently ready for sex. Interestingly enough, one of the things that engendered controversy around Édouard Manet's nudes in *Olympia* and *Le déjeuner sur l'herbe* (both 1863) was the fact that the women boldly return the gaze of the viewer. In the paintings of the Oriental *odalisque*, by contrast, no such outrage or discomfort was provoked by the bold gaze returned by the nudes because they were already assumed to be concubines, who were synonymous with prostitutes.

3. See Leslie Peirce's *The Imperial Harem* (1993) for an explanation of the formal ranks and workings of the Ottoman harem.

4. I am grateful to Bertrice Small for alerting me to this text, which was one of her historical sources for *The Kadin*.

5. I have not been given permission to reprint these covers but they are easily accessible on the following FantasticFiction websites: http://www.fantasticfiction.co.uk/l/johanna-lindsey/silver-angel.htm; http://www.fantasticfiction.co.uk/n/christina-nicholson/savage-sands.htm; http://www.fantasticfiction.co.uk/m/connie-mason/desert-ecstasy.htm.

6. Parts of this section appear in Teo 2012.

7. I am grateful to Bertrice Small for answering my questions about her novel and sharing her historical sources with me.

8. There were, however, earlier works published on women in the Ottoman Empire, such as Fanny Davis, *The Ottoman Lady* (1986).

CHAPTER 6

1. The business and financial commentator and author Paul Erdman was especially taken with this idea, and published articles on the subject in *New York Magazine* in November 1973 and June 1974. The global financial crisis of 2007–2008 saw renewed

fears in periodicals such as *Bloomberg Weekly* and *The Economist* that wealthy Arabs and sovereign-funds-rich Asian states were once again "buying up Wall Street."

2. Indeed, so widespread has its currency become in common usage that the Oxford dictionary entry on "Mills and Boon" defines it as: "A proprietary name for a (type of) popular romantic novel published by Mills & Boon Limited"; a "person or situation reminiscent of the type of fiction published by Mills & Boon Limited, esp. in its light, romantic manner or style"; or an adjective "denoting idealized and sentimental romantic situations of a kind associated with the fiction published by Mills & Boon Limited." (http://www.oed.com/view/Entry/240020?redirectedFrom=Mills%20and%20Boon#eid).

3. McAleer thought that Hilliard's manuscript was never published. I am grateful to Juliet Flesch for alerting me to Hilliard's *Land of the Sun* and for providing me with a copy of the novel.

4. In the 1970s, the Egyptian president Anwar Sadat was generally portrayed as a "good Arab" by American journalists, but Americans were not writing category romance novels at that time.

CHAPTER 7

1. Derek Hopwood's examination of Arab men's writings about European women in Chapter Ten of *Sexual Encounters in the Middle East* confirms this impression.

2. Unfortunately, I was denied permission by Harlequin Enterprises to publish the covers of these novels. They are easily accessible on the Amazon.com site.

CHAPTER 8

1. There was much more to the 1970s and 1980s than this, of course, as social historians and recent oral history projects have shown, but this picture of Britain in decline is what these sheik romance novelists focused upon.

2. Visiting Shepheard's Hotel would have been impossible. The hotel was destroyed in an arson attack in 1952, during civil unrest that led to the July 23 revolution that overthrew King Farouk and established a republic in Egypt ruled by the military, thereby bringing Colonel Gamal Abdel Nasser to power as president.

3. There have been many studies on this subject: e.g., two major surveys in New York conducted just after 9/11 showed that 10 percent of those surveyed met the full criteria for PTSD specifically related to the 9/11 events, while the figure nationwide was 2.7–4.3 percent, and mainly included those who followed the television coverage of the event extensively (Marshall and Galea, 2004).

4. In Kathleen Creighton's *Virgin Seduction* (2002), the Arab princess's father tells the American hero that if he wants to marry her, he has to "convert" to "our ways, our culture," rather than specifically to Islam (81).

5. Obviously there are also problems with realism in Orientalist discourse, as many critiques of Orientalist literature, especially travel literature, have shown.

6. Thanks to Eric Selinger for alerting me to this novel and its expressions of xenophilia.

CHAPTER 9

1. Barbara Cartland is the one significant romance novelist of the twentieth century whose works I have not discussed in this book. Her oeuvre is so extensive, and the titles of her romance novels so ambiguous, that it was difficult to establish which books were sheik or desert romances.

2. See Teo 2003 for an extended discussion of fantasies of whiteness in the romance novel.

CONCLUSION

1. See *The Ritchie Report*, produced by the Oldham Independent Review, for the Oldham Metropolitan Borough Council; December 11, 2001.

Bibliography

PRIMARY SOURCES

Anonymous. N.d. "Abduction and Forcible Confinement: Human Rights Violation or Frisky Romantic Adventure?" *Sheikhs and Desert Love* website, http://sheikhs-and-desert-love.com/feature13.html.

Anonymous. 2003. *A Night in a Moorish Harem* (n.d.). A Renaissance eBook publication.

Anonymous. N.d. "Another Great Interview with Dana Marton." *Coffee Time Romance*, http://www.coffeetimeromance.com/Interviews/DanaMarton.html.

Anonymous. 1999. *Bevis of Hampton*. In *Four Romances of England*, edited by Ronald B. Herzman, Graham Drake, and Eve Salisbury. Kalamazoo, Michigan: Medieval Institute Publications.

Anonymous. N.d. "Floris and Blancheflour." Auchinleck Manuscript, NLS Adv MS 19.2.1. National Library of Scotland. http://auchinleck.nls.uk/mss/floris.html.

Anonymous. September 17, 1988. "In a world of their own. (Arabs in Britain)." *The Economist* 67.

Anonymous. N.d. *The King of Tars*. Auchinleck Manuscript. http://www.nls.uk/auchinleck/mss/tars.html.

Anonymous. 2005. *The Lustful Turk* (1828). Olympia Press.

Anonymous. 1990. *The Sultan of Babylon*. In *Three Middle English Charlemagne Romances*. Kalamazoo, Michigan: Medieval Institute Publications. http://www.library.rochester.edu/camelot/teams/sultint.htm.

Ariosto, Ludovico. 1974. *Orlando Furioso*, translated by Guido Waldman. Oxford: Oxford University Press.

August, Melissa. August 22, 2005. "Sheikhs and the Serious Blogger." *Time*. http://www.time.com/time/nation/article/0,8599,1096809,00.html.

Barry. Kathleen. 1971. "The Vagina on Trial: The Institution and Psychology of Rape." The CWLU Herstory Website Archive of Classic Feminist Writings, http://www.cwluherstory.com/CWLUArchive/vaginatrial.html.

Beckford, William. 1887. *The History of the Caliph Vathek*. London: Cassell & Company.

Bianchin, Helen. 1996. *Desert Mistress*. Harlequin Mills & Boon.

Bickerstaffe, Isaac. 1782. "The Sultan, or, A Peep into the Seraglio" (1775). In *Collection of the Most Esteemed Farces and Entertainments Performed on the British Stage*. Vol. 1. Edinburgh: C. Elliot, 310–326.

Bode, Margo. 1981. *Jasmine Splendor*. New York: Gallen/Pocket Books.

Boiardo, Matteo Maria. 1995. *Orlando Innamorato*, translated by Charles Stanley Ross. Oxford: Oxford University Press.

Brockman, Suzanne. 2002. *Into the Night*. New York: Ballantine.

Buchan, John. 1964. *Greenmantle* (1916). Harmondsworth: Penguin.

Byron, Lord. 1898. *The Works of Lord Byron: Letters and Journals*. Vol. 2, edited by Rowland E. Prothero. London: John Murray. Project Gutenberg eBook #9921. http://www.gutenberg.org/etext/9921.

———. 1900. *The Works of Lord Byron*. Vol. 3, edited by Ernest Harley Coleridge. London: John Murray. Project Gutenberg eBook #21811. http://www.gutenberg.org/etext/21811.

Cinthio, Giraldo. 1885. *Hecatommithi* (1565), translated by J. E. Taylor, digitized by Stephen L. Parker. http://www.virgil.org/dswo/courses/shakespeare-survey/cinthio.pdf.

Civil Rights Act of 1964—CRA—Title VII—Equal Employment Opportunities—42 U.S. Chapter Code 21.

Conquest, Joan. 1920. *Desert Love*. New York: Macaulay.

———. 1922. *The Hawk of Egypt*. New York: Macaulay.

Corelli, Marie. 1892. *The Soul of Lilith*. London: Richard Bentley & Son.

———. 1897. *Ziska: The Problem of a Wicked Soul*. Bristol: Arrowsmith.

Coulter, Catherine. 2000. *Devil's Daughter* (1985). New York: Signet.

Craig, Jasmine. 1988. *The Devil's Envoy*. New York: Berkley.

Creighton, Kathleen. 2002. *Virgin Seduction*. New York: Silhouette Intimate Moments.

Crusie, Jennifer. April 14, 2007. "Please Remove Your Assumptions, They're Sitting on My Genre." *Argh Ink*, http://www.arghink.com/2007/04/14/please-remove-your-assumptions-theyre-sitting-on-my-genre/.

Darcy, Emma. 1988. *The Falcon's Mistress*. Harlequin Mills & Boon.

———. 1993. *The Sheikh's Revenge*. Harlequin Mills & Boon.

———. 1995. *Climax of Passion*. Harlequin Mills & Boon.

———. 1998. *The Sheikh's Seduction*. Harlequin Mills & Boon.

———. 2005. *Traded to the Sheikh*. Harlequin Mills & Boon.

Darrach, Brad. January 17, 1977. "Rosemary's Babies." *Time*.

Daveson, Mons. 1982. *My Lord Kasseem*. London: Mills & Boon Ltd.

Delk, Karen Jones. 1992. *The Bride Price*. New York: HarperCollins.

Diamond, Jacqueline. 1998. *How to Marry A Real-Live Sheikh*. Harlequin.

———. 2000. *Captured by a Sheikh*. Harlequin.

Diver, Maud. 1910. *Lilamani: A Study in Possibilities*. Edinburgh: William Blackwood & Sons.

———. 1921. *Far to Seek: A Romance of England and India*. Edinburgh: William Blackwood & Sons.

Dunaway, Diane. 1982. *Desert Hostage*. New York: Dell.

Dunn, Carola. 1996. *Scandal's Daughter*. New York: Zebra.

Edwards, Sarah. 1989. *Fire and Sand*. New York: St. Martin's Press.

Faith, Barbara. 1984. *Bedouin Bride*. New York: Silhouette.

———. 1988. *Flower of the Desert*. New York: Silhouette.

———. 1990. *Lord of the Desert*. New York: Silhouette.

Favart, Charles-Simon. 1817. *Les Trois Sultanes, ou, Soliman Second* (1761). Paris: Imprimerie de Fain.

Fitzgerald, Julia. 1978. *Royal Slave*. London: Troubadour.

———. 1985. *Silken Captive*. New York: Pinnacle.

Forbes, Rosita. 1921. "Where There Ain't No Ten Commandments." *Health and Physical Culture*. July 1, 45.

———. 1922. *Quest: The Story of Anne, Three Men, and Some Arabs*. London: Cassell.

———. 1925. *If the Gods Laugh*. London: Thornton Butterworth.

———. 1927. *Sirocco*. London: Thornton Butterworth.

———. 1944. *A Gypsy in the Sun*. New York: E. Dutton & Co.

Gerard, Louise. 1915. *Flower-of-the-Moon*. London: Mills & Boon.

———. 1921. *A Sultan's Slave*. London: Mills & Boon.

Glyn, Elinor. 2006. *Three Weeks* (1907). Teddington, Middlesex: The Echo Library.

Golon, Sergeanne. 1961. *Angélique and the Sultan*. London: Heinemann.

Grasso, Patricia. 1993. *Desert Eden*. New York: Dell.

Haskell, Molly. November 1976. "Rape Fantasy: The 2000-Year-Old Misunderstanding." *Ms. Magazine*, 84–86, 92–98.

Hastings, Juliet. 1996. *Forbidden Crusade*. London: Black Lace.

Hatcher, Robin Lee. 1987. *Pirate's Lady*. New York: Leisure Books.

Hazm, Ibn. 1997. *The Ring of the Dove: A Treatise on the Art and Practice of Arab Love*, translated by A. J. Arberry. London: Luzac & Co.

Herries, Anne. 1992. *Captive of the Harem*. New York: Harlequin.

Hichens, Robert. 2010. *The Garden of Allah* (1904). Forgotten Books. http://www.forgottenbooks.org/info/9781440095160.

———. 1910. *The Spell of Egypt*. London: Hodder.

Hilliard, Nerina. 1976. *The Land of the Sun*. Harlequin Mills & Boon.

Hoke, Zlatica. 2006. "America's Muslims after 9/11." *Voice of America News*. September 10, http://www.voanews.com/english/archive/2006-09/Muslims2006-09-10-voa17.cfm?CFID=8727293&CFTOKEN=80191078

Holt, Victoria. 1989. *The Captive*. New York: Doubleday.

Hujer, Marc, and Daniel Steinvorth. 2007. "A Lesson for Europe. American Muslims strive to become model citizens," translated by Christopher Sultan. *Der Spiegel*. September 13, http://www.spiegel.de/international/world/0,1518,505573-2,00.html.

Hull, E. M. 1921. *The Sheik*. New York: Bucaneer.

———. 1976. *The Sons of the Sheik* (1925). New York: American Reprint Company.

———. Papers. Reference 7EMH. The Women's Library, London Metropolitan University.

Jackson, Brenda. 2002. *Delaney's Desert Sheikh*. New York: Silhouette.

Jehl, Douglas, and Elizabeth Becker. April 16, 2003. "A Nation at War: The Looting; Experts' Pleas to Pentagon Didn't Save Museum." *The New York Times.*

Johansen, Iris. 1988. *Strong, Hot Winds*. New York: Loveswept.

Jordan, Nicole. 1992. *Lord of Desire*. New York: Avon.

Jordan, Penny. 1981. *Falcon's Prey*. Harlequin Mills & Boon.

———. 2003. *One Night with the Sheikh*. Harlequin Mills & Boon.

———. 2003. *The Sheikh's Virgin Bride*. Harlequin Mills & Boon.

Kendrick, Sharon. 2007. *The Desert King's Virgin Bride*. Harlequin Mills & Boon.

———. 2007. *The Sheikh's English Bride*. Harlequin Mills & Boon.

Kerbaj, R. 2006. "Muslim leader blames women for sex attacks." *The Australian.* October 26, http://www.theaustralian.news.com.au/story/0,20867,20646437-601,00 .html.

Krentz, Jayne Ann. 1992. "Trying to Tame the Romance: Critics and Correctness." In *Dangerous Men and Adventurous Women: Romance Writers on the Appeal of the Romance*, edited by Jayne Ann Krentz. Philadelphia: University of Pennsylvania Press.

Lamb, Charlotte. 1978. *Desert Barbarian*. Harlequin Mills & Boon.

Lawrence, Kim. 2008. *Desert Prince, Defiant Virgin*. Harlequin Mills & Boon.

Lee, Miranda. 1993. *Beth and the Barbarian*. Harlequin Mills & Boon.

———. 2006. *Love-Slave to the Sheikh*. Harlequin Mills & Boon.

Lindsey, Johanna. 1977. *Captive Bride*. New York: Avon Books.

———. 1988. *Silver Angel*. New York: Avon.

Lyons, Mary. 1986. *Escape from the Harem*. Harlequin Mills & Boon.

Malek, Doreen Owens. 1994. *The Panther and the Pearl*. New York: Dorchester.

———. 1996. *Panther's Prey*. New York: Dorchester Publishing.

Malik, Sarah. 2006. "Lakemba shakes the sheik." *Sydney Morning Herald.* October 26, http://www.smh.com.au/news/national/lakemba-shakes-the-sheik/2006/10/ 26/1161749248850.html.

Mallery, Susan. 2002. *The Sheik and the Virgin Princess*. New York: Silhouette.

———. 2005. *The Sheik and the Virgin Secretary*. New York: Silhouette.

Marmontel, Jean-François. 1824. "Soliman II." *Contes Moraux* (1761). Paris: Chèz Verdière, Libraire, 34–55.

Marsh, Richard. 1897. *The Beetle*. London: Skeffington & Son.

Marton, Dana. 2005. *The Sheik's Safety*. Toronto: Harlequin Intrigue.

———. 2008. *Sheik Protector*. Toronto: Harlequin Intrigue.

———. 2008. *The Sheikh's Wayward Wife*. Harlequin Mills & Boon.

———. 2009. *Desert Ice Daddy*. Toronto: Harlequin Intrigue.

Marton, Sandra. 2008. *The Sheikh's Rebellious Mistress*. Harlequin Mills & Boon.

Mason, Connie. 1988. *Desert Ecstasy*. New York: Leisure Books.

———. 1997. *Sheik*. New York: Leisure Books.

———. 2004. *The Pirate Prince*. New York: Dorchester.

Mather, Anne. 1980. *Sandstorm*. London: Mills & Boon.

Mayne, Elizabeth. 1996. *The Sheik and the Vixen*. New York: Silhouette.

McCullough, Christy. 2007. "Desert Hearts." *BITCH: Feminist Response to Pop Culture*. Risk Issue, 36, http://bitchmagazine.org/article/desert-hearts.

McMahon, Barbara. 1996. *Sheik Daddy*. New York: Silhouette.

Michael, Kasey. 2000. *The Sheikh's Secret Son*. Harlequin.

Miller, Linda Lael. 1993. *Taming Charlotte*. New York: Pocket Books.

Mills, Dorothy. 1922. *The Tent of Blue*. London: Duckworth.

Minger, Miriam. 1991. *Captive Rose*. New York: Avon.

Mittermeyer, Helen. 1996. *The Veil*. New York: Grand Central Publishing.

Monroe, Lucy. 2008. *Hired: The Sheikh's Secretary Mistress*. Harlequin Mills & Boon.

Montagu, Lady Mary Wortley. 1790. *The Letters of the Right Honourable Lady M-y W-y M-e Written during Her Travels in Europe, Asia and Africa to Persons of Distinction, Men of Letters, &c. in Different Parts of Europe*. London: Thomas Martin.

Montesquieu, Charles-Louis de Secondat, Baron de. 1964. *The Persian Letters* (1721), translated by George R. Healy. Indianapolis: Bobbs-Merill.

Morey, Trish. 2008. *The Sheikh's Convenient Virgin*. Harlequin Mills & Boon.

Morgan, Sarah. 2005. *In the Sheikh's Marriage Bed*. Harlequin Mills & Boon.

———. 2007. *The Sultan's Virgin Bride*. Harlequin Mills & Boon.

———. 2007. *The Sheikh's Virgin Princess*. Harlequin Mills & Boon.

Murray, Elicia. 2009. "Sydney Islamic school rejected." *Sydney Morning Herald*. June 2, http://www.smh.com.au/national/sydney-islamic-school-rejected-20090602-btfo .html.

Nicholson, Christina. 1978. *The Savage Sands*. New York: Fawcett Crest.

North, Miranda. 1989. *Desert Slave*. New York: Zebra.

Orderic Vitalis. 1968–1980. *The Ecclesiastical History of Orderic Vitalis* (1130–1135), edited and translated by Marjorie Chibnall. 6 vols. Oxford: Clarendon.

Pargeter, Margaret. 1978. *The Jewelled Caftan*. Harlequin Mills & Boon.

Powell, Enoch. April 20, 1968. "Speech to the Conservative Association Meeting in Birmingham." Reproduced in *The Telegraph*. November 6, 2007.

Raoulemont, Therese. 1931. "Captive in a Sheik's Harem." *Health and Physical Culture*. September 1, 26–7, 37, 39, 45.

Reardon, Patrick T. April 24, 2006. "The Mystery of Sheik Romance Novels." *Chicago Tribune*.

Redd, Joanne. 1989. *Desert Bride*. New York: Dell Publishing.

Rhodes, Kathlyn. 1909. *The Desert Dreamers*. London: Hutchinson.

———. 1920. *The Relentless Desert*. London: Hutchinson.

Riefe, Barbara. 1980. *So Wicked the Heart*. Chicago: Playboy Paperbacks.

Roberts, Nora. 1989. *Sweet Revenge*. New York: Bantam.

Rogers, Evelyn. 1990. *Wanton Slave*. New York: Zebra.

Rogers, Rosemary. 2002. *Wicked Loving Lies* (1976). New York: Mira.

Rome, Margaret. 1972. *Bride of the Rif*. London: Mills & Boon.

Sellers, Alexandra. 1997. *Bride of the Sheikh*. New York: Silhouette.

———. 1999. *Solitary Sheikh*. New York: Silhouette.

Seymour, Janette. 1978. *Purity's Ecstasy*. New York: Pocket Books.

Shaw, Chantelle. 2008. *At the Sheikh's Bidding*. Harlequin Mills & Boon.

Showalter, Elaine. August 10, 2002. "Rereadings." *The Guardian*.

Small, Bertrice. 1978. *The Kadin*. New York: Avon Books.

———. 1980. *Skye O'Malley*. New York: Ballantine.

———. 1995. *Love Slave*. New York: Fawcett Crest.

Smith, Bobbi. 1992. *Capture My Heart*. New York: Zebra.

Southwick, Teresa. 2003. *To Catch a Sheik*. Harlequin Mills & Boon.

———. 2003. *To Kiss a Sheik*. Harlequin Mills & Boon.

Stephens, Susan. 2005. *The Sheikh's Captive Bride*. Harlequin Mills & Boon.

———. 2007. *The Sheikh's English Bride*. Harlequin Mills & Boon.

Stopes, Marie. 1918. *Married Love, or Love in Marriage*. London: Putnam.

The Ritchie Report. December 11, 2001. Produced by the Oldham Independent Review
for the Oldham Metropolitan Borough Council.

Whitaker, Brian. 2006. "Those Sexy Arabs." *The Guardian*. March 23, http://comment
isfree.guardian.co.uk/brian_whitaker/2006/03/those_sexy_arabs.html

Wilding, Lynne. 1991. *The Sheikh*. New York: Silhouette Books.

Winspear, Violet. 1969. *Blue Jasmine*. London: Mills & Boon.

———. 1970. *Tawny Sands*. London: Mills & Boon.

———. 1976. *The Burning Sands*. London: Mills & Boon.

———. 1985. *The Sun Lord's Woman*. London: Mills & Boon.

Winstead Jones, Linda. 2002. *Secret-Agent Sheik*. New York: Silhouette.

Wood, Sara. 1986. *Perfumes of Arabia*. Harlequin Mills & Boon.

FILMS

Bolero. Directed by John Derek. 1984. Cannon Films, USA.

Harem. Directed by Arthur Joffé. 1985. Sara Films, France.

Harem. Directed by William Hale. 1986. Highgate Pictures/New World Pictures, USA.

Harum Scarum. Directed by Gene Nelson. 1965. MGM, USA.

Lost in a Harem. Directed by Charles Reisner. 1944. Metro-Goldwyn-Mayer, USA.

Sahara. Directed by Andrew McLaglen. 1983. MGM, USA.

The Man Who Knew Too Much. Directed by Alfred Hitchcock. Paramount Pictures,
USA.

The Road to Morocco. Directed by David Butler. 1942. Paramount Pictures, USA.

The Sheik. Directed by George Melford. 1921. Famous Players-Lasky, USA.

The Son of the Sheik. Directed by George Fitzmaurice. 1926. Feature Productions, USA.

PERIODICALS

Bioscope	*The Australian*
Bloomberg Weekly	*The Economist*
Der Spiegel	*The Guardian*
Kinematograph Weekly	*The Sydney Morning Herald*
New York Magazine	*The Times*
Photoplay	*Time*
Pictureplay	*Voice of America News*

WEBSITES

Australian Government Department of Foreign Affairs and Trade. 2008. "Saudi Arabia Country Brief—January 2008." http://www.dfat.gov.au/geo/saudi_arabia/saudi_brief.html.

"Bertelsmann Club Interview with Kathleen E. Woodiwiss." October 2000. Posted on Forumwise website, November 17, 2006, http://kwoodiwiss.forumwise.com/kwoodiwiss-thread39.html. Accessed November 2009.

Bolton, Gwyneth. "Reading and Writing African American Romance." Posted June 12, 2007, http://gwynethbolton.blogspot.com/2007/06/bitch-magazine-does-romance.html. Accessed November 2009.

Fielding, Liz. 2009. "The Appeal of the Sheikh." http://community.eharlequin.com/content/appeal-sheikh. Accessed July 2011.

Harlequin website, http://www.eharlequin.com/au

http://pinkheartsociety.blogspot.com/

http://romancereaderatheart.com/sheik/Authors.html

http://romancing-the-desert---sheikh-books.blogspot.com/

http://shabbysheikh.blogspot.com/

http://sheikhs-and-desert-love.com/

http://splumonium.com/DIR_romance/research.htm

http://teachmetonight.blogspot.com/

http://www.amazon.com/Captive-Bride-Johanna-Lindsey/dp/0380016974/ref=pd_bbs_sr_1?ie=UTF8&s=books&qid=1213858412&sr=1-1. Accessed November 2009.

http://www.amazon.com/Delaneys-Desert-Sheikh-Brenda-Jackson/product-reviews/0373764731/ref=dp_top_cm_cr_acr_txt?ie=UTF8&showViewpoints=1. Accessed November 2009.

http://www.amazon.com/Kadin-Bertrice-Small/dp/0727817434/ref=sr_1_1?ie=UTF8&s=books&qid=1213856041&sr=1-1. Accessed November 2009.

http://www.amazon.com/Love-Slave-Bertrice-Small/dp/0449002136/ref=pd_sim_b_2. Accessed November 2009.

http://www.amazon.com/Secret-Agent-Romancing-Silhouette-Intimate-Moments/

dp/037327212X/ref=sr_1_1?ie=UTF8&s=books&qid=1259478079&sr=1-1. Accessed November 2009.

http://www.amazon.com/Sheik-Daddy-Romance-Barbara-McMahon/dp/0263 157911/ref=sr_1_1?ie=UTF8&s=books&qid=1259484655&sr=1-1. Accessed November 2009.

http://www.amazon.com/Sheiks-Kidnapped-Bride-Desert-Rogues/dp/0373243162/ ref=pd_sim_b_2. Accessed November 2009.

http://www.amazon.com/Sheik-Seduction-Harlequin-Intrigue-Marton/dp/0373 693060/ref=sr_1_1?ie=UTF8&s=books&qid=1259483921&sr=1-1. Accessed November 2009.

http://www.amazon.com/Sheik-Vixen-Silhouette-Intimate-Moments/dp/0373 077556/ref=sr_1_1?ie=UTF8&qid=1259478043&sr=1-1-fkmro. Accessed November 2009.

http://www.amazon.com/Sheiks-Safety-Harlequin-Intrigue/dp/0373228597/ref=sr_1_ 1?ie=UTF8&s=books&qid=1259477996&sr=1-1. Accessed November 2009.

http://www.amazon.com/Sheikhs-Secret-Bride-Susan-Mallery/dp/0373049099/ref=s r_1_1?ie=UTF8&s=books&qid=1259477868&sr=1-1. Accessed November 2009.

http://www.amazon.com/Solitary-Sheikh-Desert-Silhouette-Desire/dp/0373762178/ ref=sr_1_1?ie=UTF8&s=books&qid=1259482833&sr=1-1. Accessed November 2009.

http://www.amazon.com/Sweet-Revenge-Nora-Roberts/dp/0553386417/ref=sr_1_1?ie =UTF8&s=books&qid=1259485773&sr=1-1. Accessed November 2009.

http://www.amazon.com/Wicked-Loving-Lies-Rosemary-Rogers/dp/1551669277/ref =sr_1_1?ie=UTF8&s=books&qid=1214206340&sr=8-1. Accessed November 2009.

http://www.mrsgiggles.com/books/morgan_princess.html. Accessed November 2009.

http://www.mrsgiggles.com/books/palmer_desert.html. Accessed November 2009.

http://www.romancingtheblog.com/blog/

Internet Movie Database, http://www.imdb.com/

Mrs. Giggles, http://www.mrsgiggles.com/. Accessed November 2009.

Romance Writers of America, http://www.rwanational.org/.

Shoemaker, Marilyn. http://romancing-the-desert---sheikh-books.blogspot.com/ 2006/10/sheikh-article-chicago-tribune-i-had.html. Accessed November 2009.

Tan, Candy. "Meg Cabot, Comfort Reads and Sheikh Romance." Smart Bitches Trashy Books website, http://www.smartbitchestrashybooks.com/index.php/weblog/ comments/meg_cabot_comfort_reads_and_sheikh_romance/. Accessed July 2011.

West, Annie. 2008. "The Lure of the Sheikh Hero." Down Under Desirabelles website, http://desirabelles.wordpress.com/2008/11/02/the-lure-of-the-sheikh-hero-by-annie-west/. Accessed July 2011.

"The World of Angélique." Official website of Anne Golon's historical novels, http:// www.worldofangelique.com/anneor.htm. Accessed November 2009.

SECONDARY SOURCES

Abu-Haidar, J. A. 2001. *Hispano-Arabic Literature and the Early Provençal Lyrics*. Richmond, Surrey: Curzon Press.

Adams, Michael C.C. 1990. *The Great Adventure: Male Desire and the Coming of World War I*. Bloomington: Indiana University Press.

Ahmed, Leila. 1982. "Western Ethnocentrism and Perceptions of the Harem." *Feminist Studies* 8: 521–534.

Akbari, Suzanne Conklin. 2009. *Idols in the East: European Representations of Islam and the Orient, 1100–1450*. Ithaca: Cornell University Press.

Akram, Susan M. 2002. "The Aftermath of September 11, 2001: The Targeting of Arabs and Muslims in America." *Arab Studies Quarterly* 24: 61–119.

Allen, Roger M. A. 1998. *The Arabic Literary Heritage*. New York: Cambridge University Press.

Alloula, Malek. 1986. *The Colonial Harem*. Minneapolis: University of Minnesota Press.

Alsultany, Evelyn. 2007. "Selling American Diversity and Muslim American Identity through Nonprofit Advertising Post-9/11." *American Quarterly* 59: 593–622.

———. 2008. "The Prime-Time Plight of the Arab Muslim American after 9/11." *Race and Arab Americans Before and After 9/11: From Invisible Citizens to Visible Subjects*, edited by Amaney Jamal and Christine Naber. New York: Syracuse University Press, 204–228.

Anderson, Rachel. 1974. *The Purple Heart Throbs: The Subliterature of Love*. London: Hodder & Stoughton.

Ardis, Ann. 1996. "E. M. Hull, Mass Market Romance and the New Woman Novel in the Early Twentieth Century." *Women's Writing* 3: 287–296.

Augstein, Hannah Franziska. 1996. Introduction to *Race: The Origins of an Idea, 1760–1850*, edited by H. F. Augstein. Bristol: Thoemmes Press.

Aune, M. G. 2005. "Early Modern European Travel Writing after Orientalism." *Journal for Early Modern Cultural Studies* 5: 120–138.

Bach, Evelyn. 1996. "Sheik Fantasies: Orientalism and Feminine Desire." *Hecate* 23: 9–40.

Baepler, Paul. 1999. *White Slaves, African Masters: An Anthology of American Barbary Captivity Narratives*. Chicago: University of Chicago Press.

Bailey, Beth. 1994. "Sexual Revolution(s)." *The Sixties: From Memory to History*, edited by David Farber. Chapel Hill: University of North Carolina Press, 235–262.

Baines, Barbara J. 1998. "Effacing Rape in Early Modern Representation." *ELH* 65: 69–98.

Bakalian, Anny, and Mehdi Bozorgmeh. 2009. *Backlash 9/11: Middle Eastern and Muslim Americans Respond*. Berkeley and Los Angeles: University of California Press.

Baldwin, M. Page. 2001. "Subject to Empire: Married Women and the British Nationality and Status of Aliens Act." *The Journal of British Studies* 40: 522–556.

Ballaster, Ros. 2008. *Fabulous Orients: Fictions of the East in England, 1662–1785*. New York: Oxford University Press.

Bart, Pauline B., and Patricia H. O'Brien. 1985. *Stopping Rape: Successful Survival Strategies*. New York: Pergamon.

Bartlett, Robert. 2001. "Medieval and Modern Concepts of Race and Ethnicity." *Journal of Medieval and Early Modern Studies* 31: 39–56.

Baudrillard, Jean. 1988. *America*, translated by Chris Turner. New York: Verso.

Beauman, Nicola. 1983. *A Very Great Profession: The Woman's Novel, 1914–1939*. London: Virago.

Behdad, Ali. 1994. *Belated Travelers: Orientalism in the Age of Colonial Dissolution*. Durham: Duke University Press.

Belsey, Catherine. 1994. *Desire: Love Stories in Western Culture*. Oxford: Blackwell.

Bent, J. Theodore, 1890. "The English in the Levant." *The English Historical Review* 5: 654–664.

Bernstein, M., and Gaylyn Studlar, editors. 1997. *Visions of the East: Orientalism in Film*. New Brunswick: Rutgers University Press.

Bernstein, Richard. 2009. *The East, the West, and Sex*. New York: Alfred A. Knopf.

Blake, Susan L. 1992. "A Woman's Trek: What Difference Does Gender Make?" In *Western Women and Imperialism: Complicity and Resistance*, edited by Nupur Chaudhuri and Margaret Strobel. Bloomington: Indiana University Press, 19–34.

———. 2003. "What 'Race' is the Sheik? Rereading a Desert Romance." In *Doubled Plots: Romance and History*, edited by Susan Strehle and Mary Paniccia Carden. Jackson: University Press of Mississippi, 67–85.

Bland, Lucy. 1995. *Banishing the Beast: Sexuality and the Early Feminists*. London: Penguin.

———. 2005. "White Women and Men of Colour: Miscegenation Fears in Britain after the Great War." *Gender & History* 17: 29–61.

Boase, Roger. 1977. *The Origin and Meaning of Courtly Love: A Critical Study of European Scholarship*. Manchester: Manchester University Press.

Boorstin, Daniel J. 1975. "From Traveler to Tourist: The Lost Art of Travel." In *The Image: A Guide to Pseudo-Events in America*. New York: Atheneum, 77–117.

Brenchley, Frank. 1989. *Britain and the Middle East: An Economic History 1945–87*. London: Lester Crook Academic Publishing.

Brownmiller, Susan. 1975. *Against Our Will: Men, Women and Rape*. New York: Simon and Schuster.

Brundage, James A. 1987. *Law, Sex and Christian Society in Medieval Europe*. Chicago: University of Chicago Press.

———. 1995. "Prostitution, Miscegenation and Sexual Purity in the First Crusade." In *Crusade and Settlement*, edited by Peter W. Edbury. Cardiff: University College Cardiff Press, 57–65.

Burge, Amy. 2008. "Getting Medieval: The Use of the Medieval in Modern Popular Romance Fiction." MA thesis. University of York.

———. 2011a. "Dangerous Desire: Sexuality, Ethnicity and Miscegenation in Contemporary Sheikh Mills & Boon Romance and *The King of Tars*." Conference paper presented at the Popular Culture Association Conference, San Antonio, April 20.

———. 2011b. "Desiring the East: A Diachronic Study of Middle English Romance and Modern Popular Sheikh Romance." PhD thesis. Centre for Women's Studies, University of York.

Burnham, Michelle. 1997. *Captivity and Sentiment: Cultural Exchange in American Literature, 1682–1861*. Dartmouth: University Press of New England.

Burton, Antoinette. 1994. *Burdens of History: British Feminists, Indian Women and Imperial Culture*. Chapel Hill: University of North Carolina Press.

Buzard, James. 1993. *The Beaten Track: European Tourism, Literature, and the Ways to Culture 1800–1918*. Oxford: Oxford University Press.

Cadogan, Mary. 1994. *And Then Their Hearts Stood Still*. London: Macmillan.

Cainkar, Louise. 2004. "The Impact of the September Attacks and their Aftermath on Arab and Muslim Communities in the United States." *GSC Quarterly* 13, http://www.ssrc.org.

Callaway, Helen. 1987. *Gender, Culture and Empire: European Women in Colonial Nigeria*. Urbana & Chicago: University of Illinois Press.

Cancian, Francesca M. 1987. *Love in America: Gender and Self-Development*. Cambridge: Cambridge University Press.

Cannadine, David. 2002. *Ornamentalism: How the British Saw Their Empire*. London: Penguin.

Caton, Steven C. 2000. "*The Sheik*: Instabilities of Race and Gender in Transatlantic Popular Culture of the Early 1920s." In *Noble Dreams Wicked Pleasures: Orientalism in America, 1870–1930*, edited by Holly Edwards. Princeton: Princeton University Press, 99–117.

Chaudhuri, Nupur, and Margaret Strobel, editors. 1992. *Western Women and Imperialism: Complicity and Resistance*. Bloomington: Indiana University Press.

Chow, Karen. 1999. "Popular Sexual Knowledges and Women's Agency in 1920s England: Marie Stopes's 'Married Love' and E. M. Hull's 'The Sheik.'" *Feminist Review* 63: 64–87.

Christison, Kathleen. 1987. "The Arab in Recent Popular Fiction." *Middle East Journal* 41: 397–411.

Cochran, P., editor. 2006. *Byron and Orientalism*. Newcastle: Cambridge Scholars Publishing.

Cohen, Jeffrey Jerome. 2001. "On Saracen Enjoyment: Some Fantasies of Race in Late Medieval France and England." *Journal of Medieval and Early Modern Studies* 31: 113–146.

Cohn, Jan. 1988. *Romance and the Erotics of Property: Mass-Market Fiction for Women*. Durham and London: Duke University Press.

Colley, Linda. 2002. *Captives: Britain, Empire and the World 1600–1850*. London: Jonathan Cape.

Colligan, Colette. 2003. "'A Race of Born Pederasts': Sir Richard Burton, Homosexuality, and the Arabs." *Nineteenth-Century Contexts* 25: 1–20.

———. 2006. *The Traffic in Obscenity from Byron to Beardsley: Sexuality and Exoticism in Nineteenth-Century Print Culture*. London: Palgrave.

Collins, Marcus. 2001. "Pride and Prejudice: West Indian Men in Mid-Twentieth-Century-Britain." *Journal of British Studies* 40: 391–418.

Conant, Martha Pike. 1966. *The Oriental Tale in England in the Eighteenth Century* (1908). London: Frank Cass.

Cook, Hera. 2004. *The Long Sexual Revolution: English Women, Sex and Contraception, 1800–1975*. Oxford: Oxford University Press.

Daniel, Norman. 1966. *Islam, Europe and Empire*. Edinburgh: Edinburgh University Press.

Davis, Fanny. 1986. *The Ottoman Lady: A Social History from 1718 to 1918*. Westport, CT: Greenwood Press.

Davis, Robert C. 2004. *Christian Slaves, Muslim Masters: White Slavery in the Mediterranean, the Barbary Coast and Italy, 1500–1800*. Houndsmill: Palgrave Macmillan.

Dawson, Graham. 1994. *Soldier Heroes: British Adventure, Empire and the Imagining of Masculinities*. London: Routledge.

Deacon, Desley, Penny Russell, and Angela Woollacott, editors. 2010. *Transnational Lives: Biographies of Global Modernity, 1700–Present*. London: Palgrave Macmillan.

De Groot, Joanna. 1989. "'Sex' and 'Race': The Construction of Language and Image in the Nineteenth Century." In *Sexuality and Subordination: Interdisciplinary Studies of Gender in the Nineteenth Century*, edited by Susan Mendus and Jane Rendall. London: Routledge, 89–131.

———. 2006. "Oriental Feminotopias? Montagu's and Montesquieu's 'Seraglios' Revisited." *Gender & History* 18: 66–86.

DelPlato, Joan. 2002. *Multiple Wives, Multiple Pleasures: Representing the Harem, 1800–1875*. Cranbury and London: Associated University Press.

Denzin, Norman K., and Yvonna S. Lincoln, editors. 2003. *9/11 in American Culture*. Walnut Creek, CA: AltaMira Press.

Derounian-Stodola, Kathryn Zabelle. 1993. *The Indian Captivity Narrative, 1550–1900*. New York: Twayne.

Diamond, Michael. 2006. *"Lesser Breeds": Racial Attitudes in Popular British Culture, 1890–1940*. London: Anthem.

Dixon, Jay. 1999. *The Romance Fiction of Mills & Boon 1909–1990s*. London: UCL Press.

Docker, John. 1994. *Postmodernism and Popular Culture: A Cultural History*. Cambridge: Cambridge University Press.

Dolar, Mladen. 1998. "Introduction: The Subject Supposed to Enjoy." In *The Sultan's Court: European Fantasies of the East*, by Alain Grosrichard, translated by Liz Heron. London and New York: Verso, ix–xxvii.

Donaldson, Laura E. 1992. *Decolonizing Feminisms: Race, Gender and Empire-Building*. Chapel Hill: University of North Carolina Press.

Douglas, Ann. 1980. "Soft-Porn Culture: Punishing the Liberated Woman." *The New Republic* 183: 25–29.

Dubino, Jeanne. 1993. "The Cinderella Complex: Romance Fiction, Patriarchy and Capitalism." *Journal of Popular Culture* 27: 103–118.

Dyer, Richard. 1997. *White*. London and New York: Routledge.

Edwards, Holly. 2000. "A Million and One Nights: Orientalism in America, 1870–1930." In *Noble Dreams, Wicked Pleasures: Orientalism in America, 1870–1930*, edited by Holly Edwards. Princeton: Princeton University Press, 11–57.

Eisele, John C. 2002. "The Wild East: Deconstructing the Language of Genre in the Hollywood Eastern." *Cinema Journal* 41: 68–94.

Eisenstein, Zillah. 2004. *Against Empire: Feminisms, Racisms, and the West*. London and New York: Zed Books.

Elmarsafy, Ziad. 2001. "Submission, Seduction, and State Propaganda in Favart's Soliman II, ou Les trois sultanes." *French Forum* 26: 13–26.

Emsley, Clive. 2008. "Violent crime in England in 1919: Post-War Anxieties and Press Narratives." *Continuity and Change* 23: 173–195.

Felski, Rita. 1995. *The Gender of Modernity*. Cambridge, MA: Harvard University Press.

Ferguson, Margaret W. 1999. Foreword to *Menacing Virgins: Representing Virginity in the Middle Ages and Renaissance*, edited by Kathleen Coyne Kelly and Marina Leslie. Newark: Associated University Presses, 7.

Flesch, Juliet. 2004. *From Australia with Love: A History of Modern Australian Popular Romance Novels*. Fremantle: Curtin University Press.

Foster, Shirley. 1992. *Across New Worlds: Nineteenth-Century Women Travellers and Their Writings*. London: Harvester Wheatsheaf.

Foucault, Michel. 1978. *The History of Sexuality, Vol. 1: An Introduction*. Harmondsworth: Penguin.

Fowler, Bridget. 1991. *The Alienated Reader: Women and Romantic Literature in the Twentieth Century*. London: Harvester Wheatsheaf.

Frenier, Mariam Darce. 1988. *Good-bye Heathcliff: Changing Heroes, Heroines, Roles, and Values in Women's Category Romances*. New York: Greenwood.

Fussell, Paul. 1975. *The Great War and Modern Memory*. New York: Oxford University Press.

———. 1980. *Abroad: British Literary Traveling Between the Wars*. New York and Oxford: Oxford University Press.

Gallini, Clara. 1988. "Arabesque: Images of a Myth." *Cultural Studies* 2: 168–180.

Gargano, Elizabeth. 2006. "'English Sheiks' and Arab Stereotypes: E. M. Hull, T. E. Lawrence, and the Imperial Masquerade." *Texas Studies in Literature and Language* 48: 171–186.

Garrett, Cynthia E. 2004. "Sexual Consent and the Art of Love in the Early Modern English Lyric." *SEL* 44: 37–58.

Gerges, Fawaz A. 2003. "Islam and Muslims in the Mind of America." *Annals of the American Academy of Political and Social Science* 588: 73–89.

Gerhard, Jane. 2001. *Desiring Revolution: Second-Wave Feminism and the Rewriting of American Sexual Thought, 1920 to 1982*. New York: Columbia University Press.

Giffin, Lois Anita. 1971. *Theory of Profane Love Among the Arabs: The Development of the Genre*. New York: New York University Press.

Gilman, Sander L. 1985a. "Black Bodies, White Bodies: Toward an Iconography of

Female Sexuality and Late Nineteenth-Century Art, Medicine, and Literature." *Critical Inquiry* 12: 202–242.

———. 1985b. *Difference and Pathology: Stereotypes of Sexuality, Race and Madness.* Ithaca: Cornell University Press.

Giroux, Henry A. 2003. "Terrorism and the Fate of Democracy after September 11." In *9/11 in American Culture*, edited by Norman K. Denzin and Yvonna S. Lincoln. Walnut Creek, CA: AltaMira Press, 4–8.

Glick, Thomas F. 1979. *Islamic and Christian Spain in the Early Middle Ages.* Princeton: Princeton University Press.

Goade, Sally, editor. 2007. *Empowerment versus Oppression: Twenty First Century Views of Popular Romance.* Newcastle: Cambridge Scholars Publishing.

Grabar, Oleg. 2000. "Roots and Others." In *Noble Dreams, Wicked Pleasures: Orientalism in America, 1870–1930*, edited by Holly Edwards. Princeton: Princeton University Press, 3–10.

Greer, Germaine. 1970. *The Female Eunuch.* London: McGibbon & Kee.

Grescoe, Paul. 1996. *The Merchants of Venus: Inside Harlequin and the Empire of Romance.* Vancouver: Raincoast Books.

Grewal, Inderpal. 1996. *Home and Harem: Nation, Gender, Empire, and the Cultures of Travel.* Durham, North Carolina: Duke University Press.

Griffin, Susan. 1981. *Pornography and Silence: Culture's Revenge Against Nature.* New York: Harper & Row.

Grosrichard, Alain. 1998. *The Sultan's Court: European Fantasies of the East*, translated by Liz Heron. London and New York: Verso.

Gualtieri, Sara. 2001. "Becoming 'White': Race, Religion and the Foundations of Syrian/Lebanese Ethnicity in the United States." *Journal of American Ethnic History* 20: 29–58.

Gullace, Nicoletta F. 1997. "Sexual Violence and Family Honor: British Propaganda and International Law During the First World War." *American Historical Review* 102: 714–747.

Haddad, Emily A. 2007. "Bound to Love: Captivity in Harlequin Sheikh Novels." In *Empowerment versus Oppression: Twenty First Century Views of Popular Romance Novels*, edited by Sally Goade. Newcastle: Cambridge Scholars Publishing, 42–64.

———. 2011. "The White Woman Maps the Road to Peace: Harlequin 'Presents' Anglo-American Involvement in the Middle East." Paper presented at the Popular Culture Association Conference, San Antonio, April 20.

Hall, Jacqueline Dowd. 1979. *Revolt Against Chivalry: Jessie Daniel Ames and the Women's Campaign Against Lynching.* New York: Columbia University Press.

Halliday, Fred. 2010. *Britain's First Muslims: Portrait of an Arab Community.* London: I. B. Tauris.

Hanania, Ray. N.d. "Fighting for the Last Victims of September 11." http://www.themediaoasis.com/hatevictims.html

Hansen, Miriam. 1986. "Pleasure, Ambivalence, Identification: Valentino and Female Spectatorship." *Cinema Journal* 25: 6–32.

Hansen, Randall. 2003. "Migration to Europe Since 1945: Its History and its Lessons." *Political Quarterly* 74: 25–38.

Harris, Joseph. 1994. "The Other Reader." In *Composition Theory for the Postmodern Classroom*, edited by Gary A. Olson and Sidney I. Dobrin. Albany: SUNY Press, 225–235.

Harris, Ruth. 1993. "The 'Child of the Barbarian': Rape, Race and Nationalism in France during the First World War." *Past and Present* 141: 170–206.

Heffernan, Teresa. 2000. "Feminism Against the East/West Divide: Lady Mary's Turkish Embassy Letters." *Eighteenth-Century Studies* 33: 201–215.

Helliwell, Christine. 2000. "'It's Only a Penis': Rape, Feminism, and Difference." *Signs* 25: 789–816.

Heng, Geraldine. 1998. "Cannibalism, the First Crusade, and the Genesis of Medieval Romance." *Differences* 10: 98–174.

Hermes, Joke. 2000. "Of Irritation, Texts and Men: Feminist Audience Studies and Cultural Citizenship." *International Journal of Cultural Studies* 3: 351–367.

Higham, John. 1955. *Strangers in the Land: Patterns of American Nativism 1860–1925*. New Brunswick: Rutgers University Press.

Hoeveler, Diane Long. 2006. "The Female Captivity Narrative: Blood, Water, and Orientalism." In *Interrogating Orientalism: Contextual Approaches and Pedagogical Practices*, edited by Diane Long Hoeveler and Jeffrey Cass. Columbus: Ohio State University, 46–71.

Hollinger, David A. 2003. "Amalgamation and Hypodescent: The Question of Ethnoracial Mixture in the History of the United States." *American Historical Review* 108: 1363–1390.

Homberger, Eric. 2003. "Obituary, Kathleen Winsor." *The Guardian*. June 4, http://www.guardian.co.uk/obituaries/story/0,3604,969747,00.html.

Hopwood, Derek. 1999. *Sexual Encounters in the Middle East: The British, the French and the Arabs*. Reading: Ithaca.

Hughes, Helen. 1993. *The Historical Romance*. London and New York: Routledge.

Hunt, Lynn. 1993. *The Invention of Pornography: Obscenity and the Origins of Modernity, 1500–1800*. New York: Zone Books.

Hurd, Elizabeth Shakman. 2003. "Appropriating Islam: The Islamic Other in the Consolidation of Western Modernity." *Critique: Critical Middle Eastern Studies* 12: 25–41.

Hyam, Ronald. 1990. *Empire and Sexuality*. Manchester: Manchester University Press.

Illouz, Eva. 1997. *Consuming the Romantic Utopia: Love and the Cultural Contradiction of Capitalism*. Berkeley: University of California Press.

Isom-Verhaaren, Christine. 2006. "Royal French Women in the Ottoman Sultans' Harem: The Political Uses of Fabricated Accounts from the Sixteenth to the Twenty-First Century." *Journal of World History* 17: 159–196.

Jackson, Stevi. 1993. "Love and Romance as Objects of Feminist Knowledge." In *Making Connections*, edited by Mary Kennedy, Cathy Lubelska, and Val Walsh. London: Taylor & Francis, 39–50.

Jacobson, Matthew Frye. 1998. *Whiteness of a Different Color: European Immigrants and the Alchemy of Race.* Cambridge, MA: Harvard University Press.

Jarmakani, Amira. 2008. *Imagining Arab Womenhood: The Cultural Mythology of Veils, Harems and Belly Dancers in the U.S.* New York: Palgrave Macmillan.

Jeffreys, Sheila. 1990. *Anticlimax: A Feminist Perspective on the Sexual Revolution.* London: The Women's Press.

Jensen, Margaret Ann. 1984. *Love's Sweet Return: The Harlequin Story.* Toronto: Women's Education Press.

Johnson-Woods, Toni. 2004. *Pulp: A Collector's Book of Australian Pulp Fiction.* Canberra: National Library.

Kabbani, Rana. 1994. *Imperial Fictions: Europe's Myths of Orient.* London: Pandora.

Kahf, Mohja. 1999. *Western Representations of the Muslim Woman: From Termagant to Odalisque.* Austin: University of Texas Press.

Kalb, Marvin. 1994. "A View from the Press." In *Taken by Storm: The Media, Public Opinion, and U.S. Foreign Policy in the Gulf War,* edited by W. Lance Bennett and David L. Paletz. Chicago: University of Chicago Press, 3–7.

Kamrath, Mark. 2004. "An 'Inconceivable Pleasure' and the Philadelphia Minerva: Erotic Liberalism, Oriental Tales, and the Female Subject in Periodicals of the Early Republic." *American Periodicals* 14: 3–34.

Karlsson, Ingmar. 2006. "The Turk as Threat and Europe's 'Other.'" *International Issues & Slovak Foreign Policy Affairs* 1: 62–72.

Kellner, Douglass. N.d. "The Persian Gulf TV War." http://www.gseis.ucla.edu/faculty/kellner/essays/gulfwarch2.pdf. Accessed July 8, 2009.

———. 2003. "September 11, Terrorism, and Blowback." In *9/11 in American Culture,* edited by Norman K. Denzin and Yvonna S. Lincoln. Walnut Creek, CA: AltaMira Press, 9–20.

Kelly, Kathleen Coyne. 2000. *Performing Virginity and Testing Chastity in the Middle Ages.* London: Routledge.

Kelly, Liz. 1987. "The Continuum of Sexual Violence." In *Women, Violence and Social Control,* edited by Jalna Hanmer and Mary Maynard. Basingstoke: Macmillan, 46–60.

Kennedy, Dane. 2000. "'Captain Burton's Oriental Muck Heap': The Book of the Thousand Nights and the Uses of Orientalism." *The Journal of British Studies* 39: 317–339.

Kent, Susan Kingsley. 1993. *Making Peace: The Reconstruction of Gender in Interwar Britain.* Princeton: Princeton University Press.

Khoury, Philip S. 1999. "Lessons from the Eastern Shore" (1998 Presidential Address). *MESA Bulletin* 33: 2–9.

Kietzman, Mary Jo. 1998. "Montagu's *Turkish Embassy Letters* and Cultural Dislocation." *Studies in English Literature, 1500–1900* 38: 537–551.

Krentz, Jayne Ann, editor. 1992. *Dangerous Men, and Adventurous Women: Romance Writers on the Appeal of Romance.* Philadelphia: University of Philadelphia Press.

Lampert, Lisa. 2004. "Race, Periodicity, and the (Neo-)Middle Ages." *Modern Language Quarterly* 65: 391–421.

Laqueur, Thomas. 1990. *Making Sex: Body and Gender from the Greeks to Freud*. Cambridge, MA: Harvard University Press.

Lawrence, Jon. 2003. "Forging a Peaceable Kingdom: War, Violence and Fear of Brutalization in Post-First World War Britain." *Journal of Modern History* 75: 557–589.

Leach, William. 1993. *Land of Desire: Merchants, Power, and the Rise of a New American Culture*. New York: Pantheon.

Leask, Nigel. 1992. *British Romantic Writers and the East: Anxieties of Empire*. Cambridge: Cambridge University Press.

Leed, Eric. 2000. "Fateful Memories: Industrialized War and Traumatic Neuroses." *Journal of Contemporary History* 35: 85–100.

LeGates, Marlene. 1976. "The Cult of Womanhood in Eighteenth-Century Thought." *Eighteenth-Century Studies* 10: 21–39.

Leider, Emily W. 2003. *Dark Lover: The Life and Death of Rudolph Valentino*. London: Faber and Faber.

Lerner, Daniel. 1958. *The Passing of Traditional Society: Modernizing the Middle East*. New York: Free Press.

Levine, Philippa. 1994. "'Walking the Streets in a Way No Decent Woman Should': Women Police in World War I." *Journal of Modern History*, 66: 34–78.

———, editor. 2004. *Gender and Empire*. Oxford: Oxford University Press.

Lewis, C. S. 1936. *The Allegory of Love*. Oxford: Oxford University Press.

Lewis, Reina. 1996. *Gendering Orientalism: Race, Femininity and Representation*. London and New York: Routledge.

———. 2004. *Rethinking Orientalism: Women, Travel, and the Ottoman Harem*. New Brunswick: Rutgers University Press.

Liddle, Joanna, and Shirin Rai. 1998. "Feminism, Imperialism and Orientalism: The Challenge of the 'Indian Woman.'" *Women's History Review* 7: 495–520.

Light, Alison. 1991. *Forever England: Femininity, Literature, and Conservatism Between the Wars*. London: Routledge.

Little, Douglas. 2002. *American Orientalism: The United States and the Middle East Since 1945*. Chapel Hill: University of North Carolina Press.

Lockman, Zachary. 2004. *Contending Visions of the Middle East: The History and Politics of Orientalism*. Cambridge and New York: Cambridge University Press.

Long, Andrew. 2009. "The Hidden and the Visible in British Orientalism: The Case of Lawrence of Arabia." *Middle East Critique* 18: 21–37.

Lowe, David. 2006. "From Sudan to Suez: Strategic Encounters." In *Australia and the Middle East: A Front-Line Relationship*, edited by Fethi Mansouri. London: Tauris.

Lowe, Lisa. 1990. "Rereadings in Orientalism: Oriental Inventions and Inventions of the Orient in Montesquieu's 'Lettres persanes'." *Cultural Critique* 15: 115–143.

———. 1991. *Critical Terrains: French and British Orientalisms*. Ithaca: Cornell University Press.

Lowenthal, David. 1985. *The Past is a Foreign Country*. Cambridge: Cambridge University Press.

Lutz, Deborah. 2006. *The Dangerous Lover: Gothic Villains, Byronism, and the Nineteenth-Century Seduction Narrative*. Columbus: Ohio State University Press.

Lyons, Martyn. 2001. "Britain's Largest Export Market." In *A History of the Book in Australia 1891–1945: A National Culture in a Colonised Market*, edited by Martyn Lyons and John Arnold. St Lucia: University of Queensland Press, 19–26.

Lystra, Karen. 1989. *Searching the Heart: Women, Men and Romantic Love in Nineteenth-Century America*. New York and Oxford: Oxford University Press.

MacKinnon, Catherine. 1989. *Toward a Feminist Theory of the State*. Cambridge, MA: Harvard University Press.

Maira, Sunaina. 2008. "Belly Dancing: Arab-Face, Orientalist Feminism, and U.S. Empire." *American Quarterly* 60: 317–345.

Mann, Peter H. 1969. *The Romantic Novel: A Survey of Reading Habits*, in collaboration with Mills & Boon Ltd. London: Mills & Boon.

———. 1974. *A New Survey: The Facts About Romantic Fiction*, in collaboration with Mills & Boon Ltd. London: Mills & Boon.

Mansouri, Fethi, and Sally Percival Wood. 2006. "Exploring the Australia-Middle East Connection." In *Australia and the Middle East: A Front-Line Relationship*, edited by Fethi Mansouri. London: Tauris, 1–18.

Marchetti, Gina. 1993. *Romance and the "Yellow Peril": Race, Sex, and Discursive Strategies in Hollywood Fiction*. Berkeley: University of California Press.

Marcus, Julie. 1992. *A World of Difference: Islam and Gender Hierarchy in Turkey*. London: Zed Books.

Marcus, Steven. 1966. *The Other Victorians: A Study of Sexuality and Pornography in Mid-Nineteenth Century England*. London: Weidenfeld and Nicolson.

Marshall, Randall D., and Sandro Galea. 2004. "Science for the Community: Assessing Mental Health After 9/11." *Journal of Clinical Psychiatry* 65: 37–43.

Matar, Nabil. 1998. *Islam in Britain, 1558–1685*. Cambridge: Cambridge University Press.

Matar, N. I. 1993. "The Renegade in English Seventeenth-Century Imagination." *Studies in English Literature, 1500–1900* 33: 489–505.

McAleer, Joseph. 1999. *Passion's Fortune: The Story of Mills & Boon*. Oxford: Oxford University Press.

McAlister, Melani. 2001. *Epic Encounters: Culture, Media, and U.S. Interests in the Middle East, 1945–2000*. Berkeley: University of California Press.

McClintock, Anne. 1995. *Imperial Leather: Race, Gender and Sexuality in the Colonial Context*. London: Routledge.

McInerney, Maud Burnett. 1999. "Rhetoric, Power, and Integrity in the Passion of the Virgin Martyr." In *Menacing Virgins: Representing Virginity in the Middle Ages and Renaissance*, edited by Kathleen Coyne Kelly and Marina Leslie. Newark: Associated University Presses, 50–70.

Melman, Billie. 1988. *Women and the Popular Imagination in the Twenties: Flappers and Nymphs*. New York: St Martin's Press.

———. 1995. *Women's Orients: English Women and the Middle East, 1718–1918. Sexuality, Religion and Work*. Ann Arbor: University of Michigan Press.

Menocal, Maria Rosa. 1981. "Close Encounters in Medieval Provence: Spain's Role in the Birth of Troubadour Poetry." *Hispanic Review* 49: 43–64.

———. 1987. *The Arabic Role in Medieval Literary History*. Philadelphia: University of Pennsylvania Press.

Mernissi, Fatima. 1987. *The Veil and the Male Elite: A Feminist Interpretation of Women's Rights in Islam*, translated by Mary-Jo Lakeland. Reading, MA: Addison-Wesley.

———. 2001. *Scheherazade Goes West: Different Cultures, Different Harems*. New York: Washington Square Press.

Meserve, Margaret. 2008. *Empires of Islam in Renaissance Historical Thought*. Cambridge, MA: Harvard University Press.

Metlitzki, Dorothee. 1977. *The Matter of Araby in Medieval England*. New Haven: Yale University Press.

Meyer, Eve R. 1974. "*Turquerie* and Eighteenth-Century Music." *Eighteenth-Century Studies* 7: 474–488.

Michalak, Laurence. 1988. *Cruel and Unusual: Negative Images of Arabs in American Popular Culture*, third ed. American Anti-Arab Discrimination Committee Issue Paper No. 15. Washington, D.C.: American Anti-Arab Discrimination Committee.

Michie, Helena. 1987. *The Flesh Made Word: Female Figures and Women's Bodies*. New York: Oxford University Press.

Middleton, Victor T. C. 2005. *British Tourism: The Remarkable Story of Growth*. Oxford: Butterworth-Heinemann.

Midgley, Clare, editor. 1998. *Gender and Imperialism*. Manchester: Manchester University Press.

Mills, Sara. 1991. *Discourses of Difference: An Analysis of Women's Travel Writing and Colonialism*. London: Routledge.

Mitchell, Timothy. 1988. *Colonizing Egypt*. Cambridge: Cambridge University Press.

Modleski, Tania. 1982. *Loving with a Vengeance: Mass-Produced Fantasies for Women*. Hamden, CT: Archon.

Mohanty, Chandra Talpade. 1984. "Under Western Eyes: Feminist Scholarship and Colonial Discourses." *boundary 2* 12: 333–58.

Morgan, Jennifer L. 1997. "'Some Could Suckle over Their Shoulder': Male Travelers, Female Bodies, and the Gendering of Racial Ideology, 1500–1770." *The William and Mary Quarterly* 54: 167–192.

Morsy, Soheir. 1983. "Politicization Through the Mass Information Media: American Images of the Arabs." *Journal of Popular Culture* 17: 91–97.

Mosse, George L. 2000. "Shell-Shock as a Social Disease." *Journal of Contemporary History* 35: 101–108.

Mussell, Kay. 1984. *Fantasy and Reconciliation: Contemporary Formulas of Women's Romance Fiction*. Westport: Greenwood.

Naber, Nadine. 2000. "Ambiguous Insiders: An Investigation of Arab American Invisibility." *Ethnic and Racial Studies* 23: 37–61.

Nagel, Joanne. 2003. *Race, Ethnicity, and Sexuality: Intimate Intersections, Forbidden Frontiers*. New York: Oxford University Press.

Nance, Susan. 2009. *How the Arabian Nights Inspired the American Dream, 1790–1935*. Chapel Hill: University of North Carolina Press.

Nelson, Elizabeth. 2007. "Victims of War: The First World War, Returned Soldiers, and Understandings of Domestic Violence in Australia." *Journal of Women's History* 19: 83–106.

Newman, Louise Michele. 1999. *White Women's Rights: The Racial Origins of Feminism in the United States*. New York and Oxford: Oxford University Press.

Norton, Anne. 1991. "Gender, Sexuality and the Iraq of Our Imagination." *Middle East Report* 173: 26–28.

Nye, Robert A. 2007. "Western Masculinities in War and Peace." *American Historical Review* 112: 417–438.

Oren, Michael B. 2007. *Power, Faith, and Fantasy: America in the Middle East. 1776 to the Present*. New York: Norton.

Orfalea, Gregory. 1988. "Literary Devolution: The Arab in the Post-World War II Novel in English." *Journal of Palestinian Studies* 17: 109–128.

Osborne, Gwendolyn. 2002. "How Black Romance—Novels, that is—Came to Be." *Black Issues Book Review*. January–February.

Parameswaran, Radhika. 1999. "Western Romance Fiction as English-Language Media in Postcolonial India." *Journal of Communication* 49: 84–105.

———. 2002. "Reading Fictions of Romance: Gender, Sexuality, and Nationalism in Postcolonial India." *Journal of Communication* 52: 832–851.

Paxton, Nancy L. 1999. *Writing Under the Raj: Gender, Race, and Rape in the British Colonial Imagination, 1830–1947*. Piscataway, NJ: Rutgers University Press.

Payne, James L. 2008. "What Do the Terrorists Want?" *The Independent Review* 13: 29–39.

Pearce, Roy Harvey. 1947. "The Significances of the Captivity Narrative." *American Literature* 19: 1–20.

Peirce, Leslie P. 1993. *The Imperial Harem: Women and Sovereignty in the Ottoman Empire*. New York: Oxford University Press.

Penzer, N. M. 1975. *The Harem: An Account of the Institution as it Existed in the Palace of the Turkish Sultans with a History of the Grand Seraglio from its Foundation to the Present Time* (1936). New York: AMS Press.

Perry, Adele. 1997. "'Fair Ones of a Purer Caste': White Women and Colonialism in Nineteenth-Century British Columbia." *Feminist Studies* 23: 501–524.

Poole, Robert M. February 2008. "Looting Iraq." *Smithsonian* magazine. http://www.smithsonianmag.com/arts-culture/monument-sidebar.html. Accessed July 2009.

Pratt, Mary Louise. 1992. *Imperial Eyes: Travel Writing and Transculturation*. London: Routledge.

Procida, Mary A. 2001. "Good Sports and Right Sorts: Guns, Gender, and Imperialism in British India." *The Journal of British Studies* 40: 454–488.

Purdie, Susan. 1992. "Janice Radway, *Reading the Romance*." In *Reading into Cultural Studies*, edited by Martin Barker and Anne Beezer. London: Routledge, 148–164.

Radway, Janice A. 1991. *Reading the Romance: Women, Patriarchy, and Popular Literature*. Chapel Hill and London: University of North Carolina Press.

Ramsdell, Kristin. 1999. *Romance Fiction: A Guide to the Genre*, second ed. Englewood, Colorado: Libraries Unlimited.

Raub, Patricia. 1992. "Issues of Passion and Power in E. M. Hull's *The Sheik*." *Women's Studies* 21: 119–128.

Reed, Cory A. 1999. "Harems and Eunuchs: Ottoman-Islamic Motifs of Captivity in *El Celoso Extremeño*." *Bulletin of Hispanic Studies* 76: 199–214.

Regis, Pamela. 2003. *A Natural History of the Romance Novel*. Philadelphia: University of Pennsylvania Press.

Robel, Lauren. 1989. "Pornography and the Existing Law." In *For Adult Users Only: The Dilemma of Violent Pornography*, edited by Susan Gubar and Joan Hoff. Bloomington: Indiana University Press, 178–197.

Rodinson, Maxime. 1987. *Europe and the Mystique of Islam*, translated by Roger Veinus. Seattle: University of Washington Press.

Roediger, David R. 1991. *The Wages of Whiteness: Race and the Making of the American Working Class*. London: Verso.

Rose, Jonathan. 1992. "Rereading the English Common Reader: A Preface to a History of Audiences." *Journal of the History of Ideas* 53: 47–70.

Rothman, Ellen K. 1987. *With Hands and Hearts: A History of Courtship in America*. Cambridge, MA: Harvard University Press.

Rougemont, Denis de. 1983. *Love in the Western World* (1940), translated by Montgomery Belgion. Pinceton: Princeton University Press.

Said, Edward W. 1993. *Culture and Imperialism*. New York: Alfred A. Knopf.

———. 1995. *Orientalism: Western Conceptions of the Orient* (1978). London: Penguin.

Seaman, Myra. 2001. "Engendering Genre in Middle English Romance: Performing the Feminine in Sir Beves of Hamtoun." *Studies in Philology* 98: 49–75.

Seddon, Peter. "Hull, Edith Maude—a Forgotten Derbyshire writer." *You & Yesterday*, October 30, 2007, http://www.youandyesterday.co.uk/articles/Hull,_Edith_Maude_-_A_forgotten_Derbyshire_writer. Accessed July 2009.

Segol, Marla. 2003. "'Floire et Blancheflor': Courtly Hagiography or Radical Romance?" *Alif: Journal of Comparative Poetics* 23: 233–275.

Seidman, Steven. 1991. *Romantic Longings: Love in America, 1830–1980*. New York and London: Routledge.

Selinger, Eric M. 2007. "Rereading the Romance." *Contemporary Literature* 48: 307–324.

Selinger, Eric Murphy, and Frantz, Sarah S. G., editors. 2012. *New Approaches to Popular Romance Fiction*. Jefferson, NC: McFarland.

Semmerling, T. J. 2006. *"Evil" Arabs in American Popular Film: Orientalist Fear.* Austin: University of Texas Press.

Shaheen, Jack G. 1984. *The TV Arab.* Bowling Green: Bowling Green State University Popular Press.

———. 1987. "The Hollywood Arab: 1984–1986." *Journal of Popular Film and Television* 14: 148–157.

———. 1994. "Arab Images in American Comic Books." *Journal of Popular Culture* 28: 123–133.

———. 2001. *Reel Bad Arabs: How Hollywood Vilifies a People.* New York: Olive Branch Press.

———. 2003. Reel Bad Arabs: How Hollywood Vilifies a People. *The Annals of the American Academy of Political and Social Science* 588: 171–193.

———. March 10, 2005. "Network TV Demonizes American Arabs." *The Signpost,* http://media.www.wsusignpost.com/media/storage/paper985/news/2005/03/02/Editorial/Network.Tv.Demonizes.American.Arabs-2109776.shtml. Accessed September 2009.

———. 2008. *Guilty: Hollywood's Verdict on Arabs After 9/11.* New York: Olive Branch Press.

Sharafuddin, Mohammed. 1996. *Islam and Romantic Orientalism: Literary Encounters with the Orient.* London and New York: I. B. Tauris.

Sharoni, Simona. 1995. *Gender and the Israeli-Palestinian Conflict: The Politics of Women's Resistance.* New York: Syracuse University Press.

Sharpe, Jenny. 1993. *Allegories of Empire: The Figure of Woman in the Colonial Text.* Minneapolis: University of Minnesota Press.

Shohat, Ella. 1991. "The Media's War," *Social Text* 28: 135–141.

———. 1997. "Gender and Culture of Empire: Toward a Feminist Ethnography of the Cinema." In *Visions of the East: Orientalism in Film,* edited by Matthew Bernstein and Gaylyn Studlar. New Brunswick: Rutgers University Press, 19–68.

Shumway, David R. 2003. *Modern Love: Romance, Intimacy and the Marriage Crisis.* New York: New York University Press.

Sielke, Sabine. 2002. *Reading Rape: The Rhetoric of Sexual Violence in American Literature and Culture, 1790–1990.* Princeton: Princeton University Press.

Sigel, Lisa Z. 2002. *Governing Pleasures: Pornography and Social Change in England, 1815–1914.* New Brunswick: Rutgers University Press.

Spigel, Lynn. 2004. "Entertainment Wars: Television Culture After 9/11." *American Quarterly* 56: 235–270.

Simon, Reeva S. 1989. *The Middle East in Crime Fiction: Mysteries, Spy Novels and Thrillers from 1916 to the 1980's.* New York: Lilian Barber Press.

———. 2010. *Spies and Holy Wars: The Middle East in 20th Century Crime Fiction.* Austin: University of Texas Press.

Singleton, Brian. 2004. *Oscar Asche, Orientalism, and British Musical Comedy.* Westport: Praeger.

Snitow, Ann Barr. 1979. "Mass Market Romance: Pornography for Women is Different." *Radical History Review* 20: 141–161.

Snowden Jr., Frank M. 1983. *Before Color Prejudice: The Ancient View of Blacks*. Cambridge, MA: Harvard University Press.

Spongberg, Mary. 2002. *Writing Women's History Since the Renaissance*. Houndsmill:
Palgrave Macmillan.

Stoler, Ann Laura. 1995. *Race and the Education of Desire: Foucault's History of Sexuality and the Colonial Order of Things*. Durham: Duke University Press.

———. 2002. *Carnal Knowledge and Imperial Power: Race and the Intimate in Colonial Rule*. Berkeley and Los Angeles: University of California Press.

Strassberg Donald S., and Lisa K. Lockerd. 1998. "Force in Women's Sexual Fantasies."
Archives of Sexual Behavior 27: 403–415.

Stratton, Jon. 1987. *The Virgin Text: Fiction, Sexuality and Ideology*. Brighton: Harvester Press.

Strickland, Debra Higgs. 2000. "Monsters and Christian Enemies." *History Today* 50:
45–51.

Stone, John. 1992. "The Grand Diversion: Mozart and *Die Entführung aus dem Serail*."
The Cambridge Quarterly 21: 107–119.

Strong, Pauline Turner. 1999. *Captive Selves, Captivating Others: The Politics and Poetics of Colonial American Captivity Narratives*. Boulder: Westview Press.

Studlar, Gaylyn. 1993. "Valentino, 'Optic Intoxication,' and Dance Madness." In
Screening the Male: Exploring Masculinities in Hollywood Cinema, edited by Steven
Cohan and Ira Rae Hark. London: Routledge, 23–45.

———. 2004. "'The Perfect Lover'? Valentino and Ethnic Masculinity in the 1920s."
In *The Silent Cinema Reader*, edited by Lee Grieveson and Peter Krämer. London
and New York: Routledge, 290–304.

Suleiman, Michael W. 1999. "Islam, Muslims and Arabs in America: The Other of the
Other of the Other. . . ." *Journal of Muslim Minority Affairs* 19: 33–47.

Tabili, Laura. 1994. *"We Ask for British Justice": Workers and Racial Difference in Late
Imperial Britain*. Cornell: Cornell University Press.

Taylor, Jessica. 2007. "And You Can Be My Sheikh: Gender, Race, and Orientalism in
Contemporary Romance Novels." *Journal of Popular Culture* 40: 1032–1051.

Teo, Hsu-Ming. 1998. "Exotic Excursions: British Women's Travel Writing, 1890–
1939." PhD dissertation, University of Sydney.

———. 2002. "Femininity, Modernity, and Colonial Discourse." *In Transit: Travel,
Text, Empire*, edited by Helen Gilbert and Anna Johnston. New York: Peter Lang,
173–190.

———. 2003. "The Romance of White Nations: Imperialism, Popular Culture and
National Histories." In *After the Imperial Turn*, edited by Antoinette Burton. Duke
University Press, 279–292.

———. 2004. "The Britishness of Australian Popular Fiction." In *Exploring the British
World*, edited by Kate Darian-Smith, Patricia Grimshaw, Kiera Lindsey, and Stuart
Macintyre. Melbourne: RMIT Publishing, 721–747.

———. 2007. "Orientalism and Mass Market Romance Novels in the Twentieth Century." In *Edward Said: The Legacy of a Public Intellectual*, edited by Debjani Ganguly and Ned Curthoys. Melbourne: Melbourne University Press, 241–262.

———. 2010a. "Gypsy in the Sun: The Transnational Life of Rosita Forbes." In *Transnational Lives: Biographies of Global Modernity, 1700–Present*, edited by Desley Deacon, Penny Russell, and Angela Woollacott. Houndsmill: Palgrave Macmillan, 273–285.

———. 2010b. "Historicizing *The Sheik*: Comparisons of the British Novel and the American Film." *Journal of Popular Romance Studies* 1, http://jprstudies.org/2010/08/historicizing-the-sheik-comparisons-of-the-british-novel-and-the-american-film-by-hsu-ming-teo/.

———. 2012. "'Bertrice Teaches You About History, and You Don't Even Mind!' History and Revisionist Historiography in Bertrice Small's *The Kadin*." In *New Approaches to Popular Romance Fiction*, edited by Eric Murphy Selinger and Sarah S. G. Frantz. Jefferson, NC: McFarland.

———. 2011. "Eroticising the Orient: A Survey of European Literary Representations of Cross-Cultural Encounters Between Europe and the Middle East." In *Rethinking the Racial Moment: Essays on the Colonial Encounter*, edited by Alison Holland and Barbara Brookes. Newcastle: Cambridge Scholars Publishing, 21–47.

Thébaud, Françoise. 1994. "The Great War and the Triumph of Sexual Division." *A History of Women in the West. Vol. V. Toward a Cultural Identity in the Twentieth Century*, edited by Françoise Thébaud. Cambridge, MA: Belknap Press, 21–75.

Thomas, Glen. 2008. "'And I deliver': An Interview with Emma Darcy." *Continuum* 22: 113–126.

Thorslev, Jr., Peter L. 1962. *The Byronic Hero: Types and Prototypes*. Minneapolis: University of Minnesota Press.

Thurston, Carol. 1987. *The Romance Revolution: Erotic Novels for Women and the Quest for a New Sexual Identity*. Urbana: University of Illinois Press.

Tidrick, Kathryn. 1989. *Heart Beguiling Araby: The English Romance with Arabia* (1981). London: I. B. Tauris.

Tromans, N. et al. 2008. *The Lure of the East: British Orientalist Painting*. New Haven: Yale University Press.

VanDerBeets, Richard. 1984. *The Indian Captivity Narrative: An American Genre*. Lanham: University Press of America.

Vaughn, Alden T. and Edward W. Clark, editors. 1981. *Puritans Among the Indians: Accounts of Captivity and Redemption 1676–1724*. Cambridge, MA: Belknap Press.

Vaughn, Alden T. 1983. *Narratives of North American Indian Captivity: A Selective Bibliography*. New York: Garland.

Vitkus, Daniel J. 1997. "Turning Turk in *Othello*: The Conversion and Damnation of the Moor." *Shakespeare Quarterly* 48: 145–176.

Walker, David. 2006. "Perilous Encounters: Australia, Asia and the Middle East." In *Australia and the Middle East: A Front-Line Relationship*, edited by Fethi Mansouri. London: Tauris, 19–34.

Wallace, Diana. 2005. *The Woman's Historical Novel: British Women Writers, 1900-2000*. Houndsmill, Basingstoke: Palgrave Macmillan.

Wann, Louise. 1915. "The Oriental in Elizabethan Drama." *Modern Philology* 12: 423-447.

Ward, Paul. 2001. "'Women of Britain Say Go': Women's Patriotism in the First World War." *Twentieth Century British History* 12: 23-45.

Waters, Chris. 1997. "Dark Strangers in Our Midst: Discourses of Race and Nation in Britain, 1947-1963." *Journal of British Studies* 36: 207-238.

Webster, Wendy. 2007. *Englishness and Empire 1939-1965*. Oxford: Oxford University Press.

Weiss, Judith. 1991. "The Wooing Woman in Anglo-Norman Romance." In *Romance in Medieval England*, edited by Maldwyn Mills, Jennifer Follows, and Carol M. Meale. Cambridge: D. S. Brewer, 149-161.

Wendell, Sarah, and Candy Tan. 2009. *Beyond Heaving Bosoms: The Smart Bitches' Guide to Romance Novels*. New York: Fireside.

Werbner, Pnina. 2004. "Theorising Complex Diasporas: Purity and Hybridity in the South Asian Public Sphere in Britain." *Journal of Ethnic and Migration Studies* 30: 895-911.

Wheatcroft, Andrew. 1993. *The Ottomans*. London: Viking.

Willis, Ellen. 1984. "Feminism, Moralism, and Pornography." In *Desire: The Politics of Sexuality*, edited by Ann Snitow, Christine Stansell, and Sharon Thompson. London: Virago.

Wittkower, Rudolf. 1942. "Marvels of the East: A Study in the History of Monsters." *Journal of the Warburg and Courtauld Institutes* 5: 159-197.

Woollacott, Angela. 1994. "'Khaki Fever' and Its Control: Gender, Class, Age and Sexual Morality on the British Homefront in the First World War." *Journal of Contemporary History* 29: 325-347.

Yeazell, Ruth Bernard. 2000. *Harems of the Mind: Passages of Western Art and Literature*. New Haven and London: Yale University Press.

Yermolenko, Galina. 2005. "Roxolana: 'The Greatest Empresse of the East.'" *The Muslim World* 95: 231-248.

Young, Robert J. C. 1995. *Colonial Desire: Hybridity in Culture, Theory, and Race*. London and New York: Routledge.

Zaitchik, Alexander. 2003. "The Romance Writers of America Convention is Just Super." *New York Press*, July 22, http://www.nypress.com/16/30/news&columns/feature.cfm.

Zeldin, Theodore. 1994. *An Intimate History of Humanity*. New York: HarperCollins.

Zonana, Joyce. 1993. "The Sultan and the Slave: Feminist Orientalism and the Structure of *Jane Eyre*." *Signs* 18: 592-617.

Index

CPSIA information can be obtained
at www.ICGtesting.com
Printed in the USA
BVHW030243301121
622859BV00016B/265

9 780292 756908